FERRUCCIO BUSONI AND HIS LEGACY

FERRUCCIO BUSONI
and HIS LEGACY

Erinn E. Knyt

INDIANA UNIVERSITY PRESS

This book is a publication of

INDIANA UNIVERSITY PRESS
Office of Scholarly Publishing
Herman B Wells Library 350
1320 East 10th Street
Bloomington, Indiana 47405 USA

iupress.indiana.edu

© 2017 by Erinn E. Knyt

All rights reserved

No part of this book may be reproduced or utilized in any form or by any means, electronic or mechanical, including photocopying and recording, or by any information storage and retrieval system, without permission in writing from the publisher. The Association of American University Presses' Resolution on Permissions constitutes the only exception to this prohibition.

The paper used in this publication meets the minimum requirements of the American National Standard for Information Sciences—Permanence of Paper for Printed Library Materials, ANSI Z39.48-1992.

*Manufactured in the
United States of America*

*Library of Congress
Cataloging-in-Publication Data*

Names: Knyt, Erinn E., author.
Title: Ferruccio Busoni and his legacy / Erinn E. Knyt.
Description: Bloomington ; Indianapolis : Indiana University Press, 2017. | Includes bibliographical references and index.
Identifiers: LCCN 2016059667 (print) | LCCN 2017000759 (ebook) | ISBN 9780253026286 (cloth : alk. paper) | ISBN 9780253026842 (pbk. : alk. paper) | ISBN 9780253026897 (e-book)
Subjects: LCSH: Busoni, Ferruccio, 1866-1924—Influence. | Music—20th century—History and criticism.
Classification: LCC ML410.B98 K59 2017 (print) | LCC ML410.B98 (ebook) | DDC 780.92—dc23
LC record available at https://lccn.loc.gov/2016059667

1 2 3 4 5   22 21 20 19 18 17

For Eric

CONTENTS

Acknowledgments ix

Introduction 1

1. Unconventional Maestro 11
2. Janus-Faced Modernism 45
3. New Instruments, New Sounds, and New Musical Law 89
4. From Opera to Films 136
5. New Sonic Landscapes 189
6. New Music of the Weimar Republic 232
7. Conclusions: "Passing the Torch" 277

Selected Bibliography 341
Index 359

ACKNOWLEDGMENTS

THIS BOOK WOULD not have been possible without the support and encouragement of numerous scholars, colleagues, friends, and family members. I wish to thank my undergraduate and graduate professors for inspiring me to pursue a career in musicology and for awakening my interest in new music: George Barth, Karol Berger, Anna Maria Busse Berger, Sandra Graham, Tom Grey, Heather Hadlock, Stephen Hinton, and Christopher Reynolds. I also appreciate the advice of my colleague and mentor at UMass Amherst, Ernest May, who first inspired me to examine the Busoni-Varèse connection, and to Neil Lerner for drawing my attention to Louis Gruenberg. One of my piano teachers, Julian White, who studied with Egon Petri, awakened my interest in Busoni. I also appreciate those who were willing to critique drafts: Austin Clarkson, Louis Epstein, Matthew Mugmon, Robert Nisbett, Raina Polivka, Emiliano Ricciardi, Marc-André Roberge, Suzanne Ryan, and other, anonymous readers. I am also indebted to my editor, Janice Frisch, for her advice and counsel. This project would not have been as complete without the assistance of those who helped me locate obscure letters, document, or scores, including Joan Gruenberg Cominos (daughter of Louis Gruenberg), Jean-Christophe Gero (Staatsbibliothek zu Berlin), Jonathan Hiam (New York Public Library), Ulrike Jarnach (daughter of Philipp Jarnach), Pam Juengling (University of Massachusetts Amherst), Henrica Lillsjö (Åbo Akademi Archives), Felix Meyer (Paul Sacher Stiftung), Laura Mills (Roosevelt University), Jerry McBride (Stanford University), Leo Monenen (Sibelius Academy),

Judith Picard (Lienau Publishing House), Marja Pohjola (National Archives of Finland), Theresa Rowe (McGill University), Bradley Short (Washington University in St. Louis), Judith Grant Still (daughter of William Grant Still), and Petri Tuovinen (National Library of Finland). Also indispensable were the memories shared by Joan Gruenberg Cominos, Paul de Jong, Joel Feigin, Catherine Luening, Severine Neff, Eric Salzman, Harvey Sollberger, Richard Taruskin, Andrew Violette, Michael Finnissy, Alistair Hinton, Larry Sitsky, and Charles Wuorinen. Many thanks to Laura Arpiainen for her help with Finnish and Swedish translations and to Benjamin Ayotte for typesetting the music examples. This book would not have been possible without the generous support of a Faculty Research Grant from the University of Massachusetts Amherst, and I gratefully acknowledge the support of the AMS 75 PAYS Endowment of the American Musicological Society, funded in part by the National Endowment for the Humanities and the Andrew W. Mellon Foundation. Finally, I would like to express gratitude to my husband, Eric, and children, Kristof, Astrid, Erling, and Florian, for their endless patience as I worked on book drafts and went on numerous trips to archives and libraries.

FERRUCCIO BUSONI AND HIS LEGACY

Introduction

> Ultimately it is always in a man's impact and not in his successes that his value is determined. And the influence that Busoni has had on our generation, not just as a pianist as most people take him to be, but as theoretician, teacher, innovator, creator—in short as a master in the old sense of the word which made the man and his work one—will perhaps be fully appreciated only by the next.
>
> Stefan Zweig, *Neue Freie Presse*

AT THE TIME of his death, Ferruccio Busoni (1866–1924) was widely remembered as a pianist with legendary technique, but his activities as composer and author usually received only passing mention, while his role as a teacher was largely forgotten, except by his pupils.[1] He was widely praised for performances of his own J. S. Bach transcriptions, the late Beethoven sonatas, and complete cycles of works by Franz Liszt. By contrast, his compositions were little understood even by some of his students. Teeming with allusions to the past that were audibly juxtaposed to passages displaying new timbres, textures, harmonies, and scales, they seemed to stand outside main musical trends of his era. His aphoristic, mystical, and suggestive writings were inspirational but difficult to understand, and could be interpreted in any number of ways.[2] At the same time, his work as a composition teacher in the first decades of the twentieth century was overshadowed by the activities of other contemporaneous or near contemporaneous teachers, such as Arnold Schoenberg (1874–1951), who succeeded him in the Berlin master classes at the

Akademie der Künste, and Nadia Boulanger (1887–1979), to whom hundreds flocked as Paris became an important musical center after World War I.

Busoni's importance not only as a pianist, but also as an aesthetician, composer, piano teacher, and mentor of composition pupils during his Berlin master class (1921–1924) at the end of his life, is now beginning to be recognized.[3] Tamara Levitz, for instance, has documented the importance of Busoni's teaching on the lives and careers of his students (Kurt Weill, Wladimir Vogel, Walther Geiser, Robert Blum, Luc Balmer, Svetislav Stančić, Erwin Bodky, Hans Hirsch, and Heinz Joachim-Loch), the types of exercises he prescribed, and the class's cultural and political ramifications in the early Weimar Republic. In addition, as Levitz has shown, Busoni impacted many others during informal coffee hours (*Schwarzer Kaffee*) held in his home, including Stefan Wolpe, Dimitri Mitropoulos, Ernst Krenek, and Alois Hába.[4]

However, Busoni's mentorship of composition pupils extended throughout his career, and well beyond the small circle of masterclass pupils. Even though Busoni was only officially affiliated with a single institution as a composition professor during this master class at the Akademie der Kunste in Berlin, Busoni had previously been connected to several institutions as a professor of piano, including the Helsinki Music Institute (1888–1890), the Moscow Conservatory (1890–1891), and the New England Conservatory (1891–1892).[5] He unofficially taught composition to students at most of the institutions where he worked, including at the Liceo musicale in Bologna from 1913 to 1914, where he was officially an administrator.[6] In addition, his teaching of composition extended beyond the confines of traditional institutional settings—he taught and mentored composition students privately throughout his career.

Looking beyond the Berlin masterclass pupils offers a fuller vision of Busoni's activities as composition teacher. By documenting the relationship between Busoni and some of his significant pre-Berlin masterclass pupils, this book seeks to enrich understanding about his pedagogical activities, to reassess his importance as a composition teacher, and to contribute new knowledge to previously little-understood periods in the lives and careers of several significant composers of the early twentieth century. It documents how his teaching contributed to experimental strands of composition as his students pioneered new sounds and styles of music, such as electronic and film music, as well as new structures in more traditional genres.

Several of Busoni's pre-Berlin masterclass students went on to pursue successful careers in composition and teaching, and they credited Busoni with having been one of the most important influences on their development as composers. Among the more significant are Jean Sibelius, Edgard Varèse, Otto Luening, Louis Gruenberg, and Philipp Jarnach. Other lesser-remembered figures include Guido Guerrini, Gino Tagliapietra, Bernard van Dieren, Gisella Selden-Goth, and Reinhold Laquai.[7] At the same time, Busoni mentored and promoted several composers who would become central figures in early twentieth-century music, including Schoenberg, Béla Bartók, and Percy Grainger.

Studying Busoni's early- and mid-career composition pupils is especially significant because of his evolution as a thinker and composer. By the end of his life, his thoughts had turned inward, and he was preoccupied with theories of Young Classicality, that is, the transformation of music of the past into music of the present and future. This was his alternative to the ideals of both the conservatives and the avant-garde of the 1920s, and it represents an evolution of the ideas he expressed in the previous decade. At that time he was viewed as forward thinking and adventurous, in part because of the experimental theories he published in 1907 in the *Entwurf einer neuen Ästhetik der Tonkunst* about new instruments, new scales, and new means of music organization. His own compositions had also simultaneously evolved from being experimental, such as the nearly atonal Sonatina seconda, BV 259 (1912), notated without bar lines, to stylistically eclectic works that embraced musics of the past, present, and future equally in a stylistic montage foreshadowing the postmodernist approach of the 1960s and beyond. This shift in emphasis is reflected in his teaching and in the output of his pupils.

It would be impossible to cover the entire topic of his early composition teaching in the space of a single book. Thus I do not aim here for comprehensive coverage, but instead provide focused vignettes exploring Busoni's individualized pedagogical approaches with Sibelius, Varèse, Luening, Gruenberg, and Jarnach. These vignettes are framed by an opening chapter discussing Busoni's general approach to teaching composition and a closing chapter exploring his continued influence on subsequent generations of composers. The closing chapter also documents the long-lasting influence of Busoni's ideas as they were passed on to his composition grand pupils, such as Bernd Alois Zimmermann, William Grant Still, Charles Wuorinen, John Corigliano, and many others. At the same time, it draws connections between Busoni's stylistically disparate composition disciples based on his aesthetic ideals that aroused shared interest in sonority, stylistic heterogeneity, and unique structures.

Busoni's mentorship of young composers and musicians was effective if one judges by the careers of his pupils and the quality of their compositions. This book shows how his teachings and aesthetic ideas were catalysts for Varèse's, Luening's, and Gruenberg's experiments with new electronic mediums, Sibelius's play with sounds and textures, and Jarnach's use of polystylism and experimentation with forms. In addition, it contributes knowledge about little-understood developmental periods in the lives of each of the composers, including Sibelius's evolution as a composer after his graduation from the Helsinki Music Institute, Varèse's and Gruenberg's student years in Berlin, and Luening's and Jarnach's development in Zurich during World War I.

The book also reveals that Busoni's teaching style was unconventional. Busoni never became a composition teacher in the strictest sense of the word.[8] Meetings were irregular and he did not charge for private lessons. He did not systematically guide students through technical drills, nor focus on specific ways to combine musical materials. He had no set method that he imposed upon his pupils, and he favored the exchange of ideas through dialogue rather than an authoritarian imparting of facts or rules. Kurt Weill (1900–1950) reportedly claimed that he never had a "lesson" with Busoni in the traditional sense, even though he was his composition pupil:[9]

> He called us disciples and there were no actual lessons, but he allowed us to breathe his aura, which emanated in every sphere, but eventually always manifested itself in music. These hours spent daily in his company are still too recent for me to be able to speak about them. It was a mutual exchange of ideas in the very best sense, with no attempt to force an opinion, no autocracy, and not the slightest sign of envy or malice; and any piece of work that revealed student talent and ability was immediately recognized and enthusiastically received.[10]

Guido Guerrini (1890–1965) recorded similar thoughts in his memoirs, adding that in order to study with Busoni, one already had to have mastered the fundamentals: "Of course, his were not, and could not be, lessons in the pedagogical sense of the word. (Defined here as lessons in composition, because we do not know how things were in the field of piano). Whoever came to him to learn, had to have passed all the purely mechanical aspects of composition."[11]

According to Egon Petri (1881–1962), who called him "the most inspiring teacher of our time," if Busoni was not a traditional teacher, his lessons were unforgettable.[12] He did not progressively guide pupils' technical development, but he did provide them with an inspirational vision of art.[13]

Because he did not focus on technical methods but on abstract ideals about music, the output of his students is so stylistically diverse it is hard to believe they all studied with the same teacher. If there were distinctive aspects shared by his pupils, they were, according to Guerrini, "the logic of construction, the experience and the flavor of counterpoint, and the search for harmony and timbre."[14] Such elements, however, are not always readily apparent to the listener or analyst, and there are many ways to explore them. Thus it is difficult to think of Busoni's students as forming a unified stylistic school or as sharing any common methodology. Indeed, even though his students were populating the musical scenes in the United States and Europe in the 1920s, their music was quite diverse, as Austin Clarkson has already observed.[15]

Busoni embraced many different styles and eschewed any specific method of instruction; thus this book does not aim to present a stylistic genealogy. Instead, it focuses on the transmission of Busoni's aesthetic ideals to his pupils. Through close readings and comparisons of letters, essays, scores, and other documents, it unveils his unconventional pedagogical methods and reveals ideological connections between Busoni, his pupils, and subsequent generations of composers. My book describes how he tailored general teaching approaches and aesthetic ideologies to the work of individual students; it examines specific advice rendered via letters and annotations in scores; it documents his approach to mentorship through concert promotion and discussions with publishers; and—through score analyses—it reveals specific manifestations of Busoni's aesthetic ideals in the compositions of his students.

Many of the documents and scores consulted are still unpublished and found in archives or private collections, including at the Busoni-Nachlass and the Jarnach-Nachlass, Preussischer Kulturbesitz, Musikabteilung, Staatsbibliothek (Berlin), the Galston-Busoni Archive (University of Tennessee), the Louise Varèse Papers, the Sophia Smith Collection (Smith College), the Gruenberg Papers and Luening Papers (New York Public Library), the Private Gruenberg Collection of Joan Gruenberg Cominos (Martinez, CA), the Gruenberg Papers (Syracuse University), the National Library of Finland, the Sibelius Academy Archives (Helsinki), the Åbo Academy University/Sibelius Museum Archive (Helsinki), the Harry Ransom Humanities Research Center (University of Texas), the Varèse Collection, Paul Sacher Stiftung (Basel), and the Edward Dent Papers, Rowe Library, Kings College (Cambridge). Primary documents from these collections are discussed throughout each of the chapters.

OVERVIEW OF CHAPTERS

Chapter 1 provides an overview of how Busoni taught composition based on student memoirs and Busoni's writings. It also compares Busoni's approach with near contemporaries, such as Boulanger and Schoenberg, and considers how Busoni's ideas related to contemporaneous aesthetic trends. It concludes that Busoni's approach was idiosyncratic in its emphasis on aesthetic ideals rather than on methodologies or techniques.

Chapter 2 explores the numerous ways that Busoni impacted the creative activities of Sibelius. Based on analyses of letters, memoirs, archival documents, and scores, the chapter reveals that Busoni was the main catalyst for some of the most progressive elements in Sibelius's music, including experimentation with sound as an organizational feature, new methods of orchestration, ahistoricism, and new structural approaches. At the same time, it documents how Busoni helped shape Sibelius's aesthetic ideals and launch his international career. In the process, the text enriches understanding about Sibelius's compositional development while contributing to ongoing discourse about the evolution of timbral-based music in the twentieth century.

Chapter 3 documents Busoni's impact on Varèse, revealing that it was Busoni who provided the aesthetic stimuli for features of his experimental compositional style: rhythmic simultaneity, expansion of the tonal system, the use of non-traditional instruments, and new means of formal organization. Based on concert programs, letters, lectures, scores, interviews, and annotations in Varese's copy of Busoni's *Sketch of a New Aesthetic of Music*, the chapter exposes Busoni's significance as Varese's teacher, mentor, and friend, while analyzing parallels between aesthetic ideals, compositional styles, and concert organizing activities. In so doing it not only provides missing information about Varèse's little-documented musical activities in Berlin, but also much-needed context for his compositional innovations and for the development of experimental music in the early twentieth century.

Chapter 4 analyzes Busoni's importance for the development of one of the United States' early nationalist composers, Louis Gruenberg. It reveals that Busoni, with whom Gruenberg studied in Europe from 1908 to 1914, helped him discover his own artistic voice and launched his career. This chapter shows that, largely because of Busoni, Gruenberg began writing operatic and symphonic works and began dreaming of new ways to meld technology and music. Busoni also laid the foundation for Gruenberg's search for a new "American" style of music.

Chapter 5 discusses the Busoni-Luening connection. The chapter reveals that Busoni was the main catalyst for Luening's interest in acoustical harmony as well as polytonality and tape music. Although Luening did not start experimenting with electronic music until 1951 when he had access to the necessary equipment, the seeds of interest were planted by Busoni in Zurich during World War I. Documenting the nature and scope of the relationship not only sheds light on Luening's development, but also enriches discussions about the international exchange of ideas during World War I and the evolution of electronic music.

Chapter 6 considers the importance of Busoni on the life and career of Jarnach, who was considered by his contemporaries to be one of the most important young composers in Germany during the 1920s and early 1930s. As a member of the *Novembergruppe*, he was part of the avant-garde of the Weimar Republic, and his music is characterized by novel treatments of the musical language, form, and style, even if it is simultaneously described as intellectual, classy, spiritual, timeless, noble, and technically proficient. This section reveals Busoni's importance for the development of the most experimental aspects of Jarnach's music, including his idiosyncratic approach toward form, style, and musical language.

The final chapter addresses the issue of whether or not there is a "Busoni School" of composition. It also considers specific ways Busoni's ideas were transmitted to his grand pupils and beyond. It contributes to a richer understanding of the breadth of Busoni's influence, his importance as a composition teacher, and the genealogy of experimental music in the early twentieth century. It attempts to enrich current understandings of the scope of Busoni's legacy.

As my book reveals, Busoni's early- and mid-career pupils pioneered new sounds, styles, and forms; they explored how technology and new instruments could expand musical possibilities, how sonority could become an integral material of music, and how stylistic heterogeneity could be used to break away from traditional forms. Although his students were certainly not the only ones experimenting in these areas, they were some of the first and most important pioneers. If one of the significant developments in twentieth-century music was the recognition that sonority and timbre could be considered basic materials of music on par with tones and harmonies, then Busoni's early students were leaders. Examining Busoni's pre-Berlin masterclass pupils thereby contributes to a richer understanding of the breadth of Busoni's influence, his importance as a composition teacher, and the genealogy of experimental music in the early twentieth century.

NOTES

1. See, for instance, the following obituary that praises his pianism but discounts his other professional activities: "Ferruccio Benvenuto Busoni," *The Musical Times* 65:979 (September 1, 1924), 847.

2. Two of his most important texts are Busoni, *Sketch of a New Esthetic of Music* (1907), trans. Dr. Th. Baker (New York: Schirmer, 1911); and Busoni, "The Essence and Oneness of Music" (1922), in *The Essence of Music and Other Papers*, trans. Rosamund Ley (London: Salisbury Square, 1957).

3. See, for instance, Martina Weindel, *Ferruccio Busonis Ästhetik in seinen Briefen und Schriften*, ed. Richard Schaal (Wilhelmshaven: Heinrichsofen-Bücher, 1996); Paul Fleet, *Ferruccio Busoni: A Phenomenological Approach to His Music and Aesthetics* (Cologne: Lambert Academic Publishing, 2009); Antony Beaumont, *Busoni the Composer* (Bloomington: Indiana University Press, 1985); Larry Sitsky, *Busoni and the Piano: The Works, the Writings, and the Recordings*, 2nd ed., Distinguished Reprints 3

(Hillsdale, NY: Pendragon Press, 2009); Albrecht Riethmüller, *Ferruccio Busonis Poetik* (Mainz: Schott, 1988); Albrecht Riethmüller and Hyesy Shin, eds., *Busoni in Berlin: Facetten eines kosmopolitischen Komponisten* (Stuttgart: Franz Steiner, 2004). Marc-André Roberge, *Ferruccio Busoni: A Bio-Bibliography*, Bio-Bibliographies in Music 34 (Westport, CT: Greenwood Press, 1991), lists numerous other sources. In relation to Busoni and pedagogy, consult Joseph Matthews, "Busoni's Contribution to Piano Pedagogy" (PhD diss., Indiana University, 1977); Roberto Wis, "Ferruccio Busoni and Finland," *Acta Musicologica* 49:2 (July–December 1977), 250–269; Erinn Knyt, "Ferruccio Busoni and the New England Conservatory: Piano Pedagogue in the Making," *American Music* 31:3 (Fall 2013), 277–313; Tamara Levitz, "Teaching New Classicality: Busoni's Master Class in Composition, 1921–24" (PhD diss., University of Rochester, 1993). Levitz later converted her dissertation into a book, *Teaching New Classicality: Ferruccio Busoni's Master Class in Composition*, European University Studies, Series 36, vol. 152 (Berlin: Peter Lang, 1996). The content is substantially the same in both versions, except for some abridged passages in the published book. I have chosen to refer to the dissertation as opposed to the book throughout this text, unless otherwise indicated, because some of the material omitted from the book version is valuable for this study. Other sources discussing the masterclass pupils include Gianmario Borio, "Sul concetto di scuola nella musica del Novecento e sulla scuola di Busoni in particolare," in *Ferruccio Busoni e la sua scuola*, ed. Gianmario Borio, Mauro Casadei, and Turroni Monti, Nuovi percorsi musicali (Lucca: Una cosa rara, 1999), 3–18; Stephen Hinton, *Weill's Musical Theater: Stages of Reform* (Berkeley: University of California Press, 2012); Carlo Piccardi, "Wladimir Vogel: La cifra Politica Berlinese oltre l'insegnamento di Busoni," in Borio et al., *Ferruccio Busoni e la sua scuola*, 89–105.

4. For an explanation of which students studied which years in the master class, consult Levitz, "Teaching New Classicality," 82. For a richer discussion of the black coffee hours (*Schwarzer Kaffee*), consult Levitz, "Teaching New Classicality," 115–133 and 232. Busoni regularly invited artists, publishers, and scholars to his home. In 1910, he instituted a practice of holding regular social hour each week, often on Wednesdays or Thursdays, so that everyone could gather at the same time. The tradition of the social hour continued throughout his time in Zurich and once again in Berlin. The gatherings regularly included eating, drinking, game playing, and artistic exchanges. Busoni reportedly used the term to describe the social hours (e.g., "Come drink Schwarzer Kaffee with me tomorrow"). Robert Blum, quoted in Levitz, "Teaching New Classicality," 232. Blum (1900–1994) was a member of Busoni's Berlin master class.

5. Busoni also led piano master classes at the Vienna Conservatory (1907–1908) and at the Hochschule für Musik in Basel (1910). In addition, he led a piano master class in Weimar during the summers of 1900 and 1901, but it was not affiliated with a music institution.

6. This institution is now known as the Conservatorio di Musica Giovan Battista Martini.

7. Consult the following source for information about Busoni and Reinhold Laquai: Clara Laquai, *Kultur und Gesellschaft seit der Jugendstilzeit: Musiker-Memoiren von Reinhold und Clara Laquai* (Zurich: Kreis-Verlag, 1979), 14–16.

8. Busoni's teaching of composition might have been unconventional—in part—because of his own musical training. He never had an obvious role model himself. He did not study with a famous composition teacher himself, nor was he taught according to a specific compositional system or school. Much of Busoni's early skill in piano and composition was supervised by his father, Ferdinando Busoni (1834–1909), a clarinetist, and acquired through trial and error. A short time at the Vienna Conservatory in 1875 proved less than satisfactory due to the regimented course of instruction, which Busoni believed was impeding his progress. His main instruction in composition took the form of a brief apprenticeship (1879–1881) under Wilhelm Mayer-Rémy (1831–1898), who provided him with a thorough grounding in counterpoint and a love for the music of Mozart. For a more complete introduction to Busoni's early education, consult Beaumont, *Busoni the Composer*. Busoni produced an elaborately calligraphed handwritten book of exercises and short compositions during his studies with Mayer-Rémy.

9. Kurt Weill studied with Busoni during the Berlin composition master class (1921–1924).

10. Weill, quoted in H. H. Stuckenschmidt, *Ferruccio Busoni: "Chronicle of a European,"* trans. Sandra Morris (New York: St. Martin's, 1970), 196.

11. "S'intende che le sue non erano, e non potevano essere, lezioni nel senso pedagogico della parola. (Si parla qui di lezioni di composizione, ché non sappiamo come le cose si svolgessero nel campo del pianoforte). Chi si rivolgeva a lui per apprendere, doveva aver superato tutta la parte puramente mecanica della composizione." Guido Guerrini, *Ferruccio Busoni: La vita, la figura, l'opera* (Firenze: Casa Editrice Monsalvato, 1944), 232. Guerrini (1890–1965) studied composition with Busoni at the Bologna Liceo musicale from 1913 to 1914, and continued to send him scores until his death.

12. Egon Petri, "How Ferruccio Busoni Taught: An Interview with the Distinguished Dutch Pianist," interview by Friede F. Rothe, *Etude* 58 (October 1940), 657.

13. Ibid., 657.

14. "La logica della costruzione, la esperianza e il gusto contrappuntistico, la ricerca armonica e timbrica." Guerrini, *Ferruccio Busoni*, 232.

15. Austin Clarkson, "Wolpe, Varèse, and the Busoni Effect," *Contemporary Music Review* 27:2/3 (April/June 2008), 364. Mitropoulos (1896–1960) and Wolpe (1902–1972) frequented Busoni's Berlin master class even if they were not "officially enrolled" in it. For more information, consult Levitz, "Teaching New Classicality." Steuermann (1892–1964) studied with Busoni for years in Berlin. For more information consult Eduard Steuermann, *The Not Quite Innocent Bystander: Writings of Edward Steuermann*, ed. Clara Steuermann, David H. Portner, and Gunther Schuller, trans. Richard Cantwell and Charles Messner (Lincoln: University of Nebraska Press, 1989).

1

Unconventional Maestro

To say that Busoni was a teacher, is both an understatement and an overstatement, depending upon one's viewpoint. In the sense of guiding a pupil's technical and artistic problems in a steadily progressive manner, he was not a teacher at all. But in the higher sense of imparting to a pupil a consummate understanding of art, and the need for cultural and spiritual completion, he was the most inspiring teacher of our time.

Egon Petri, "How Ferruccio Busoni Taught"

HOW BUSONI TAUGHT COMPOSITION: THE MUSIC OF THE MASTERS AS MODELS

AS A TEACHER of composition, Busoni imparted his vision of great music to his students, even if he did not require the systematic completion of exercises to improve technical skill.[1] When he did give practical musical advice, it was based on the music of the masters—especially the compositions of Johann Sebastian Bach and Wolfgang Amadeus Mozart. He disliked abstract exercises, and instead encouraged students to devise their own technical drills from other compositions. Score study was therefore a major part of his instruction, as he encouraged students to seek out and study unfamiliar music, as well as to thoroughly parse well-known pieces. Bach's music was used to teach counterpoint, fugue, and variation form, while Mozart was a model for opera and orchestration. Bach's Passacaglia in C Minor for Organ, BWV 582, the Chaconne from the Violin Sonata in D Minor, BWV 1004, and the Aria mit 30 Veränderungen, BWV 988

("Goldberg Variations") served as examples of variation form. Busoni also revealed characteristics in the music that he considered to be timeless and universal, such as the counterpoint.

Busoni's only important surviving "composition treatise," if it can be called that, his edition of Bach's *Das Wohltemperierte Klavier*, book II, BWV 870–893, is neither systematic nor comprehensive. First published in 1915, it represents his attempt to illuminate principles of good composition derived from Bach's preludes and fugues. As such, it contrasts considerably with his edition of *Das Wohltemperierte Klavier*, book I, BWV 846–869 (1894), in which he sought to illustrate masterful keyboard technique. Busoni described his aims for book II in the preface: "As editor I have devoted some diligence to establishing a definite connection between prelude and fugue, occasionally showing this by means of examples. In the later examples I believe I have overstepped Bach's intentions. All changes and additions, however, follow the educational intention of giving the learner an insight into the mechanism of the composition."[2]

One of the principles Busoni sought to illustrate using Bach fugues as examples was the close relationship between the subject and overall form. Similarly, he focused on thematic interrelatedness between the preludes and fugues. Organic connectedness was a key component of his compositional ideal, and Bach served as a prime example for him. For instance, he noted thematic connections between the Prelude and Fugue no. 2 in C Minor, BWV 871, even if, as he noted, the interrelatedness might have been unintentional.[3]

Busoni was especially interested in explicating the exceptions Bach made to generally accepted contemporaneous practices of counterpoint and fugal writing. He claimed that some foreshadowed practices of his own era: "In the present-day art of composition, which is descended in a straight line from that of Bach (in so far as it strives more and more consciously through polyphony to become feeling in sound) the course of moving towards the middle point of the modulation circle—dependence on key—and objective symbolism both fall out of the plan which makes way for the subjective temperament. Consequently the Master's rights have been extended; he may now take possession of the Bach exceptions as rules."[4]

Throughout the edition, he considered form, motivic treatment, counterpoint, and scoring. In Prelude no. 1 in C Minor, BWV 870, for instance, he wrote about Bach's ability to evoke unusual sonorities through spacing and registration. He specifically mentioned that Bach's treatment of register and voicing creates unusual timbral effects, such as the evocation of manual changes on the organ.[5]

Busoni also taught about form, counterpoint, thematic construction, and scoring through extensive commentary. In Prelude no. 3 in C-Sharp Major, BWV 872, for instance, he analyzed and divided the form into sections, showed thematic relationships between the main sections, and suggested instrumental doublings evoking the sonority of a string quintet (see music example 1.1).[6]

If Busoni included his own ideas in commentary, he also encouraged his students to be active learners by creating personal composition exercises based on Bach's music; he illustrated the process with several of his own composition etudes. For instance, he showed how to study the fugal subject by separating the voices onto separate staves with Fugue no. 2 in C Minor, BWV 871 (see music example 1.2).[7] In another exercise, he rewrote Bach to illustrate the construction of good melodic material and included his own revised version alongside Bach's as a point of comparison. In Prelude no. 3 in C-Sharp Major, BWV 872, for instance, he "reconstructed" the final bars, relying in part on an older version of the prelude, in which some of the harmonies were notated using only block chords. All three voices contain notes that are altered in terms of pitch and register, although rhythmic similarities persist in the bass, and the rhythm of constant sixteenth notes remains unaltered. He felt his version was better (!) than Bach's, but left it up to the student to determine why (see music example 1.3).[8]

For Busoni, transcription was also important for the educational process, as was a study of a piece's genealogy and transformation. Bach had learned composition by transcribing the works of others, and Busoni taught his students to do the same. He encouraged them to become more critical composers by identifying multiple ways of approaching the same piece. Thus, in his edition, he did not seek to provide a single definitive version, but included multiple versions of Bach's preludes when available, such as the Prelude no. 5 in D Minor, BWV 874.

While Busoni used Bach's pieces as models for form, counterpoint, and thematic interrelatedness, he relied on Mozart's music as a model for orchestration. In an age dominated by Mahlerian and Wagnerian lushness, his call to return to Mozartian principles of orchestration was

Anmerkungen

Dies praeludium besteht aus einem ersten Abschnitt von zweimal drei Takten, einem zweiten von viermal zwei und wieder zweimal drei Takten und einer Gruppe von vier weiteren Takten, die zum Fughette führen. Die fughette, dreiteilig gestaltet, setzt sich zusammen aus neun, sieben, und zehn Takten: Exposition, Durchführung und Coda en miniature. Die melodische Linie, die aus den obersten Noten des Soprans am Ende des ersten und des zweiten Teils des Vorspiels sich ergibt

gibt die Veranlassung zum Fughetten-Thema; eine verborgene Beziehung, die man nicht verkennen sollte.

Zur Hebung des Klanges wäre die Verdoppelung des Basses   oder der Mittelstimme von guter Wirkung

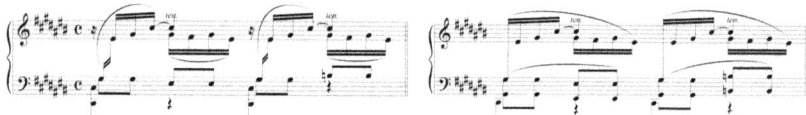

wobei man allerdings die weiche Tongebung der Violen und Violoncelle in einem Streichquintettsatz sich zu vergegenwärtigen hätte.

MUSIC EXAMPLE 1.1. Busoni's adaptation of and commentary about J. S. Bach's Prelude no. 3 in C-Sharp Major, BWV 872, from *The Well-Tempered Clavier*, book II. The German text can be translated as follows: "This prelude consists of a first section of twice three bars, a second section of four times two bars, and a return of twice three bars, before a group of four other bars that lead to a fughetta. The fughetta, a tripartite design, is made up of 9, 7, and 10 measures: exposition, development, and coda in miniature. The melodic line of the uppermost notes of the soprano at the end of the first and second parts of the prelude is the source of the fughetta theme—a hidden relationship you should not ignore. In order to enhance the sound, the doubling of the bass or of the middle would create a good effect, whereby one generally recalls the soft tone of the violas and cellos in the string quintet."

[1] Die Kompositionsstudie will eine deutliche Darstellung aller thematischen Stimmen, häufig ihre Zurückführung auf den ursprünglichen Sinn sowie eine Vervollständigung der Vierstimmigkeit in der Exposition darlegen. Dadurch soll dem Studierenden die Bedeutung aller Einschränkungen und Umbildungen des Originals zum Bewußtsein gebracht werden. Das Thema ist überall durch Bögen kenntlich gemacht.

MUSIC EXAMPLE 1.2. Busoni's re-staving of J. S. Bach's Fugue no. 2 in C Minor, BWV 871, from *The Well-Tempered Clavier*, book II. A translation of the footnote is as follows: "This composition study seeks to present a clear depiction of all the thematic voices, expose their meaning in their original context, as well as demonstrate the perfection of the four voices in the exposition. Through this study, the meaning of all fragmentations and transformations [of the subject] are brought to consciousness. The subject is made evident by slurs."

1) Wir versuchen die thematische Idee, deren teuere Gestaltung zugunsten der chromatischen Melodieführung aufgegeben ist, zu rekonstruieren und gewinnen in dem folgenden Beispiel eine Fassung, die zwischen der älteren Version und dem Haupttext die Mitte einnimmt.

MUSIC EXAMPLE 1.3. Busoni's reworked version of the end of the ending of Prelude no. 3 in C-Sharp Major, BWV 872, from J. S. Bach's *Well-Tempered Clavier*, book II. A translation of the note is as follows: "We seek to reconstruct the thematic idea, whose structure is subsumed in the chromatic melody, and to portray a version in the following example that captures a middle ground between the older version and the main text."

unconventional. For Busoni, Mozart was the ideal orchestrator. He claimed that all orchestral works needed to directly refer back to Mozart. Busoni especially admired Mozart's approach toward spacing and voice leading, which contributed to transparent but resonant textures that took advantage of diverse instrumental timbres and colors:[9]

> Hardly explored yet today are the secrets of spacing in Mozart's works. Broadly demonstrated: a) the influence of voice leading on the choice of instrumentation. Mozart often uses double counterpoint. This causes the most striking feature of his scores: the leading voice is simultaneously above and below the accompaniment (or the other way around); b) his pedal notes; c) the wide position in the strings; a free space to give the harmonies room to breathe, in other words allowing space for the overtones of the lower voices, including the unimposing horns and bassoons. An important point: melodic strings always play through closed chords in the brass, not the other way around, because doubling

in order to penetrate is foreign to Mozart. He would double something only to achieve a distinct instrumental color (e.g., flutes and oboes, flutes and bassoons, etc.) or to support the dynamic intensification of a theme.[10]

Orchestration was an integral (rather than ancillary) part of the compositional process for Busoni, and he spent much time with his students discussing the topic, frequently using Mozart as the main example. He was known to ask students to orchestrate a passage from a Mozart concerto and then compare their versions to the original. Selden-Goth describes one such assignment that included orchestrating sixty-four bars of a piano arrangement of a Mozart concerto without looking first at the complete score. Then students compared their version with Mozart's in order to better understand the techniques of the master. The goal was not to imitate Mozart, but rather, by comparing solutions, to gain a richer vision of the possibilities of orchestration. He urged his students to systematically repeat this process until they understood the intricacies of Mozart's orchestrations.[11]

Busoni considered writing an orchestration treatise relying on ideas from Mozart, Wagner, and his own experience, and he published an outline in 1905, but he never completed the project. Even so, the 1905 draft, and subsequent detailed unpublished sketches recorded in Philipp Jarnach's handwriting, provide a good idea as to the advice he gave to composition students. In particular, he stressed the connectedness of the instruments, stating that they should function like a single unit, like a piano with an expansive register, yet with the added advantage of differing timbral qualities. He maintained that all the instrument types should regularly participate, that there should not be long stretches of music featuring a single orchestral group. He thought spatially when discussing register, and he sought to counter the notion that soft dynamics required few instruments. Most importantly, he discussed what he called "absolute instrumentation," that is, when the timbre is viewed as essential to a work's identity—as opposed to the view that instrumentation can be added at the end of the compositional process.[12]

Mozart served as a model not only for orchestration, but also for dramatic principles. Busoni encouraged his students to study Mozart's operas, in particular, *Die Zauberflöte*, *Le Nozze di Figaro*, and *Don Giovanni*.[13]

He turned to Mozart for models of dramatic pacing, characterization of characters, and stylistic heterogeneity.

Although Bach and Mozart were the main composers that Busoni covered with his composition students, he also referred to Italian opera composers, especially Bellini, Donizetti, and Verdi, as models of melodic writing. For Busoni, melody was the fundamental building block of music from which the harmony could be organically derived. Yet although he admired the long melodies of the Italian opera masters, he also began developing his own theories about melody and harmonic derivation not long after learning of Bernhard Ziehn's principles of melodic and harmonic integration from Frederick Stock in Chicago: "This 'absolute' melody, at first a self-sufficient formation, united itself subsequently with accompanying harmony, and later melted with it into oneness; out of this oneness the continually progressive poly-harmony aims to free and liberate itself."[14]

HOW BUSONI TAUGHT COMPOSITION: SCORE CRITIQUE

If Busoni's students studied the music of the masters, they also clamored for his comments on their work. He looked at the scores of his pupils, sometimes right away, while at other times he would keep the scores and look at them in private. He did not always notate comments in the scores; he often provided suggestions in person or in letters, and he would frequently relate the comments to his aesthetic vision of music. On the other hand, he sometimes rewrote whole passages. According to Stuckenschmidt, Walther Geiser once brought him a score; he took it, disappeared, and came back having rewritten and orchestrated it.[15] Busoni was more than happy to critique scores even after his students had moved away, either in person during visits or via mail, and in that way he maintained lasting relationships with many of them. Guerrini, for instance, only studied with the composer in Bologna from 1913 to 1914, but he continued sending pieces to him until Busoni's death in 1924. Busoni reportedly responded with detailed and insightful comments.[16] Dieren also bought pieces to Busoni for advice, including a piano piece on March 11, 1912.[17] Letters between Dieren and Busoni that span from 1910 to 1921 provide some evidence of suggestions about compositions. When Dieren asked for advice about opera, Busoni suggested that it needs to be based on fantastic subjects (as opposed to historical figures, which—according to Busoni—must not sing).[18] In 1913, the two discussed Dieren's first string quartet and plans for a second quartet.[19] In 1919, Dieren sent Busoni the score of a composition entitled *Carnavalesque*, which he had dedicated to him. Busoni specifically praised the transparency of the orchestration.[20]

Some of the most detailed surviving records of Busoni's score critiques appear in the form of two pages of manuscript paper featuring comments about compositions by Louis Gruenberg, who studied with him in Berlin.[21] When Gruenberg submitted a piano sonata for critique, Busoni responded on August 11, 1908, with copious suggestions. In addition to requesting orthographic clarification, he also sketched out possible alternative realizations. On a separate page, he offered ideas about instrumentation and texture for an unspecified orchestral piece from around the same time period, including that the unbroken fugal subject at the beginning of the scherzo would be better served by more contrapuntal movement. In another passage, he suggested a scoring of cellos, trombones, and basses. To add greater spirit to the finale, he encouraged Gruenberg to score the trumpets one octave higher (see figure 1.1).

HOW BUSONI TAUGHT COMPOSITION: AESTHETIC VISION

If Busoni imparted practical ideas about the craft of composition through the lens of music masterpieces and score critique, he shared his esoteric vision of music through conversations during private lessons or social gatherings. In addition, students read his published writings about music.[22] For most of his students, it was his aesthetic ideas that had the greatest impact.

These ideas were informed by an intellectual culture that included German idealists, such as Arthur Schopenhauer (1788–1860), who preached the preeminence of music and its close association with nature, as well as the writings of Johann Wolfgang von Goethe (1749–1832) and Friedrich Nietzsche (1844–1900), whose ideas about organicism and eternal reoccurrence were foundational for Busoni's theories of form and Young Classicality.[23] German Romantic authors, such as E.T.A. Hoffmann, who glorified the fantastic, also informed his theories about opera. In addition,

FIGURE 1.1. Busoni, notes for Gruenberg's sonata-in-progress. Private collection of Joan Gruenberg Cominos, Martinez, CA.

his ideas were impacted by contemporaneous artistic movements, including Futurism and *Jugendstil*. Like others influenced by the brief *Jugendstil* movement, Busoni wanted to break away from traditional forms and move to a more organic and abstract art characterized by color, uniqueness, and asymmetry.[24] His contributions to the magazine *Pan*, which was published in Berlin from 1895 to 1900 and again from 1910 to 1915, reveal direct connections to the movement. Along with other *Jugendstil* authors, poets, and artists, he published his ideas at least three times in the magazine from 1911 to 1912.[25] Although not an advocate of noise music, like Luigi Russolo (1885–1947) nor interested in making a complete break with music of the past, as many Futurists were, he nevertheless also embraced the Futurist fascination with new technology. As a friend of Umberto Boccioni (1882–1916), Busoni had ample time to exchange ideas with Futurists.

As a syncretist, Busoni's ideas were inclusive. Consequently, his instruction was rarely dogmatic. It often took the form of witty dialogues between teacher and pupil in the manner of Plato. He did not want to impose opinions on students in an authoritarian manner, but he did make his views known. At the same time, he welcomed differences of opinion, and he often talked about composers and pieces from diverse vantage points, thus resulting in seemingly paradoxical or inconsistent points of view. One conversation with Dieren began with Verdi's *Falstaff* and ended with Puccini's *Madama Butterfly*, but turned to Beethoven and Liszt in the middle. The two discussed orchestration and staging, among other topics:

BUSONI: I am looking for the first time at a full score of *Falstaff*
MYSELF: Oh! Ah!
B. I am greatly disappointed.
M. !?!
B. Honestly—don't be upset—his brass writing is too...
M. Oh, please don't. Think of the richness...
B. Yes, but perhaps that reminds me too much of the Italian brass band of his day. That is what he imagined; that is what he wrote for.
M. Can't we give him the benefit of the doubt, and believe he foresaw what sound we should hear later?
B. Let us—but what about the "one-two-three," "one-two-three"?

M. What about the agonizing brass of the "Emperor" Concerto, and those recurring entries in imitation?

B. (*who has just played the work*) Let's not talk about it. But what do you think of the other work on the programme, I mean the "Totentanz"?

M. I think Liszt...

B. Yes, I know all that—one time I think he is more than capable, more capable than anyone has need to be, and at other times that he is technically not quite competent. What *is* one to think?

M. That is not what people like or disdain him for. See how they are all crazy about Puccini now; here is a modicum of incompetence for you all the time, and yet...

B. All the same, last season when I was in Milan I walked in at the opera and I heard "Butterfly"—and it was all so well put on and so well done; I thought it was really quite charming.

M. !!![26]

In yet another conversation, they discussed orchestration and registration based on Wagner's *Tristan* prelude. Busoni's disdain for Wagner's writing, which he considered formulaic, is thinly veiled by sarcasm:

MYSELF: I have been carefully studying the "Tristan" Prelude today.

BUSONI. And...

M. One must admit...

B. Ah, mustn't one...

M. Only, when one by one they all come in doing the same thing.—these crushing, crashing octaves...

B. Oh, but you must leave him that. That was his special acoustic discovery. One can understand his making the most of the sonority he got by it.[27]

Topics were not just focused on music. Busoni took a holistic approach, teaching that the artist needed more than technical prowess to write masterpieces. He had to be a well-rounded *mensch*, with a rich understanding of the humanities—especially literature, architecture, and the other arts.[28] Busoni had wide-ranging interests, and he tried to expand the intellectual and artistic horizons of his students—he disliked focusing merely on craftsmanship.[29] Discussions often turned to Goethe's *Faust*, Miguel de Cervantes's *Don Quixote*, or other important pieces of literature. Dieren remembers, for instance, how one conversation that started with Giacomo Meyerbeer shifted to Hector Berlioz and ended with references to English literature and culture.[30] Guerrini similarly recalls that Busoni saw music as connected to culture. To discuss music was to discuss all of the arts: "In his courses he not only cared about the instrument or the music, but always aimed at the totality of the arts and of humanity. So the lessons were a bit in all areas: from the literary to the philosophical to the aesthetic to the moral-social. And even more than with the spoken word, he loved to spread his knowledge and advise and guide you through epistolary correspondence, which is often a very minor aspect of pedagogy."[31]

The visual and plastic arts were especially important to Busoni, who encouraged his students to think of music in spatial terms.[32] In addition, he stressed the importance of the visual presentation of scores as part of the complete artwork.

Busoni's aesthetic thoughts also formed an integral part of the conversations, and none of his students left without being familiar with his texts and ideas. He imparted a vision of music that he hoped would guide students' aesthetic and technical decisions. In this way he communicated avant-garde and experimentalist thoughts about electronic instruments and the expansion of the tonal system. During student gatherings, he discussed his idiosyncratic ideas about music and sometimes read from his libretti or aesthetic texts as a form of instruction. Some of his students' personal copies of Busoni's writings, replete with personal annotations, have survived, thereby offering glimpses into what they gleaned from the text.[33] His writings also provide a vivid glimpse into some of the topics he must have discussed with his pupils.

Busoni's *Entwurf einer neuen Ästhetik der Tonkunst* starts with a vision of abstract music in nature before moving to a more tangible discussion of the art of composing. He did not propose any methods, claiming that music was abstract, free, and limitless, like nature itself, in contradistinction to the other arts that were fettered by the imitation of text or image: "Music was born free, and to win freedom is its destiny. It will become the most complete of all reflexes of nature by reason of its untrammeled immateriality."[34] Instead, in a series of aphoristic sections, he poses suggestive possibilities that can be applied in numerous ways.[35]

Throughout his writings, Busoni stressed that the human artwork should reflect music in nature through style, content, and form. According to Busoni, the essence of music, also called "Ur-Musik" and "Eternal harmony" in his writings, was an unheard source of music resounding in the vibrating universe that provided germinal material for all compositions. Weindel likened it to *musica mundana*, and Crispin notes its existence outside time and its similarity to nature.[36] The composer's job, according to Busoni, was that of a prophet—to divine the mysteries of music in nature and to translate them into audible sounds. For that reason, he did not believe that art music could be truly original. In phrases reminiscent of the harmony of the spheres, he claimed that everything already exists in the vibrating universe—all scales and all combinations of sounds. The clearer the vision of true music, the better the translation and the more perfect the artwork, which he felt should be stylistically inclusive, thus reflecting the oneness of the styles in nature.

Busoni's theory of musical oneness had important ramifications for his teachings on stylistic pluralism and the exploration of new scales and harmonies. He argued that since music is pure tone and all-encompassing in its primordial state, audible music should embrace all scales, harmonies, and styles of music. It should not be subjected to stylistic, historical, and genre divisions, which he claimed limited musical possibilities: "The time has come to recognize the whole phenomenon of music as a 'oneness' and no longer split it up according to its purpose, form, and sound-medium. It should be recognized from two premises exclusively, that of its content and that of its quality."[37] He did not encourage his students to forge a new style of music, which he believed would age quickly, nor to imitate the new styles of any contemporaries, but rather to embrace the stylistic characteristics of all the compositions they admired and to combine them, reflecting the multiplicity of musics in the sounding universe: "I believe one should attempt to put into one's own music all that is assimilable of the composers one admires most and loves best. That is a sensible procedure, and a better tribute than uncritical veneration. Surely better than to ape a style and then set this up as the exclusive model for others."[38] He especially urged his mentees not to get caught up in the styles of the present. As he wrote to Jarnach, "One has to laugh, people have increasingly closed vision. They understand the value of the present, but not one second beyond that."[39]

Busoni's vision extended to scalar systems and instrumental sounds. He embraced the newest ideas about instruments, scales and music organization, suggesting they could be combined with the scales and instruments of the past and present.[40] In particular, he talked about the possibilities of microtonal scales and new divisions of the octave as a reflection of the unlimited possibilities of music. He helped his students dream of new sounds beyond traditional acoustic ones. In particular, he talked about Thaddeus Cahill's electronic telharmonium.[41] In practice, he also experimented with polytonality, music without bar lines, and new scales.

Because of Busoni's views about the role of the composer as a diviner of inaudible music already in existence, he communicated countercultural views about originality to his students. His theory of Young Classicality reached maturity just after World War I, even if the roots of the theory were germinating already at the beginning of the twentieth century.[42] Young Classicality is not primarily a looking back to the past, but a fusion of past musical experiments with current ones to create new and unique forms: "By 'Young Classicism' I mean the mastery, the sifting and the turning to account of all the gains of previous experiments and their inclusion in strong and beautiful forms. This art will be old and new at the same time."[43]

As Fleet notes, Busoni was part of a larger trend of composers and authors (especially from *the Jung-Wien* movement) in Central Europe seeking to situate their works within historical traditions.[44] With a sense of youthful optimism, he believed that art was continually evolving to greater perfection, even as he elevated melody and thin textures.[45] He believed that what is truly classical will never age, and that it is characterized by timeless compositional traits (e.g., counterpoint), solid but unique forms, objectivity, and stylistic plurality.

Unlike many of his contemporaries, Schoenberg included, Busoni did not place a high value on originality. In a dialogue with Dieren, he claimed that the possibility of originality was doubtful, at best, and was certainly not the main goal of artwork: "Originality is a strange thing. Ponder it as you will, it is deceptive, fugitive. An intractable, elusive quality. A creative artist should not be consciously occupied with it."[46] Great compositions did not need to be new, but rather, of high quality, according to Busoni. Thus it was not a philosophical or aesthetic problem for Busoni and his students to create transcriptions or to borrow from and build upon previous compositions.[47] He illustrated this process of musical evolution using the model of his own *Fantasia contrappuntistica*, BV 256 (1910, 1912, 1922), which many of his composition students heard, and which was a completion of Bach's *Die Kunst der Fuge*, BWV 1080, coupled with new added material, including an introductory fantasia.[48] Busoni considered the work his own, even despite the reuse of Bach's material:

> There is no new and old. Only known and not yet known. Of these, it seems to me that the known still forms by far the smaller part. A *Fantasia Contrappuntistica* was the first item on the program of 19th January. This work grew out of the attempt to complete J. S. Bach's last unfinished fugue. It is a study. (Every self-portrait of Rembrandt's is a study; every work is a study for the next one; every life's work a study for those who come after.) The Bach fragment is planned on four fugue subjects, of which two are complete and the third commenced. The fragment breaks off when the three of these meet together for the first time, but the "development" of these three themes is lacking.... The fourth subject, on the other hand, had to be a completely new creation; there was no clue as to its character.... The old does not yield to the new but to the better.[49]

Busoni particularly discouraged working measure to measure; he also preferred to evaluate complete compositions. For this reason, he liked to hold irregular lessons separated by rather large spans of time, as Guerrini remembers:

> The primary condition imposed by the Maestro to his disciples was to bring to a lesson a certain amount of work. He did not admit (I think of the composition student of today) students that came with a folio of eight to sixteen bars. One went to class maybe once a month, but with a finished work, it was one time a sonata, or a symphonic piece, or a scene from an opera. This is because the lesson consisted of, and "had to consist of," above all, an aesthetic discussion between Master and disciple. Indeed, the Maestro almost always started with the resolve not to get into questioning technique; therefore—he said—"the aesthetic result can justify use of all technical means."[50]

Busoni claimed that every composition should begin with an overarching vision for that particular work and that it could be informed by human experience. The vision, in turn, had to be translated into audible musical ideas that are then arranged into complete works of art reflecting the ideals of "abstract music":[51] "First comes the idea, then the conception, or one seeks for it, then follows the execution."[52] He taught that the vision should determine the formal structure of a piece—and not traditional forms taken from the *Formenlehre* tradition. While traditional forms played an important role in the majority of composition instruction at the time, for Busoni they only held historical interest. He called for strong and beautiful forms derived organically from opening themes, but sought them through a melding of forms normally kept separate, such as fantasia, sonata, palindrome, and variation, for instance. He idealized unique forms and instructed his students to strive for the same: "I am a worshipper of form! I have remained sufficiently a Latin for that. But I demand—no! the organism of art demands—that every idea fashions its own form for itself; the organism—not I—revolts against having one single form for all ideas."[53]

Busoni frequently modeled form after architectural structures rather than traditional musical forms, which he considered too systematic. As an avid lover of architecture, he collected books with floor plans, created his own architectural drawings, and also discussed architecture with his students. In one conversation with his students, he reportedly stated: "Form in music can often be compared with form in architecture. Thus three-part form is analogous to the Greek temple. There are other Greek buildings that are not based on a central idea, but have decoration and motifs going right round, often in the form of a frieze in bas-relief depicting historical or mythological scenes, each one quite different, but all united on the same plane."[54]

In the Germanic tradition, the symphony was considered the crowning genre. By the mid-1910s, however, Busoni began to view opera, or some combination of music, scenery, and vocalization, as the highest art form. He envisioned a complete musical work in which the visual and drama explicate what is happening musically and provide a context for stylistic pluralism.[55] For him, opera most closely approached music in nature because it invited many different styles of music and because it could transport the listener out of the everyday through supernatural subjects.[56]

HOW BUSONI TAUGHT COMPOSITION: PERFORMANCE AS INSTRUCTION AND AN AVOIDANCE OF ROUTINE

Busoni's instruction was not always esoteric and idealistic. For the composer, music was also to be heard, and performance and listening were integral parts of the compositional process. Thus he also encouraged free improvisation as part of the creative process. In addition, he often demonstrated at the piano. Once students had created pieces, he sometimes made them perform them, even if they were not professional musicians. In his Berlin master class, he had students create piano transcriptions of their compositions for performance. In addition, students attended performances of new music. He sponsored concerts in his home to which he invited students, and he also directed an orchestra concert series in Berlin from 1902 to 1909 for the purpose of promoting new music. During the Berlin master class, on November 2, 1921, he revived the practice of educating through concert music with a program of both old and new music:

> Sibelius, Symphony no. 5 in E-Flat Major, op. 82
> Monteverdi, Assorted Madrigals
> Beethoven, Symphony no. 3 in E-Flat Major, op. 55 ("Eroica")
> Busoni, Suite from Mozart's *Idomeneo*, K. 366[57]

He had an insatiable curiosity for the unknown—older music and modern music—and he tried to instill that curiosity in his pupils as well. As Dieren remembers, he could not rest until he had programmed pieces that he found interesting.[58] His students also attended concerts of his own music when the pieces were finished, even if Busoni was reticent to show his own works in progress.

If there was anything predictable about his teaching, it was that of unpredictability. One never knew what he would talk about during the social hours and he did not follow a set and incremental course of assignments. Whatever impressed him or was on his mind would be brought up. This pedagogical style dovetailed with his own view of composition, which, he believed, should be unsystematic. According to Busoni, the creator should not follow any laws, but rather create anew his own each time: "But I think in this way about music: that every case should be a new case, an 'exception.' That every problem, once solved, should experience no repeated attempts at solution."[59]

He criticized systematization as deficient and impoverished; Wagner's system of leitmotifs thus received scathing criticisms from him as formulaic, even if he admired some of his orchestrations. For Busoni, routine was destructive. He claimed that the systematic transformed the masterpiece into little more than a mass-produced commodity. For one who strongly criticized writing music for money, and who held an otherworldly vision of music, this was a scornful criticism. In particular, he criticized routine as practiced in schools and institutions as detrimental to true art: "Routine transforms the Temple into a factory. It destroys all creativeness. For creation means bringing form out of the void. But routine is the factory for mass production. It is 'poetry made to order.' It prevails because it suits the generality. It flourishes in the theatre, in the orchestra, with virtuosi and in the 'Schools of Art,' that is to say those institutions which are arranged excellently for the maintenance of the teachers."[60]

If Busoni was unpredictable in what he spoke about, he also seemed paradoxical to those who knew him. Hardly anything was black and white for him, so seeming or actual contradictions abounded in what he said. For instance, he had a strong antipathy for Wagner, not least because of his "routine" use of leitmotif technique. He might refer to him in a positive light, however, when discussing orchestration, and he also liked *Parsifal*.[61] It was up to students to try to reconcile things that seemed dialectically opposed on the surface but that were logically synthesized in Busoni's mind.

COMPARISON OF TEACHING STYLES AND METHODS

Busoni's unsystematic teaching style, which focused on aesthetic ideas rather than the material of music, was unconventional at the time, as a brief comparison with the pedagogical methods of his contemporaries and near contemporaries illustrates. Because he had largely concentrated on concertizing and teaching piano early on, the majority of his composition teaching activities took place after he reached the age of forty (in the years 1906–1924). For that reason, Nadia Boulanger and Arnold Schoenberg, both of whom were slightly younger yet who began teaching seriously around the same time as Busoni, provide comparative examples. The fact that Schoenberg succeeded Busoni in leading a Berlin composition master class at the Akademie der Künste in 1925 strengthens the comparison.[62] Although Boulanger and Schoenberg, like Busoni, considered the masterpieces to be central to instruction, and also recognized the importance of the individuality of each student, style and technique were the main foundations of their composition instruction.[63] So was regular systematic training.

Boulanger believed that technique was a foundation upon which students could discover personal style. She thus insisted students systematically study and practice basic technical skills, such as counterpoint, harmony, score reading, or figured bass, until they had completely mastered the subjects.[64] Additionally, she required students of all ability levels to take remedial courses if she perceived deficiencies. Virgil Thomson remembers that her goal was solid technique: "Her teaching of the musical techniques is . . . full of rigor, while her toleration of expressive and stylistic variety in composition is virtually infinite."[65] Stylistic variety was a byproduct that she not only tolerated but also embraced, within some bounds. She had definite stylistic ideals closely aligned with French Neoclassical ideals, such that some of her students adopted similar stylistic approaches. Matthew Mugmon has argued that her tolerance of Austro-Germanic music after Beethoven was limited. In particular, she disliked the twelve-tone music of Schoenberg even while favoring the music of Igor Stravinsky.[66]

Students remember that it took six to eight hours per day just to prepare for the lessons with Boulanger, which consisted largely of abstract exercises. Philip Glass, for instance (who had already trained with a Boulanger pupil in America), had to go back to the basics of harmony and counterpoint when he studied with Boulanger for two years (1963–1965). He states that all the students took part in regularly scheduled instruction with her and with her assistant, Mademoiselle Dieudonné: "You took three classes with her a week. One was a private class, the second was the class you took with Mademoiselle Dieudonné, which was also private. Then there was a third class called the Wednesday Class, which was a general class of all of her students who were with her at the time."[67] The most challenging Black Thursday classes, "by invitation only," consisted of six to eight students and met for three hours. Subjects varied but often included assignments in which the goal was to recreate exact harmonizations by the masters without having prior knowledge of the pieces. Boulanger also gave composition lessons privately, and, according to Virgil Thomson, they consisted largely of score critique with Boulanger at the piano: "The lessons take place with the teacher at the piano, the student in a chair at her right. She reads the score before her silently at first, then little by little begins to comment, spontaneously admiring here and there a detail of musical syntax or sound, expressing temporary reservations about another. Suddenly she will start playing (and perfectly, for she is a fabulous sight-reader) some passage that she needs to hear out loud or that she wishes the student to hear as illustration to her remarks."[68]

Of particular contrast to Busoni's approach was Boulanger's attention to detail. While Busoni focused on meta-suggestions and rewrote pieces away from the piano, Boulanger focused on specific concrete technical problems at the piano.[69] Joel Feigin remembers that Boulanger emphasized craft and how to move notes around and that she taught voice leading through harmony.[70]

Like Boulanger, Schoenberg, who succeeded Busoni as master class instructor at the Akademie der Künste in 1925, regularly taught the basics of harmony and counterpoint to his students, insisting that they establish a firm foundation before branching off into free composition. During one of his earlier teaching positions, when he first began instructing Alban Berg and Anton Webern as part of the *Freies Konservatorium*, which was started by reform pedagogue Eugenie Schwarzwald in the facilities of a girls' school in October 1904, Schoenberg reportedly oriented harmony training after Simon Sechter and used Johann Joseph Fux for counterpoint.[71] Instruction began with three years of harmony and counterpoint. His own *Harmonielehre* (1911), which was not intended to spell out the rules of correct writing but to explain the logic underlying tonal harmony, was born from his experiences as a teacher. Moreover, the *Formenlehre* tradition based on Adolf Bernhard Marx's writings was integral to Schoenberg's teaching.[72] Free composition assignments included three- and four-voice choral arrangements and four- and five-voice double fugues. He insisted that mere technique was not enough to make someone great, but it was *necessary* for greatness, and he made sure his students had a firm technical foundation.[73] In his Berlin master class, Schoenberg reportedly also included detailed assignments in music analysis and critiqued his students' works. Marc Blitzstein (1905–1964), who studied orchestration, counterpoint, and free composition with Schoenberg in Berlin for about five months, maintains that Schoenberg was "married" to his theories, which he taught in his master classes, and that he severely criticized works that went beyond his own theories and Germanic aesthetic ideals.[74] He took a very "left-brained" approach, with an interest, above all, in the process or the working out of theories. The class analyses of pieces like Mahler's Symphony no. 6 in A Minor ("Tragische") and *Das Lied von der Erde*, along with Schoenberg's Wind Quintet op. 26, consisted largely of parsing the structure apart from any musical or sonorous considerations. Blitzstein remembers looking at many diagrams and schemes, for instance, that Schoenberg used to create his Quintet.[75]

While many contemporaneous pedagogues drilled technique into their students, they also encouraged learning from the great masterpieces, but they did so through traditional analytical means. Boulanger, in particular, wanted students to have a good understanding of tradition and how their compositions fit into that tradition. Lennox Berkeley, claiming that exposure to the music of the masters helped develop personal taste and an understanding of form, summarizes:[76] "She was an inspiring force, and her inspiration consisted in making us aware of the necessity of acquiring the technique which is indispensible for a composer.... Apart from that, she helped us to form our own tastes by insisting that we had to know music by composers of the past in depth; on this foundation she could help us to develop our sense of form."[77] She had her classes analyze the masterpieces and she presented material topically, rather than chronologically. For instance, she devoted one season to analyzing the cantatas of Bach and one to the Mozart concerti.[78] In Boulanger's lessons, she taught technical skills using the great masters as reference, but with a reverence lacking in Busoni's teaching. Bach's counterpoint, according to Elliott Carter, was held as a standard to which Boulanger's students aspired. To do it the same way Bach did was an accomplishment. Altering Bach would have been unthinkable.[79]

The basis of Schoenberg's teaching was also the music of the masters. Schoenberg insisted that his students be thoroughly familiar with musical masterpieces through analysis in order to understand how their compositions related to tradition and differed from it. He wanted his students to understand how historical composers tackled the problems of working with and shaping the materials of music, and then to come up with their own novel solutions. Busoni, by contrast, wanted his disciples to revise and build upon the musics of the past. Whereas Schoenberg utilized analysis for the sake of revolution and originality, Busoni was interested in evolution:

> Often, a young man who wants to study with me expects to be taught in musical modernism. But he experiences a disappointment. Because in his compositions I usually recognize the absence of an adequate background. Superficially investigating I unveil the cause: the student's knowledge of musical literature offers the aspects of Swiss cheese—almost more holes than cheese. Then I ask the following question: "If you wanted to build an aeroplane, would you venture to invent and construct by yourself every detail of which it is composed, or would you not better first try to acknowledge what all men did who designed aeroplanes before you? Don't you think the same idea is correct in music?"[80]

Despite fundamental differences with regard to technique and analysis of the masters, similarities can also be observed. As with Busoni's students, so also with Boulanger's and Schoenberg's, lessons extended beyond the confines of official classes to social events. Schoenberg, Busoni, and Boulanger were concerned about their students as individuals, and the students became their friends. Berg helped Schoenberg with details related to his move and an American pupil reportedly taught Boulanger to drive, while Busoni's pupils helped him with editions, piano reductions, rehearsals, and issues related to his final illness. Boulanger, like Busoni, promoted her students as well, introducing Aaron Copland to Serge Koussevitzky, for instance, who later performed his music.

In addition, Schoenberg, Boulanger, and Busoni all insisted that students should always start with a vision for a complete piece. However, Schoenberg's and Boulanger's visions were musical ones, even while Busoni's was initially an aesthetic one. Schoenberg stated, like Busoni, that it is detrimental to plot out a few measures per day without a larger plan for the piece: "A composer must not compose two or eight or sixteen measures today and again tomorrow and so on until the work seemed to be finished, but should conceive a composition as a totality, in one single act of inspiration. Intoxicated by his idea, he should write down as much as he could, not caring for the little details. They could be added, or carried out later."[81] Boulanger, for her part, insisted that a composition needed to have *la grande ligne*, a term which no one knows how to translate, but which has something to do with linear and organic unfolding. Although it is not clear that this *grande ligne* needed to be completely conceived before a piece was started, it was a purely musical conception.[82]

For Boulanger, performance was also an important part of instruction. She had her students conduct, sing, and play, but in a pedantic way, as a means of gaining mastery over musical material. For his part, Busoni taught through performance in his new music concerts in Berlin from 1902 to 1909. He also insisted that student compositions be performed (often in piano reductions) in his Berlin master class.

Busoni's pedagogical approach was spontaneous and focused on ideology, as opposed to musical material. This was blatantly different than the teaching style of his contemporaries. Moreover, it went against the grain of most of the instructional treatises of the age, which focus on techniques for combining the materials of music. Composition treatises or method books usually covered the topics of harmony, counterpoint, and/or form methodically and in detail. Sometimes the topics are covered comprehensively in multi-volume methods by single authors. Other times, authors focus on a single topic. Popular texts at the time included Johann Joseph Fux for counterpoint and Simon Sechter for harmony. Hector Berlioz was seen as a model for orchestration and A. B. Marx for form.[83] Before meeting Busoni, Jean Sibelius worked through the comprehensive four-volume *Lehrbuch der musikalischen Komposition* by Johann Christian Lobe, which progresses incrementally from basic concepts, such as the treatment of diatonic harmony, part writing, motive formation, and forms (vol. 1), to instrumentation (vol. 2), counterpoint (vol. 3), and opera composition (vol. 4).[84] Like Busoni, Lobe relies heavily on exemplary compositions to teach compositional technique. He also upholds Mozart as the quintessential example for opera and Bach for counterpoint. Haydn, Mozart, and Beethoven feature prominently in the volume on harmony and motive formation and Berlioz serves as a model for orchestration. However, Lobe's emphasis is on the treatment of music material, and his presentation of ideas is fairly methodical. His volume on orchestration, for instance, lists each instrument individually—systematically discussing range, timbral qualities, and uses. Rather than communicating color as an integral fiber of compositional identity, Lobe urges students to practice doublings first in keyboard score before considering timbre and color.[85] In volume 1, he covers scales, cadences, and phrasing, for instance. Information about aesthetics is relegated to an ancillary closing section entitled "addendum," in which he includes compositional maxims. For his part, Varèse chose to have his early composition students in Berlin work through harmony books by Ludwig Thuille/Rudolf Louis and Schoenberg, both of which offer compositional advice through presentations of basic principles of harmony and voice leading. The texts might have appealed to Varèse, because they feature innovative treatments of chromaticism or dissonance resolution. Thuille, for instance, offers the usual advice about triadic harmony and voice leading. However, he also includes information about complex chromatic modulations that stretched the boundaries of tonality, such as movement from A minor to C-sharp minor.[86] In addition, his book contains extensive information about chromatic chords. Schoenberg, who sought in his text to teach composition through harmony, covers consonance and dissonance, modes, voice leading, cadences, modulation, and non-harmonic tones, among other topics. Schoenberg's sometimes discursive but almost always deep writing style interweaves philosophy of music with guidelines for treating the material of music. Yet unlike Busoni, Schoenberg's end goal is not to communicate esoteric aesthetic ideas but practical compositional principles. He stresses throughout that he is interested in tones and their combinations. He avoids figured bass realizations—asking students instead to devise their own harmonic progressions, phrases, and forms—a difference, he claims, that mandates the fusion of harmony and composition from the beginning.

Busoni's teaching style was thus fundamentally different from some of the most influential contemporaneous teachers. Moreover, it did not reflect the thorough, systematic training in most composition method books in circulation at the time. While Boulanger and Schoenberg focused on the materials of music and systematically conveyed a thorough technical foundation, Busoni focused on aesthetic ideas and connected music to the other arts. He left the fundamentals up to others and inspired his students with esoteric ideas. Lessons were intermittent, and there were no assignments that built up in an incremental manner. Although he used the music of the masters as teaching tools, he did not consider it sacrosanct. He was always ready to point out sections of tremendous competence in Bach's music, but he encouraged his students to rewrite the music as well. He had no distinctive pedagogical method of his own, as he eschewed routine and tried to do things differently every time. Busoni thought his students could figure out the fundamentals on their own as their vision of what music should be like directed them.

CLOSING THOUGHTS

Despite the idiosyncrasy of Busoni's approach, it had a profound effect on many of the youths who studied with him. At the same time, the students also had a positive effect on Busoni. To the end of his life, he surrounded himself with young people, and he enjoyed exchanging ideas with them. He was enthused by their ideas and their energy—their ideas reminded him to never become complacent: "The fact, that both as an artist and as a human being, I prefer looking forward rather than backward, explains why I like having young people around me. So may it continue until the end—because if that ceases to be the case, it is very sad."[87]

According to Guerrini, Busoni not only basked in the presence of youth, but he also had young people's best interests in mind, even if this meant stating what they did not want to hear: "Busoni's love for young people was the true love of teacher, the one that in order to educate is not afraid to hurt. Ruthless criticism was in him the greatest sign of consideration and affection. For this reason, only a few of his disciples followed him, then, in life. In general, the young people of his time did not understand him or were averse to him, in part, because [they were] intolerant of his brusque means of educating."[88]

To those who followed him, he became a father figure—a priest—revealing the secrets of art. He encouraged them to tap previously unexplored creative regions in their minds and souls. Thus some statements by Busoni pupils must be read with reservation, as it was common for mentees to put their teachers on pedestals, especially in Germany, where hagiography and an obsession with greatness colored the way of writing about well-respected figures. Moreover, Busoni, like Schoenberg, consciously cultivated a sense of authority. Schoenberg did this through the dogmatic assertion of his theories, and Busoni fostered an aura of otherworldliness, further contributing to the awe with which their students held them. As Levitz has already noted, although jovial and human during social hours, Busoni sometimes portrayed an air of authority during lessons by modeling his teaching behavior and style of communication on literary characters. For instance, he dialogued with his students like Mephistopheles had done with Faust, thereby assuming the role of the wise and all-knowing master.[89] At times, he could be condescending and sarcastic.

Busoni never wanted his role as pedagogue to be pedantic; rather, he saw himself as a motivator and a visionary. He believed anyone could develop the technical craft of composition, but only those with true ability could understand the vision of music and how to translate that into the vision for an individual composition. He thus tried to bring out the best of the gifted and to help them develop their individual style, but he had little to offer the less talented or the beginner, except for his own charisma. While his pedagogical approach was not successful with all of his pupils, many claim that they were inspired by it. Moreover, although the styles of his students are so diverse that it is difficult to identify a stylistic school, it does not preclude the fact that Busoni's idiosyncratic approach was meaningful and effective, leading to the development of a nexus of composers with a shared vision of music that influenced new trends in early twentieth-century music, including experimentalist ones. This nexus of students explores new sonorities, new ways of organizing sound, and stylistic heterogeneity, even as the students embraced a variety of musical and artistic traditions and reached toward a future of music that reflected their own appropriations of Busoni's vision of the essence of music. In Stuckenschmidt's words: "Pupils of his pupils continue to carry the flame that [Busoni] kindled in the distant past," and it is the story of the kindling of the flame and the passing of the torch that unfolds in more detail in the following pages.[90]

NOTES

1. I am grateful to Matthew Mugmon for his comments on an earlier version of this chapter, as well as to Joel Feigin for sharing his memories of studies with Nadia Boulanger.

2. Busoni, "Introduction to Bach Edition" (1915), in *The Essence of Music and Other Papers*, trans. Rosamund Ley (1922; London: Salisbury Square, 1957), 99.

3. "Hier ist der thematische Zusammenhang mit der Fuge offenbar: trotzdem hält ihn der Herausgeber für unbeabsichtigt; aber die beiden Motive sind aus demselben Geiste heraus geboren." J. S. Bach, *Das wohltemperierte Klavier*, vol. II, ed. Busoni (Leipzig: Breitkopf und Härtel, 1916), 10.

4. Busoni, "Introduction to the Bach Edition" (1915), in *The Essence of Music and Other Papers*, 98.
5. Bach, *Das wohltemperierte Klavier,* vol. II, ed. Busoni, 3.
6. Ibid., 20.
7. Ibid., 14.
8. Ibid., 19.
9. Busoni, "Aesthetik des Orchesters," Staatsbibliothek zu Berlin, Preußischer Kulturbesitz, Musikabteilung mit Mendelssohn-Archiv, Mus. Nachl. F. Busoni, CI-135.
10. "Beinahe unerforscht sind heute noch die Geheimnisse der Lage bei Mozart. Breite Demonstration: a) der Einfluss der Stimmführung auf die instrumentale Zeichnung; Mozart wendet doppelten Kontrapunkt häufig an; daher die frappanteste Erscheinung in seinen Partituren: die führende Stimme gleichzeitig ober- und unterhalb der Begleitung (oder umgekehrt); b) Seine Pedalnoten; c) die breite Lage bei den Streichern, beständiges Sorgen, einen freien Raum für die füllende Harmonie zu erhalten, d.h. Obertone der unteren Stimmen, unaufdringliche Hörner oder Fagotte. Ein wichtiger Moment: melodische Streicher gehen durch geschlossene Blaserakkorde; nie umgekehrt, denn Verdoppelung zum Zweck des Durchdringens sind Mozartfremd. Er wendet solche nur der Klangfarbe wegen an, (Flöte und Oboen—Flöte und Fagotte, u.s.w.) oder zum dynamischen Anwachsen des Themas." Ibid.
11. Gisella Selden-Goth, *Ferruccio Busoni: Der Versuch eines Porträts* (1922; Firenze: Leo S. Olschki, 1964), 130.
12. Busoni, "The Theory of Orchestration," (1905), in *The Essence and Oneness of Music,* 35–36.
13. Busoni encouraged Jarnach to study *Le Nozze di Figaro* in 1916. Busoni to Jarnach, April 4, 1916. Jarnach Nachlass, uncatalogued, Staatsbibliothek zu Berlin, Preußischer Kulturbesitz, Musikabteilung mit Mendelssohn-Archiv, N. Mus. Depos 56.
14. Busoni, "An Attempt at a Definition of Melody" (1913), in *The Essence of Music and Other Papers,* 33.
15. H. H. Stuckenschmidt, *Ferruccio Busoni: "Chronicle of a European* [1967]*,"* trans. Sandra Morris (New York: St. Martin's, 1970), 200–201. Geiser was one of Busoni's Berlin masterclass pupils. For more information about Geiser, consult Tamara Levitz, "Teaching New Classicality: Busoni's Master Class in Composition, 1921–24" (PhD diss., University of Rochester, 1993), 229–230.
16. Guerrini to Busoni, February 3, 1924, Berlin Staatsbibliothek zu Berlin, Preußischer Kulturbesitz, Musikabteilung mit Mendelssohn-Archiv, Mus. Nachl. F. Busoni, BII, 1998. Guerrini still addresses Busoni as "my dearest master" and writes that he has not forgotten Busoni's advice. A letter dated February 6, 1923, from Guerrini states that he meditated on Busoni's every word. In addition, his most recent works, he claimed, had profited from his advice. Staatsbibliothek zu Berlin, Preußischer Kulturbesitz, Musikabteilung mit Mendelssohn-Archiv, Mus. Nachl. F. Busoni, BII, 1998. Guerrini, *Ferruccio Busoni: La vita, la figura, l'opera* (Firenze: Casa Editrice Monsalvato, 1944), 232.
17. Busoni, "Tagesbuch, Staatsbibliothek zu Berlin, Preussischer Kulturbesitz, Musikabteilung mit Mendelssohn Archiv, N. Mus. Nachl. 4, 98.

18. Busoni to Dieren, April 26, 1913, Staatsbibliothek zu Berlin, Preussischer Kulturbesitz, Musikabteilung mit Mendelssohn Archiv, N. Mus. Bachl. F. Busoni, BI, 525. Perhaps these discussions were important for Dieren's only surviving opera, *The Tailor* (1917–1930).

19. Dieren to Busoni, April 18, 1913, Staatsbibliothek zu Berlin, Preussischer Kulturbesitz, Musikabteilung mit Mendelssohn Archiv, N. Mus. Nachl. F. Busoni, BII, 1449.

20. Busoni to Dieren, October 26, 1919, Staatsbibliothek zu Berlin, Preussischer Kulturbesitz, Musikabteilung mit Mendelssohn Archiv, N. Mus. Nachl. F. Busoni, BI, 526.

21. Busoni, notes for Gruenberg's compositions in progress, private collection of Joan Gruenberg Cominos, Martinez, CA.

22. Busoni avoided everyday topics of politics or economics and created a utopian otherworldly atmosphere that put many students in awe of him.

23. Busoni owned several copies of the complete works by Goethe as well as Nietzsche's *Als sprach Zarathustra* (1904), *Der Fall Wagner* (1888), and *Die Geburt der Tragödie* (1907). See Max Perl, Antiquariat, *Bibliothek Ferruccio Busoni: Werke der Weltliteratur in schönen Gesamtausgaben und Erstdrucken; Illustrierte Bücher aller Jahrhunderte*, Auction 96, March 30–31, 1925 (Berlin: Max Perl, 1925).

24. Consult the following sources for more information: Walter Frisch, "Music and Jugendstil," *Critical Inquiry* 17:1 (Autumn 1990), 138–161; Andrew McCredie, ed., *Art Nouveau and Jugendstil and the Music of the Early 20th Century*, Miscellanea Musicologica, Adelaide Studies in Musicology, vol. 13 (Adelaide: University of Adelaide, 1984); Hans Hollander, *Musik und Jugendstil* (Zurich: Atlantis-Verlag, 1975).

25. Busoni, "Routine," *Pan* 1:20 (August 16, 1911), 654–655; Busoni, "Schönberg-Matinée," *Pan* 2:11 (February 11, 1912), 327–330; Busoni, "Selbst-Rezension," *Pan* 2: 11 (February 1, 1912), 327–330.

26. Bernard van Dieren, *Down among the Dead Men and Other Essays* (London: Oxford University Press, 1935), 65–66.

27. Ibid., 65

28. The use of the masculine pronoun is intentional here. Busoni doubted the intellectual and artistic potential of women in the professional realm. He specifically disliked females in authority positions and those who came across as strong or intellectual. He considered some women childish and underdeveloped socially, psychologically, and intellectually. At the same time, he felt bereft without their graces. For additional information of Busoni's views about women, consult Levitz, "Teaching New Classicality," 117–118; Knyt, "Ferruccio Busoni and the
New England Conservatory: Piano Pedagogue in the Making," *American Music* (31:3), 292.

29. Petri, "How Ferruccio Busoni Taught: An Interview with the Distinguished Dutch Pianist," interview by Friede F. Rothe, *Etude* 58 (October 1940), 710.

30. Dieren, *Down among the Dead Men and Other Essays*, 68.

31. "Nei suoi corsi d'insegnamento egli non curava soltanto lo strumento o la musica, mireva sempre alla totalità dell'arte e dell'umanità. Perciò la lezioni si svolgevano un po' in tutti i settori: da quello letterario a quello filosofico, da quello estetico

a quello morale-sociale. E più ancora che con la parola detta, egli amò propagare il suo sapere e consigliare e guidare attraverso corrispondenze epistolare, che sono spesso dei veri piccoli Trattati di pedagogia." Guerrini, *Ferruccio Busoni*, 233.

32. Levitz, "Teaching New Classicality," 303.

33. For instance, Edgard Varèse's personal copy of the *Entwurf einer neuen Ästhetik der Tonkunst* is housed at the Harry Ransom Humanities Research Center at the University of Texas at Austin. Louis Gruenberg's copy can be found in the private collection of Joan Gruenberg Cominos. Arnold Schoenberg also was influenced by the text, as evident by his personal annotated copy of it. Busoni, *Entwurf einer neuen Aesthetik der Tonkunst*, facsimile of the 1916 edition with annotations by Schoenberg (Frankfurt: Insel, 1974).

34. Busoni, *Sketch of a New Esthetic of Music* (1907), trans. Dr. Th. Baker (New York: Schirmer, 1911), 5.

35. For a fuller vision of Busoni's views about absolute music and program music, consult Erinn Knyt, "Ferruccio Busoni and the Absolute in Music: Form, Nature and Idee," *Journal of the Royal Musical Association* 137:1 (May 2012), 35–69.

36. Martina Weindel, *Ferruccio Busonis Ästhetik in seinen Briefen und Schriften*, ed. Richard Schaal (Wilhelmshaven: Heinrichsofen-Bücher, 1996); Judith Michelle Crispin, *The Esoteric Musical Tradition of Ferruccio Busoni and Its Reinvigoration in the Music of Larry Sitsky: The Operas Doktor Faust and the Golem*, preface by Larry Sitsky (Lewiston, ME: Edwin Mellen Press, 2007), 23–25. See also Knyt, "Ferruccio Busoni and the Absolute in Music."

37. Busoni, "The Essence and Oneness of Music," in *The Essence of Music and Other Papers*, 1.

38. Dieren, *Down among the Dead Men and Other Essays*, 76.

39. Busoni, quoted in Levitz, "Teaching New Classicality," 148. Based on a letter from Busoni to Jarnach, April 20, 1921, Staatsbibliothek zu Berlin, Preußischer Kulturbesitz, Musikabteilung mit Mendelssohn-Archiv, N. Mus. Depos. 56.

40. Drafts leading up to Busoni's *Entwurf* indicate that his experimental ideas about microtonal systems date back to at least 1888. Staatsbibliothek zu Berlin, Preußischer Kulturbesitz, Musikabteilung mit Mendelssohn-Archiv, Mus. Nachl. F. Busoni, CI, 115.

41. Thaddeus Cahill (1867–1924) invented one of the first electronic instruments, the massive telharmonium. Although its size (seven tons) and cost (about $200,000) made the use and production of the instrument prohibitive, the idea of the instrument captured Busoni's imagination. For more information about the instrument consult Reynold Weidenaar, *Magic Music from the Telharmonium* (London: Scarecrow Press, 1995).

42. Messing's book deals more generally with neoclassicism and mentions Busoni's views of young classicality in a small but well thought out analysis of Busoni's aesthetic texts: Scott Messing, *Neoclassicism in Music: From the Genesis of the Concept through the Schoenberg/Stravinsky Polemic* (Rochester: University of Rochester Press, 1998), 65–74.

43. Busoni, "Young Classicism" (Busoni to Paul Bekker, February 7, 1920), in *The Essence of Music*, 20.

44. Paul Fleet, *Ferruccio Busoni: A Phenomenological Approach to His Music and Aesthetics* (Cologne: Lambert Academic Publishing, 2009), 17–19. Young Vienna was a group of writers in Vienna at the turn of the twentieth century that turned from naturalism to symbolism or impressionism.

45. Messing, *Neoclassicism in Music*, 74.

46. Dieren, *Down among the Dead Men and Other Essays*, 77.

47. True, Schoenberg encouraged transcriptions as a means to learn about music and to make it more accessible. However, unlike Busoni, he was offended by the idea that a transcription could be better than the original. See Erinn Knyt, "How I Compose: Ferruccio Busoni's Views about Invention, Quotation, and the Compositional Process," *Journal of Musicology* 27:2 (Spring 2010) 224–263. Levitz also discusses the role of transcription in Busoni's composition master class, in "Teaching New Classicality," 171–174.

48. Busoni created several versions of this piece. The 1912 version is shortened considerably, and the 1922 version is scored for two pianos. The piece combines Busoni's freely adapted and completed version of Bach's *Die Kunst der Fuge* and a modified version of his own piano elegy no. 3. The titles of the three versions are as follows: *Fantasia contrappuntistica (Preludio al corale "Gloria al Signore nel Cieli" e Fuga a quattro soggetti obbligati sopra un frammento di Bach)* (1910); *Fantasia contrappuntistica: Kleine Ausgabe (Choral-Vorspiel und Fuge über ein Bachsches Fragment* (1912); and *Fantasia contrappuntistica (Choral Variationen über "Ehre sei Gott in der Höhe" gefolgt von einer Quadrupel-Fuge über ein Bachsches Fragment: für Zwei Klaviere)* (1922). For comparisons of the three versions, consult Larry Sitsky, *Busoni and the Piano: The Works, the Writings and the Recordings*, 2nd ed., Distinguished Reprints, no. 3 (Hillsdale, NY: Pendragon Press, 2009), 139–161, and Antony Beaumont, *Busoni the Composer* (Bloomington: Indiana University Press, 1985), 160–177.

49. Busoni, "Self Criticism" (1912), in *The Essence and Oneness of Music*, 46–47, 50.

50. "Prima condizione imposta dal Maestro ai discepoli, era quella di portare a lezione una certa quantità di lavoro. Egli non ammetteva (lo ricordino gli studenti di composizione di oggi) che ci si recasse a scuola col fogliolino delle otto e sedici battute. Si andasse a lezione magari una volta al mese, ma con un lavoro finito, fosse un Tempo di Sonata, o un pezzo sinfonico o una scena d'opera. Perché la lezione consisteva, 'doveva consistere' sopratutto in una discussione estetica fra Maestro e discepolo. Anzi il Maestro partiva quasi sempre dal proponimento di non voler entrare in questioni tecniche, poiché—diceva lui—'il risultato estetico può giustificar l'impiego di tutti i mezzi tecnici.' Pel contrappunto, non occorre dirlo, la pietra di tutti i paragoni era Giov. Sebastiano Bach." Guerrini, *Ferruccio Busoni*, 233–234.

51. For a more detailed explanation about Busoni's compositional process, consult Knyt, "How I Compose: Ferruccio Busoni's Views about Invention, Quotation, and the Compositional Process."

52. Busoni, "How I Compose" (1907), in *The Essence of Music and Other Papers*, 50–51.

53. Busoni, "Open Letter to Hans Pfitzner" (1917), in *The Essence of Music and Other Papers*, 18.

54. Busoni, quoted in Stuckenschmidt, *Ferruccio Busoni*, 181. That architecture and the architectural shaping of sound or composition was a frequent topic of his conversations is supported by many of his students and friends in their memoirs, diaries, and letters. It was a topic that brought him great joy, and it surfaces in many of his letters. In a letter to Hugo Leichtentritt, Busoni stated, for instance: "I am becoming increasingly convinced that musical forms feel the *need* to be moulded adjustably, according to content and motif; just as a building, according to its given purpose and terrain." Busoni to Leichtentritt, September 21, 1918 in *Selected Letters*, 274.

55. Busoni, "The Essence and Oneness of Music," in *The Essence of Music and Other Papers*, 14.

56. Busoni, "The Future of Opera" (1913), in *The Essence of Music and Other Papers*, 39–40.

57. Levitz, "Teaching New Classicality," 154.

58. Dieren, *Down among the Dead Men and Other Essays*, 73.

59. Busoni, "Routine" (1911), in *The Essence of Music and Other Papers*, 184–185. Originally published without title in *Pan* 1:20 (August 16, 1911), 645ff.

60. Busoni, "Routine" (1911), in *The Essence of Music and Other Papers*, 185.

61. Busoni's views about *Parsifal* are preserved in a short unpublished essay in the Staatsbibliothek zu Berlin, Preußischer Kulturbesitz, Musikabteilung mit Mendelssohn-Archiv, Mus. Nachl. F. Busoni, CI, 19.

62. It is worth noting that a revival of the master-apprentice model developed from European Guilds of the Middle Ages took place in Germany in the 1920s. This trend was modeled at the Bauhaus, where workshops were led by master craftsmen and artists. Busoni also favored the master-apprentice model by choosing the masterclass format over more standardized institutional instruction.

63. For more information about Boulanger's teaching, consult Don G. Campbell, *Master Teacher: Nadia Boulanger* (Washington, DC: Pastoral Press, 1984), 5.

64. Boulanger taught from 1904 to 1979 and eventually gave up composition to devote herself to the life of a pedagogue. She gave instruction in counterpoint, harmony, organ, score reading, figured bass, and analysis in a number of institutions, including the Conservatoire Femina-Musica, the École Normale, the Conservatoire American in Fontainebleau, and the Conservatoire de Paris. Her assistant, Mademoiselle Dieudonné, taught ear training and score reading.

65. Virgil Thomson, quoted in Alan Kendall, *The Tender Tyrant: Nadia Boulanger, A Life Devoted to Music* (London: Macdonald and Jane's, 1976), 59.

66. Matthew Mugmon, email to the author, March 23, 2014. See also Virgil Thomson, "'Greatest Music Teacher' at 75," *Music Educator's Journal* 49:1 (September-October 1962), 43.

67. Ev Grimes, "Interview: Education," in *Writings on Glass: Essays, Interviews, Criticism*, ed. Richard Kostelanetz and Robert Flemming (New York: Schirmer Books, 1997), 30–31.

68. Thomson, quoted in Alan Kendall, *The Tender Tyrant: Nadia Boulanger, A Life Devoted to Music* (London: Macdonald and Jane's, 1976), 59.

69. I am grateful to Matthew Mugmon for making this comparison explicit. Mugmon, email to the author, March 23, 2014.

70. Joel Feigin, phone communication with the author, May 22, 2014.

71. Eugenie Schwarzwald (1872–1940) was an Austrian author and pedagogue who was interested in providing quality education for girls. Simon Sechter (1788–1867) was a prolific composer. Sechter's most important pedagogical text is *Die richtige Folge der Grundharmonien*, a three-volume treatise on composition. Johann Joseph Fux (1660–1741) is the author of *Gradus ad Parnassum*, one of the most influential books on Renaissance counterpoint.

72. Ulrich Krämer, *Alban Berg als Schüler Arnold Schönbergs: Quellenstudien und Analysen zum Frühwerk*, Alban Berg Studien, vol. 4, ed. Rudolf Stephan (Vienna: Universal Edition, 1996). Adolf Bernhard Marx (1795–1866) wrote an influential four-volume treatise about music composition that presented a systematic discussion of traditional forms: *Die Lehre von der musikalischen Komposition*.

73. Schoenberg, "Problems in Teaching Art" (1911), in *Style and Idea: Selected Writings of Arnold Schoenberg*, ed. Leonard Stein, trans. Leo Black (New York: St. Martin's, 1975).

74. Blitzstein stopped taking private composition lessons with Schoenberg after about three months, but continued attending the masterclass sessions.

75. Marc Blitzstein to Nadia Boulanger, October 18, 1927, Bibliothèque Nationale de France, NLA 56, pieces 290–299. For a more comprehensive description of Blitzstein's lessons with Schoenberg, consult Howard Pollack, *Marc Blitzstein: His Life, His Work, His World* (New York: Oxford University Press, 2012), 66–68.

76. Lennox Berkeley (1903–1989) was an English composer who went to Paris in 1927 to study with Boulanger.

77. Caroline Potter, *Nadia and Lili Boulanger* (Abingdon: Ashgate, 2008), 139. Also refer to Joseph Epstein, *Masters: Portraits of Great Teachers* (New York: Basic Books, 1981); Jérôme Spycket, *Nadia Boulanger*, trans. M. M. Shriver (Stuyvesant, NY: Pendragon Press, 1992); Alan Kendall, *The Tender Tyrant;* Robin Orr, "A Note on Nadia Boulanger," *Musical Times*, 120:1642 (December 1979), 999; George Steiner, *Lessons of the Masters* (Cambridge, MA: Harvard University Press, 2003).

78. Ev Grimes, "Interview: Education," in *Writings on Glass*, 30–31.

79. Elliott Carter and Jonathan W. Bernhard, "An Interview with Elliott Carter," *Perspectives of New Music* 28:2 (Summer 1990), 199–200.

80. Schoenberg, "Teaching and Modern Trends in Music" (1938), in *Style and Idea*, 376–377.

81. Schoenberg, "The Blessing of the Dressing" (1948), in *Style and Idea*, 385.

82. Matthew Mugmon, email to the author, March 23, 2014.

83. See Johann Joseph Fux, *Gradus ad Parnassum: sive Manuductio ad compositionem musicæ regularem, methodo novâ ac certâ, nondum antè tam exacto ordine in lucem edita* (Vienna: Joannis Petri van Ghelen, 1725); Simon Sechter, *Die Grundsätze der musikalischen Komposition* (Leipzig: Breitkopf und Härtel, 1853–1854); Adolf Bernhard Marx, *Die Lehre von der musikalischen Komposition, praktisch-theoretisch, zum Selbstunterricht, oder als Leitfaden bei Privatunterweisung und öffentlichen Vorträgen* (Leipzig: Breitkopf und Härtel, 1837); Hector Berlioz, *Grand traité d'instrumentation et d'orchestration modernes* (Paris: Schonenberger, c. 1844). For information about A. B. Marx and the Formenlehre tradition (as well as English translations of selected

passages from his composition method), see Scott G. Burnham, *Musical Form in the Age of Beethoven: Selected Writings on the Theory and Method* (Cambridge: Cambridge University Press, 1997).

84. J. C. Lobe, *Lehrbuch der musikalischen Komposition*, 4 vols. (Leipzig: Breitkopf und Härtel, 1858–1867).

85. Busoni's incomplete (and unpublished) orchestration treatise, by contrast, focuses on randomly organized aesthetic ideals of sound and color, and observations about effective orchestration techniques in the music of Mozart. The basics—such as instrument range, character, or capabilities, do not feature in the discussion.

86. See Rudolf Louis and Ludwig Thuille, *Harmonielehre*, 7th ed. (Stuttgart: Carl Gruninger, 1920), and Arnold Schoenberg, *Theory of Harmony* (1922), 3rd ed., trans. Roy E. Carter (Berkeley: University of California Press, 1983).

87. Busoni quoted in Stuckenschmidt, *Ferruccio Busoni*, 178.

88. "L'amore di Busoni per i giovani fu il vero amore di Maestro, quello ciò che per educare non teme di ferire. La critica più spietata era in lui il maggior segno di considerazione e di affetto. Per questo, soltanto pochi de suoi discepoli lo seguirono, poi, nella vita. In generale la gioventù del suo tempo non lo comprese o gli fu avversa, in parte proprio perché intollerante dei suoi rudi mezzi educatavi." Guerrini, *Ferruccio Busoni*, 236–237.

89. Levitz, "Teaching New Classicality," 139–142.

90. Stuckenschmidt, *Ferruccio Busoni*, 178.

Janus-Faced Modernism

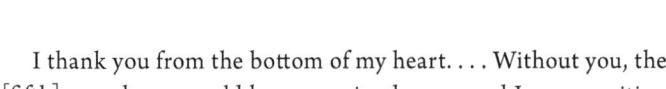

> I thank you from the bottom of my heart.... Without you, the [fifth] symphony would have remained paper and I an apparition from the forest.
>
> Letter from Jean Sibelius to Ferruccio Busoni, November 20, 1921

BEGINNINGS OF SIBELIUS'S COMPOSITION CAREER

JEAN SIBELIUS (1865–1957) wrote in a style that has defied categorization. His predominantly tonal compositions seemed anachronistic in the early twentieth century.[1] At the same time, scholars have increasingly recognized his play with texture, timbre, and form as innovative.[2] In addition, it has been argued that Sibelius's music contains "prototypes of what later became postmodernism."[3] Approaching music ahistorically, Sibelius drew upon Bachian counterpoint, Mozartian equilibrium, and Lisztian treatments of melody and color while forging sounds that were distinctively his own.

Although several teachers impacted Sibelius's compositional development, including Martin Wegelius (1846–1906), Albert Becker (1834–1899), Karl Goldmark (1830–1915), and Robert Fuchs (1847–1927), it was Ferruccio Busoni, with whom he never officially studied, but to whom he went for compositional advice and mentorship from 1888 to 1921, who was Sibelius's muse. Busoni stimulated Sibelius's imagination and was a catalyst for his experimentation with sound, color, and structure. He helped Sibelius discover a distinctive style that was an alternative to both the avant-garde and the conservative trends of the day.[4] At the same time, he promoted his music across Europe.

Several biographers and scholars, including Erik Tawaststjerna, Tomi Mäkelä, Cecil Gray, and Karl Ekman, feature detailed discussions of Busoni's importance for Sibelius's artistic development.[5] Yet, scattered as they are throughout biographical narrative, these descriptions of the Busoni-Sibelius connection must be pieced together by the reader. Busoni scholarship touches only lightly upon the topic. Barbara Hong, for instance, has documented the friendship of Busoni and Sibelius in Helsinki from 1888 to 1890.[6] Antony Beaumont's article about the Busoni-Sibelius connection, although a valuable source of information, is hardly complete, and is dismissive of stylistic connections.[7] Roberto Wis's and Petri Sariola's articles focus mainly on Busoni's creative activities in Finland.[8] Most recently, Chiara Bertoglio has published an article on the Sibelius and Busoni friendship, yet without exploring in detail the importance of that friendship for Sibelius's compositional style.[9] Thus there is still no single comprehensive source that considers the extent of Busoni's impact on Sibelius's development.

BUSONI'S INFLUENCE ON SIBELIUS'S CAREER PATH

Although Sibelius had studied music theory on his own and composed a few chamber pieces, he did not initially aspire to the career of a composer; instead, he was intent upon becoming a concert violinist.[10] By spring 1887, Sibelius began to compose more seriously, officially studying the subject for the first time. However, he still had no intention of pursuing a career in composition.[11] True, he visited Wegelius's summer home. There he spent mornings working on counterpoint and composition while performing in the afternoons. Yet Sibelius doubted his abilities as a composer and did not see it in his future, even as Wegelius was initially only cautious in his support.

The turning point for Sibelius happened during the 1888–1889 academic year, when Busoni arrived in Helsinki. Although there were a number of factors contributing to Sibelius's switch from violin performance to composition, including reported sickness, recurring problems from an arm injury, and Wegelius's growing encouragement of his composition studies, Busoni helped him come to the realization that composition could become more than an avocation. He also helped him discover a personal compositional voice.

Even though Sibelius did not officially study with Busoni, the two met almost daily to talk about music. Through discussions and impromptu performance sessions, Sibelius matured as a composer.[12] Busoni's and Sibelius's correspondence reveal that they talked about compositional and performance projects, composers of interest, and other non-musical matters too. Busoni mentioned these times in Helsinki with Sibelius in a letter to Egon Petri on June 13, 1908: "When I was younger than you, in Helsingfors, Sibelius and the Jaernefelt brothers formed a stimulating association."[13] The meetings included impromptu performances and the critique of compositions. Busoni also shared details about his life as a touring virtuoso. Sibelius remembers the gatherings as informal, but formative:

> In spite of his being a teacher and I a pupil, we met almost daily. Besides, I was not his pupil, as lessons in piano playing did not form part of my curriculum at the musical academy; we were drawn together by our common musical interests in general. Our usual meeting-place was Ericson's café, very popular at that time, where Armas Järnefelt, my future brother-in-law, and Adolf Paul, both of them Busoni's pupils, also used to turn up regularly. When Busoni was in the humor for it, and that happened pretty often, he invited the three of us to supper at Kämp's. His was a generous nature, cordial and impulsive. He played a good deal to us during our meetings, either the works of his favorite composers or improvisations of his own. He encouraged us, too, to improvise to him, and I readily took advantage of his indulgence to defects in my skill on the piano.... He displayed an interest in my music that both pleased and flattered me.[14]

Especially since Wegelius was an ardent follower of new German composers, Busoni's views about absolute music must have made an impact on the group.[15] In addition, Busoni encouraged free improvisation as a way to arrive at musical ideas regardless of how skilled one was in piano playing. This was a valuable suggestion for Sibelius, who was a great improviser, even if he possessed only basic skills at the piano.[16] Busoni also shared his own vision of great music, which emphasized formal originality and timbral color.

Sibelius's student compositions showed a sudden new maturity beginning in April 1889. The Suite in A Major for String Trio, the first performance of which took place on April 13, 1889, represented a breakthrough moment for Sibelius and impressed Busoni so deeply that he mentioned it in his written remarks when conducting Sibelius's Symphony no. 2 in D Major, op. 43, twenty-seven years later, calling it "far above the level of a pupil's work."[17] Already some characteristic traits appear in the suite, including long pedal points that serve several harmonic functions and aphoristic writing in which textures shift rapidly. Another exceptional student composition from around the same time was Sibelius's String Quartet in A Minor, appearing just one month later. The quartet contains rapidly changing textures, clearly differentiated instrumental timbres, and the use of open spacing with expansive registers. The two discussed this piece in detail and Busoni was possibly the first to study it in its entirety, if Sibelius's account is to be trusted: "He looked forward eagerly to my A minor quartet, my last composition at the musical academy, and when I had completed it and showed him the score, he seated himself at once at the piano and played through the whole quartet from beginning to end without previously having had an opportunity of glancing at the music. And how he played it!"[18]

Busoni was one of the first to recognize Sibelius's compositional talent and he helped stimulate his musical imagination. At the same time he exposed his weaknesses as a performer. Although he impressed his teachers in Helsinki, Sibelius had a long way to go technically before he would have been able to win over an international audience. He recognized that only after witnessing Busoni's impressive technique, encyclopedic memory, and thoughtful interpretations.

While he was a student, Sibelius had ample opportunity to hear Busoni perform, and his performances were an inspiration to him. In the first year, Busoni gave five solo recitals. The first, which took place on October 4, 1888, in the Assembly Hall of the Swedish Normal High School, featured a variety of composers and was well received:

> J. S. Bach, Toccata und Fuge in D-moll for piano
> Edvard Grieg, Sonata no. 3 in C-moll for violin and piano (H. Csillag, violin)
> Busoni, Studie (from op. 3)
> Busoni, Ballettszene (op. 6)
> Richard Strauss: Waltz: *Man lebt nur einmal!*
> Richard Wagner, arr. by Carl Tausig, *Ride of the Valkyries*

He also gave a series of concerts, each devoted to a single composer. The first of these took place on October 13, 1888. In total, he participated in eleven of the fourteen evening recitals of the institute his first year in Helsinki and nine of the evenings his second year. In addition, he played in concerts outside the institute, such as with the Helsinki Symphony Orchestra on February 28, 1889.[19] After leaving Helsinki in June 1890, Busoni returned to give concerts in March 1891, May 1895, September 1898, and October 1912. Sibelius was there in May 1895 and again in October 1912 (see figure 2.1). Since he was not abroad in September 1898, it is also likely he attended that recital as well.[20]

Busoni's playing was a revelation for Sibelius, who stated: "When I think of Busoni shining fully as an artist, I understand my ode, my infinite tragic ode!"[21] When Sibelius heard the 1912 recitals in Helsinki, he was overcome with emotion.[22] After the first concert, Sibelius wrote: "Busoni played Bach, Beethoven, Op. 111 in C minor. An inimitable artist! An unforgettable moment!"[23] He was even more overwhelmed by the second recital: "Busoni played the B Major [sic] Sonata (op. 106). I will treasure this my whole life! Never has man's greatness and power appeared to me with such clarity and in so convincing a manner."[24]

BUSONI'S CONTINUED GUIDANCE

Although Busoni was never "officially" Sibelius's composition teacher in an institutional setting, he offered feedback on his compositions throughout his life. After moving away from Helsinki, both men met numerous times in Berlin and elsewhere in Europe. Moreover, he was his mentor, suggesting names of potential teachers, writing letters of recommendation, and guiding him in new artistic directions.

Busoni initially suggested that Sibelius should study with Nikolai Rimsky-Korsakov (1844–1908), but studying with a Russian teacher was reportedly not deemed appropriate by Wegelius.[25] When Sibelius ended up studying with Albert Becker in Berlin (1834–1899) at the suggestion of Wegelius, Busoni recognized the mistake and noticed that it was stifling Sibelius's creativity.[26] By the time Busoni visited him in December 1889, Sibelius had produced no new important compositions. For the following academic year, Busoni suggested a change and wrote a letter of

HELSINGFORS MUSIKINSTITUTS

14:de (182:dra) Musikafton.

Lördagen den 25 Maj 1895 kl. 8 e. m.

i Normallyceum.

Program.

1) *Kvintett* op. 81 (A-dur) för piano och stråkinstrumenter . . . . **Dvorak.**
I. Allegro, ma non tanto. II. Dumka (Andante con moto). III. Scherzo (Furiant). IV. Finale (Allegro).
Herrar *Ekman, Kihlman, Sante, König* och *Martin.*

2. *Concertstück* op. 79 (F-moll) . . . . **Weber.**
I. Larghetto affettuoso. II. Allegro agitato. III. Marcia. IV. Rondo gjoioso
Herr **Feruccio B. Busoni** ackomp af Herr *Ekman.*

3. *Benediction* de Dieu dans la solitude . . . . . **Liszt.**
(efter en dikt ur Lamartines „Harmonies poëtiques et religieuses").*)
I. Moderato. II. Andante. III. Piu sostenuto quasi preludio. Tempo 1:mo.
Herr **Busoni.**

4. *Variations de Bravoure* sur le marche des Puritains. **(Bellini.)**
a) Introduction et Thema . . . . **Liszt.**
b) Variation I. . . . . **Thalberg.**
c) „ II. . . . . **Liszt.**
d) „ III. . . . . **Pixis.**
e) „ IV. . . . . **Henri Herz.**
f) „ V. . . . . **Carl Czerny.**
g) „ VI. . . . . **Chopin**
h) Finale . . . . **Liszt.**
Herr **Busoni.**

Konsertflygeln är af Steinway et Sons.

*) Se andra sidan.

Helsingfors Tryckeriet Unionsgatan 20, 1895.

FIGURE 2.1. Program of May 25, 1895, Sibelius Academy Archives.

recommendation for Sibelius to study in Berlin with Heinrich Freiherr von Herzogenberg (1843–1900), who had been a professor at the Hochschule für Musik since 1885: "The person in question, Mr. Jean Sibelius, is a very talented composer who, in my opinion, may best be able to achieve his development with you. In keeping with his Northern homeland, he has come to maturity later than usual, but in return he has remained unusually unspoiled for his age."[27]

Although Sibelius stopped in Berlin for a few days, he ultimately ended up studying in Vienna with Robert Fuchs,[28] who taught at the Vienna Conservatory, and with Karl Goldmark.[29] Yet even when studying with his Viennese teachers, Sibelius held Busoni as a yardstick of accomplishment. He left the following rather strange assessment of his own Overture in E Major (1891) after taking it to Goldmark for critique, setting up a pattern of longstanding comparison between his and Busoni's compositions: "My new Ouverture is better, for example, than Busoni's *Concertstück* for orchestra, but worse than his Toccata and Fugue. Goldmark said that I need to come now only on a quarterly basis to get his advice."[30] They were contemporaries, but Sibelius had far to go to gain the popularity of Busoni in his own age. Little did he know that his fame would one day far surpass Busoni's.

BUSONI'S INFLUENCE ON SIBELIUS: MUSIC, AESTHETICS, AND INSTRUCTION

Busoni's mentorship of Sibelius continued in Berlin, London, Helsinki, and elsewhere to nearly the end of Busoni's life (see table 2.1).[31] Sibelius brought scores for compositional advice, socialized, attended concerts, and discussed aesthetic ideas. Although Sibelius held little admiration for Busoni's compositions, contact with them and with Busoni's aesthetic ideas did have a marked effect on Sibelius's development. This included not only the composition of pieces in direct response to Busoni's performances, but also the assimilation of Busoni's artistic ideals. Most notably, Busoni's ideas about sound/orchestration, form, and style influenced Sibelius.

Busoni directly inspired at least two of Sibelius's early compositions, *Florestan* (1889), a suite for piano, and the Piano Quintet in G Minor (1890); both display experimentation with form. While Busoni was in Helsinki,

TABLE 2.1. CONTACT BETWEEN SIBELIUS AND BUSONI

DATES	LOCATION
September 1888–September 1889	Helsinki
December 1889	Berlin and Leipzig
May/June 1890	Helsinki
September 1894	Berlin
May 1895	Helsinki
May–June 1896	Berlin*
July 1897	Berlin*
February–May 1898	Berlin
September 1898	Helsinki
July–August 1900	Weimar
October 1900–May 1901	Berlin*
May–June 1901	Berlin*
June 1902	Vienna
November 1902	Berlin
January–March 1905	Berlin
January 1906	Birmingham
August 1907	Berlin
May 1909	Berlin
September–October 1910	Berlin
November–December 1911	Berlin
October 1912	Helsinki
January–February 1914	Berlin
January–April 1921	London

* I have been unable to definitively verify meetings between Sibelius and Busoni at these times in letters or other documents, even though it is highly probable that they met due to their geographic proximity.

he performed the music of Robert Schumann (1810–1856) several times, thereby exposing Sibelius to his music with its unconventional formal structures. His music began to serve as a model for Sibelius's formal innovations. Together with Busoni, Sibelius played the second violin with the faculty for a performance of Schumann's Piano Quintet in E-Flat Major, op. 44, on February 14, 1889. Busoni also performed the then little known *Kreisleriana*, op. 16, and *Symphonic Etudes*, op. 13, in a recital on December 11, 1888.[32] On March 16, 1889, he also performed Schumann's Sonata in

D Minor for Violin and Piano, op. 121, together with Hermann Csillag, and on September 30, 1889, he performed Schumann's "Belshazzar" Ballad, op. 57, with Abraham Ojanperä.[33] Sibelius's exposure to Schumann through Busoni is not to be underestimated, since Wegelius was an ardent follower of Wagner and the New German School.[34]

Sibelius composed his *Florestan* piano suite in the spring of 1889, likely under the inspiration of Busoni's performances, and there are clear musical parallels to Schumann's *Kreisleriana*, which Busoni performed the previous December. Although this similarity has been mentioned in several biographies, no detailed analyses have been provided. Clearly one of Sibelius's early works, *Florestan* already displays several Schumannesque features that later became characteristic of Sibelius's writing, including experimentation with form and harmonic color. A few of the more obvious parallels between the works include a hovering between keys (G minor and B-flat major), harmonic ambiguity, the juxtaposition of contrasting fragmentary sections, and formal disruptions.[35] With its contrasting keys and moods, Schumann's *Kreisleriana* alludes subtly and without explicit program to E.T.A. Hoffmann's eccentric Kapellmeister, Herr Kreisler. Sibelius, on the other hand, left an explicit program and focused exclusively on the impulsive Florestan:

1. Florestan wanders in the forest unhappy and depressed. Scents of wild moss and wet tree bark are in the air.
2. Florestan comes to a large waterfall whose foaming waters transform under his eyes into water nymphs. There is a scent of water lilies in the air.
3. One of the water nymphs has dank, black eyes, and golden yellow hair. Florestan falls in love with her.
4. Florestan tries to lure her to come to him, but she disappears. Dejected and unhappy, Florestan returns through the forest.[36]

Sibelius's suite contains four movements, as opposed to Schumann's eight. The piano writing is primitive in Sibelius's suite, a testament to his weak technical skills at the piano. Nevertheless, the piece displays several ingenious features—especially in relation to form. Sibelius's suite is unified as a cycle through repetition and variation. The opening number is repeated at the conclusion of the final number with a slightly elongated conclusion. A descending stepwise melodic line (D, C, B-flat, A, G)

MUSIC EXAMPLE 2.1. a) Sibelius, *Florestan*, mvt. 1, mm. 1–4; b) Sibelius, *Florestan*, mvt. 2, mm. 1–2; c) Sibelius, *Florestan*, mvt. 3, mm. 1–5.

underlies the thematic material of all of the movements. These are structural pitches occurring on beats 1 and 3 in the opening melodic material in the first movement; they reappear at the beginning of the second and third movements as well, although in some cases they are altered chromatically (see music example 2.1. a and b).

The structure of individual movements is irregular, much like Schumann's, due to fragmentary interruptions and harmonic ambiguity. Throughout the movements, Sibelius's almost irritatingly regular phrasing obscures the irregularity of the large-scale structure. The second movement, for instance, contains elements of variation form coupled with ABA form—opening material is fragmented and interrupted throughout (see music example 2.2). It begins with clear antecedent and consequent phrases (4 +4) followed by nine bars of contrasting material (5+4). Opening material (4+4) returns in measure 18, however changed in register

MUSIC EXAMPLE 2.2. Sibelius, *Florestan*, mvt. 2, mm. 1–17.

and texture. It is then repeated again in measure 26 but interrupted after four bars by developmental material that is treated sequentially. The far out point harmonically occurs in measures 41 and 42 with movement to D-flat major, before a return to B-flat and material from the antecedent phrase of A (bars 5–8).

Busoni's influence remained important for Sibelius throughout his career. During his visits, Sibelius brought scores for compositional advice to Busoni. He leaves the following brief account of his 1894 visit in Berlin, noting Busoni's interest in his scores: "I am now with Busoni, Nováček and Paul. They are very friendly, although it is not like old times. . . . I could not be reached as Busoni necessarily wanted to see what I had been working on."[37] That Busoni continued to look at Sibelius's scores and offer advice during his many visits is evident from his diary. An entry on October 16, 1910, for instance, describes his progress on *Tulen Synty*, op. 32, and Busoni's encouragement: "Been with Busoni. He gave me much through his admiration for my art, especially for the orchestral parts. Advised me to stick with it. It worked fine. Finished writing the piano draft for 'Tulen synty,' op. 32."[38]

During the visits, Sibelius also became acquainted with Busoni's most recent compositions. He was, for instance, present in 1914 at a Berlin concert featuring Busoni's Piano Concerto in C Minor, BV 247 (Egon Petri, soloist), J. S. Bach's Concerto in D Minor, BWV 1052, arranged by Busoni, BV B28 (Egon Petri, soloist), and Busoni's Violin Concerto in D Major, BV 243 (Josef Szigeti, soloist).[39] Sibelius also noted that he studied Busoni's *Fantasia contrappuntistica*, BV 256, in some detail, and he must have been present at the reading of Busoni's *Berceuse élégiaque*, BV 252, by Oskar Fried with the Berlin Philharmonic in 1910.[40] Of these pieces, he disliked the *Fantasia contrappuntistica*, BV 256, which he found to be too thin-textured, but he liked the *Berceuse élégiaque*, BV 252, even if he considered it relatively insignificant: "Studied Busoni's *Fantasia contrappuntistica*. Why does this great pianist bother to compose? It is always interesting to hear a great an artist to work—but—this 'music.' 'Thin and ugly.' Without movement!! His *Berceuse élégiaque* is another matter, as it has color and scenery. But that is all!"[41]

Continued conversations with Busoni impacted Sibelius in a number of ways. For instance, they helped cement his gradual turning of loyalty away from Wagner toward Liszt in 1894. This was especially significant given that Wegelius was an ardent Wagnerian and that Sibelius ultimately found his own voice in the symphony and symphonic poem. He set out on a trip to the Wagner festival in Bayreuth in July 1894 with the purpose of becoming better acquainted with Wagner's music.[42] However, he only ended up becoming disillusioned with Wagner and developed an aversion that extended to the end of his life.[43] Afterward, Sibelius visited Busoni in Berlin, where he discovered Liszt's *Faust Symphony*, S. 108.[44]

Sibelius found Liszt's approach to be more similar to his own musical ideals than Wagner's: "I think that I really am a musical painter and poet. I mean that music brings Liszt's position closest to me. That Symphonic poem (in the way I was nearly a 'poet') I am working on is very dear to me."[45]

Busoni also showed him music that was virtually unknown in Helsinki, such as compositions by Claude Debussy (1862–1918) and Arnold Schoenberg (1874–1951). Sibelius left this memory of his introduction to Schoenberg's music:[46] "I was one of the first to get hold of Arnold Schoenberg's works for himself. I bought them on Busoni's advice, to learn something."[47] Although he downplayed the significance of this encounter with Schoenberg's music, he continued to study Schoenberg's music and stated that he had been deeply impressed with Schoenberg's *Kammersymphonie* no. 1 in E Major, op. 9, after hearing it in Berlin on February 4, 1914.[48] Busoni also conducted Debussy's *Nuages* and *Fêtes* from the set of three Nocturnes, L. 91, and, as Tawaststjerna points out, probably showed Sibelius the score.[49]

Above all, Busoni shared his aesthetic ideas, and these affected Sibelius's approach toward form and orchestration. Like Busoni, Sibelius called for a breaking away from traditional forms. In Busoni's *Entwurf einer neuen Ästhetik der Tonkunst*, "old-fashioned" critics of his ideas are called "lawgivers." Sibelius similarly refers to "old gentlemen" in his writing, to describe old-fashioned critics who take issue with non-conventional structures and calls for an expansion of musical forms: "Strange that the name of my symphonies should be their greatest enemy. These old gentlemen with their 'concepts' would of course prefer to call them 'fantasies' or something else—what do I know? ... The name 'symphony' can be expanded in its meaning. It has always been that way. An example of infinity."[50]

Busoni had previously written in a similar manner that the concept of forms as fixed molds into which ideas were poured was not fitting for an evolving art: "Our lawgivers have identified the spirit and emotion, the individuality of these composers and their time, with 'symmetric' music, and finally, being powerless to recreate either the spirit or the emotion, or the time, have retained the Form as a symbol and made it a fetish, a religion."[51]

Idealizing free improvisatory passages, Busoni preferred unique structures not bound by *Formenlehre* molds: "Indeed, all composers have drawn nearest the true nature of music in preparatory passages (preludes and transitions), where they felt at liberty to disregard symmetrical proportions, and unconsciously drew free breath."[52]

Sibelius, likewise, believed unique structures would result from unique content. He became obsessed with the concept of motivic growth in spring 1912, after he had spent extended time in Berlin with Busoni the previous fall:[53] "I intend to let the musical thoughts and their development in my mind determine the form. There is no other solution to these conflicts!"[54] Sibelius's thoughts about motivic growth to create unique formal structures appear to gloss Busoni's ideas on the subject: "Every motive—so it seems to me—contains, like a seed, its life-germ within itself. From the different plant-seeds grow different families of plants, dissimilar in form, foliage, blossom, fruit, growth, and color. Even each individual plant belonging to one and the same species assumes, in size, form, and strength, a growth peculiar to itself. And so, in each motive, there lies the embryo of its fully developed form; each one must unfold itself differently, yet each obediently follows the law of eternal harmony. *The form is imperishable, though each be unlike every other.*"[55] Both men thought of the composition process as one of arranging themes and motives in varying formats to achieve unique forms: 'In the evening [I worked on] the symphony. Arrangements of themes. This important task, which fascinates me in a mysterious way.'[56] Busoni likewise described composition as a process of arranging motives and themes into complete compositions:

> The very intention to write down the musical concept [*Einfall*] compels a choice of measure and key. The form, and the sound means [*Klangmittel*], which the composer must decide upon, still more closely define the way and the limits.... From the moment of decision, although much that is original and imperishable in the musical concept [*Einfall*] may live on, it is pressed [*herabgedrückt*] into the type of a genre [*Klasse*]. The musical concept [*Einfall*] becomes a sonata or a concerto; the man a soldier or a priest. That is an arrangement [*Arrangement*] of the original.[57]

Besides impacting Sibelius's ideas about form and content, Busoni taught Sibelius about the importance of sound and timbre. Busoni believed in what he called "absolute orchestration," namely that instrumental color and timbre were an essential part of a musical work. Arranging for another instrument meant altering the work: "Above all it must be emphasized and impressed upon the learner from the beginning that there are two kinds of instrumentation: that which is demanded and directed by musical thought—absolute orchestration—and the instrumentalization of what was originally only an abstract musical composition—one conceived for another instrument. The first is the only genuine one, the second belongs to 'arrangements.'"[58]

In an unpublished two-chapter essay about the aesthetics of the orchestra, Busoni claimed that the orchestration should be integral and not ancillary (see figure 2.2).[59] "Orchestration is composition, not 'instrumentation.' The choice of medium: precision of the thought, shape of the form, form itself."[60] This set of ideas had a profound impact on many of his students, leading them to experiment in new ways with sonority, treating it as a fundamental component of music. Sibelius, who in his maturity rarely created a piano score and then orchestrated it, usually filled in instruments as he composed, rather than saving orchestration for the end. Color and timbre were already in his head. Sibelius stated to Levas: "Actual 'orchestration' is something with which I am quite unfamiliar. I let the musical ideas develop of their own accord."[61] He was adamant that he did not want his songs orchestrated, as that would change the works.[62] Bengt von Törne, one of the few able to call Sibelius a "teacher," recorded some memories of practical orchestration advice from the master that bears striking similarity to Busoni's description of the pedal, as Tawaststjerna has noted. In 1905, Busoni discussed the need for continuous use of pedal as a connective tissue even in an orchestra: "At times one plays the piano without the pedal, but for the most part, the right foot is continually active, helping, filling out the tone, binding the texture together; not to mention the typically big pedal effects. This 'right foot' is also indispensible in the orchestra."[63]

Sibelius also described the need for a "pedal" when orchestrating, especially when moving from one instrumental color to the next. His writing on this subject appears to be a gloss on Busoni's: "The orchestra, you see, is a huge and wonderful instrument, that has got everything—except the pedal. You must always bear this in mind. You see, if you don't create an artificial pedal for your orchestration, there will be holes in it, and some passages will sound ragged."[64]

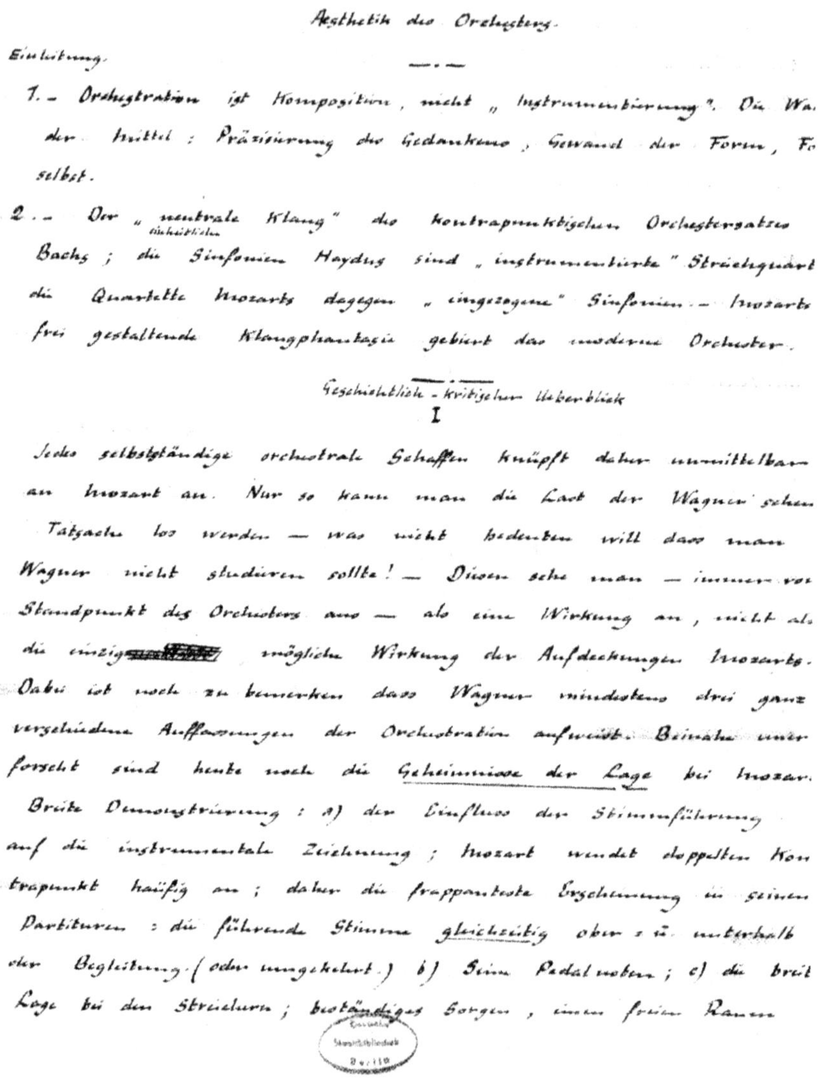

Aesthetik des Orchesters.

Einleitung.

—.—

1.– Orchestration ist Komposition, nicht „Instrumentierung". Die Wa
der Mittel: Präzisierung des Gedankens, Gewand der Form, Fo
selbst.

2.– Der „neutrale Klang" (einheitliche) des kontrapunktischen Orchestersatzes
Bachs; die Sinfonien Haydns sind „instrumentierte" Streichquart
die Quartette Mozarts dagegen „eingezogene" Sinfonien.– Mozarts
frei gestaltende Klangphantasie gebiert das moderne Orchester.

Geschichtlich-kritischer Ueberblick

I

Jedes selbstständige orchestrale Schaffen knüpft daher unmittelbar
an Mozart an. Nur so kann man die Last der Wagner'schen
Tatsache los werden — was nicht bedeuten will dass man
Wagner nicht studieren sollte! — Diesen sehe man — immer vo
Standpunkt des Orchesters aus — als eine Wirkung an, nicht als
die einzig mögliche Wirkung der Aufdeckungen Mozarts.
Dabei ist noch zu bemerken dass Wagner mindestens drei ganz
verschiedene Auffassungen der Orchestration aufweist. Beinahe uner
forscht sind heute noch die Geheimnisse der Lage bei Mozar.
Breite Demonstrierung: a) der Einfluss der Stimmführung
auf die instrumentale Zeichnung; Mozart wendet doppelten Kon
trapunkt häufig an; daher die frappanteste Erscheinung in seinen
Partituren: die führende Stimme gleichzeitig ober- u. unterhalb
der Begleitung. (oder umgekehrt.) b) Seine Pedalnoten; c) die breit
Lage bei den Streichern; beständiges Sorgen, einen freien Raum

FIGURE 2.2. Busoni, "Einleitung," in *Aesthetik des Orchesters*, Berlin Staatsbibliothek, Preussischer Kulturbesitz, Musikabteilung mit Mendelssohn Archiv, Busoni-Nachlass, C1–135.

While contemporaries looked to Berlioz and Wagner as model orchestrators, Busoni considered Mozart to be the greatest model of instrumentation. He claimed that Mozart gave birth to modern orchestration.[65] He praised Mozart for many aspects of orchestration, but especially his use of color and chordal spacing. He specifically revered the water and fire scene in *Die Zauberflöte* and the serenade in *Don Giovanni*.[66] He also advocated allowing each instrument to be heard and overtones to resonate. Doublings, he asserted, should be used to achieve particular colors.[67]

Sibelius came to venerate Mozart as a model of good orchestration as well. Not long after completing the fifth symphony, he reportedly stated: "Do you know . . . whom I consider the two greatest geniuses of the orchestra? You will be surprised to hear it: Mozart and Mendelssohn."[68] Both Busoni and Sibelius used instrumental color with transparency and clarity, like Mozart. At the same time, timbre and chord spacing were not just superficial features, but primary structural elements. This is embodied in Busoni's *Berceuse élégiaque,* which Sibelius admired, where each instrumental timbre receives special attention and is arguably as important as the pitches and harmonies. Each instrument has its own part, even if the thematic material is minimalist. The changing timbres are the central focus. Timbre and chord spacing were not just superficial features, but primary structural elements. But Sibelius took this even further than Busoni. Patterns of orchestration intersect with rhythmic/harmonic/thematic designs in unpredictable ways. Proto-minimalist or almost static sound sheets featuring actively moving timbre surfaces over deep-current slow motion are characteristic of Sibelius's music. Sometimes he creates a crush of sound in the bass regions due to adjacent pitches making a dense screen of sound through which thematic fragments in higher registers emerge and recede. He sometimes varies instrumentation in the recapitulation in the same way that earlier composers, like Mozart, varied tonal regions. In the opening of his Symphony no. 5, for instance, thematic material is varied timbrally as flutes, oboes, bassoons, and trade thematic material.

In addition, Busoni imparted veneration for classical composers, genres, and ideals. His sometimes thinner-textured, contrapuntal approach differed from many of his German contemporaries—Gustav Mahler, Richard Strauss, and Schoenberg included. Although the ideas were already expressed in the first edition of the *Entwurf einer neuen Ästhetik der Tonkunst,* with its emphasis on form and organicism, his theories of Young Classicality solidified throughout the 1910s.[69] In addition to strong and beautiful forms, Busoni called for a more intellectual and objective approach and a distillation of historical musical styles into an almost postmodernist stylistic potpourri:

> I have been misunderstood, in that the multitude construed Classicality as something retrospective.... My idea (or rather perception, personal necessity rather than fabricated principle) is that *Young Classicality* should signify completion in two senses: as *perfection* and as ending, as the *conclusion* to all preceding experiments. I lay stress on the importance of the word *Young* in order to distinguish Classicality from conventional classicism. Every recent or new means, should it be capable of expressing something which cannot be expressed in any other way, ought to be adopted and employed; intentional disdain of effective new achievements strikes me as unreasonable and impoverished.[70]

Busoni's Young Classicality, unlike Stravinsky's neoclassicism, is proto-postmodernist. While Stravinsky used the past as a muse to address old problems in new ways with defamiliarized harmonies, instrumentation, and melody in older forms, Busoni embraced musics of all time periods. True, Busoni looked back to Mozart as a model for form, and Sibelius said: "To my mind, a Mozart allegro is the most perfect model for a symphonic movement. Think of its wonderful unity and homogeneity! It is like an uninterrupted flowing, where nothing stands out and nothing encroaches upon the rest."[71] But they reinterpreted Mozartian ideals according to the expression of their own age and blended Mozartian transparency with elements from several historical periods. Rather than imitating the forms of the past using a defamiliarized set of instruments and harmonies, Busoni's notion, and subsequently Sibelius's as well, was a more spiritual one, in which there is not exterior conformity with the models of the past, but rather internal equilibrium and intellectual balance as well as an atemporal embracing of musics from various time periods. It is not a return to the *Formenlehre* tradition, but rather a transcendence of it. Mozartian transparency of orchestration opened the possibility for new treatments of sound and color. Breaking away from sonata structures allowed for new treatments of form, organization according to the gradual evolution of rhythms, harmonies, textures, and timbres, yet with an underlying intellectuality and order and with an expanded tonal vocabulary. It was in Busoni that Sibelius found a model for his proto-postmodernist style that combined Bachian counterpoint, Lisztian color, Brucknerian registrations, newer experiments with harmonies, and rhythmic displacement.

While many of Sibelius's aesthetic ideals derived from conversations with Busoni, the two differed significantly in the genres in which they chose to write. Sibelius excelled in the symphony and symphonic poem; Busoni mainly wrote small orchestral suites, piano pieces, and operas. Yet this does not preclude certain compositional similarities based on shared aesthetic ideals. In terms of form, both sought to create unique structures in which the content shaped the form. Numerous scholars have discussed Sibelius's approach to form, most notably James Hepokoski, who has stressed the notion of Sibelius as a modern classicist, a composer who strove to produce unique structures dictated by Sibelius's listening to the "*will* of the material."[72] According to Hepokoski, Sibelius's post-1912 compositions are sound objects producing larger architectural shapes.[73] Sibelius is merely in dialogue with sonata traditions. Hepokoski specifically observes a conflation of sonata principles and rotational forms—insistent repetition of a short melodic phrase or set of phrases combined with the forward motion of the sonata. This circular stasis can already be observed in the 1898 song *Illale*, op. 17, no. 6. The fourth symphony generates a theme out of disparate fragments that repeat and evolve. Sibelius's Symphony no. 5 in E-flat major, op. 82, is also based on fragments with a rotational structure that gradually become more complex. Motivic hints grow in later reiterations until fully unfurled. Julian Anderson describes the process as "simply letting a melodic-rhythmic cell grow progressively by gradual changes—bypassing the dialectical tension of developing variation."[74]

Sibelius's approach has led to divergent formal analyses. In the first movement of Symphony no. 5, for instance, which Hepokoski has described as a mixture of sonata and scherzo form, the repeat of expositional material in bars 36–71 with varied textures and instrumental colors, the double function of the first movement, the "non-developmental" aspects of the development section, and the unclear point of return are rarely analyzed the same way by different theorists.[75] Indeed, the structure bears only distant relation to the classical sonata-allegro symphony form.

While Sibelius's Symphony no. 5 reflects Busoni's ideals of unique formal structures, the Symphony no. 4 in A Minor, op. 63, shows the influence of Busoni's experimentalist bent in the early 1900s and his emphasis on timbre (see music example 2.3). Although the form is more straightforward than Sibelius's fifth symphony, the musical language is experimental, while the themes develop by a process of continuous thematic metamorphosis.[76] The tonal language is expanded, as the opening motive C-D-F#-E has modal (C Lydian) and whole-tone implications while blurring the predominant tonality of A minor. The opening motive also sets up a tritone relationship that is prominent throughout all of the movements. Only in measure 7 does the tonality become clear, even despite a bimodal accompaniment. Octatonic and whole-tone implications reach their full potential in the development section, but the entire movement is based on the conflict between whole tone and major/minor scales. The subsidiary theme appears in the "wrong key" of F-sharp minor after a canonic development bypasses C Major. In addition, instrumental color plays a structural role. Both themes are then fragmented and developed while instrumental "chamber" groups play off each other and contribute to a sense of structural disjunction. Even despite advanced musical language, the orchestration is Mozartian in its transparency and clarity.

It was in Berlin in 1909 that Sibelius started thinking deeply about the change of style so clearly manifested in the fourth symphony, precisely when Busoni was also embarking on his most experimental compositions, including his *Berceuse élégiaque*, BV 252, his piano sonatinas, and his *Nocturne symphonique*, BV 262. Busoni had also recently completed seven piano elegies, which marked a new style reflecting the aesthetic ideas expressed in his *Entwurf einer neuen Ästhetik der Tonkunst*. That Sibelius was familiar with many of these pieces is documented in his diary and letters.

That Sibelius studied the *Fantasia contrappuntistica*, BV 256, while he was composing the fourth symphony is especially significant, as the opening section, largely a quotation of the piano elegy no. 3, *Meine Seele bangt und hofft zu dir*, BV 249, displays similar tonal and formal tensions. Originally an independent composition that served as the central and (arguably) the most complex and experimental piece in a published collection of seven elegies, the piece was written shortly after the publication of the

MUSIC EXAMPLE 2.3. Sibelius, Symphony no. 4 in A Minor, op. 63, mvt. 1, mm. 1–11.

first version of the *Entwurf einer neuen Ästhetik der Tonkunst*. It is based on a chorale melody, but Busoni's treatment of the melody is experimental.[77] The majority of the composition develops fragmented portions of the quoted section of the chorale melody, and the piece consistently draws upon unconventional scales and arpeggios based on unrelated triads. There are excursions into bitonality, when a Lydian A major chorale melody appears over an E-flat pedal point in the bass, a tritone relation that serves an important structural function in the piece. This mixture of modality, bitonality, experimental scales, and organization around a tritone within a more conventional formal framework is too similar to Sibelius's approach in the fourth symphony to ignore. Indeed, Sibelius's approach to form and sonority were informed by his composition mentor, Busoni, and the extent of his influence is perhaps more significant than previously acknowledged.

BUSONI'S MENTORSHIP AND CONCERT PROMOTION OF SIBELIUS

Busoni impacted Sibelius's compositional style, serving as a catalyst for some of his most innovative ideas about sound and form, and he also consistently promoted his music even when it was strongly criticized; he helped him navigate the often difficult business of the professional musician and introduced him to the international music scene.

Sibelius had struggled to find a publisher on his own. His first publication, *Serenad* for voice and piano, the first of many settings of texts by Johan Ludvig Runeberg, the Finnish national poet, was completed in 1888.[78] It was published in a collected edition of Finnish songs.[79] Sibelius had no additional success until 1892 when Otava published a collection of seven songs. Sibelius notes that Busoni suggested contacting Max Abraham (1831–1900), who founded the Peters edition in Leipzig on January 2, 1894:[80] "Indeed, I would go to Leipzig, and there's a method to get a publisher. This is Busoni's advice. I heard it through Nováček in Leipzig that [Max] Abraham (patron) is not there; but maybe he will be. Busoni suggests I go today. Then I will write about how it all goes."[81]

Busoni also tried to help get Sibelius's music published with a Russian publisher, Baeiloff. He hoped it would work, because at that time Finland was a Duchy of Russia:

> The Russians have a publisher that I have always envied them. . . . One day the thought occurred to me that when it comes to something like this, the Finns should surely be counted as Russians and I raised the matter with Glazunov who visited me here and if Rimsky is his right hand, then Glazunov is his left. The latter promised to raise the subject with Belaiev and has kept his word. He writes to the effect that the question has been resolved in your favor and suggests that you send some of your work to Belaiev. The outcome will be decided by a committee of three distinguished and fair-minded artists so that I don't doubt that it will be satisfactory. I should advise you to send Beliaev *En Saga, Vårsång, Skogsrået* and to send them straight away.[82]

However, the attempts were unsuccessful. Sibelius's connection with Breitkopf und Härtel was not established until 1898, and Beaumont surmises that when Sibelius finally had his first piece published with Breitkopf und Härtel in 1898, *King Christian II*, op. 27, Busoni was probably instrumental in making this happen. This hypothesis, however, is not supported by any of the letters or documents that have survived.[83] At the very least, Busoni defended and recommended Sibelius to Breitkopf und Härtel, even after Sibelius received scalding criticism from the press, as evident from the letter Busoni penned in Zurich on January 27, 1916:

> Although I graciously escaped, I was painfully disappointed in the attitude of the criticism of *Sibelius's fourth symphony*. I allow myself to give the assurance that the judgment of the *Berliner Blätter*, in my opinion, is fallacious. The fourth symphony of Sibelius is no small wonderful source of feeling, of sound, and of form, and one of his most mature creations. (That a man as P.E. in the local newspaper, himself a composer, whose low-grade popular quality remains, devalues him as a musician.) Of the style of this review there is unfortunately also nothing good to mention. That is the entirety of the disagreeable subject.[84]

After this incident, Busoni also wrote to Breitkopf und Härtel in April 1916: "I would like to know whether you acquired and will publish Sibelius's fifth symphony?"[85] Although the answer was negative—in fact, Sibelius had not even brought up the subject with the publisher—Busoni persisted in the matter, contacting them again in 1918 when he could not find a copy of the score anywhere else.

Busoni also helped Sibelius attain public performances of his compositions, and this was crucial, as Sibelius would probably never had become so widely known outside of Finland during his lifetime had it not been for Busoni's efforts. While Wegelius introduced Sibelius to the national scene, Busoni paved the way on the international scene. Coming from Finland, Sibelius was at the outskirts of musical life and had trouble gaining international recognition, especially in Germany. Although Germans were curious about his music, and adored *Finlandia*, op. 26, the interest dissipated after Busoni's death. Sibelius claimed: "When Busoni died [1924], I knew where I stood,... Busoni was the only person in Germany who was really interested in my music. He was my friend."[86] Sibelius relied upon Busoni to get his music performed abroad. In 1894, when he was still relatively unknown, he believed he could only hope for a performance in Germany with a recommendation from Busoni:[87] "I have been meaning to go to Dresden, and give something of note, *Lemminkäisestä*. Nováček claims that Nicodé will perform it if Busoni gives the recommendation."[88]

Sibelius's big break came when Busoni invited him to participate in his Berlin contemporary orchestra music series on several occasions. Busoni's twelve concerts took place between 1902 and 1909; Sibelius's music was featured in three of them.[89] The concerts were especially novel at the time, not just because they focused on contemporary music, but because they featured cutting edge composers from around the world, such as Debussy and Béla Bartók (1881–1945). By contrast, Richard Strauss's orchestra series contained adventurous music by German-speaking composers, such as Gustav Mahler (1860–1911) and Hugo Wolf (1860–1903), but conservative music by composers of other nations, such as Vincent d'Indy (1851–1931) and Edward Elgar (1857–1934).

Busoni kept Sibelius in mind from the beginning when planning these concerts, and he suggested featuring one of Sibelius's more neo-Germanic works, *En Saga*, op. 9, during the second orchestra evening:[90] "I am planning a number of concerts of new music in Berlin with orchestra whose purpose will be to introduce little-known music of real merit. You shall in this scheme play a leading part in one of them. Will you do me the honour of conducting *En Saga*? At the beginning of November. The Philharmonic Orchestra. Two rehearsals. I beg you to give me your word not to disappoint my hopes. I watch with the greatest delight your German successes, which I foresaw as a certainty."[91]

Sibelius was thrilled to receive the invitation, as he stated in his reply to Busoni, not just because it was an international concert, but also because it was with the Berlin Philharmonic Orchestra: "Naturally, I am pleased to serve personally as well as with my compositions. It will be a great honor and a pleasure to comply with your exceedingly friendly invitation in November. I hope still to speak to you in the course of this week here in Berlin and ask you to kindly notify me when you arrive!"[92]

Busoni and Sibelius corresponded for several months about the details, including the dates and scores. Sibelius, for instance, wrote the following in September, noting that he was revising the piece specifically for Busoni's concert.[93] The concert, which took place in the Beethoven-Saal, was a huge success for Sibelius and featured the following works:[94]

> Edmund von Mihalovich: *Pans Tod*—Symphonische Dichtung
> Jean Sibelius: *En Saga*, op. 9
> Théophile Ysaÿe: Piano Concerto (Soloist: the composer)
> Frederick Delius: *Paris: The Song of a Great City*—Nocturne for Orchestra
> Franz Liszt: *Mephisto Waltz* no. 2 (Nocturnal Procession)

Sibelius gushed endlessly in letters to his wife about how the concert went: "Went very well. Was called back 5 times. My *Saga* was, in my opinion, the best composition. I was very calm and very focused. Do they really understand the *Saga*? It's too good for them. I am sending you the only criticism I could get a hold of (Lokalanzeiger). . . . Busoni congratulates on my 'great success' More soon!"[95]

This concert led to other performance opportunities in Germany. Ferdinand Neisser, for instance, conducted *Finlandia*, op. 26, in 1904 in Berlin and the *Valse triste*, op. 44, no. 1, in 1906,[96] and Richard Strauss conducted the Violin Concerto in D Minor, op. 47, in 1905.[97]

In December 1904, Busoni again asked Sibelius to participate, this time to conduct the second symphony, which he did on January 5, 1905. What he might not have known is that Busoni privately studied several scores of Sibelius's published compositions from Breitkopf und Härtel beginning as early as June 1903 to select one for his upcoming concerts.[98] Busoni considered the Violin Concerto,[99] but ultimately decided to program one of his personal favorites, the second symphony.

This concert, as the previous one, was a great success for him.[100] His music attracted much attention and he became a controversial figure overnight in Germany. Sibelius expressed it this way: "Here I am at the centre of the battle. Fired at or praised. Mostly the latter."[101] Afterward, Max Lewinger conducted the Violin Concerto in 1907, which would be performed again in 1909 under Franz von Vecsey.[102] The String Quartet in D Minor, op. 56 ("voces intimae"), premiered in 1911 and Oskar Fried introduced the fourth symphony to Germany with the Berlin Philharmonic in 1916.[103]

In the penultimate orchestral evening, Busoni programmed *Pohjola's Daughter*, Symphonic Fantasy, op. 49, and conducted it himself. Since Sibelius could not be there, Busoni's conducting caused him much anxiety, perhaps well founded. He wrote on January 3, 1908: "I am a little anxious about Busoni. He is no great conductor and *Pohjola's Daughter* in particular calls for a really good one. May God protect it from being placed at the beginning of the program."[104] The piece, in fact, did go first on the program and was almost unnoticed by reviewers.[105] Sibelius could hardly contain his disappointment, but apparently did not tell Busoni.[106]

Busoni continued to program and direct Sibelius's music until nearly the end of his life in countries throughout Europe, such as Switzerland, the Netherlands, Italy, and Germany (see table 2.2). The most frequently programmed pieces were the second, fourth, and fifth symphonies, which were favorites of Busoni. Although Sibelius expressed concern about Busoni's conducting capabilities on several occasions, he was grateful for Busoni's tireless efforts to promote his music. He also tried to program Sibelius's second symphony in Bologna, toward the end of his time at the Liceo musicale (now the Conservatorio di musica Giovan Battista Martini), as evident from a request to Breitkopf und Härtel for scores and parts: "Please send (without commitment on my part) the parts of Sibelius's second symphony. If it goes well, I will conduct it."[107] Unfortunately, the planned performance never took place, probably due to a need for more rehearsal time. Since Busoni left the Liceo shortly thereafter, it was impossible to reschedule the performance. However, Busoni was able to convince the Liceo to purchase a copy of the score for the library.[108]

As late as 1920, Sibelius still needed Busoni's help in promoting his music. Busoni considered programming Sibelius's fourth symphony in Zurich and also in Paris.[109] He also included Sibelius's music in an orchestral concert in Berlin in 1921 that also featured Busoni's concert suite based

TABLE 2.2. PERFORMANCES OF SIBELIUS SYMPHONIES CONDUCTED BY BUSONI

DATE	LOCATION	COMPOSITION
January 25, 1913	Berlin	Symphony #4
March 29/30, 1913	Amsterdam	Symphony #4
January 16, 1916	Zurich	Symphony #4
March 13/14, 1916	Zurich	Symphony #2
November 1916	Rome	Symphony #2
November 1919	Berlin	Symphony #5
May 1, 1920	Rome	Symphony #2
Summer 1920*	Zurich	Symphony #4
Summer 1920*	Paris	Symphony #4
November 2, 1921	Berlin	Symphony #5

* It is unclear whether or not these performances took place. Busoni wrote about the possibility in a postcard to Sibelius, but I have been unable to locate programs or reviews confirming that the performances took place.

on Mozart's *Idomeneo*, Monteverdi madrigals, and Beethoven's Symphony no. 3, op. 55 ("Eroica"). Busoni left this description in a letter to Adolf Paul in which he not only mentions his concert promotion, but also his frustration that the relationship still seemed so one sided:

> Once again it has fallen to me to help Sibelius a step forward on his path (even though this ought not be necessary! But such are the ways of the world!) and I am glad that everything went so well. I hope you have given him your impressions of the occasion (would really like to know what he makes of this act of devotion; he is so complex and difficult to make out, and our relationship remains one-sided). They are all the same. I know their work, but none of them knows mine. I think highly of the Fifth Symphony. The Fourth is closer to my heart. The Third I don't know. The Second I performed last April [actually 1 May] in Rome.[110]

Knowing Busoni also expanded Sibelius's musical contacts. Because Busoni's house was a musical center to which many composers came while in Berlin, Sibelius met Edgard Varèse (1883–1965), Hans Pfitzner (1869–1949), Louis Gruenberg (1884–1964), Philipp Jarnach (1892–1982), and Frederick Delius (1862–1934), among others. Tawaststjerna describes the meeting between Sibelius and Varèse thus: "On one occasion when Sibelius and Busoni met, the latter had the young Edgard Varèse in his company. As a youth, Varèse had heard the *Swan of Tuonela* in Turin, most likely in the performance conducted by Arturo Toscanini, and had been enchanted by the mystery and sense of space in that work. Even in later years he retained his admiration for the Finnish composer."[111]

Although Varèse and Sibelius would pursue very different career trajectories, and work with different combinations of instruments, there are also parallels—especially in terms of a shared interest in the ways textures, timbres, and sonorities can serve organizational functions.

RECEPTION

The relationship between Sibelius and Busoni was friendly to the end. Busoni was always looking out for Sibelius, mentoring and helping him, actively exposing him to new music and people, promoting him, and critiquing his work. The friendship was so strong that the two usually lost all track of time when they met. Henry Wood left the following recollection of their final meeting in 1921 (see figure 2.3).

> I could generally manage Busoni when I had him to myself, but my heart was always in my mouth if he met Sibelius. I never knew where they would get to. They would forget the time of the concert at which they were to appear; they hardly knew the day of the week. One year I was directing the Birmingham Festival and had to commission a friend never to let those two out of sight. He had quite an exciting time for two or three days following them about from restaurant to restaurant. He told me he never knew what time they went to bed or got up in the morning. They were like a couple of irresponsible schoolboys.[112]

If Busoni was a compositional muse for Sibelius, Busoni, for his part, found equal inspiration from Sibelius. In his second orchestral suite, BV 242 (1895, rev. 1903), each of the movements is dedicated to one of his friends from Finland:[113]

1. Vorspiel (Jean Sibelius)
2. Kriegstanz (Adolf Paul)
3. Grabdenkmal (Armas Järnefelt)
4. Ansturm (Eero Järnefelt)

As Glenda Goss has pointed out, the subtitle, *Geharnischte Suite* (The Armoured Suite), bears reference to Don Quixote, to whom Sibelius and

FIGURE 2.3. Ferruccio Busoni and Jean Sibelius in London (1921). Staatsbibliothek Berlin, Preussischer Kulturbesitz, Musikabteilung mit Mendelssohn Archiv, Busoni Nachl. PI, 214a.

Adolf Paul both compared themselves multiple times.[114] Busoni, for his part, owned numerous editions of Cervantes's *Don Quixote* in his personal library, and left program notes describing the image of a knight in a distant era.[115]

The Vorspiel aptly depicts Sibelius and his music with its startling harmonic colors, repetitions that distort traditional formal structures, gradually unfolding motivic material, starkly contrasting textural and musical sections, and colorful instrumental timbres (see music example 2.4). An opening motive consisting of an ascending half-step on a half-note, eighth on top of timpani sixteenth notes in the winds and strings that appears in diminution beginning in measure 5, suggests the plodding of Rosinante, the horse. Although hinting at E major in the voice leading, the harmonies fail to establish a clear tonal center. The rhythmic and harmonic prancing abruptly stops in measure 8 with sustained pitches in the brass leading to a timpani solo. A witty and comical brass and percussion chromatic march begins in measure 14. Although march rhythms continue in the bassoon and timpani, a lyrical oboe solo emerges in measure 35 while the accompaniment roams chromatically through harmonic regions as unrelated as A major and C minor, with suggestions of C-sharp minor. The tempo relaxes (*più lento*) in measure 54 as imitation and development begins first in the strings and them moves to the brass. The ending, although a return to opening militant material followed by material from the slower and more lyrical section, represents an intensification rather than resolution. Ascending chromatic figures overlay running notes in the strings that migrate chromatically further from the main key with excursions into G-flat, E-flat, A, D, and several other keys. Winds and strings toss the theme back and forth as the movement comes to a peaceful close on C-sharp Major.

By contrast, the second movement depicting Adolf Paul is more firmly rooted in the key of F major. The third movement, representing Arnas Järnefelt, a devoted Wagnerian, features brass, pedal points, and Wagnerian themes. The fourth movement, portraying the painter Eero Järnefelt, plays with different instrumental colors and time signatures to create a musical portrait in sound.[116]

True, the friendship experienced a few bumps along the way. In a letter to his wife, Sibelius accused Busoni of coldness in 1894. In reality, he was

MUSIC EXAMPLE 2.4. Busoni, Second Orchestral Suite ("Geharnischte"), BV 242, mvt. 1, mm. 1–8.

merely overworked with preparing for his Liszt recitals and composing at the same time: "Listen, Busoni seems so cold now. Yes, he is a great champion and has achieved great things, but his soul is lacking!! At least it seems that way to me. Otherwise it would be a 'breakthrough' winter and only think about it. We don't really fit together anymore."[117]

Sibelius was also jealous that Busoni's compositions, which he considered to be inferior, were sometimes better received: "Busoni is being praised as a composer. Delius has one great triumph after another. Even Bantock! Even Juon in Danzig! But me?—"[118] Busoni, for his part, felt the relationship to be one-sided.

Despite these bumps in an otherwise lengthy friendship, Busoni undertook the risk of launching little-known composers, and he invested time in promoting Sibelius, time that he did not have to spare. However, he found a friend and colleague during his lonely sojourn in Helsinki. Moreover, the conversations must have been stimulating for Busoni as well. Louis Gruenberg mentioned in his memoirs that Busoni admired Sibelius's technical proficiency and frequently praised him in conversations:

> His [Sibelius's] technic is adequate (Busoni often spoke of the assurance and certainty of his technic) but by no means extraordinary. When I remarked upon the fact that Sibelius was a national figure, that already every servant girl knew him in 1913, when I was in Finland, Busoni, with a malicious grin, answered: "I can readily believe it." ... Speaking of the fourth symphony to Busoni, I remarked on the skeletonized form of the construction and the effect of the impression of wide spaces in the music in spite of this. Busoni answered: "Sibelius is a great master of economy. A third flute stuck in the score among many stronger instruments makes the impression on paper that it cannot possibly be heard above the mass. However, on more careful examination, it will be found that the note of the flute is the strongest on the instrument, and so placed that it makes an individual impression."[119]

Sibelius, for his part, kept Busoni's image over his desk, and he realized his indebtedness to his lifelong mentor, teacher, and friend. Busoni had been a muse and source of inspiration: "Over my desk is Eero's portrait of you, and when I received your very welcome letter, it was as if the picture began to speak. It has been silent for many years now but has always prompted me to work. You do me the great kindness to ask about my fifth symphony. It is not yet in print as I have not been able to publish anything since 1914. I am so proud of the interest you show in me."[120]

The reception of their music also seems to have followed a similar trajectory. As Carl Dahlhaus has observed, confusion about how to situate both of them historically has led to their neglect. Neither romantic nor avant-garde, they shared a tenuous position in the historiographic narrative: "Composers as Jean Sibelius and Ferruccio Busoni, which undoubtedly belonged to the moderns—as one understood at that time—but were afraid to implement the writings on new music, were subjected to a critique, which hardly succeeded in aesthetic judgment, because it failed to ascertain their historical place, and through this they ended up in aesthetic "no-man's land," and were deprived of historiographical formulae."[121]

Both men's music declined in popularity when the avant-garde was on the ascendancy, experiencing revivals only with the birth of postmodernism. After his death in 1924, Busoni was largely forgotten until the centennial of his birth (1966). Sibelius experienced a similar fate, with a major decline in popularity, especially in Germany, beginning in the 1920s, only to experience a revival in the 1970s and 1980s. Although complex political and aesthetic issues were partially to blame, not least Busoni's eccentric views about originality and Sibelius's failure to embrace Nazi solicitations of his music, at the heart of the issue was difficulty appreciating the innovative aspects of their music—especially in relation to form and sonority.

Of course, Busoni was not the only important influence on Sibelius. Sibelius would never have succeeded without the technical expertise provided by Wegelius and the solid but dull training in counterpoint by Becker. It was Goldmark who first introduced him to orchestral writing. Growing up in Finland exposed Sibelius to landscapes and natural sounds, to folk melodies that gave much of his music distinctive characteristics and that contributed to his choice of unusual harmonies and tone colors. Yet Busoni also shared aesthetic ideas that contributed some of Sibelius's most innovative compositional characteristics.

Sibelius's music, like the music of other Busoni pupils, in turn has deeply impacted contemporary composers interested with sound and experimental formal processes, as Julian Anderson has documented. French spectral music, in which the acoustic structure of sounds and the acoustics of human perception have been taken as starting points for the music, is, for instance, indebted to Sibelius.[122] Equally fascinated with Sibelius and Varèse because of their unique treatment of sound, Hughes Dufort, Tristan Murail, Pascal Dusapin, Gérard Grisey, and Alain Bancquart forged new sounds in their compositions.[123] A pupil of Grisey, Magnus Lindberg held a similar opinion, going on to make the claim that Sibelius was not only thinking along the same lines as Varèse, but also more innovative in some respects:

> While his [Sibelius's] language was far from modern, his thinking, as far as form and the treatment of materials is concerned, was ahead of its time. While Varèse is credited with opening the way for new sonorities, Sibelius has himself pursued a profound reassessment of the formal and structural problems of composition.... His harmonies have a resonant, almost spectral quality. You find an attention to sonority in Sibelius's works which is not actually so far removed from that which appeared long after in the work of Grisey or Murail.[124]

Sibelius also influenced composers of Scandinavian and Nordic regions interested in the linking of distinct thematic areas through processes of evolution or metamorphosis. Per Nørgård, in particular, was fascinated with Sibelius's melodic processes, especially in the fifth symphony, which he used as a model for his own "infinity row" that explores harmonic, melodic, and rhythmic stratification.[125] At the same time, American and British composers such as Peter Maxwell Davies and George Benjamin were fascinated by Sibelius's treatment of form and Morton Feldman by his orchestrations.

It was indeed a paradoxical tension between the classic and the innovative that marked Sibelius's music as enigmatic in his own age; yet his compositional style has finally received its due recognition in our own. Understanding Sibelius's compositional style in the context of one of his most imaginative teachers, Busoni, enriches understanding about Sibelius's development and reveals parallels with even some of the most adventurous composers of his time, including Varèse, who was similarly interested in sound as a structural feature and who sought to create new forms based on human ideas. It also enlarges understanding about the flexible aesthetic ideas underlying the creative activities of Busoni's diverse pupils even as Sibelius's Janus-faced music can be seen as looking not only backward to Classicism and Romanticism, but also forward to a future characterized by new sounds, new forms, and the dissolution of temporal boundaries.

NOTES

1. See Theodor Adorno, "Gloss on Sibelius," in *Jean Sibelius and His World*, ed. Daniel Grimley (Princeton, NJ: Princeton University Press, 2011), 333–334. On the other hand, Cecil Gray stated in 1931: "The symphonies of Sibelius represent the highest point attained in this form since the death of Beethoven." Cecil Gray, *Sibelius* (London: Oxford University Press, 1934), 181. I am grateful to Emiliano Ricciardi for commenting on an earlier version of this chapter.
2. See, for instance, Daniel Grimley, ed., *The Cambridge Companion to Sibelius* (Cambridge: Cambridge University Press, 2004), and Grimley, ed., *Jean Sibelius and His World*.
3. Tomi Mäkelä, "The Wings of a Butterfly: Sibelius and the Problems of Musical Modernity," in Grimley, *The Cambridge Companion to Sibelius*, 93.
4. See the following source for a discussion of Sibelius as a progressive composer: Tim Howell, *Progressive Techniques in the Symphonies and Tone Poems* (New York: Garland, 1989).
5. Erik Tawaststjerna, *Sibelius*, trans. Robert Layton, 3 vols. (Berkeley: University of California Press, 1976); Tomi Mäkelä, *Jean Sibelius*, trans. Steven Lindberg (Woodbridge: Boydell Press, 2007); Cecil Gray, *Sibelius*; Karl Ekman, *Jean Sibelius: His Life and Personality*, trans. Edward Birse (London: A. A. Knopf, 1938). As much of the information in the Tawaststjerna and Ekman biographies is based on personal interviews with the composer, some of which were not recorded right away, there might be some inaccuracies. Moreover, the biographers' lack of experience with Busoni's aesthetics and music is evident. Of these sources, Mäkelä's provides the most comprehensive and thoughtful analysis of connections between Busoni's aesthetics and Sibelius's compositional philosophies.
6. Barbara Hong, "The Friends of Lesko, the Dog: Sibelius, Busoni, Armas, and Eero Järnefelt," in *Sibelius in the Old and New World: Aspects of His Music, Its Interpretation, and Reception*, ed. Timothy L. Jackson, Veijo Murtomäki, Colin Davis, and Timo Virtanen, Interdisziplinäre Studien zur Musik, ed. Tomi Mäkelä und Tobias R. Klein, vol. 6 (Frankfurt am Main: Peter Lang, 2010).
7. Antony Beaumont, "Sibelius and Busoni," in *Proceedings from the First International Jean Sibelius Conference, Helsinki* (Helsinki: Sibelius Academy, 1995), 14–20.
8. Roberto Wis, "Ferruccio Busoni and Finland," *Acta Musicologica* 49:2 (July–September 1977), 250–279; Petri Sariola, "Doktor Faustus of the Keyboard and the Discreet Charm of Stella Polaris," *Finnish Music Quarterly* 1 (1999), 46–51. Inaccessibility of primary source documents has inhibited detailed discussions of this topic. In addition, Sibelius corresponded in numerous languages, but most frequently in either Finnish or Swedish. Sibelius's diary and many letters were only recently published. Jean Sibelius, *Dagbok: 1909–1944*, ed. Fabian Dahlström, Skrifter utgivna av

Svenska litteratursällskapet i Finland, no. 681 (Helsingfors: Svenska litteratursällskapet i Finland, 2005); Aino Sibelius and Jean Sibelius, *Tulen synty: Aino ja Jean Sibeliuksen kirjeenvaihtoa 1892–1904*, ed. Suvisirkku Talas, Suomalaisen Kirjallisuuden Seuran toimituksia, no. 910 (Helsinki: Suomalaisen Kirjallisuuden Seura, 2003); Aino Sibelius and Jean Sibelius, *Syysilta: Aino ja Jean Sibeliuksen kirjeenvaihtoa, 1905–1931*, ed. Suvisirkku Talas Suomalaisen Kirjallisuuden Seuran toimituksia, 1133 (Helsinki: Suomalaisen Kirjallisuuden Seura, 2007); Aino Sibelius and Jean Sibelius, *Sydämen aamu: Aino Järnefeltin ja Jean Sibeliuksen kihlausajan kirjeitä*, ed. Suvisirkku Talas, Suomalaisen Kirjallisuuden Seuran toimituksia, 821 (Helsinki: Suomalaisen Kirjallisuuden Seura, 2001); Glenda Dawn Goss, *Jean Sibelius and Olin Downes: Music, Friendship, Criticism* (Boston: Northeastern University Press, 1995); Jean Sibelius and Rosa Newmarch, *The Correspondence of Jean Sibelius and Rosa Newmarch*, ed. Philip Ross Bullock (Rochester: Boydell Press, 2011); Jean Sibelius and Axel Carpelan, *Högtärade Maestro!, högtärade Herr Baron!: Korrespondensen mellan Axel Carpelan och Jean Sibelius 1900–1919*, ed. Fabian Dahlström, Skrifter utgivna av Svenska litteratursällskapet i Finland, no. 737 (Helsingfors: Svenska litteratursällskapet i Finland; Stockholm: Atlantis, 2010). Many other letters and other primary documents remain unpublished. Moreover, many of Sibelius's compositions were kept by family members until their donation to the Helsinki University Library in 1971—the recent publication of Sibelius's collected works is therefore of great value to Sibelius scholarship. Sibelius, *Jean Sibelius: Complete Works*, The National Library of Finland and the Sibelius Society of Finland, 28 vols. (Leipzig: Breitkopf und Härtel, 1996–present). Goss describes the donation in her article summarizing the contents of the Sibelius collection. The date of the donation differs from source to source. Glenda Dawn Goss, "Sibelius Letters in the Helsinki University Library," *Fontes artis Musicae* 52:3 (July-September 2005), 145–156. Other letters and Sibelius documents have been found in numerous private and public Finnish collections. See "Jean Sibelius," accessed December 29, 2012, http://www.sibelius.fi/english/omin_sanoin/index.htm. Major archival sources include the the Helsinki University Library, Sibelius Academy Archive, the National Library of Finland, and the Åbo Akademi archive. The National Archives of Finland has the family letters and the diary.

9. Chiara Bertoglio, "Four Hands and Fur Paws: Sibelius, Busoni, and Lesko the Dog," *Trio* 5:1 (June 2016), 6–33.

10. In particular, he studied Johann Christian Lobe's four-volume *Lehrbuch der musikalischen Composition*. Sibelius obtained a copy in 1884. Sibelius, letter to his Uncle Pehr of February 24, 1884, in Glenda Dawn Goss, ed., *Jean Sibelius: The Hämeenlinna Letters: Scenes from a Musical Life 1874–1895* (Helsinki: Schildts, 1997), 64. Lobe's volumes start with basic harmony and culminate with instruction about the composition. Sibelius also looked at Adolf Bernhard Marx's *Lehrbuch der musikalischen Komposition*. Goss, ed., *Jean Sibelius: The Hämeenlinna Letters*, 27. He began studying in the Physical-Mathematical Department at the Imperial Alexander University in 1885 with the idea of studying medicine before switching to law, but his passion was for the violin. By the 1886–1887 academic year, he devoted himself full-time to music studies at the Helsinki Music Institute.

11. Sibelius to Pehr, September 27, 1887, in Goss, *The Hämeenlinna Letters*, 89.

12. Tawaststjerna claims Busoni's influence during these meetings was largely responsible for Sibelius's dramatic compositional growth in 1889. Tawaststjerna, *Sibelius*, vol. 1, 45.

13. "Als ich, jünger als Du jetzt, in Helsingfors war, da bildeten Sibelius und die beiden Brüder Jaernefelt einen anregenden Umgang; von meinem Director Martin Wegelius, einem höchst feincultivirten Mann, lernte ich Manches." Busoni, to Egon Petri, June 13, 1908 in Busoni, *Briefe an Henri, Katharina und Egon Petri*, ed. Martina Weindel, Taschenbücher zur Musikwissenschaft, ed. Richard Schaal (Wilhelmshaven: Florian Noetzel, 1999), 94. Eero Jaernefelt was a painter. His brother was a composer, conductor, and Wegelius's successor as director of the Helsinki Music Institute. Adolf Paul, a writer, and one of Busoni's piano pupils at the Helsinki Music Institute, was another member of the group.

14. Sibelius did take rudimentary piano lessons with Martin Wegelius. Leo Mononen, email to the author, January 9, 2013. Sibelius, quoted in Ekman, *Sibelius: His Life and Personality*, 61–62.

15. Tawaststjerna, "The Two Leskovites," *Finnish Musical Quarterly* 3 (1986), 2.

16. Ibid., 2.

17. Busoni, quoted in Ekman, *Sibelius: His Life and Personality*, 60–61.

18. Sibelius, quoted in ibid., 61–62.

19. Ibid., 264. Busoni's performances impressed the pupils and music lovers in Helsinki, as they did Sibelius as well. Ibid., 260.

20. For a list of Sibelius's journeys abroad, consult "Jean Sibelius," accessed January 22, 2013, http://www.sibelius.fi/english/erikoisaiheet/matkat/matk_kronologinen.htm.

21. "Då jag tänker på Busonis glansfulla ställning som konstnär förstår jag mitt öde Mitt oändligt tragiska öde!" Sibelius, *Dagbok*, February 25, 1912, 128.

22. Busoni expressed excitement that Sibelius would be present for his 1912 concerts, claiming that he wanted to play his best for Sibelius. Busoni to Sibelius, October 29, 1912, quoted in Wis, "Ferruccio Busoni and Finland," 266.

23. "Busoni spelade Bach, Beethoven, Op. 111 c-moll. En oförliknelig konstnär! En oförgätlig stund!" Sibelius, *Dagbok*, October 23, 1912, 155.

24. "Busoni spelade B dursonaten (Op. 106). Ett minne för hela lifvet synnes mig! Aldrig har menniskans storhet och kraft fremstått för mig med sädan tydlighet och sä öfvertygande." Ibid., October 28, 1912, 155.

25. Guy Rickards, *Jean Sibelius* (London: Phaidon Press, 1997).

26. Sibelius would have previously met Becker during the faculty concert of February 14, 1889, at the Helsinki Music Institute.

27. Busoni to Heinrich Freiherr von Herzogenberg, quoted in Mäkelä, *Sibelius*, 172. Tawaststjerna and Ekman claimed there existed a similar letter intended for Brahms, but if so, it has never surfaced.

28. Sibelius to Aino Sibelius, October 24, 1890, in Sibelius, *Sydämen aamu*, 20. If Sibelius did visit Herzogenberg, he does not mention it in the letter.

29. Goldmark paid little attention to the details, but was good at giving general criticism. Fuchs provided detailed advice about technical craftsmanship. On Febru-

ary 12, 1890, Sibelius showed a new Overture in E Major to Goldmark, who criticized the themes and suggested taking Haydn, Mozart, and Beethoven as models rather than Wagner and Berlioz.

30. "Täma minun uusi ouverturini on parempi kuin vaikkapa Busonin konserttikappale orkesterille mutta huonompi kuin hänen toccatensa ja fuugansa. Goldmark sanoi, että minun pitää enää vain neljännesvuosittain viedä jotakin hänen nähtäväkseen." Sibelius to Aino Sibelius, February 13, 1891, in *Sydämen aamu*, 170. This is a reference to Sibelius's Overture in E Major (1890), Busoni's *Consertstück*, BV 236 (1890), and perhaps Busoni's transcription of J. S. Bach's Toccata and Fugue in D Minor (1890). A reference to a piano transcription seems out of place here.

31. Sibelius visited Berlin at least thirty-six times between 1890 and 1931. Mäkelä, "Sibelius and Germany: *Wahrhaftigkeit* beyond *Allnatur*," in Grimley, *The Cambridge Companion to Sibelius*, 169.

32. Wis, "Ferruccio Busoni and Finland," 267. The program is preserved in the Staatsbibliothek zu Berlin, Preußischer Kulturbesitz, Musikabteilung mit Mendelssohn-Archiv, Mus. Nachl. F. Busoni, E 1888, 5.

33. Ibid., 267. Abraham Ojanperä taught voice from 1885 to 1915 at the Helsinki Music Institute.

34. Some of Wegelius's views about Wagner can be read in the following text: Martin Wegelius, *Konstnärsbrev* (Helsingfors: Senare Delan, 1919).

35. The descending scales in the second movement also resemble the *Papillons* quotation in the Florestan movement from Schumann's *Carnaval*, op. 9 (also in G minor).

36. Eero Heinonen, "Introduction," trans. Jaakko Mäntyjärvi, in Sibelius, *Florestan* (1889) (n.p.: Warner/Chappell Music, 2001), 1 (trans. modified by Erinn Knyt).

37. "Täällä olen nyt Busonin, Novatcekin ja Paulin kanssa. Ovat hyvin ystävällisiä. Waikka ajat ei ole niinkuin ennen. Kaikki oomme muuttuneet. Omat intressit ovat lähinnä. Se oli niin surkeata nähdä ja huomata sitä.... Eilen olin mielioopperaa, Carmenia, kuulemaassa. Minä nyt sitä rakastan.... En voinut olla telegrafeeraamatta koska Busoni niin välttämättömästi tahtoi nähdä teostani jotain." Sibelius to Aino Sibelius, August 30, 1894, in *Tulen Synty*, 97–98. There is no evidence that Sibelius visited Breitkopf und Härtel until 1898.

38. "Varit hos Busoni. Han gaf mig mycket genom sin beundran för min konst. Den orkestrala. Rådde mig att hålla mig därtill. Arbetat bra. Skrifvit färdig klaverutdraget till 'Tulen synty' [op. 32]." Sibelius, *Dagbok*, October 16, 1910, 57.

39. The concert took place on February 14, 1914.

40. The piece did not receive its public premiere until February 21, 1911, in New York under the baton of Gustav Mahler.

41. "Studerat Busonis 'Fantasia contrappuntistica.' Hvarför vill denna stora klaverkonstnär komponera? Intressant är ju alltid att höra en stor konstnär jobba—men—denna 'musik.' 'Fattig och ful.' Utan fart!!! Hans 'Berceuse élégiaque' har som färg och kuliss, sitt berättigande. Men det är också allt!" Sibelius, *Dagbok*, November 3, 1910, 59. Sibelius continued to be inspired by Busoni's piano playing when he was abroad. He heard the second of Busoni's all-Liszt recitals in Berlin on January 21, 1905, and mentions hearing another of Busoni's new piano pieces in a letter. Sibelius to Axel Carpelan, January 19/26, 1914, in *Högtärade Maestro!*, 347.

42. For a more detailed description of the trip consult "Jean Sibelius," accessed January 11, 2013, http://www.sibelius.fi/english/erikoisaiheet/matkat/matk_03.htm

43. Walter Legge, "Conversations with Sibelius," *Musical Times* 76:1105 (March 1935), 218.

44. Sibelius to Aino Sibelius, September 7, 1894, in *Tulen Synty*, 106.

45. "Luulen että minä oikeastaan olen musiikki maalari ja runoilia. Tarkoitan että tuo Listz'in musiikki kanta on minulle lähintä. Tuo symfoninen runo (sillä tavalla meinasin 'runoilija') Minä käsittelen hyvin rakasta ainetta nyt." Sibelius to Aino Sibelius, August 19, 1894, in *Tulen Synty*, 84.

46. Mäkelä has left a more detailed account of the connection in *Jean Sibelius*, 265–269.

47. Sibelius, quoted in Santeri Levas, *Sibelius: A Personal Portrait* (Lewisburg, PA: Bucknell University Press, 1973), 74.

48. Sibelius, *Dagbok*, February 4, 1914, 184.

49. Tawaststjerna, *Sibelius*, vol. 2, 25. Kajanus conducted the Helsinki Orchestra.

50. "Egendomligt att mina symfoniers namn skall vara deras största fiende. Dessa gamla herrar med 'begrepp' skulle naturligtvis helst kalla dem fantasier eller annat— hvad vet jag.—Från sin nedärfda åskådning kunna de ej komma. Namnet symfoni [oläsligt] ju till dess betydelse vidgas. Så har det alltid varit. Exempel i oändligh[et]." Sibelius, *Dagbok*, February 5, 1918, 269–270.

51. Busoni, *Sketch of a New Esthetic of Music*, trans. Theodore Baker (New York: Schirmer, 1911), 7.

52. Ibid., 8.

53. Sibelius, *Dagbok*, April 22, 1912, 135.

54. "Jag tanker låta de musikaliska tankarna och deras utveckling i min anda, bestämma formen. Någon annan lösning på dessa strider finnes nog ej.—Arnold Schönberg's teorier intressera mig. Dock finner jag honom ensidig! Kanske ej då jag närmare lär mig känna honom! Sic!" Sibelius, *Dagbok*, May 8, 1912, 138–139.

55. Busoni, *Sketch*, 10–11.

56. Sibelius, *Dagbok*, April 10, 1915, quoted in James Hepokoski, *Sibelius: Symphony No. 5*, Cambridge Music Handbooks, ed. Julian Rushton (Cambridge: Cambridge University Press, 1993), 32.

57. Busoni, *Sketch of a New Esthetic of Music* (1911). My revised translation is based on that by Theodor Baker in *Three Classics in the Aesthetic of Music* (New York: Dover Publications, 1962), 84–85.

58. Busoni, "The Theory of Orchestration," (1905) in *The Essence of Music and Other Papers*, 36.

59. He expressed great authority in approaching scores of even the acknowledged masters and taught his students to do the same using what would seem to be this very orchestration treatise, as Levitz notes: "Shortly before the master class began, Philipp Jarnach copied out the start of what Busoni planned as an aesthetic of orchestration, in which he defined orchestration as more than mere instrumentation: it was a form of composition, a means of more precisely expressing musical thoughts (*Gedanken*) and creating form." Tamara Levitz, "Teaching New Classicality: Busoni's Master class in Composition, 1921–24" (PhD diss., University of Rochester, 1993), 174.

60. "Orchestration ist Komposition, nicht 'instrumentierung.' Der Wahl der mittel: Präzisierung des Gedankens, Gewand der Form, Form selbst." Busoni, "Aesthetik des Orchesters," Staatsbibliothek zu Berlin, Preußischer Kulturbesitz, Musikabteilung mit Mendelssohn-Archiv, Mus. Nachl. F. Busoni, CI, 135.

61. Levas, *Sibelius: A Personal Portrait*, 88–89.

62. "I don't want them orchestrated . . . for they completely lose their individual character." Sibelius, quoted in ibid., 85–86.

63. Busoni, quoted in Tawaststjerna, *Sibelius*, vol. 2, 26.

64. Bengt de Törne, *Sibelius: A Close Up* (Boston: Houghton Mifflin, 1938), 31.

65. Busoni, "Aesthetik des Orchesters," 1.

66. Ibid., 2.

67. Ibid., quoted in Levitz, "Teaching New Classicality," 175. In his Berlin master class (1921–1924), Busoni used Mozart as a basis for instruction about orchestration. Levitz, "Teaching New Classicality," 174–176.

68. Sibelius, quoted in de Törne, *Sibelius: A Close Up*, 47. Although Wegelius, Fuchs, and Goldmark revered the Viennese masters, they did not single out Mozart the way Busoni had done. Goldmark, for instance, suggested that Sibelius should stay away from Bizet and Wagner for a time and study the works of the Viennese trilogy, but he did not mention Mozart specifically. Tawaststjerna, *Sibelius*, vol. 2, 88.

69. Busoni, "'Neue Klassizität?': Offener Brief an Paul Bekker," *Frankfurter allgemeine Zeitung*, February 7, 1920; "Young Classicism" in *The Essence and Oneness of Music and Other Papers*, 19/23; "Vom Wesen der Musik: Anbahnung einer Verständigung für den immerwährenden Kalender," *Melos*, 4:1 (August 1, 1924), 7/13. Busoni states he first used the term more than two years prior to writing the letter. Busoni to Raffaello Busoni, June 18, 1921, in Beaumont, *Selected Letters*, 342.

70. Beaumont, *Selected Letters*, 342.

71. De Törne, *Sibelius: A Close Up*, 48.

72. Hepokoski, *Sibelius: Symphony No. 5*, 60.

73. It is unclear whether or not Sibelius read Busoni's book. Regardless, the two would have discussed many of the ideas contained in it.

74. Julian Anderson, "Sibelius and Contemporary Music," in Grimley, *The Cambridge Companion to Sibelius*, 198.

75. Hepokoski, *Sibelius: Symphony No. 5*, 60.

76. Consult the following article for a diagram of the formal structure: Elliott Antokoletz, "The Musical Language of the Fourth Symphony," in *Sibelius Studies*, ed. Timothy Jackson and Veijo Murtomäki, Cambridge Composer Studies (Cambridge: Cambridge University Press, 2001), 299–300.

77. George A. Winfield claims that the melody was a tenth-century plainsong, the "Et in terra pax" segment of the "Gloria" from the Easter Mass (Mass I, "Lux et Origo") found in the *Liber Usualis*. George A. Winfield, "Ferruccio Busoni's Compositional Art: A Study of Selected Works for Piano Solo Composed Between 1907 and 1923" (PhD diss., Indiana University, 1982), 32–35.

78. For a more thorough explanation of Sibelius's publishers consult Fabian Dahlström, *Jean Sibelius: Thematisch-bibliographisches Verzeichnis seiner Werke* (Wiesbaden: Breitkopf und Härtel, 2003), 23–27.

79. Wegelius was editor of *Det sjunde Finland*, in which it was published.
80. Andreas Soport, email to the author, January 16, 2013.
81. "Menisin nimittäin Leipzigiin ja siellä koettaisin saada 'forlag.' Tämä on kaikki Busonin neuvoa. Nyt kuulin Leipzigista Novacekin kautta että Abraham (maecenati) ei ole siellä; vaan ehkä hän tulee. Busonin luo menen tänään. Kirjoitan sitten kuinka kaikki käy." Sibelius to Aino Sibelius, September 1894, in *Tulen synty*, 102.
82. Busoni to Sibelius, quoted in Tawaststjerna, vol. 1, 166. Mitrofan Beliaev (1836–1904) played piano, violin, and viola. Professionally, he worked for his father's lumber business, but he also organized Russian concert series and Russian chamber music series in the last two decades of the nineteenth century. His publishing company, M. P. Belaieff, was established in 1885 in Leipzig and St. Petersburg and eventually succeeded by C. F. Peters after passing under control of the state.
83. Beaumont, "Sibelius and Busoni," 16.
84. "Wenngleich ich selber noch gnädig davongekommen bin, so hat mich die Haltung der Kritik gegenüber der IV. Sibelius'schen Symphonie schmerzlich enttäuscht. Ich erlaube mir, Ihnen die Versicherung zu geben, dass das Urtheil der Berliner Blätter—meines Glaubens—durchaus irrig ist. Die 'Vierte' von Sibelius ist eine kleine Wunderblüthe der Empfindung, des Klanges u. der Form, u. eine seiner gereiftestesten Schöpfungen. (Dass ein Mann wie P.E. im Lokalanzeiger, selber ein Komponist, diesen Eigenschaften gegenüber taub bleibt, richtet ihn als Musiker.) Von dem "Styl" dieser Besprechungen ist leider auch Nichts Gutes zu sagen; das Ganze ist eine unliebsame Angelegenheit." Busoni to Breitkopf und Härtel, January 27, 1916, in *Ferruccio Busoni im Briefwechsel mit seinem Verlag Breitkopf und Härtel*, ed. Eva Hanau. 2 vols., Busoni-Editionen, ed. Albrecht Riethmüller (Wiesbaden: Breitkopf und Härtel, 2012), vol. 2, 112.
85. "... zugleich möchte ich wissen, ob sie Sibelii 5. Symph. erwarben u. veröffentlichen werden?" Busoni to Breitkopf und Härtel, April 12, 1916, in Hanau, *Ferruccio Busoni im Briefwechsel*, vol. 2, 135.
86. Sibelius, quoted in Harold E. Johnson, *Jean Sibelius* (New York: Faber and Faber, 1959), 91.
87. For a more complete account of Sibelius and Germany consult Mäkelä, "Sibelius and Germany," 169–181.
88. "Olen aikonut mennä Dresdeniin ja antaa esitää jotain Lemminkäisestä. Novaçek väittää että Nicódé sen tekee jos Busoni antaa rekommendationinsa." Sibelius to Aino Sibelius, April 13, 1898, in *Tulen Synty*, 144. Jean Louis Nicódé (1853–1919) was a Prussian pianist, composer, and conductor. He also became a professor at the Royal Conservatory in Dresden.
89. Sibelius conducted *En Saga*, op. 9, on November 15, 1902. During the sixth concert on January 12, 1905, Sibelius's second symphony was performed. The eleventh concert, which took place on January 3, 1908, featured *Pohjolas Tochter*, op. 49.
90. *En Saga*, op. 9, is a tone poem that Sibelius began in 1890 as an octet for strings, flute, and clarinet; it evolved into a septet by September 1892, was titled Ballet Scene no. 2 in November 1892, and eventually received its current title by the time of the first performance in 1893. Tawaststjerna, *Sibelius*, vol. 1, 130.
91. Busoni, quoted in ibid., vol. 1, 257. The original letter is written in German and is located in the Sibelius Family Papers Collection in the Finnish National Archives.

92. "Selbstverständlich bin ich sowohl persöhnlich als wie mit meinen Kompositionen zu Diensten. Es wird mir eine grosse Ehre und ein Vergnügen sein deiner überaus freundlichen Aufforderung im November nachzukommen. Ich hoffe dich noch im Laufe dieser Woche hier in Berlin zu sprechen und bitte höflichst mir benachrichtigen zu wollen wenn Du hier eintriffst!" Sibelius to Busoni, June 22, 1902, in Martina Weindel, ed., "Busonis 'Berlin Orchesterabende': Eine Nachlese Unveröffentlichter Briefe von Schönberg, Mahler, Bartók und Sibelius," *Schweizer Jahrbuch für Musikwissenschaft* 23 (2003), 323.

93. "Danke herzlichst für d. Brief.—Für mich wäre d. 15. November das beste. Mit deiner Erlaubniss werde ich d. 'Saga' aufführen. Doch muss ich sie etwas umarbeiten und könnte deswegen nicht sogleich d. Partitur und Stimmen absenden. Die kommen doch sicher zeitig genug! ... Die 'Saga' dauert kaum 25 Minuten, (Vielleicht doch!)." Sibelius to Busoni, September 15, 1902, in Weindel, "Busonis 'Berlin Orchesterabende,'" 323.

94. Dent, *Ferruccio Busoni*, 332.

95. "Meni oikein hyvin. Minua huudettin esille viisi kertaa. Minun saga oli mielestäni paras noviteetti. Olin hyvin levollinen ja dirigeerasin hyvin. Eivät ne oikein ymmärrä saaga. Den är för fin för dem. Jag sänder Dig här den enda kritik jag fått tag uti (Lokalanzeiger).... Busoni gratuleerar till min 'grosse Succès.' Mera snart!" Sibelius to Aino Sibelius, November 16, 1902, in *Tulen synty*, 301.

96. Mäkelä, "Sibelius and Germany," 169.

97. Ibid., 169.

98. Busoni to Breitkopf und Härtel, June 9, 1903, in Hanau, *Ferruccio Busoni im Briefwechsel*, vol. 1, 123.

99. Busoni to Breitkopf und Härtel, July 6, 1904, in ibid., vol. 1, 129.

100. Sibelius to Aino Sibelius, January 12, 1905, in *Syysilta*, 11.

101. Tawaststjerna, *Sibelius*, vol. 2, 24.

102. Mäkelä, "Sibelius and Germany," 170.

103. Ibid.

104. Sibelius, in Tawaststjerna, *Sibelius*, vol. 2, 84.

105. Dent, *Ferruccio Busoni*, 335–336. The program consisted of the following pieces: Jean Sibelius: *Pohjola's Daughter*: Symphonic Fantasy, op. 49; Ferruccio Busoni: Violin Concerto, op. 35a (Soloist: Émile Sauret); Franz Liszt-Busoni: *Tre Sonetti di Petrarca* (orchestrated by Busoni, Singer: Felix Senius); Paul Ertel: *Harald-Symphonie*, op. 2, 3rd mvt. Bacchanal; Franz Liszt: *Tre Sonetti di Petrarca*: nos. 2 and 3 (original songs) (Busoni acc. at piano, Senius, singer); Franz Liszt: *Mazeppa*—Symphonic Tone Poem no. 6.

106. Sibelius in Tawaststjerna, *Sibelius*, vol. 2, 110.

107. "Bitte schicken Sie (ohne Verbindlichkeit meinerseits) Part. u. Stimmen der II. Symph. von Sibelius. Wenn es noch geht, würde ich sie spielen." Busoni to Breitkopf und Härtel, April 14, 1914, in Hanau, *Ferruccio Busoni im Briefwechsel*, vol. 1, 634.

108. Breitkopf und Härtel to Busoni, May 16, 1914, in Hanau, *Ferruccio Busoni im Briefwechsel*, vol. 1, 637.

109. Busoni mentions the scheduled performances in a postcard to Sibelius. It is unclear whether or not the performances actually took place. Busoni to Sibelius, June 1920, Sibelius Finnish National Archives.

110. Busoni to Adolf Paul, November 10, 1921. Paul quoted the letter and sent it to Sibelius. A copy of Paul's letter to Sibelius with the Busoni quote is found in the Åbo Academi Archive. A translation is found in Tawaststjerna, *Sibelius*, vol. 3, 212.

111. Tawaststjerna, *Sibelius*, vol. 2, 147.

112. Henry Wood, quoted in Della Couling, *Ferruccio Busoni: A Musical Ishmael* (Lanham, MD: Scarecrow Press, 2005), 176.

113. Busoni, *Zweiter Orchester-Suite* ["Geharnischte-Suite"], BV 242 (Leipzig: Breitkopf und Härtel, 1905).

114. Goss, *Sibelius: A Composer's Life*, 95.

115. Max Perl, Antiquariat, *Bibliothek Ferruccio Busoni: Werke der Weltliteratur in schönen Gesamtausgaben und Erstdrucken; Illustrierte Bücher aller Jahrhunderte*, Auction 96. March 30–31, 1925 (Berlin: Max Perl, 1925), 20–25; Busoni, program notes to the *Geharnischte Suite*, King's College Archive Centre, Cambridge, Papers of Edward Joseph Dent, EJD.

116. It is also possible that Sibelius's *Pohjola's Tochter: Eine sinfonische Fantasie*, op. 49, informed Busoni's *Indianische Fantasie*, BV 264. Busoni conducted Sibelius's composition in January 1908 in one of his orchestra evenings, and worked on the *Indianische Fantasie* from April 1913 to February 1914. The first performance took place in the Beethovensaal on December 3, 1914, and was published by Breitkopf und Härtel in 1915. Although Antony Beaumont has already documented Busoni's indebtedness to another of his American pupils, Natalie Curtis, for supplying him with Native American Indian melodies, no one has yet made the connection between these two pieces, which open with similar stylistic and instrumental characteristics. Both are based on extra-musical folk ideas.

117. "Kuules Busoni on minun mielestäni niin kylmäksi tullut. Kyllä se on suuri mestari ja on mennyt eteenpäin paljo mutta sielua siltä puuttuu arveluttavassa määrissä!! Se nyt on ainakin minun arvosteluni. Muuten se tulee 'slå igenom' tänä talvena ja ajattelee vaan sitä. Emme me enään oikein sovi yhteen." Sibelius to Aino Sibelius, September 2, 1894, in *Tulen synty*, 100.

118. "Busoni höjes till skyarna som komponist. Delius har den ena stora triumfen efter den andra. Äfvenså Bantock! Äfvenså i Danzig Juon! Mais moi?" Sibelius, *Dagbok*, June 13, 1912, 141. Granville Bancock (1868–1946) was a British composer. Paul Juon (1972–1940) was a Russian composer who wrote in a Germanic style.

119. Louis Gruenberg, "Conversations," Gruenberg Papers, Special Collections Research Center, Syracuse University Libraries, 26–27.

120. Sibelius, quoted in Tawaststjerna, *Sibelius*, vol. 3, 145.

121. "Komponisten wie Jean Sibelius und Ferruccio Busoni, die zweifellos der Moderne—wie man sie damals verstand—angehörten, sich jedoch scheuten, den Schritt zur Neuen Musik zu vollziehen, gerieten für eine Kritik, die kaum noch ästhetisch zu urteilen vermochte, ohne sich des geschichtlichen 'Stellenwerts' einer Erscheinung zu vergewissern, dadurch in ästhetisches Niemandsland, dass sie sich den historiog-

raphischen Formeln entzogen." Carl Dahlhaus, *Die Musik des 19. Jahrhunderts: Mit 75 Notenbeispielen, 91 Abbildungen und 2 Farbtafeln,* Akademische Verlagsgesellschaft Athenaion (Wiesbaden: Laaber Verlag, 1980), 309.

122. Anderson, "Sibelius and Contemporary Music," 197.

123. Ibid., 196.

124. Marcus Lindberg, quoted in ibid., 207. Lindberg, a pupil of Grisey, like Sibelius, was born in Helsinki.

125. Nørgard stated that he had, in Sibelius's music, discovered a "genuinely symphonic principle fully blossoming in the works normally labeled under the heading of an earlier historical period of music!" Nørgard to Sibelius, quoted in *The Forest's Mighty God,* ed. Edward Clark (n.p.: British Sibelius Society, 1997), 66–68.

3

New Instruments, New Sounds, and New Musical Laws

> Personally, I know he [Busoni] crystalized my half-formed ideas, stimulated my imagination, and determined, I believe, the future development of my music.
>
> Edgard Varèse, *Varèse: A Looking-Glass Diary*

ENLARGEMENT OF VARÈSE'S MUSICAL ALPHABET

WHEN EDGARD VARÈSE (1883–1965) burst on the musical scene in America in December 1915, he held radical ideas about music that, as yet, were largely unrealized in his compositions. In his first newspaper interview after embarking in New York, he stated several of these ideas; they became his compositional and artistic credo:

> Our musical alphabet must be enriched. We also need new instruments very badly.... New instruments must be able to lend varied combinations and must not simply remind us of things heard time and time again. Instruments, after all, must only be temporary means of expression. Musicians should take up this question in deep earnest with the help of machinery specialists. In my own work I have always felt the need of new mediums of expression. I refuse to limit myself to sounds that have already been heard. What I am looking for is new mechanical mediums which will lend themselves to every expression of thought and keep up with thought.[1]

Varèse's vision was to enlarge the musical alphabet and to explore new musical sounds and new instruments. That he attempted to put his ideas into practice from *Amériques* (1918–1922) to the incomplete *Nocturnal* (1961) is documented by Malcolm Macdonald, Louise Varèse, Fernand Ouellette, and many other scholars.[2] Yet the apparent disparity between his early compositions, all but one destroyed by fire or Varèse himself, and his innovative American compositions has led to the presumption that Varèse was a musical orphan, as Larry Stempel has described:

> As it has stood since his death in 1965, the complete Varèsian oeuvre, glistening with the newness of its tensile phonology, seems to have sprung out of music history like Athene born full-grown and battle-clad. From its first rude utterances in the 1920s the repertoire of sound we now hear as so distinctively Varèse not only induced few sympathetic vibrations in his contemporaries, but still defies our efforts to unmask resonances from any real musical progeny or pro-genitors.[3]

Louise Varèse remembers that contemporaneous composers, including Pierre Boulez (1925–2016), also recognized the novelty of Varèse's mature style, claiming he stood outside any recognizable schools of composition: "In his associations as well as in his music, Varèse was, as Boulez would say, *marginale,* in the sense of belonging to no system, no coterie. He was a lone wolf, but a friendly one."

The gap between Varèse's early compositions, which are described by listeners as Romantic or Impressionistic, and his experimental mature works is vast and contributes to the notion of a reinvented Varèse. The lone surviving composition from the pre-American years, the French melodie, "Un grand sommeil noir (c. 1906)," based on poetry by Paul Verlaine (1844–1896), is written in an Impressionistic style and includes a quotation from Claude Debussy's *Pelléas et Mélisande*. Opening chords move in parallel motion even while the main key, E-flat minor, is established through pitch repetition. Vocal material featuring mainly stepwise motion floats above a simple chordal accompaniment, and the piece ends after a mere thirty-two bars with two delicate reiterations of the tonic pitch. A review in *La Rénovation esthétique* of January 1906 describes Varèse's other lost early compositions in romantic terms, noting richness of sonority as well as beautiful and powerful themes.[4]

Even despite the disparity between Varèse's early and experimental compositions, the notion of Varèse as a "lone wolf" is a romantic one that is not substantiated by his writings or music. Correcting this vision contributes to better understanding about the development of experimentalist music and its evolution in the United States. Varèse was indeed influenced by several composers of his age, including Richard Strauss (1864–1949) and Claude Debussy (1862–1918).[5] Stempel, for instance, has documented Debussian harmonic progressions and scales even in the American works, such as *Arcana* (1925–1927) and *Amériques* (1918–1921, rev. 1927).[6] Strauss influenced his choice of genre and instrumentation. However, his second wife, Louise Varèse, remembers that his admiration for Strauss's music faded quickly: "By the time I met Varèse many years later, and after I came to know his musical predilections and aversions, his enthusiasm for Strauss' music had abated. Not that he admired less the virtuosity of Strauss's orchestration, but he found the themes, the motifs, really too 'cheap.' *Elektra* he still enjoyed, while the *Rosenkavalier* was in his own simple words, 'de la merde.'"[7]

Arnold Schoenberg and Igor Stravinsky have also been mentioned as minor influences on Varèse's musical style, but he never belonged to either modernist school. In a popular music history textbook, his minor connection to these schools is glossed as follows: "Varèse celebrated his adopted country in his first major work, *Amériques* (1918–1921). Its fragmentary melodies and loose structure betray links to Debussy. He was also influenced by Schoenberg, notably in the use of strong dissonance and chromatic saturation, and by Stravinsky, including the association of a musical idea with instrumental color, the avoidance of linear development, and the juxtaposition of disparate elements through layering and interruption."[8]

In all these discussions of influence, Ferruccio Busoni is rarely given more than passing mention—especially in English-language scholarship. This is despite the fact that Varèse repeatedly referred to Busoni as one of the most seminal influences on his experimental music and on his career: "Personally, I know he [Busoni] crystalized my half-formed ideas, stimulated my imagination, and determined, I believe, the future development of my music."[9] Louise Varèse reiterates: "One cannot over assess the importance of Busoni's influence on Varèse in his twenties. Varèse was not only stimulated as never before by Busoni's brilliant personality and caustic intelligence but in Busoni Varèse found the first musician whose ideas on the future of music were, as Varèse has said, like an echo of his own thoughts."[10]

Varèse's descriptions about Busoni's influence are enthusiastic, much more so than for any other musical figure. When mentioning Debussy, Varèse, for instance, notes Debussy's introductions and recommendations, and he recollects his kindness.[11] His writing is full of respect, admiration, and gratitude. However, Varèse does not claim he had seminal importance for his artistic innovations: "I had the privilege of knowing Debussy when I was still a student in Paris and from the many long talks I had with him I have kept the image of a man of great kindness, intelligence, fastidiousness, and wide culture."[12]

SUMMARY OF SCHOLARSHIP AND SOURCE MATERIAL

Existing scholarship about the Busoni-Varèse connection is minimal to date. The influence of some of Busoni's aesthetic ideas on Varèse has been cursorily mentioned in a number of sources, including those by Otto Luening, Andrea Antonini, Olivia Matthis, Helga de la Motte-Haber, Malcolm Macdonald, and Jürg Stenzl.[13] Austin Clarkson's article "Wolpe, Varèse and the Busoni Effect" mentions the influence of Busoni on Varèse as part of a larger argument about his importance as the father of a modernist strand of composition; however, his main focus is on Stefan Wolpe.[14] Currently, no single source documents the scope, nature, and evolution of the relationship, nor presents a picture of the impact of Busoni's ideas on Varèse's aesthetics, compositions, and career. In filling this gap, the chapter not only provides missing information about Varèse's little-documented musical activities in Berlin (1907–1913), but also much-needed context for his compositional innovations and for the development of experimental music in the early twentieth century.

This neglect of the Busoni-Varèse connection can be attributed, in part, to a paucity of source materials from the time Varèse was actively studying with Busoni in Berlin. All of Varèse's scores are lost or destroyed, and no documents contain indications of Busoni's compositional suggestions. If he and Busoni corresponded, none of the letters have surfaced.[15] Although his second wife, Louise Varèse, actively sought to preserve her husband's letters, his first wife, Suzanne Bing, to whom he was married for nearly the entire time he was in Berlin, left few memoirs of their brief marriage, and any letters remain unpublished.[16] Varèse also did not actively record his aesthetic ideas until his time in America. Indeed, Varèse's years in Berlin, when he interacted most closely with Busoni, are shrouded in mystery. Additionally, few stylistic parallels are readily apparent between the somewhat conservative compositions of Busoni and the experimentalist music of Varèse.

Based on Varèse's personal and annotated copy of Busoni's *Entwurf einer neuen Ästhetik der Tonkunst*, in addition to concert programs, letters, lectures, scores, and interviews, this chapter seeks to provide the first detailed account of the Busoni-Varèse connection. It documents Busoni's role as teacher, mentor, collaborator, and friend, while analyzing parallels between aesthetic ideals and compositional styles. In so doing it shows the impact Busoni had on Varèse's professional career as pedagogue, concert organizer, and composer, and thereby contributes further knowledge not only about Varèse, but also about the history of modern music and concert life in the United States during the first decades of the twentieth century.

BEGINNINGS OF THE BUSONI-VARÈSE CONNECTION

According to biographical accounts, the Busoni-Varèse connection most likely began in Berlin in late 1907 or early 1908. It started as a pupil-teacher relationship, with Varèse bringing scores for Busoni's critique, but later developed into a friendship. Although the exact date of the initial meeting might never be determined, it is possible to identify windows of time when it might have occurred. Varèse's move from Paris to Berlin took place shortly after his marriage to his first wife in November 1907, and the meeting with Busoni probably took place early on during Varèse's stay in Berlin—he had already read Busoni's *Entwurf einer neuen Ästhetik der Tonkunst* and was anxious to meet its author.[17] Louise Varèse has stated: "I don't know how long Varèse was in Berlin before he went to see Busoni. Probably not long. Busoni's little book, *Sketch for a New Aesthetic of Music*, seemed a sufficient introduction."[18] The two had established a good working relationship by spring 1909 when Busoni wrote a letter recommending Varèse for a prestigious grant.[19] Varèse's own statements suggest that the meeting took place soon after he moved to Berlin. He remembers showing either *Les Cycles du Nord* or *Ödipus* to Busoni after knowing him for at least three years. He was working on *Ödipus* from 1909 to 1914 and *Les Cycle du Nord* around 1911 or 1912, suggesting an initial meeting date during his first or, at the very latest, second year in Berlin.[20]

Busoni's busy schedule, documented by a paper trail of letters, helps further narrow potential windows when meetings could have taken place.[21] While Varèse was in Berlin, Busoni was actively pursuing a career as a touring virtuoso and composer. It was common for him to devote summers to composition in Berlin. He also frequently returned to Berlin in late December for Christmas. From fall to spring he was usually active teaching or taking extended concert tours. For instance, he went on two extended concert tours in America during the winter and spring in 1910 and 1911:

1. January 3, 1910–April 28, 1910
2. December 28, 1910–April 8, 1911[22]

At the end of April 1912, he gave a concert tour in Italy (Bergamo, Milan, Turin, Ferrara, Rome, and Bologna) before moving to Bologna in September 1913 to direct the *Liceo Musicale* (now called the Conservatorio di Musica "Giovan Battista Martini").

Busoni was also busy teaching. In September of 1907, he was selecting students for a master class at the Vienna Conservatory. Instruction began in October 1907 and continued through the end of the year. After a brief concert tour of Switzerland, Paris, and London in February, he returned to complete his master class from April through July 1908. In addition, he conducted a master class in Basel in the summers of 1909 and 1910.[23]

Busoni was thus in Berlin for only short periods from late 1907 to summer 1913. Letters document that he was there in early January 1908, and it is likely that he came home for Christmas in late December 1907, as was his custom. Varèse and Busoni could have met for the first time then. Busoni conducted an orchestral concert on January 3, 1908, and this might have provided a perfect opportunity for the two to meet. He also stayed in Berlin from late January to early February, but he was ill and preoccupied with preparing for his concerts in Switzerland.[24] Letters also document his return at the end of March, but he only came back to Berlin for a more extended period of time at the conclusion of the Vienna master class in late July.[25]

While Busoni remained preoccupied with concertizing and teaching throughout the years Varèse was in Berlin, Varèse also took several trips back to France where he frequented salons and mingled with the artists and musicians of Paris. Varèse tended to travel in the summer months, precisely when Busoni spent extended time in Berlin. His first journey to France took place from fall 1908 to January 1909.[26] He returned to France again during the summer of 1909, leaving in late July or early August for Le Villars.[27] He also visited Vienna in May 1909 and went to Paris for three months in 1912 beginning in June.[28] He left Berlin for good (not to visit again until 1922) in the summer of 1913 after separating from his first wife earlier that year.[29]

BUSONI'S TEACHINGS

Despite irregular meetings, the teaching relationship was fruitful and eventually blossomed into friendship and broader professional support. Busoni functioned as teacher and mentor by offering compositional advice, launching Varèse's teaching career, promoting him financially and professionally, and enlarging his sphere of acquaintances and knowledge of contemporary music.

Composition lessons with Busoni were free of cost.[30] Varèse remembers that Busoni did this as a matter of principle, as he had trouble connecting art with remuneration: "Busoni gave generously of himself. I know that not one of the pupils of his whom I knew personally ever paid for their lessons with him. Connecting music and money he found distressing. He also had an almost exaggerated sense of what he owed pupils and colleagues."[31]

Holding irregular but intense lesson sessions had been Busoni's modus operandi since at least 1896 for both piano and composition, because he preferred to see and hear only finished works or finished performances. Augusta Cottlow, who studied piano with Busoni from 1896 to 1899, remembers that months sometimes separated lessons, which could then last for hours.[32] Busoni's practice seemed to have worked well for Varèse, who reportedly came up with innovative ideas, but he took time to bring them to fruition, as Nadia Boulanger, a fellow student at the Paris Conservatoire, remembers:

Varèse would come into the class with one measure of a composition and explain to Widor, their teacher, how it was going to go on—that there was going to be a big tutti after a few measures and so forth. And Widor would say, "Well now, this sounds fine. Write it!" And then the next week he'd arrive with another measure, and another explanation, for a different piece. Finally Widor got angry at him, because he never brought in any more than a very few measures with enormous explanations of what the pieces were going to be like!

Varèse did bring his scores to Busoni for compositional suggestions and general advice when the pieces were ready, and his lessons consisted mainly of in-depth discussions about music aesthetics and score critique. Lessons were not systematic, as Busoni did not like to be bothered with technical subjects, such as harmony or counterpoint, subjects Varèse had already studied at the Schola Cantorum and the Conservatoire de Paris. He preferred to discuss esoteric and abstract concepts about music rather than provide concrete practical advice. Near the end of his time in Berlin, Varèse reportedly became more confident and independent, which pleased Busoni, whose goal for his students was not imitation, but musical creativity and individuality. Varèse remembers the incident in detail:

> From the beginning Busoni took an interest in my work and let me bring my scores for criticism. But one day—by then I had known him for three years or more—I brought him my latest scores—whether *Les Cycles du Nord* for orchestra, or an opera based on Hugo von Hoffmannsthal's *Oedipus und die Sphinx*, I cannot remember. In any case he seemed surprised and expressed pleasure at the way I had developed. He went over the score with special attentiveness and asked many questions. At certain places he suggested certain modifications which I found contrary to my composition. He asked me if I didn't agree with him, and I said emphatically, "No, maestro," and gave him my reasons. "So," he said, "you will not make these changes." "No, Maestro," I repeated, somewhat belligerently. He looked at me for a moment and I thought he resented my rejection of his recommendations as youthful conceit. But then he smiled and, putting his hand on my shoulder, said, "From now on it is no longer *Maestro* but *Ferruccio* and *Tu*."[33]

The scores that Varèse brought to Busoni are now lost. Moreover, no written records of the specific comments Busoni made about his compositions have surfaced. However, the genres and styles of the compositions

TABLE 3.1. COMPOSITIONS BY VARÈSE, 1907–1913

DATE	TITLE
1907	*Le délire de Clytemnestre*
1907–1908	*Bourgogne*
1909	*Gargantua*
1909–1914	*Ödipus und die Sphinx*
c. 1911	*Mehr Licht*
c. 1912	*Les Cycles du Nord*[1]
various	other unnamed chansons
various	other unnamed percussion pieces

[1] Varèse also referred to this piece as his "eighth symphonic poem, Von der Nordsee" in the biographical notes for a concert he conducted in Prague on January 4, 1914. An alternate title is *Les Cycles de la mer du Nord*.

can be deduced based on Varèse's descriptions of the lost compositions (see table 1). These pieces, which consist mainly of symphonic poems for orchestra, operas, and French songs, suggest an overall romantic compositional approach—at least in terms of genre.[34] Varèse was also working on some percussion pieces in Berlin, which he discussed in an interview with Gunther Schuller:

> SCHULLER: How do these compositions of the twenties compare with your earlier works?
>
> VARÈSE: I believe they reflect a greater refinement of my earlier conceptions. I also became increasingly interested in internal rhythmic and metric relationships, as in *Ionisation*. I was also interested in the sonorous aspects of percussion as structural, architectonic elements. But this was not my first percussion piece. I had already done some in Berlin and Paris, especially in connection with the choruses I conducted in Berlin. These works used special percussion instruments that I had collected myself, which the singers often played themselves.[35]

Busoni offered advice about many of Varèse's Berlin compositions and attended the first performance of *Bourgogne*, a tone poem, in the Blüthner-saal in Berlin. Premiering just eight days after the death of his grandfather, Claude Cortot, and inspired by the region of Burgundy where his grandfather had lived, the piece was dedicated to him, and based on the following descriptive program: "From the Plain—and along the River—comes something like a calm Spring... immense—and through the murmur of life resounds the cry of my childhood: the Future!... the Future!... //... Now I am marching with the Spring towards goodness and light!...)."

Busoni reportedly attended the premiere while battling an illness, claiming it was his duty to listen to the works of his pupil. Varèse provides the following account of Busoni's attendance at his concert, which took place on December 15, 1910.

> When a composition of mine, *Bourgogne*, was to be played by the Blüthner Orchestra—the first orchestral work I had ever performed—I was, of course, anxious for Busoni to hear it, and he promised to be present. But when I phoned the day of the concert, Mrs. Busoni, who answered, told me it would be impossible as her husband was in bed with a fever and his doctor had forbidden him to go out. It was a terrible disappointment. To my great surprise that evening I saw Busoni enter the concert hall, supported on either side by Zadora and Petri, two of his pupils. In spite of my joy, I protested that he should not have come, to which he replied simply: *"C'est mon devoir"* [It is my duty].[36]

Busoni never recorded his impressions of the piece, but it was not well received by critics who could not make sense of it. Reviewers indicate that the piece was unconventional in construction and instrumentation. A report from the Berlin Börsen-Courier dismissed it as "nonsensical," and a reviewer for the *Vossische Zeitung* was even less impressed, calling the music kitschy, immature, and technically "mangled." In retrospect, Varèse described the piece in his Schuller interview in rather experimental terms, stating that sound was already an organizing factor as it was in later compositions as well. However, his description must have been colored by the passage of time. At the premiere, the analytical description by Ernest Ansermet printed in the concert booklet describes the music in terms of traditional themes, harmony, and instrumental color. Varèse's early career is thus clouded by a lack of information, but it appears to have been characterized by a gradual shifting away from rather traditional roots toward a more experimental approach. Busoni was an integral part of this shift.

Compositions and Aesthetics

Busoni taught Varèse through score critique, but he had a more profound impact on the future direction of his music when he shared aesthetic ideas.

Varèse had already read Busoni's *Entwurf einer neuen Ästhetik der Tonkunst* before arriving in Berlin, but because he struggled with the German language, it is unclear how much he initially understood.[37] Conversations held with Busoni in Italian or French would have clarified any confusion. Varèse called the text a "milestone" in his musical development: "In 1907, still in my twenties, I went to Berlin, where I spent most of the next seven years, and had the good fortune of becoming (in spite of disparity of age and importance) the friend of Ferruccio Busoni, then at the height of his fame. I had read his remarkable little book, *A New Esthetic of Music* (a milestone in my musical development), and when I came upon 'Music is born free; and to win freedom is its destiny,' it was like hearing the echo of my own thought."[38]

Varèse also owned a copy of the English version translated by Dr. Theodor Baker and published in 1911.[39] His copy shows careful study of the text and contains numerous annotations.[40] For instance, he etched bracket marks in the left margins to set apart passages that were especially meaningful. He also cared enough about the text to note quoted authors (Busoni frequently omitted citations). For instance, for the opening quotation Varèse not only bracketed the quotation, but also penciled in the name of the author: Adam Gottlob Oehlenschläger (1779–1850). He would later use the same quote in one of his own lectures: "As an epigraph to his book, Busoni uses this verse from a poem by the Danish poet, Oehlenschläger: 'What seek you? Say! And what do you expect? I know not what; the Unknown I would have: What's known to me, is endless; I would go Beyond the known: the last word still is wanting.'"[41]

Although penciled lines, "x" marks, and brackets can be found throughout most pages, Varèse indicated excerpts that made a strong impression using double diagonal lines placed just over the page numbers.[42] These diagonal lines appear on just five pages, and feature themes of musical freedom, form, and the expansion of the tonal system, all themes that would later appear regularly in his interviews and lectures.[43] Page 5 contains an underlined passage about musical freedom that was quoted frequently by Varèse: "Music was born free; and to win freedom is its destiny. It will become the most complete of all reflexes of Nature by reason of its untrammeled immateriality. Even the poetic word ranks lower in point of incorporealness." (see figure 3.1)[44] Page 7 deals with the issue of form. Varèse bracketed the following: "Is it not singular, to demand of a composer originality in all things, and to forbid it as regards form? No wonder that, once he becomes original, he is accused of 'formlessness.'" (see figure 3.2)[45] Page 22 deals with the role of the composer and the necessity of creating new rules, rather than adhering to tradition:

> The creator should take over no traditional law in blind belief, which would make him view his own creative endeavor, from the outset, as an exception contrasting with that law. For his individual case he should seek out and formulate a fitting individual law, which, after the first complete realization, he should annul, that he himself may not be drawn into repetitions when his next work shall be in the making.... The true creator strives, in reality, after *perfection* only. And through bringing this into harmony with *his own* individuality, a new law arises without premeditation.[46]

Page 24 discusses new tonal systems. He bracketed two key passages on that page: "How strictly we divide 'consonances' from 'dissonances'—*in a sphere where no dissonances can possibly exist!*" and "Keyboard instruments in particular, have so thoroughly schooled our ears that we are no longer capable of hearing anything else—incapable of hearing except through this impure medium. Yet Nature created an *infinite gradation—infinite!*" Then in the footnote, he bracketed the following as well: "The diplomatic 'Twelve-semitone system' is an invention mothered by necessity; yet nonetheless do we sedulously guard its imperfections." (see figure 3.3)[47] The final page in Varèse's copy of Busoni's book with this double emphasis mark, page 28, had to do with musical progress and a vision for the composer-reformer. He placed a line next to the following passage:

> The Reformer of any given period excites irritation for the reason that his changes find men unprepared, and, above all, because these changes are appreciable. The Reformer, in comparison with Nature, is undiplomatic; and, as a wholly logical consequence, his changes do not win general acceptance until Time, with subtle, imperceptible advance, has bridged over the leap of the self-assured leader. Yet we find cases in which the reformer marched abreast of the times, while the rest fell behind. And then they have to be forced and lashed to take the leap across the passage they have missed. I believe that the major-and-minor key with its transpositional relations, our "twelve-semitone system," exhibits such a case of falling behind.[48]

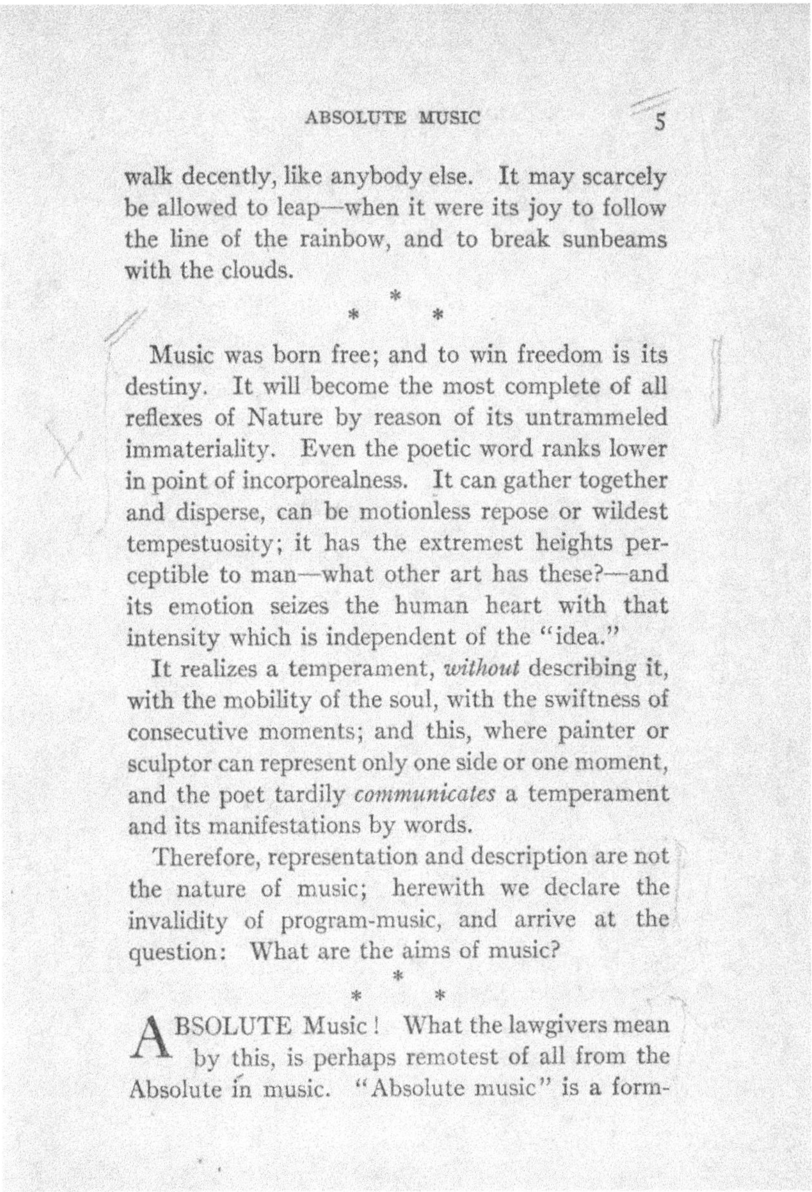

ABSOLUTE MUSIC 5

walk decently, like anybody else. It may scarcely be allowed to leap—when it were its joy to follow the line of the rainbow, and to break sunbeams with the clouds.

* * *

Music was born free; and to win freedom is its destiny. It will become the most complete of all reflexes of Nature by reason of its untrammeled immateriality. Even the poetic word ranks lower in point of incorporealness. It can gather together and disperse, can be motionless repose or wildest tempestuosity; it has the extremest heights perceptible to man—what other art has these?—and its emotion seizes the human heart with that intensity which is independent of the "idea."

It realizes a temperament, *without* describing it, with the mobility of the soul, with the swiftness of consecutive moments; and this, where painter or sculptor can represent only one side or one moment, and the poet tardily *communicates* a temperament and its manifestations by words.

Therefore, representation and description are not the nature of music; herewith we declare the invalidity of program-music, and arrive at the question: What are the aims of music?

* * *

ABSOLUTE Music! What the lawgivers mean by this, is perhaps remotest of all from the Absolute in music. "Absolute music" is a form-

FIGURE 3.1. A page from Varèse's copy of Busoni's "Sketch of a New Esthetic of Music," 5. Harry Ransom Center, University of Texas at Austin.

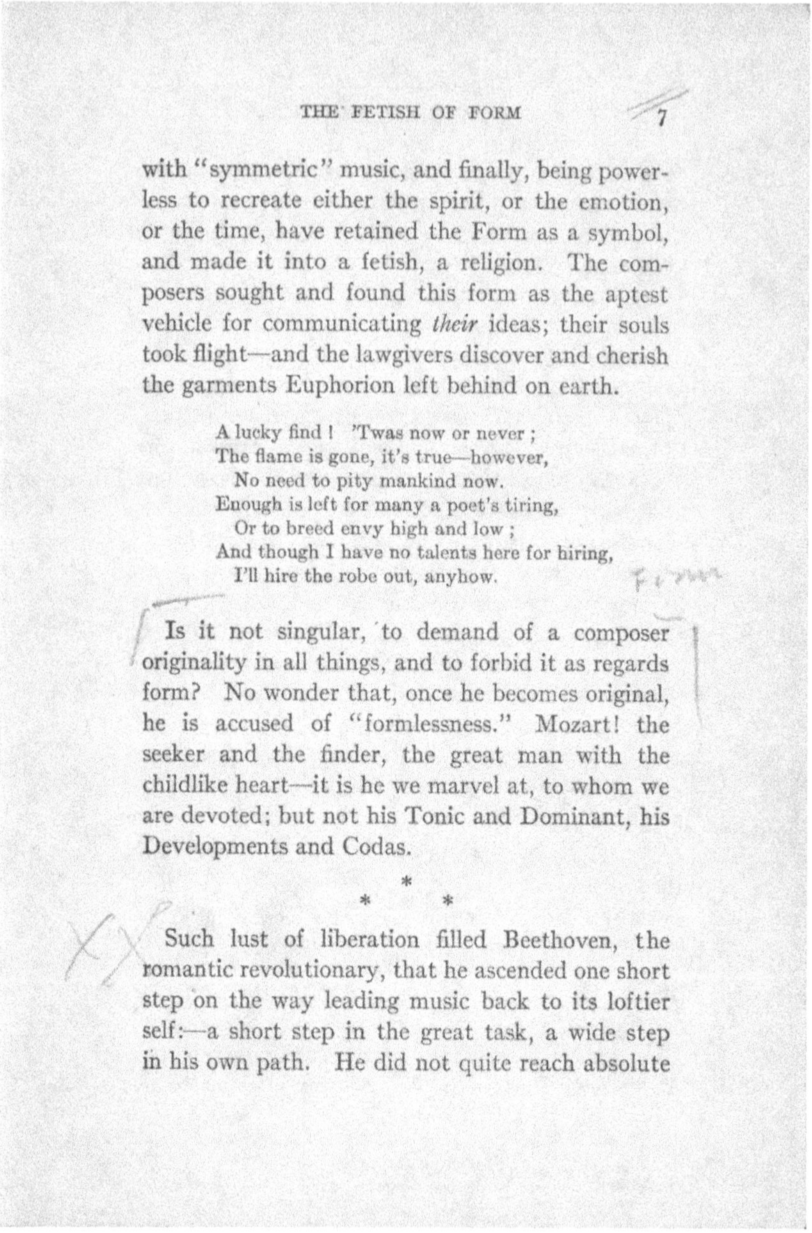

THE FETISH OF FORM 7

with "symmetric" music, and finally, being powerless to recreate either the spirit, or the emotion, or the time, have retained the Form as a symbol, and made it into a fetish, a religion. The composers sought and found this form as the aptest vehicle for communicating *their* ideas; their souls took flight—and the lawgivers discover and cherish the garments Euphorion left behind on earth.

> A lucky find ! 'Twas now or never ;
> The flame is gone, it's true—however,
> No need to pity mankind now.
> Enough is left for many a poet's tiring,
> Or to breed envy high and low ;
> And though I have no talents here for hiring,
> I'll hire the robe out, anyhow.

Is it not singular, to demand of a composer originality in all things, and to forbid it as regards form? No wonder that, once he becomes original, he is accused of "formlessness." Mozart! the seeker and the finder, the great man with the childlike heart—it is he we marvel at, to whom we are devoted; but not his Tonic and Dominant, his Developments and Codas.

* * *

Such lust of liberation filled Beethoven, the romantic revolutionary, that he ascended one short step on the way leading music back to its loftier self:—a short step in the great task, a wide step in his own path. He did not quite reach absolute

FIGURE 3.2. A page from Varèse's copy of Busoni's "Sketch of a New Esthetic of Music," 7. Harry Ransom Center, University of Texas at Austin.

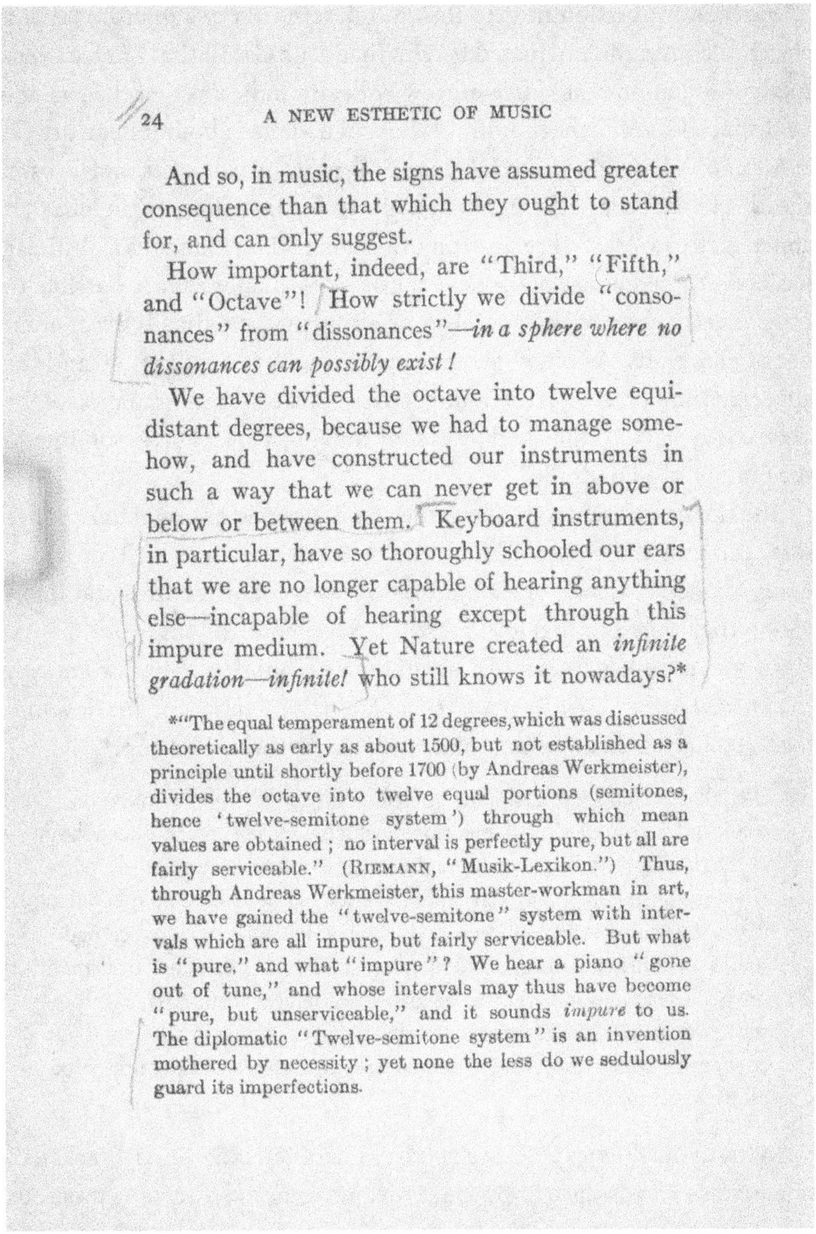

And so, in music, the signs have assumed greater consequence than that which they ought to stand for, and can only suggest.

How important, indeed, are "Third," "Fifth," and "Octave"! How strictly we divide "consonances" from "dissonances"—*in a sphere where no dissonances can possibly exist!*

We have divided the octave into twelve equidistant degrees, because we had to manage somehow, and have constructed our instruments in such a way that we can never get in above or below or between them. Keyboard instruments, in particular, have so thoroughly schooled our ears that we are no longer capable of hearing anything else—incapable of hearing except through this impure medium. Yet Nature created an *infinite gradation—infinite!* who still knows it nowadays?*

---

*"The equal temperament of 12 degrees, which was discussed theoretically as early as about 1500, but not established as a principle until shortly before 1700 (by Andreas Werkmeister), divides the octave into twelve equal portions (semitones, hence 'twelve-semitone system') through which mean values are obtained; no interval is perfectly pure, but all are fairly serviceable." (RIEMANN, "Musik-Lexikon.") Thus, through Andreas Werkmeister, this master-workman in art, we have gained the "twelve-semitone" system with intervals which are all impure, but fairly serviceable. But what is "pure," and what "impure"? We hear a piano "gone out of tune," and whose intervals may thus have become "pure, but unserviceable," and it sounds *impure* to us. The diplomatic "Twelve-semitone system" is an invention mothered by necessity; yet none the less do we sedulously guard its imperfections.

FIGURE 3.3. A page from Varèse's copy of Busoni's "Sketch of a New Esthetic of Music," 24. Harry Ransom Center, University of Texas at Austin.

Varèse's annotation next to Busoni's description of a microtonal and electronic instrument created by Dr. Thaddeus Cahill that Varèse eventually saw demonstrated live in New York also indicates that the passage held special significance for him.[49] Busoni had read about it in an article in *McClure's Magazine* from July 1906 by Ray Stannard Baker, and he used the idea to encourage the use of new electronic instruments, an idea that appealed to Varèse:[50] "I refer to an invention by Dr. Thaddeus Cahill. He has constructed a comprehensive apparatus which makes it possible to transform an electric current into a fixed and mathematically exact number of vibrations. As pitch depends on the number of vibration, and the apparatus may be 'set' on any number desired, the infinite gradation of the octave may be accomplished by merely moving a lever corresponding to the pointer of a quadrant."[51]

The themes presented in the numerous annotated passages in Busoni's text, and that the two, no doubt, discussed in person as well, provided main aesthetic strands of thought for Varèse's many lectures and interviews; they were seminal for Varèse's development and his experimental style. Varèse himself created a list of themes found in Busoni's *Entwurf einer neuen Ästhetik der Tonkunst* that had a major impact on his development, including, in addition, the element of rhythmic layering:

> We talked at length of the many questions suggested by his remarkable book and of those I already mentioned which were my chief preoccupation at the time and ever since. Although our opinions were often poles apart (he was, for instance, a Mozart addict and I was not), I am convinced that it was those long talks with Busoni, during which new horizons seemed to be constantly opening, that helped crystallize my ideas and confirmed my belief that new means must be found to liberate sound, to free it from the limitations of the tempered system, make it possible to arrive at the conception of rhythm as an element of stability, and to achieve unrelated metrical simultaneity.[52]

Many of the themes discussed above, and other underlined, bracketed, or emphasized passages in Busoni's text, resurface in Varèse's numerous interviews and lectures as quotations or paraphrases, some acknowledged and some not. Varèse preferred speaking to writing. For that reason, the majority of primary sources documenting his thoughts are in the form of interviews or lectures. Many repeat the same ideas several times expressed with only slight variation. Stenzl attributes the lack of written work, in part, to the fact that he learned several languages through conversation, including English.[53] This diversity of language has, at the very least, made it difficult to compile the source material, and there is still no source combining all the primary material.[54]

Throughout Varèse's lectures and interviews, themes of new instruments, new scales, new approaches to formal organization, musical freedom, and new directions for music, themes that contain echoes of Busoni's aesthetic writings, pervade. Varèse's writings about many fundamental aspects of music, including melody and rhythm, resemble Busoni's. That his aesthetic ideals changed little from the time he came to America in 1915 to his death in 1965 is all the more remarkable, and illustrates the long-lasting significance of Busoni on his creative activity.

The theme of the need for new instruments, and especially new electronic instruments, permeates many of Varèse's writings. In the 1916 newspaper interview quoted at the beginning of the chapter, he stated his quest for new instruments, despite the fact that he had not yet encountered an electronic instrument in person yet:

> We also need new instruments very badly. In this respect Futurists (Marinetti and his "bruiteurs") have made a serious mistake. New instruments must be able to lend varied combinations and must not simply remind us of things heard time and time again. Instruments, after all, must only be temporary means of expression. Musicians should take up this question in deep earnest with the help of machinery specialists. In my own work I have always felt the need of new mediums of expression. I refuse to limit myself to sounds that have already been heard. What I am looking for is new mechanical mediums which will lend themselves to every expression of thought and keep up with that thought.[55]

Like Busoni, Varèse called for the use of scientific knowledge to create these new instruments. However, he went beyond Busoni by using nontraditional instruments in his compositions. In addition to using everyday sounds, such as the siren, Varèse also employed electronic instruments, and specifically commissioned two instruments from Léon Theremin that were intended to display an "infinite gradation of pitch, intensity, and timbre".[56] "My first experience with an electronic instrument was in Paris in 1927 when I learned something about the possibilities and difficulties of electronics as a musical medium from René Bertrand, the inventor of the 'Dynamophone,' which was a precursor of the Martenot instrument. A few years later I experimented with Theremin, who built two instruments on my specifications for my work 'Ecuatorial' with a range of up to 6000 cycles."[57]

With his capacious mind and insatiable quest for new sounds, Varèse sought out and experimented with new means of making sounds through a combination of art and science: "Personally, for my conceptions, I need an entirely new medium of expression: a sound-producing machine (not a sound-reproducing one). Today it is possible to build such a machine with only a certain amount of additional research."[58] Eric Salzman remembers that Varèse consistently attributed his interest in new electronic sounds directly to Busoni:

> Varèse always attributed his interest in electronic music to the influence of Busoni who, in his famous "Sketch for a New Aesthetic in Music" but also in person, advocated new musical means that would enable composers to escape the tempered scale in a universe of new instrumental means. As you may know, Varèse thought that the means for this was going to be the film sound track but he could never interest any of the film studios in backing this idea. Later (like [Otto] Luening but in a much more radical way), he turned to the tape recorder and a kind of musique concrète approach. He also was eventually able to get some basic electronic equipment for his own studio. But even before his search for new musical technologies, the impact of Busoni on Varèse can be understood and felt in his orchestral and percussion music.[59]

Varèse's *Ecuatorial* (1934), originally scored for 4 trumpets, 4 trombones, percussion, organ, piano, 2 theremins, and bass voice, was the first composition for electronic and acoustic instruments. He later substituted ondes martenot by the French instrument maker Maurice Martenot. Varèse continued his experiments, bringing orchestral instruments and new scientific technology together again in *Déserts* (1954). Organized sound on three tapes appears together with an ensemble of winds, percussion, and piano.

Varèse also wrote extensively about the need for new scales, paraphrasing Busoni frequently in this context. For instance, in an interview in 1936, he talked about experimentation with microtonal harmonies and the need to break away from the tonal system: "Our present chromatic scale of half-tones can, with the aid of electricity, be broken down into almost infinite gradations of vibrations."[60] This bears striking resemblance to Busoni's description of microtones and the division of the scale into all possible combinations as infinite: "Yet Nature created an *infinite gradation—infinite!*"[61] Varèse, like Busoni, claimed, "It must not be forgotten that the division of the octave into twelve half-tones is purely arbitrary. There is no good reason why we should tolerate this restriction."[62]

While Busoni had an unspecified New York keyboard manufacturer build a harmonium with three manuals featuring tripartite tones in 1910, he did not implement microtones in his compositions, perhaps because he found the instrument cumbersome and impractical.[63] He also reportedly commissioned a second harmonium in Germany in the 1920s.[64] Harry Partch describes it as having two manuals, each featuring alternating black and white keys. Both manuals play third tones, and the second manual is tuned a sixth higher than the first.[65] Varèse, however, tried out new microtonal scales in his compositions. His first composition after arriving in America, *Amériques* (1918–1921), features quarter tones in the viola parts. For this, he had to develop his own notation system using fractions. Varèse continued to experiment with quartertones throughout his career, as is evident by the quarter tones in the bass vocal part in *Nocturnal* (1961).

Paraphrases of and allusions to Busoni's writings extend beyond these themes to many other fundaments of music, including notation, form, and melody as well. Varèse, for instance, held the view that notation could only approximate a composer's intentions. The real life of the composition, for Varèse, resided in the sounding art: "A composition is only a blue-print, a graph, which awaits mechanical means for its sonorous realization. The responsibility of a performer is consequently very gray. But he cannot go beyond the work."[66] Busoni held a similar view that sound was essential to the identity of the work. His mention of notation as vague and in need of interpretation and his use of visual metaphors are strikingly similar to Varèse's. For both men, the work was organic and living and could not be adequately represented by stale etchings on paper. However, Busoni, a pianist emerging from the Romantic virtuoso tradition had few qualms about "going beyond" the work: "Notation, the writing out of compositions, is primarily an ingenious expedient for catching an inspiration, with the purpose of exploiting it later. But notation is to improvisation as the portrait to the living model. It is for the interpreter to *resolve the rigidity of the signs* into the primitive emotion."[67]

For both men, this view of music as sounding art invited constant revisions even after publication, resulting in multiple versions (e.g., Varèse's *Amériques* and Busoni's *Fantasia contrappuntistica*, BV 256).[68] It also led to an aesthetic in which the sonorous experience was highly valued.

When discussing form, Varèse explicitly acknowledged his indebtedness to Busoni, especially in relation to a quest for structural originality and a synthesis of form and content:

> As for form—Busoni said: "Is it not singular to demand of a composer originality in all things and to forbid it as regards form? No wonder that if he becomes original he is accused of formlessness." The misunderstanding has come from thinking of form as a point of departure, a pattern to be followed, a mold to be filled. Form is the result of a process. Each of my works discovers its own form. I have never tried to fit my conceptions into any known container. If you take a rigid box of a definite shape (call it a sonata box) and you want to fill it you must have something that is the same shape and size or that is elastic or soft enough to be made to fit. But if you try to force into it something of a different shape and harder substance even if its volume and size are the same, it will break the box. . . . Connected with this contentious subject of form in music is the really futile question of the difference between form and content. There is no difference. Form and content are one. Take away form and there is no content.[69]

Like Busoni, who was preoccupied with creating strong and beautiful forms, Varèse acknowledged the importance of form for his compositions and tried to debunk the myth that his new compositions lacked formal coherence, even despite their episodic manner of organization:[70] "Form is the dominating factor in any work of art, and my chief preoccupation in composing is the form, the structure of the work I have conceived. The form of a work results from the density of the content."[71]

Despite stark differences in sound, Varèse's formal approach bears similarity to Busoni's. Both men distanced themselves from traditional forms and tried to create unique structures. Both believed in absolute music, Busoni denigrating program music, and Varèse, at least after his time in America, claiming that the titles were added to his compositions at the end and had no direct connection to the compositional process. Even so, both frequently cite extra-musical ideas for formal inspiration. Busoni attempted to achieve new formal structures by patterning his structures after architecture, literature, or nature, for instance. One of the best-known examples is his drawing of a Gothic architectural structure replete with pillars and hallways as an explanation for the structure of his two-piano version of his *Fantasia contrappuntistica* (1921). The three fugues and three sets of variations function like structural pillars. Interspersed in between, cadenzas and intermezzi act like passageways, and the final fugue is the most significant pillar.

With his background in science and math, Varèse also attributed the working out of his formal structure to extra-musical ideas—especially scientific ones. These, he claimed, were not programmatic, merely important conceptually for the ways he chose to combine the pitches and rhythms. Extra-musical topics that inspired his formal structures included crystallography (*Hyperprism*, 1922–1923), plants (*Octandre*, 1923), and mathematics (*Intégrales*, 1924–1925). In the program notes to *Intégrales*, he claimed: "The music is not a story, is not a picture, is not a psychological nor a philosophical abstraction. It is quite simply my music. It has definite form which may be apprehended more justly by listening to the music than by rationalizing about it. I repeat ... analysis is sterile. To explain by means of it is to decompose, to mutilate the spirit of the work. As to the title of a score, it is of no importance. It serves as a convenient means of cataloguing a work."[72]

Varèse has additionally attributed to Busoni his discovery of rhythmic simultaneity, considered so fundamental to his musical style. He has described his approach that is amply evident in his compositions as the play of elements in time as opposed to placing them into more rigid metric molds:

> Rhythm is so often confused with metrics that I think it is a good thing to redefine it from time to time, and worth dwelling on for a moment in connection with my music. Rhythm is the element in music that not only gives life to a work but holds it together. It is the element of stability. Cadence or the regular succession of beats and accents has really little to do with the rhythm of a composition. In my own works, for instance, rhythm derives from the simultaneous interplay of unrelated elements that intervene at calculated, but not regular, time lapses.[73]

Although Busoni wrote less about the subject of rhythm in his published texts than about scales and notation, he did use metaphors of nature to describe rhythm as a life-giving organic force, and some of these describe a conception of simultaneity of rhythm that parallels Varèse's, yet in more metaphorical terms: "Listen, every star has its rhythm and every world its measure. And on each of the stars and each of the worlds, the heart of every separate living being is beating in its own individual way. And all the beats agree and are separate and yet are a whole."[74]

Busoni never fully realized this rhythmic simultaneity in practice. Perhaps he was attempting to approach it with the orchestral version of the *Berceuse élégiaque*, BV 252, completed October 27, 1909, and which he gave to Varèse with this dedication:[75] "All'illustro Futuro, l'amico Varèse, affezionatamente, F. Busoni, 1910."[76] It is not only one of his first ventures into polytonality, and explores the possibilities of orchestral color, but it also displays rhythmic independence between parts, even if the sense of a regular metric pulse is never fully obscured (see music example 3.1). In the opening, for instance, the clarinet in A and bass clarinet share a rhythmic motive of a half note and quarter note followed by a quarter rest, but the figure is rhythmically displaced. The harp has a rhythmic pattern of a quarter note, quarter rest, quarter note, quarter rest, while the strings have individual recurring rhythmic patterns entering on diverse beats of the measure. The bass enters on the pickup to beat one with repeated pitches, the second cello enters on the pickup to beat two with a leaping figure. The second viola enters on the pickup to beat three, playing a single tied eighth note per measure. The complete sound comprises many instruments with individual parts functioning simultaneously. Fleet has also argued that this timbral displacement contributes to a sense of harmonic displacement as well: "The effect is a dissipation of the F major harmony which complements the dispersal of melodic content across the orchestra."[77]

Varèse also frequently employed rhythmic cells paired with specific instruments or groups of instruments that function simultaneously, but independently (see music example 3.2). In *Ionisation* (1931), for instance, the wood blocks play a rhythmic cell of a thirty-second, dotted sixteenth, and eighth note in measure 1. This is varied and developed in a number of ways, including as three equal eighth-note triplets in measure 44. Also

MUSIC EXAMPLE 3.1. Busoni, *Berceuse élégiaque*, BV 252, mm. 1–6.

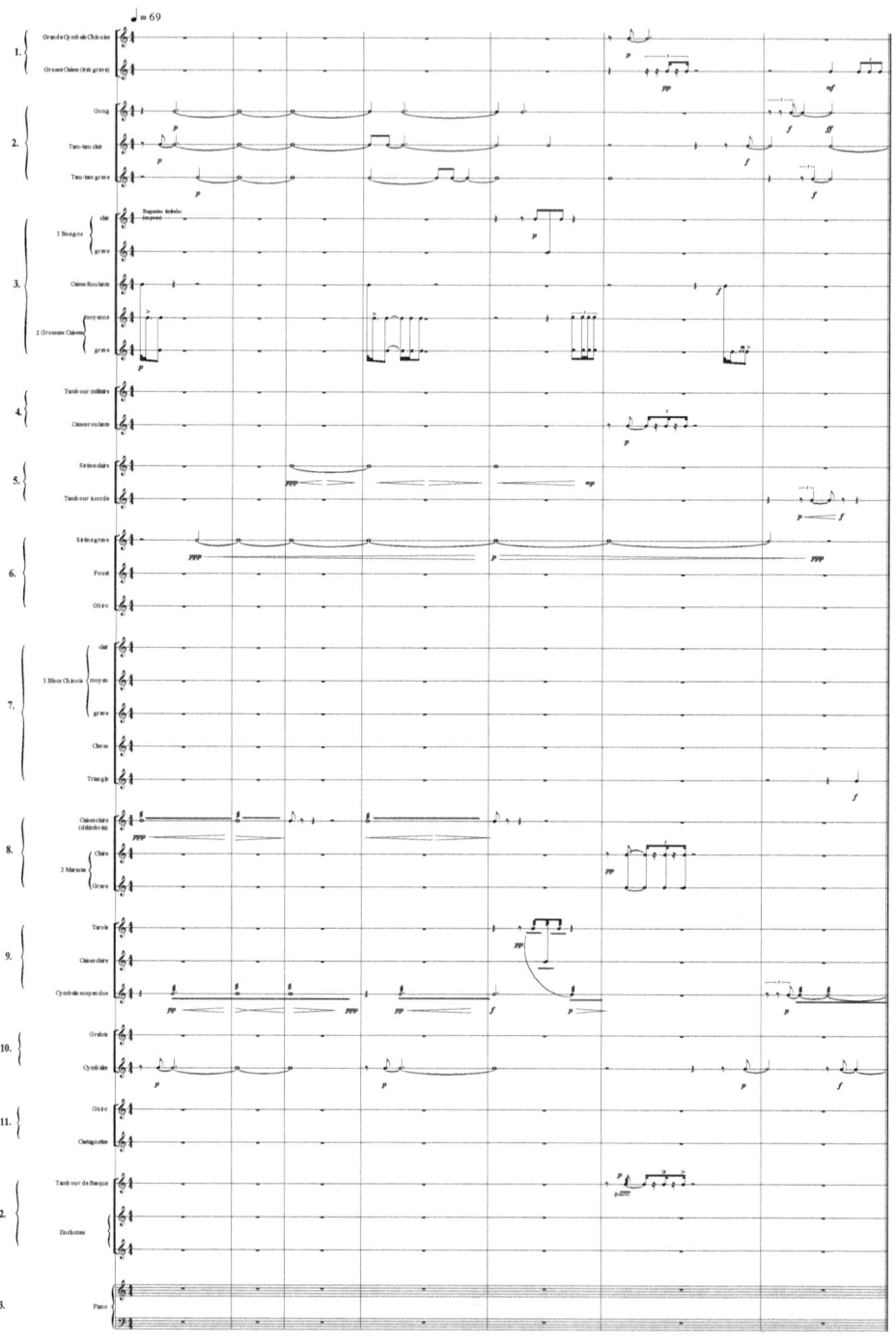

MUSIC EXAMPLE 3.2. Varèse, *Ionisation*, mm. 1–7.

MUSIC EXAMPLE 3.3. Busoni, *Fantasia Nach Bach*, BV 253, mm. 14–15.

in the first measure, the sirens begin an extended held note on beat three while the snare drum plays a tremolo. The cymbals start on the pickup to beat two and the sustained symbol begins a crescendo on beat two.

Varèse's view of the integration of musical elements was also largely borrowed from Busoni, who described melody as a totality out of which all the other compositional elements flow: "A ROW of repeated (1) ascending and descending (2) intervals which (3) organized and moving rhythmically (4) contains in itself a latent harmony and (5) which gives back a certain atmosphere of feeling; which can and does exist (6) independent of text expression and (7) independent of accompanying voices for form; and in the performance of which the choice of pitch (8) and of instrument (9) exercise no change over its essence.... This 'absolute' melody, at first a self-sufficient formation, united itself subsequently with the accompanying harmony, and later melted with it into oneness."[78]

Busoni specifically envisioned that the melody, self-sufficient in and of itself, would inform the harmony and other compositional choices. He was likely thinking of ways to derive harmony and new harmonic progressions out of the melodic flow, a practice he employed in his mature compositions, to lead to unexpected new chords and key areas or combinations. In his *Fantasia nach Bach*, BV 253 (1909), for instance, a piece composed in memory of his father and which also quotes extensively from Bach, harmonies derive from melodic figures (see music example 3.3).[79] One concise example can be observed in the *espressivo dolente* section beginning in measure 14, a descending stepwise melodic motive in the alto voice derived from a chorale melody quotation appears over an arpeggiated A-flat triad. As the middle note of the arpeggiated figure imitates the alto voice, the quality of the chord changes from A-flat augmented to A-flat major to A-flat minor over an F pedal tone.[80]

Varèse's theory about melody sounds almost identical to Busoni's upon first reading; he stated he wanted all musical elements to flow out of melody. However, he applied it in a new way, because for him the fundamental unit was sound rather than pitch. In a 1936 lecture he claimed: "There will no longer be the old conception of melody or interplay of melodies. The entire work will be a melodic totality. The entire work will flow as a river flows."[81] He was not referring in this lecture to the development of a traditional harmony from a melody, but to the generation of new sounds:[82] "Not only will the harmonic possibilities of the overtones be revealed in all their splendor, but the use of certain interferences created by the partials will represent an appreciable contribution. The never before thought of use of the inferior resultants and of the differential and additional sounds may also be expected. An entirely new magic of sound."[83]

Varèse's melodies taken in and of themselves are rarely extraordinary; motives commonly consist of chromatically decorated repeated pitches augmented by pungent dissonances, such as sevenths, ninths, or semitones. A sense of cadence is usually obliterated and chords are repeated, albeit in ever-changing registers. The interest in Varèse's music lies in the sound quality generated by the unfolding of these motives in time in various instruments. For instance, in the opening of *Octandre* (1923), the plaintive opening line, characterized by seconds (and, by extension, ninths and sevenths), is split between the oboe and clarinet (see music example 7.4). Repetitions of note groups, intervals, and pitches draw attention to the unique timbral colors of the instruments and the evolving rhythmic figurations.

PROFESSIONAL CONNECTIONS

Busoni's ideas about form, instruments, and scales had a profound impact on Varèse's artistic vision, and he also helped him personally and professionally. Varèse's life in Berlin was full of hardships—he struggled with finances, marital problems, and the German language.[84] Busoni, along with Hugo von Hoffmannsthal, Richard Strauss, and others, tried to help his young student through these difficulties. One particularly notable

MUSIC EXAMPLE 3.4. Varèse, *Octandre*, mm. 1–6.

event was when Busoni wrote a letter dated April 10, 1909, to help Varèse obtain a grant from the Kuczynski Foundation:[85]

> To the venerable President of the Paul Kuszynski Foundation
>
> Dear Sir,
>
> I take the freedom—in the interest of my dear young friend, Mr. Varèse from Paris, to call your attention to the intelligence and giftedness of this young artist. These marked characteristics deserve to be recognized and supported.
>
> Yours respectfully and entirely devoted,
Ferruccio Busoni
Imperial and Royal Professor
Great Kingdom Court Pianist
Berlin, April 10, 1909

Busoni's support was a key factor in Varèse's receipt of the grant, which was provided thanks to the generosity of Pawel Kuczynski (1846–1897), who was part of an influential and wealthy family of Polish immigrants to Berlin.[86] Family members were not only very productive, but also leaders in economics, banking, and the arts.[87] With prizes up to 250,000 marks in 1919, this was a coveted award.[88]

Pedagogy

Busoni helped the young Varèse not only by offering compositional advice and by helping him win grants, but also by launching his career as a pedagogue. Varèse would ultimately teach some important composers of American music, and it was Busoni who first sent pupils to Varèse. No doubt, he was not only trying to help him gain valuable teaching experience, but also to alleviate his very tight finances.

Varèse's first pupil was Ernst Schoen (1894–1960), a friend of Busoni's son, Benvenuto, and a piano pupil of Busoni. Schoen would have been too young and inexperienced to study composition with Busoni, who did not like to teach basic technical skills, such as harmony and counterpoint. He also referred two rich American pupils to Varèse, although their names remain undocumented.[89] That the relationship was long-lasting is also evident from the fact the Schoen was selected to be the secretary for a German International Composers' Guild centered in Berlin and founded in 1922 by Varèse. Ouellette also documents a conversation between the two as late as October 12, 1959.[90]

Schoen created a few compositions reflecting his teacher's experimental aesthetics. As a German musician, poet, and translator, Schoen would later become director of Radio Frankfurt.[91] As a tireless advocate of the radio and new technology, his ideas reflect some of Varèse's. Schoen specifically experimented with new ways to combine the best aspects of radio technology and musical theater, writing two radio cantatas, *Die Kleine Tagesserenade* (1930) and *Der Tag des Herrn Karl* (1932).[92]

Lessons with Varèse combined traditional methods, including discussion of the rules of harmony, and more esoteric aesthetic discussions about the future of music. Schoen described the traditional aspects of the lessons, and this is related by his biographer, Ouellette:

> "I was Varèse's first and worst pupil. In 1910, at the age of sixteen, I decided to become a composer of music. At that time I used to visit a lot at Busoni's house, since his eldest son, Benvenuto, was a schoolfriend of mine." Then, Schoen went on, his mother asked Busoni to find him a teacher. Busoni recommended the young Varèse, who agreed to teach him "for either ten marks a lesson or nothing." Since the first alternative was out of the question he taught me on the basis of the second. He took me through the harmony course devised by Luis-Thuille (followed later by Schoenberg).[93]

Schoen also remembers more radical ideas shared by Varèse, including that of starting a sound laboratory and a composition class for the production of electronic music.[94]

Expanding Musical Horizons

Busoni also acted as a hub in Varèse's social network, providing introductions that would further the younger composer's career. Interactive "salon-style" gatherings were a regular part of instruction. Students from both piano and composition master classes describe regular tea/coffee hours where Busoni, pupils, and other artists or scholars would discuss all things artistic. These gatherings provided exposure to the newest musical experiments and were also interdisciplinary.

It was during the gatherings at Busoni's house that artistic and intellectual exchange happened between composers, musicologists, musicians, and artists. Discussion often extended well beyond musical subjects to literature, painting, history, or other arts. That Varèse attended such gatherings at Busoni's home is remembered by musicologist Egon Kenton (1897–1987). He notes, in particular, that Varèse heard a private performance of Schoenberg's *Pierrot Lunaire* at Busoni's house:[95]

> Varèse had been invited to Busoni's to hear a private performance of Schoenberg's new work, *Pierrot Lunaire*, and he took me along. When we arrived the salon was crowded. Varèse made his way to the end of the room where Schoenberg was standing near the players. He introduced me and we stood there, Varèse, Schoenberg, and the violinist Arrigo Serrato [sic], during the performance. Afterward, when the applause had subsided, Schoenberg, timid and a little awkward, started toward the players, but Busoni, handsome and imposing, was already there, congratulating them. Then Schoenberg, screwing up his clever monkey face in a wry smile, turned to Varèse and said: "And now he's distributing the decorations."[96]

Busoni's description of the event, which matches Kenton's in many details, is dated June 17, 1913, just shortly before Varèse left Berlin for good. Although he does not list Varèse as a guest, he does mention that Steuermann was the pianist and that Schoenberg was conducting. Busoni specifically also mentioned the exchange of ideas after the concert. Such afternoons combining new music, live performances, and aesthetic exchange, were his ideal for the presentation and teaching of art music.[97]

New Music Concerts

If Busoni helped stimulate Varèse's imagination and exposed him to a variety of important people and composers, he also provided a model of promoting new music through public concerts. From 1902 to 1909, he actively promoted new music by organizing and financing a series of concerts in Berlin. It was not easy to find performance venues for new music at the time, and many pieces were first performances in Berlin, Germany, or the world. Concert programs emphasized the newness of the pieces in bold type on the first page of concert programs. The program for the December 1, 1904, concert, for instance, reads:

> Orchestra Evening
> (New and Seldom Performed Works)
> With the Philharmonia Orchestra
> Organized by
> Ferruccio Busoni[98]

Varèse must have been aware of the two concerts that took place while he was living in Berlin, and it is likely that he would have attended the concert that took place on January 3, 1908.[99] The 1908 program featured the following pieces:

XI. Beethoven-Saal, 3 January 1908[100]
1. Jean Sibelius, *Pohjolas Tochter*, Sinfonische Fantasie (First Performance)
2. Ferruccio Busoni, Concert for violin, Op. 35a (Solo Violin, Émile Sauret)
3. F. Liszt, *Tre Sonetti di Petrarca* (1) Pace non trovo, orchestrated by Ferruccio Busoni (Singer: Felix Senius) (First Performance)
4. Paul Ertel, *Bacchanal* (third movement of the *Harold-Symphonie*, Op. 2) (First Performance)
5. F. Liszt, *Tre Sonetti di Petrarca:* (2) and (3) with pianoforte accompaniment (Felix Senius) (Accompanist Busoni)
6. F. Liszt, *Mazeppa*

Another distinctive aspect of Busoni's concerts was that he actively encouraged composers to participate in the performances (see table 3.2). In the 1909 concert, for instance, Béla Bartók conducted his own scherzo. In earlier concerts a number of composers, including Jean Sibelius, Rudolf Nováček, Eugène Ysaÿe, and Vincent d'Indy, performed their own works. Although it was not uncommon for composers to participate in the premieres of their own compositions, this conscious emphasis on the composer and composition rather than the interpreter was unusual at the time.[101] Exceptions included Richard Strauss's new music concerts, but these focused on the avant-garde in Germany and more traditional compositions by foreign composers. It is important to note that Strauss also conducted the concerts.

Varèse followed Busoni's model when he founded several organizations devoted to promoting new music, including the New Symphony Orchestra (1919), the International Composers' Guild (1921), the Internationale Componisten-Gilde (1922), and the Pan American Association of Composers (1928).[102] Varèse's International Composers' Guild focused on premiering new works and featured the composers as performers or conductors. He made it a requirement that pieces would be performed for the first time (except for programs sponsored by the Pan American Association of Composers) and made it clear that the composition and composer would be the central focus of the programs: "Our plan is to present the

TABLE 3.2. COMPOSERS PERFORMING IN BUSONI'S ORCHESTRAL CONCERT SERIES

DATE	PERSON AND ROLE	TITLE
November 15, 1902	Jean Sibelius, conductor and composer	En Saga
November 10, 1904	Ferruccio Busoni, pianist and composer	Concerto for pianoforte, orchestra, and male chorus, BV 247
December 1, 1904	Rudolf Nováček, conductor and composer	Sinfonietta in D Minor, op. 48
January 12, 1905	Albéric Magnard, conductor and composer	Troisième Symphonie
January 5, 1905	Hans Pfitzner, conductor and composer	Scherzo for Orchestra
January 5, 1905	Jean Sibelius, conductor and composer	Symphony no. 2 in D Major, op. 43
October 21, 1905	Otto Singer, conductor and composer	Concerto in A major for Pianoforte and Orchestra, op. 8
December 9, 1905	Eduard Behm, conductor and composer	*Im Frühling:* Tonstück für Orchester, op. 4
December 9, 1905	Eugène Ysaÿe, conductor and composer	*Rêve d'enfant,* op. 14, and *Poème élégiaque,* op. 12
November 8, 1906	Vincent d'Indy, conductor and composer	*Symphonie sur un chant montagnard* pour piano et orchestra, op. 25

composer, not the interpreter. We will give lesser-known interpreters a chance to appear, and they, with the composers themselves, will present the works."[103] The first concert of the International Composers' Guild, for instance, took place on February 19, 1922, and featured world premieres in which some of the creators also participated as performers:

Emerson Whithorne.................... *Three Greek Impressions for String Quartet* (The I.C.G. String Quartet)
Louis Gruenberg..................... *Polychrome* (Pieces for Piano)
Alfredo Casella..................... *O toi suprême*
Gian Francesco Malipiero..................... Ariette
Ildebrando Pizzetti.................... I Pastori; La Madre al figlio lontano
Arthur Honegger..................... Three Fragments

Eugene Goossens..................... Sonata no. 1 for Violin and Piano
Greta Torpadie, voice; Andre Polah, violin; Louis Gruenberg, piano;
Carlos Salzedo, piano; Bachmann String Quartet[104]

Varèse's societies were not only based on similar principles as Busoni's, but also involved his collaboration. Varèse returned to Berlin in 1922, sailing in the summer and staying until November 20, 1922, intent upon launching a Berlin branch of the Composers' Guild, the Internationale Componisten-Gilde. He was desirous of Busoni's assistance and support, and Louise Varèse writes that they visited him soon after arriving in Berlin to explain his project: "Busoni turned to Varèse, questioning him about his music, his activities. Eagerly Varèse began to talk about the ICG and finally, inevitably, with his passion for starting things, suggested they form a German ICG. Busoni liked the idea."[105]

Varèse's daybook provides more detail about the dates and frequency of meetings, showing that Varèse met with Busoni at least five times during the trip.[106] When the two met, Busoni decided to accept Varèse's invitation to become president in the guild, but illness prevented him from taking an active role. Although Busoni provided names of composers for the organization, he was not even well enough to attend the premiere performance on November 1, 1922 (see figure 3.4a, b). Other members of the society included Alfredo Casella, Ernst Schoen, and Arthur Lourié, thereby bringing together composers from Italy, Germany, France, and Russia, among others. The complete list of members is as follows:[107]

> President, Ferruccio Busoni
> Vice-President, Heinz Tiessen
> Directors, Alois Hába, Philipp Jarnach, Hermann Springer, and Werner Wolffheim
> Business Manager, Constantin David
> Lawyer, Fritz Kalischer
> Secretary, Ernst Schoen
> Committee, Alfredo Casella, Bernard van Dieren, Eduard Erdmann, Alois Hába, Paul Hindemith, Philipp Jarnach, Ernst Krenek, Arthur Lourié, Felix Petyrek, Heinz Tiessen, and Edgard Varèse

The goal of the Berlin branch was to establish more international collaborations, and this is expressed in the motto published in the inaugural concert program.[108] Varèse's *Dedications* (later named *Offrandes*), a set of

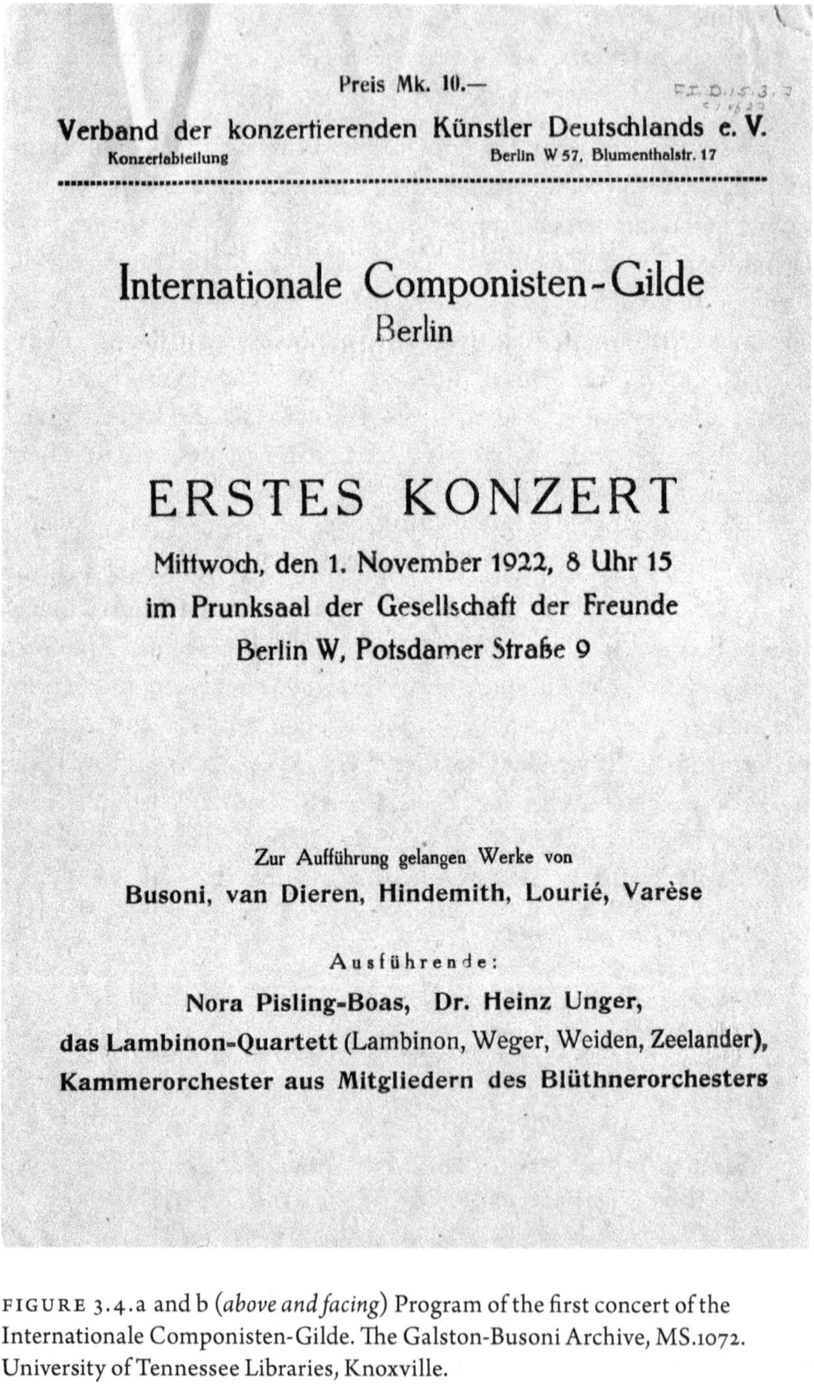

Preis Mk. 10.—

Verband der konzertierenden Künstler Deutschlands e. V.
Konzertabteilung   Berlin W 57, Blumenthalstr. 17

Internationale Componisten-Gilde
Berlin

ERSTES KONZERT

Mittwoch, den 1. November 1922, 8 Uhr 15
im Prunksaal der Gesellschaft der Freunde
Berlin W, Potsdamer Straße 9

Zur Aufführung gelangen Werke von
Busoni, van Dieren, Hindemith, Lourié, Varèse

Ausführende:
**Nora Pisling-Boas, Dr. Heinz Unger,
das Lambinon-Quartett** (Lambinon, Weger, Weiden, Zeelander)**,
Kammerorchester aus Mitgliedern des Blüthnerorchesters**

FIGURE 3.4.a and b (*above and facing*) Program of the first concert of the Internationale Componisten-Gilde. The Galston-Busoni Archive, MS.1072. University of Tennessee Libraries, Knoxville.

Programm

1. Streichquartett opus 16 C-dur .... Paul Hindemith
   1) lebhaft und energisch
   2) sehr langsam
   3) äußerst lebhaft

   Pause

2. Wolga-Pastorale .... Arthur Lourié
   (für 2 Violen, Cello, Oboe, Fagott)

3. Gesang vom Reigen der Geister .... Ferruccio Busoni
   (für eine Flöte, Clarinette, Oboe, Fagott, Horn, Trompete, Pauke u. Streichquintett)

4. Dedications .... Edgar Varèse
   (für Sopran, 2 Flöten, Oboe, Clarinette, Fagott, Horn, Trompete, Posaune, Harfe, 2 Violinen, Viola, Cello, Contrabaß, Schlagzeuge)
   a) Chanson de là-haut (Gedicht von Vicente Huidobro)
   b) La Croix du Sud (Gedicht von José Juan Tablada)

5. Ouverture op. 7 .... Bernard van Dieren
   (für eine Flöte, Oboe, engl. Horn, 2 Clarinetten, Fagott, 2 Hörner, 1 Trompete, Harfe, Pauke und Streichquintett)

In den nächsten Konzerten

der

Internationalen Componisten-Gilde

werden u. a. zur Aufführung gelangen
Werke von

JARNACH (Sonatina für Violine und Klavier)
MYASKOWSKY (Lieder)
RAVEL (Sonate für Violine und Cello)
SCHOENBERG
TIESSEN (Streichquintett, Uraufführung)

Alle Anfragen sind zu richten an den Sekretär der I. C. G. Herrn Ernst Schoen, Charlottenburg, Droysenstraße 14; Telephon: Steinplatz 11134.

two chansons, was well received by the audience at the inaugural concert, if reviews are to be trusted: "Varèse was enthusiastically applauded by the international audience and achieved the chief success of the evening."[109] Other pieces did not fare as well from reviewers. Although a second concert was planned, and pieces and composers chosen, it never took place. The next concert was to include music by Philipp Jarnach, Nikolai Mysakowsky, Maurice Ravel, Arnold Schoenberg, and Heinz Tiessen.[110] Without an active president, and with Varèse in New York, the organization dissolved as quickly as it began. Hyperinflation in Germany also created insurmountable financial problems for the society. However, the New York society remained strong until 1927.

CODA

Varèse found the aesthetic ideas of Busoni to be stimulating catalysts for new means of musical expression. It is sometimes startling how similar their statements sound—at least on paper. In one statement, Varèse declares his admiration and respect for him and his music: "A man of considerable musical culture and virtuosity. He was the first at the beginning of this century to conceive a new technique of art. He envisioned all that was to come." Varèse's experimental music would have been unthinkable without the aesthetic influence of Busoni, and for that reason he was perhaps the most influential teacher Varèse would ever have. Although it would be naïve to downplay the importance of Debussy or Strauss, it was Busoni's rather radical but as yet unrealized ideas that were catalysts for Varèse's most original musical experiments.

It was Varèse who first made the direct connection between Busoni's aesthetic influence and his American experimentalist compositional style. In his remarks on Busoni at Princeton University in 1959, after a lengthy eulogy to Busoni, and without a transitional sentence, he launched into a description of his new experiments in *Amériques*, implying that Busoni had been the seminal influence on that composition, especially in terms of new sounds: "The first time I made use of the siren to obtain hyperbolic and parabolic trajectories was in 1921, in the score of *Amériques*. Later I used one siren in *Hyperprism* and two in *Ionisation*."[111] Indeed, Busoni had a gift for fostering Varèse's most creative impulses, impulses that had not been given free rein in Paris: "He not only corroborated, clarified, and encouraged my ideas, but being as magical a talker as he was a brilliant thinker, he had the gift of stimulating my mind to feats of prophetic imagination. I became a sort of diabolical Parsifal looking not for a Holy Grail but for a bomb that would blow wide open the musical world and let in sound—all sounds, at that time called 'noise'—and sometimes even today."[112]

True, Varèse did take issue with a few of Busoni's ideas, and especially his stance on musical evolution. Although many of Varèse's ideas seem to be paraphrases of Busoni's, the application of the ideas were radically different. Both men thought of musical works as living organic creations. But for Busoni, this led to a belief in Young Classicality, or the subsuming of the past in the present as a means for reaching toward the future. Varèse stated: "Having become acquainted with Busoni through his extraordinarily prophetic musical theories in his *New Esthetic of Music*, I was surprised to find his musical tastes and his own music so orthodox."[113] While Varèse admired historical music, especially idealizing Renaissance choral music as a conductor, he believed new compositions should reflect new musical expressions of the age: "Many of the old masters are my intimate friends—all are respected colleagues. None of them are dead saints—in fact, none of them are dead—and the rules they made for themselves are not sacrosanct and everlasting laws. Listening to music by Machaut, Pérotin, Monteverdi, Bach, or Beethoven, we are conscious of living substances; they are alive in the present. But music written in the manner of another century is the result of culture and desirable and comfortable as culture may be, an artist should not lie down in it."[114]

Busoni's compositional approach was looking in the wrong direction, according to Varèse, and he was surprised that a man with so many radical ideas could write such conservative music. He criticized him for this and rejected Young Classicality, falsely equating it with neoclassicism:

> To Ferruccio Busoni must be given credit for the inception of this idea [neoclassicism] around 1917. It was taken up later in the twenties by such composers as Hindemith in Germany and Stravinsky in France. With Busoni it was originally a protest against the late nineteenth-century Romanticism, a tendency he disliked. For Busoni, who adored Mozart, Neo-Classicism was a return to clarity, elegance, logic, a return to ideals

of the eighteenth century. Now in spite of the very fine works which have been done by gifted composers who have chosen to limit themselves by this formula, it is, it seems to me, a dangerous and pernicious principle. For good or bad, it seems to me that it looks in the wrong direction.[115]

Despite some differences, the influence of Busoni's music on Varèse's development cannot be discounted entirely, however. The years 1907 to 1913, when Varèse knew Busoni in Berlin, mark his experimentalist period when he was trying out some of his new ideas. His atonal *Sonatina seconda*, BV 259 (1912), without bar lines and his polytonal *Berceuse élégiaque*, BV 252 (1910), struck out in new directions leading to some of his greatest masterpieces, such as his great *Doktor Faust* (posthumous), of which Varèse was aware. He would have heard Busoni's new experiments with instrumental color in the *Berceuse élégiaque*, BV 252, and noticed how he layered diverse music horizontally and vertically, including atonal and tonal music in *Doktor Faust*, which Luigi Dallapiccola remembers listening to with Varèse.[116] At the same time, Busoni began embracing color and timbre as essential to a work's identity—he called this absolute orchestration.[117] This is embodied clearly in the *Berceuse élégiaque*, BV 252, where each instrumental timbre receives special attention and is arguably as important as the pitches and harmonies. From a mass of hazy and ambiguous sound in the opening, an oboe solo harmonized with descending seventh chords and individual timbre eventually emerges at measure 20. For Varèse, sound and timbre were to become so central that they became the preeminent features of music organization.

Busoni, for his part, was surprisingly silent about his youthful protégé. In her diary, Louise Varèse, who returned to Berlin with Varèse in 1922 to garner the support of Busoni for the Internationale Componisten-Gilde, also recorded Busoni's impressions of Varèse in Berlin: "I remember a rainy day. I saw him pass in the street. He was pale, he was beautiful, he ran in the rain."[118] But this quote answers few questions as to Busoni's impressions of his music. There is also the letter to the Paul Kuczynski Foundation. Aside from that, there is silence. Busoni's sons, Rafaello and Benvenuto Busoni, also respected Varèse enough to maintain contact with him for several decades after the death of their father. When Benvenuto ("Benni") was in New York in 1919, he attended one of Varèse's concerts. Writing to Varèse afterward, he mentioned that the concert was simply fabulous.[119] As late as 1948, Rafaello ("Lello") still maintained contact with Varèse. On July 6, 1948, he wrote to Edward Dent about Varèse's lectures on modern music, some of which were devoted to Busoni's music. In the same letter he displayed knowledge of Varèse's recent musical experiments, noting especially Varèse's use of his wife's silverware and cooking utensils for musical purposes:

> Edgard Varèse is going to have a course of 30 lectures at Columbia, on modern music. Much of it will center around F.B. and he starts with having the 2nd Sonata for piano and violin performed. He then proceeds. I do not know if he counts F.B. as the spiritus rector of his (Varèse's) disconcerting concerts; as for violence he uses with one violin some kitchenware as percussion composing. The voice of the violin is amplified via loudspeaker and very imperatively while pots and pans, fryers and skillets (though the cutlery of the composer's wife) cause a backdrop noise of anything confusion. But Varèse is not as crazy as this may sound, proof: his 30 lectures pivoting around Busoni.[120]

While Busoni's music would largely fall into oblivion as he became marginalized and overlooked by scholars and performers, the music of his youthful protégé would endure and eventually become widely accepted as influential and groundbreaking. By a strange twist of fate, even Busoni's mentorship would be largely forgotten. Yet Varèse, like several of Busoni's other pupils, including Louis Gruenberg and Otto Luening, implemented many of the ideals of his teacher even while creating new laws of which Busoni could only dream, thereby helping to forge new directions in art music.[121]

NOTES

1. Varèse, *New York Telegraph*, March 1916, reprinted in Louise Varèse, *A Looking Glass Diary*, vol. 1: 1883–1928 (New York: W. W. Norton and Co., 1972), 123. I am grateful to Louis Epstein for commenting on a draft of this chapter.

2. Malcolm Macdonald, *Varèse: Astronomer in Sound* (London: Kahn and Averill, 2003); Louise Varèse, *Looking Glass Diary*; Fernand Ouellette, *Edgard Varèse*, trans. Derek Coltman (New York: Orion Press, 1966).

3. Larry Stempel, "Not Even Varèse Can Be an Orphan," *Musical Quarterly* 60:1 (January 1974), 46.

4. Armande de Polignac, "Musique," *La Rénovation Esthétique: Revue de l'Art le Meilleur* 9 (January 1906), 165.

5. Varèse studied briefly at the Schola Cantorum, leaving in the fall of 1905.

6. Stempel, "Not Even Varèse Can Be an Orphan," 55–59.

7. Ibid., 86.

8. J. Peter Burkholder, Donald J. Grout, and Claude V. Palisca, *A History of Western Music* (New York: W. W. Norton, 2010), 895. Varèse recorded a list of the people he considered seminal in his development as follows: "The composers I admired in those early days were Debussy, especially for his *Pelléas*, and then Strauss and Busoni, both of whom were very influential in my career after I went to Berlin in 1905 [sic]. But I also respected composers like Satie and Scriabin." Gunther Schuller, "Conversation with Varèse," *Perspectives of New Music* 3:2 (1965), 33.

9. Varèse, quoted in Louise Varèse, *Looking Glass Diary*, 50.

10. Ibid., 48.

11. Debussy wrote letters on Varèse's behalf for a directorship of music at the opera in Bordeaux and to Camille Chevillard (1859–1923), French conductor and composer. The letters, from 1914 and 1908, respectively, are preserved in the Varèse collection in the Paul Sacher Stiftung, Basel.

12. Varèse, "Notes on the Centenary of Debussy's Birth," quoted in Louise Varèse, *Looking Glass Diary*, 45.

13. Otto Luening, "Varèse and the Schola Cantorum, Busoni and New York," *Contemporary Music Review* 23:1 (March 2004), 13–16; Olivia Matthis, "Edgard Varèse and the Visual Arts" (PhD diss., Stanford University, 1992); Andrea Antonini, "Busoni and Varèse," http://www.rodoni.ch/busoni/telharmonium.html, accessed October 8, 2012; Helga de la Motte-Haber, "Blurred Traces: Varèse's Years in Berlin," in *Edgard Varèse: Composer, Sound Sculptor, Visionary*, ed. Felix Meyer and Heidy Zimmermann (Woodbridge: Boydell Press, 2006), 35–52; Macdonald, *Varèse: Astronomer in Sound*; Jürg Stenzl, "Busonis Sohn: Zur Genese von Varèses Musikästhetik," in *Edgard Varèse: Die Befreiung des Klangs: Symposium Edgard Varèse*, ed. Helga de la Motte-Haber (Hofheim: Wolke, 1992), 17–27.

14. Austin Clarkson, "Wolpe, Varèse and the Busoni Effect," *Contemporary Music Review* 27:2–3 (April/June 2008), 361–381.

15. A letter from each of Busoni's sons to Varèse is preserved in the Varèse collection at the Paul Sacher Stiftung, Basel. Benvenuto Busoni wrote a letter postmarked April 17, 1919, in which he praised a Varèse concert he attended as marvelous. Rafaello Busoni's sole remaining letter to Varèse discusses literature and music. Both letters are preserved in the Varèse Collection at the Paul Sacher Stiftung, Basel.

16. One sole postcard from Suzanne Bing (written to Varèse after the divorce) is preserved in the Varèse Collection at the Paul Sacher Stiftung, Basel. Varèse's letters to his grandfather, Claude Cortot, also preserved in the Paul Sacher Stiftung, largely cover personal and familial (i.e., non-musical) topics.

17. Louise Varèse, *Looking Glass Diary*, 47. Varèse moved to Berlin in November 1907 with an art scholarship. He stayed in Gartenhaus 1 in Kantstrasse 138 Charlottenburg. A letter from Varèse's grandfather, dated November 22, 1907, was sent to Varèse's new Berlin address (Paul Sacher Stiftung, Basel, Varèse Collection). In February 1908 he moved to Württembergische Strasse 34 in Wilmersdorf. The Varèses moved into Nassauische Strasse 61 in Wilmersdorf in December 1908. They lived in Markgraf-Albrecht-Strasse 2 in Halensee from June 1911 until the summer of 1913. See catalogue 14 in Haber, *Edgard Varèse: Composer, Sound Sculptor Visionary*, 59.

18. Louise Varèse, *Looking Glass Diary*, 48–49. That the meeting took place rather soon after Varèse moved to Berlin is supported by Varèse's own statements. Varèse remembers showing either *Les Cycles du Nord* or *Ödipus* to Busoni after knowing him for *at least* three years. Varèse was actively working on *Ödipus* from 1909 to 1914 and *Les Cycles du Nord* around 1911 or 1912, suggesting an initial meeting during his first, or at the very latest second, year in Berlin.

19. The letter is mentioned in several sources including in Louise Varèse, *Looking Glass Diary*, 86. The original is located in the Varèse collection in the Paul Sacher Stiftung, Basel.

20. Louise Varèse, *Looking Glass Diary*, 49.

21. Edward Dent, *Ferruccio Busoni: A Biography* (London: Eulenburg Books, 1974), 158.

22. Marc-André Roberge, "Busoni in the United States," *American Music* 13:3 (Autumn 1995), 323n.5.

23. Busoni's more talented Vienna masterclass pupils included Leo Sirota, Gregor Beklemishewv, Vera Maurina Press, and Georgina Nelson. H. H. Stuckenschmidt, *Ferruccio Busoni: Chronicle of a European*, trans. Sandra Morris (New York: St. Martin's Press, 1970), 43.

24. Dent states that Busoni left Vienna in late January and that his secretary from Berlin wrote about his illness in a letter dated February 10. Dent, *Ferruccio Busoni*, 161–162. A letter from Busoni to Volkmar Andreae dated February 5, 1908, in which Busoni discusses his impending trip to Zurich (departure scheduled for February 9) includes details about Busoni's upcoming concerts and his plan to perform the twenty-four preludes of Chopin and Liszt's *Totentanz*.

25. Dent notes Busoni's return to Berlin in late July 1908. Dent, *Ferruccio Busoni*, 166.

26. Louise Varèse, *Looking Glass Diary*, 56–57. Ravel held Sunday evening gatherings for Parisian intellectuals and artists, and Varèse was a regular guest. A letter from Claude Cortot to Suzanne Bing dated August 26, 1908, was sent to Paris, rather than Berlin, as were all of Cortot's letters until January 27, 1909. Varèse Collection, Paul Sacher Stiftung, Basel.

27. In a letter to Hoffmannsthal dated July 26, 1909, Varèse mentioned his intention to leave for Burgundy in a few days. A letter from Claude Cortot to Varèse of September 6, 1909, was sent to Berlin. Varèse Collection, Paul Sacher Stiftung, Basel.

28. Louise Varèse, *Looking Glass Diary*, 87. This Paris visit is documented by a letter dated June 17, 1912, from Debussy, inviting Varèse to a concert and giving him two tickets: "Here are two seats for tonight with my affectionate cordiality." Debussy, quoted in Louise Varèse, *Looking Glass Diary*, 99. The original is in the Varèse Collection, Paul Sacher Stiftung, Basel.

29. Louise Varèse, *Looking Glass Diary*, 101.

30. This appears to have been normal for Busoni, who had difficulty equating art and money and claimed that it was immoral to commodify art. Busoni, untitled comment from 1912, Busoni Nachlass, Staatsbibliothek zu Berlin, Preußischer Kulturbesitz, Musikabteilung mit Mendelssohn-Archiv, Mus. Nachl. F. Busoni, CI, 123.

31. Varèse, in Louise Varèse, *Looking Glass Diary*, 51.

32. Augusta Cottlow, "My Years with Busoni," *Musical Observer* 24:6 (June 1925), 28.

33. Varèse, in Louise Varèse, *Looking Glass Diary*, 49.

34. Reviewers describe his style as a synthesis of Debussy and Strauss, which is not surprising, given that both were influential mentors. "Theater und Musik," in *Vossische Zeitung* (December 17, 1910), reprinted in *Edgard Varèse: Dokumente zu Leben und Werk*, 54.

35. Gunther Schuller, "Conversation with Varèse," *Perspectives of New Music* 3 (1965), 36.

36. Louise Varèse, *Looking Glass Diary*, 51.

37. Helga de la Motte-Haber, for instance, asserts: "Given his poor command of German, he was hardly likely to have assimilated the original edition of 1907." Helga de la Motte-Haber, "Blurred Traces," 37.

38. Louise Varèse, *Looking Glass Diary*, 49.

39. Busoni, *Sketch of a New Esthetic of Music*, trans. Th. Baker (New York: G. Schirmer, 1911), 1. Edgard Varèse's version is located in the Harry Ransom Humanities Research Center, the University of Texas at Austin. Varèse wrote his name on the title page.

40. It is not clear when he made these annotations. They could have been made in the United States many years after Busoni's death.

41. Varèse, "Autobiographical Remarks" dedicated to the memory of Ferruccio Busoni, from a talk given at Princeton University, September 4, 1959, reprinted in Christine Flechtner, "Die Schriften von Edgard Varèse (1883–1965)" (PhD diss., Universität Freiburg, 1983), 347.

42. The lines appear on pages 5, 7, 22, 24, 28.

43. Pages without annotations of any kind are as follows: 19–20, 25–27, 31–32, 34, 36–37, 41, 45.

44. Busoni, *Sketch of a New Esthetic of Music*, trans. Th. Baker, annotated by Edgard Varèse (New York: G. Schirmer, 1911), 5, Harry Ransom Humanities Research Center, the University of Texas at Austin.

45. Ibid., 7.

46. Ibid., 22.

47. Ibid., 24.

48. Ibid., 29.

49. It is unclear when the performance occurred, but it must have been soon after Varèse arrived in New York. The most famous New York concerts took place in 1906, and the instrument ceased to be operated in 1918. For more detail about the instrument see Reynold Weidenaar, *Magic Music from the Telharmonium* (London: Scarecrow Press, 1995); pp. 254–255 mention Varèse's hearing of and subsequent disappointment with the instrument.

50. Louise Varèse, *Looking Glass Diary*, 50.

51. Ibid., 33. Cahill (1867–1934) is believed to have invented the first electromechanical musical instrument, the telharmonium, and he established a laboratory in Holyoke, Massachusetts. The instrument was very heavy and expensive to make, and thus never reached widespread acceptance. However, the idea was inspirational for Busoni and countless others.

52. Varèse, "Electronic Music," lecture from November 9, 1958, reprinted in Flechtner, "Die Schriften," 330.

53. Stenzl, "Busonis Sohn," 19. As with his compositions, there is virtually no record of his musical aesthetics before his time in America.

54. Important sources include Louise Hirbour's *Écrits* in French, Christine Fletchner's "Die Schriften von Edgard Varèse (1883–1965)" in their original languages, and Giacomo Manzoni's *Il suono organizzato: scritti sulla musica* (Milan: Ricordi, 1985) in Italian.

55. Varèse, *New York Telegraph* (March 1916), reprinted in Louise Varèse, *Looking Glass Diary*, 123.

56. Alfred Frankenstein, "Varèse, Worker in Intensities," *San Francisco Chronicle*, November 28, 1937, "This World Section," 13.

57. Varèse, "Electronic Music," in Flechtner, "Die Schriften," 331.

58. Varèse, "Freedom for Music," lecture given at the University of Southern California, 1939, published in *The American Composer Speaks*, ed. Gilbert Chase, Louisiana State University Press, 1966, 185–192, reprinted in Flechtner, "Die Schriften," 221.

59. Salzman, email to the author, May 14, 2014. Salzman is a composer working in new music theater as well as a writer about twentieth-century music.

60. "Varèse Envisions 'Space' Symphonies," *New York Times*, December 6, 1936, sec. 2, p. 7.

61. Busoni, *Sketch*, 24.

62. Edgard Varèse, "The Music of Tomorrow," *Evening News*, June 14, 1924, 4.

63. Busoni, "Futurism in Music" (1922), reprinted in *The Essence of Music and Other Papers*, 29–30. He did, however, try out many non-traditional scales within the chromatic system. Busoni mentions the harmonium in a letter to Egon Petri dated August 23, 1910, in Busoni, *Selected Letters*, 112. See also Busoni, "Report on the Division of the Whole Tone into Three Parts" (1922), in *The Essence of Music and Other Papers*, 29–30.

64. Tamara Levitz, "Teaching New Classicality: Busoni's Master Class in Composition, 1921–24" (PhD diss., University of Rochester, 1993), 315.

65. Harry Partch, *Genesis of a Music*, 2nd ed. (New York: Da Capo Press, 1974), 429–431.

66. Edgard Varèse, "Performer's Choices—A Symposium," *Listen* (June 1946), 3.

67. Busoni, *Sketch*, 15.

68. Varèse revised *Amériques* (1918–1921) in 1927 and rescored *Ecuatorial* (1932–1934) for Ondes Martenot in 1961. Busoni creation a condensed and revised version of the *Fantasia contrappuntistica* (1910) in 1912 and a two-piano version in 1921.

69. Varèse, "Autobiographical Remarks," reprinted in Flechtner, "Die Schriften," 345–346. Busoni not only called for formal originality, as Varèse notes. He also insisted on congruence between content and form. Using a common analogy from nature, Busoni described this perfect congruence thus: "Every motive—so it seems to me—contains, like a seed, its life-germ within itself. From the different plant seeds come different families of plants, dissimilar in form, foliage, blossom, fruit, growth, and color. Even each individual plant belonging to one and the same species assumes, in size, form and strength a growth peculiar to itself. And so, in each motive, there lies the embryo of its fully developed form; each one must unfold itself differently." Busoni, *Sketch*, 10–11.

70. Severine Neff has suggested that symmetries in Varèse's *Density 21.5* might relate to Busoni's communication of Bernhard Ziehn's theories of symmetrical inversion. Neff, phone conversation with the author, May 22, 2014.

71. "Edgard Varèse" in David Ewen, *American Composers Today* (New York: H. W. Wilson Co., 1949), 250. Varèse considered it outrageous that anyone would assume new music did not have formal structure simply because it did not follow traditional forms. "Interview with Edgard Varèse about the International Composers' Guild," *New York Times*, December 22, 1923.

72. Louise Varèse, *Looking Glass Diary*, 227–228.

73. Edgard Varèse, "Autobiographical Remarks," 344.

74. Busoni, "The Realm of Music: An Epilogue to the New Aesthetic," based on a letter to his wife from 1910, reprinted in *The Essence of Music and Other Papers*, 189.

75. The orchestral version is an expanded version of the final piano elegy and was inspired by the death of his mother. The title was *Berceuse élégiaque*, BV 252, subtitled, "Des Mannes Wiegenlied am Sarge seiner Mutter" (The man's lullaby at his mother's coffin). It was dedicated to his mother, who died on October 3, 1909. The piece initially met with surprise and shock during a reading with the Berlin Philharmonic in 1910. Beaumont, *Busoni the Composer*, 145. Its Berlin premiere did not take place until January 19, 1912, in a concert sponsored by the Berlin Gesellschaft der Musikfreunde devoted to Busoni's compositions.

76. Varèse quoted in Louise Varèse, *Looking Glass Diary*, 52. Varèse's copy is preserved in the Edgard Varèse Collection, Paul Sacher Stiftung, Basel.

77. Paul Fleet, *Ferruccio Busoni: A Phenomenological Approach to His Music and Aesthetics* (Cologne: Lambert, 2009), 186.

78. Busoni, "An Attempt at a Definition of Melody." The first sketch was a letter to his wife dated July 22, 1913. It was published in *Von der Einheit der Musik* in 1922, and reprinted in *The Essence of Music and Other Papers*, 33.

79. Busoni's father died May 12, 1909.

80. For additional analyses of the piece, consult Larry Sitsky, *Busoni and the Piano: The Works, the Writings, and the Recordings*, 2nd ed., Pendragon Distinguished Reprints no. 3 (Hillsdale, NY, 2009), 204–206; Knyt, "How I Compose: Ferruccio Busoni's Views about Invention, Quotation, and the Compositional Process," *Journal of Musicology* 27:2 (Spring 2010), 256–261; Fleet, *Ferruccio Busoni*, 145–164; and Beaumont, *Busoni the Composer*, 137–140.

81. Varèse, "New Instruments and New Music," lecture at the Mary Austin House, Santa Fe, 1936, printed in Varèse and Chou Wen-Chung, "The Liberation of Sound," *Perspectives of New Music* 5:1 (Autumn/Winter 1966), 11–12.

82. Ibid.

83. Ibid.

84. He was apparently still not fluent in German several years after his sojourn there: Motte-Haber, "Blurred Traces," in *Edgard Varèse: Composer, Sound Sculptor, Visionary*, 35.

85. The spelling in Louise Varèse's *Looking Glass Diary* and other sources was altered to "Paul Kusynski." The unpublished copy of the biography also contains the alternate spelling Paul Kusnynski. Louise Varese Papers, Sophia Smith Collection, Smith College, Northampton, MA.

86. Spellings of first and last names vary from source to source. Busoni addressed his letter to "Kuszynski."

87. For more information about the family refer to Hans H. Lembke, *Die Schwarzen Schafe bei den Gradenwitz und Kuczynski: Zwei Berliner Familien im 19. Und 20. Jahrhundert* (Berlin: Verlagsgruppe Dr. Wolfgang Weist, 2008). For more information about Kuczynski, also refer to Arnold Niggli, *Arnold Jensen: 1843–1927* (Berlin: Harmonie, 1900), 52. Also see Paul Kuczynski, *Erlebnisse und Gedanken. Dichtungen zu Musikwerken* (Berlin: Concordia Deutsche Verlags-Anstalt, 1898).

88. Hugo Riemann, *Hugo Riemann's Musik-Lexicon*, 9th ed., ed. Alfred Einstein (Berlin: Max Hesses Verlag, 1919), 926.

89. Louise Varèse, *Looking Glass Diary*, 88. Louise Varèse also mentions a Swede who paid Varèse for lessons for a short time. In the draft of *Looking Glass Diary*, she mentions that the Swedish student studied only until Christmas 1910, when he was scheduled to return to Sweden. Louise Varèse, *Looking Glass Diary* draft, Louise Varèse Papers, Sophia Smith Collection, Smith College, Northampton, MA, 118–119.

90. Fernand Ouellette, *Edgard Varèse*, trans. Derek Coltman (New York: Orion Press, 1966), 208.

91. He also studied philosophy, art history, and history from 1911 to 1914 in Berlin, Marburg, and Bern and was a journalist in the Wolff Telegraphic Bureau after 1918 and chief artistic assistant at the Ferman Broadcasting Corporation in 1924. He also worked as a translator for the BBC after immigrating to London.

92. *Die kleine Tagesserenade* premiered on November 20, 1930, in Berlin for a November Group Musikabend. *Der Tag des Herrn Karl* premiered May 30, 1932, in Darmstadt. Tobias Liebert et al., "Ernst Schoen: Biographische Skizze und Nachlass," *Studienkreis Rundfunk und Geschichte Mitteilungen* 2/3 (April-July 1994), n. 15, http://rundfunkundgeschichte.de/assets/RuG_1994_2–3.pdf. accessed October 26, 2012.

93. Ouellette, *Edgard Varèse*, 34. This paragraph is based on a letter to Ouellette dated May 30, 1960. Ludwig Thuille (1861–1907) co-authored a harmony textbook together with Rudolf Louis (1870–1914), *Harmonielehre* (1907).

94. Schoen, quoted in Ouellette, *Edgard Varèse*, 102–103.

95. Kenton was a violist and musicologist of Hungarian descent. He studied at the Royal Academy of Music, Budapest, in 1911 before studying at the University of Berlin until 1914. He was also a member of the Hungarian string quartet from 1911 to 1923. Paula Morgan, "Egon F. Kenton," *Grove Music Online, Oxford Music Online*, http://www.oxfordmusiconline.com/subscriber/article/grove/music/14897, accessed October 24, 2012.

96. Louise Varèse, *Looking Glass Diary*, 98–99. Based on Varèse's assertion that he had attended the Berlin premiere of *Pierrot Lunaire* in conjunction with Kenton's account, Louise Varèse mistakenly jumped to the conclusion that Varèse must have attended the gathering at Busoni's house in October just before the public premiere. *Looking Glass Diary*, 98–99.

97. The guests included the Dutch composer Willem Joseph Mengelberg (1871–1951), the Austrian pianist Artur Schnabel (1881–1951), and the Italian violinist Arrigo Serato (1877–1948).

98. "Orchester-Abende (Neue u. selten aufgeführte Werke) mit dem Philharmonischen Orchester veranstaltet von Ferruccio Busoni."

A copy of the concert program can be viewed at the Busoni Nachlass in the Staatsbibliothek zu Berlin, Preußischer Kulturbesitz, Musikabteilung mit Mendelssohn-Archiv. The program is also listed in Dent, *Ferruccio Busoni*, 335–336.

99. He would have been unable to attend the final orchestra evening on January 2, 1909, as he was in Paris at the time.

100. The concert programs are published in Dent, *Ferruccio Busoni*, 335–336.

101. For instance, on January 10, 1909, a Boston Symphony Orchestra concert featured Beethoven's Symphony no. 3, Brahms's Violin Concerto in D Major, op. 35, and an excerpt from Dukas's *The Sorcerer's Apprentice*. By 1921, concert programming had changed little. The January 3, 1921, concert by the Boston Symphony Orchestra, for instance, featured the following pieces, both written in a more traditional manner: Tchaikovsky's "Manfred" Symphony, op. 58 (after Byron's dramatic poem) and Saint-Saëns's Pianoforte Concerto no. 5 in F Major. Boston Symphony Orchestra Concert Programs, Season 40, 1920–1921, http://archive.org/details/bostonsymphonyor-2021bost, accessed October 26, 2012.

102. For more information about Varèse's activities, see R. Allen Lott, "'New Music for New Ears': The International Composers' Guild," *Journal of the American Musicological Society* 36:2 (Summer 1983), 266–286. The International Composers' Guild also became associated with similar organizations across the globe, including in Italy and Moscow, for instance.

103. "Composers Form Guild to Bring New Works to Public Hearing," *Musical America* 34:13 (July 23, 1921), 6.

104. There are discrepancies between the program listed in Louise Varèse's *Looking Glass Diary* on page 171, based on an announcement she helped distribute to promote the concert, and the actual concert program found in the Music Division of the New York City Public Library and reprinted in R. Allen Lott's article, 282. The most notable differences are the inclusion of Casella and Pizzetti on the actual program.

105. Louise Varèse, *Looking Glass Diary*, 180.

106. Daybooks beginning in 1922 are preserved in the Paul Sacher Stiftung, Varèse Collection. The recorded meeting times are as follows: August 8, August 30, September 5, September 7, and October 3. In addition, he met with Tiessen numerous times: August 29 and 31, September 1, and October 28.

107. Heinz Tiessen (1887–1991) was a German composer, conductor, and music critic for the *Allgemeine Musikzeitung*. Alois Hába (1893–1973) was a Czech composer, music theorist, and teacher. He is famous for his experimentation with microtones. Philipp Jarnach (1892–1982) was an important modernist composer and a pupil of Busoni. Werner Wolffheim (1877–1930) was a German music bookseller. Hermann Springer (1872–1945) was a German professor and director of the Society of German Music Critics. Alfredo Casella (1883–1947) was an Italian composer, pianist, and conductor. Bernard van Dieren (1887–1936) was a Dutch composer and author. Eduard Erdmann (1896–1958) was a German pianist and composer. Paul Hindemith (1895–1963) was a German composer, violist, and conductor. Ernst Krenek (1900–1991) was an author and composer famous for his *Zeitopern*. Arthur Lourié (1892–1966) was a Russian composer. Felix Petyrek (1892–1951) was an Austrian composer, a pupil of Franz Schreker and Guido Adler.

108. Concert Program of November 1, 1922. The Galston-Busoni Archive, MS.1072. University of Tennessee, Knoxville—Libraries. Translation by Erinn Knyt.
109. *Musical Courier,* November 20, 1922, quoted in Louise Varèse, *Looking Glass Diary,* 184.
110. Nikolai Myaskovsky (1881–1950) was a Russian composer.
111. Edgard Varèse, "Autobiographical Remarks," 340.
112. Ibid., 341.
113. Varèse, quoted in Louise Varèse, *Looking Glass Diary,* 49.
114. Varèse, "Autobiographical Remarks," 339.
115. Olin Downes, "Music in the Future: Edgard Varèse Attacks Neo-Classicism and Suggests Electronics," *New York Times,* July 25, 1948, sec. 2, p. 1.
116. In his diary, in an entry dated February 11, 1957, Dallapiccola writes: "In the home of our friends Red and Ernest Heller, at one of their typically brilliant dinners, we meet the Varèses. It seems that a recording of Busoni's *Doktor Faust* has arrived from Zurich. Among the guests only my wife and I have seen this extraordinary and unique opera on the stage. A hearing of the tape is planned in a few days hence. Varèse is most interested, and will not fail to be present. He tells us how he met Busoni in Berlin after the First World War, and how much he learned from him, both directly and indirectly." "In Memoriam: Edgard Varèse (1883–1965): Encounters with Edgard Varèse," *Perspectives of New Music* 4:2 (Spring-Summer 1966), 5.
117. Busoni, "The Theory of Orchestration," *Die Musik,* 1905. Reprinted in *The Essence of Music and Other Papers,* trans. Rosamund Ley (New York: Dover Publications, 1957), 35.
118. "Je me rappelle un jour de pluie. Je le voyais qui passait dans la rue; il était pale, il était beau, il courrait dans la pluie." A copy of the original "Red Book Diary" in which Louise Varèse recorded this quotation is located in the Louise Varèse Papers, Sophia Smith Collection, Smith College, Northampton, MA.
119. Benvenuto Busoni to Edgard Varèse, November 4, 1919, Edgard Varèse Collection, Paul Sacher Stiftung, Basel.
120. Raffaello Busoni to Edward Dent, July 6, 1948, King's College Archive Centre, Cambridge, Papers of Edward Joseph Dent, EJD.
121. It was Busoni who coined the expression "The New Classicism," and classicism new or old was what I was bent on escaping. But it was also Busoni who said, "The function of the Creative Artist consists in making laws, not in following laws already made." Edgard Varèse, "Autobiographical Remarks," 340.

4

From Opera to Films

> I had to call on Busoni 19 times before I succeeded in reaching him, who for me will always remain an ideal figure—Ferruccio Busoni, the most noble human and far-sighted artist, the greatest I have encountered in my life.
>
> Louis Gruenberg, *25 Jahre neue Musik*, 1926

GRUENBERG'S DREAMS

WHEN LOUIS GRUENBERG (1884–1964) won the Flagler Prize (1920) in composition for his symphonic work *The Hill of Dreams*, op. 10, the career of one of America's earliest nationalist composers was launched.[1] He pioneered a distinctively American musical style through the melding of jazz and classical idioms in the 1920s, and he also actively promoted the music of American composers. By 1924, two of his compositions inspired by jazz, *The Daniel Jazz*, op. 21, and *The Creation*, op. 23, achieved international recognition.[2] A career characterized by awards and commissions, such as Jascha Heifetz's request for an "American" violin concerto (1944), the RCA Victor Composition Prize (1930), and three Oscar nominations for film scores, came to an unexpected halt in the 1950s and 1960s as avant-garde aesthetics antithetical to his ideal of musical "beauty" predominated.

Gruenberg's initially limited musical education made his many composition successes unexpected, but he possessed determination and natural talent. At the same time, he claimed that Ferruccio Busoni, with whom he studied in Europe from 1908 to 1914, helped him discover his unique artistic voice and launched his career as a pianist and composer. He sent the following expression of gratitude on Busoni's birthday in 1915: "It is with profound regret, that I find myself unable to give expression of my gratitude to you for the many signs of friendship you have shown me, and for the one extraordinary feature of my life, the awakening of my artistic sense."[3] After studying with Busoni, Gruenberg began writing operatic and symphonic works, and adopted aesthetic ideas that mirror Busoni's. Busoni laid the foundation for Gruenberg's search for an American style of music and his experimentation with polystylism, film music, and new technology.

Despite the significance of Busoni's impact on Gruenberg, little scholarship has even touched upon the subject. Hans Heinz Stuckenschmidt cites cosmopolitan, humanitarian qualities as well as formal clarity resulting from Gruenberg's studies with Busoni.[4] Robert Franklin Nisbett notes greater sophistication of intervallic choices and of cadences as well as an exploration of American nationalistic sounds.[5] Other articles discussing his compositions only tangentially reference Busoni as being an influential teacher.[6] More specific details about Busoni's mentorship can be gleaned from unpublished primary source material, including at the New York Public Library, the Syracuse University Library, the Library of Congress, the Staatsbibliothek zu Berlin, and the private collection of Joan Gruenberg Cominos.

GRUENBERG'S BACKGROUND AND EDUCATION

Busoni was Gruenberg's first and last significant composition instructor. Gruenberg received initial piano lessons from his father, a violinist, before studying piano with Adele Margulies at the National Conservatory of Music in New York until 1893.[7] Gruenberg's education in composition was even more minimal. He states that his only lessons in theory in America occurred informally, and after he had dropped out of school at the age of fifteen in order to work as a freelance artist.[8] Like many of his contemporaries, Gruenberg eventually went to Europe to complete his education. Although his goal when he departed for Europe in late 1905 was to study with Busoni in Berlin, Busoni was too busy concertizing to work with him at the time. Studying with Friedrich Koch (1862–1927) for nine months instead was a disappointment. He finally met Busoni in 1908 during his second trip to Europe. Busoni then taught, mentored, and promoted his young protégé. By the time Gruenberg left Europe hastily in 1914 due to the outbreak of World War I, he had become a rising star in both piano and composition.

BUSONI'S INSTRUCTION AND MENTORSHIP

Having heard that Busoni was offering a piano master class in Vienna, Gruenberg hoped to study piano with him upon his return to Europe.[9] However, Busoni held no clear boundaries between performance and composition, and it would eventually be composition instruction that would have the greater impact. Gruenberg was finally successful, after numerous attempts, in getting an audition with Busoni and in joining the master class. (see figure 4.1)[10] Although the class began in October 1907, Gruenberg must only have participated in the second half, as he did not arrive in Europe until February 1908.[11] Busoni was touring from February 10 through April 21, with only a brief return in mid-March. The class continued from April 21 through July 15. According to Nisbett, the first meeting took place in April 1908, just as the master class was resuming, and Busoni immediately accepted Gruenberg.[12]

The master class theoretically consisted of regular bi-weekly meeting times, but there was also socialization, especially at dinners outside of class time, which allowed for an additional exchange of ideas. Gruenberg fondly recalls these social hours in Vienna, and then again later in Berlin:

> There are still other Busoni recollections. What about the evenings in Vienna, when after the day class the entire batch marched to Huebner's, near the opera house, and sat down at a special table, and ate and drank our full, and Busoni paid the entire bill. Ah, youth, youth! Why don't you come some times to us old duffers? And then again, this time in Berlin, when I run in at all times of the day in his penthouse, ever welcomed by the magnificent Gerda, with her famous smile, and a drink by Busoni—Yes, sir, these were the days![13]

In practice, lessons were also sometimes irregular, with four-hour lessons on consecutive days that were then separated by periods without any instruction.[14]

FIGURE 4.1. Busoni's Vienna master class, 1908. Busoni is in the first row in the center. Gruenberg is in the last row, fourth from the left. Staatsbibliothek zu Berlin—Preussischer Kulturbesitz, Musikabteilung mit Mendelssohn Archiv, Staatsbibliothek zu Berlin, Busoni-Nachl. PII, 48.

Busoni's performances and those of his invited guests were especially inspirational for Gruenberg. One of his recitals, which included the twelve transcendental etudes of Liszt (June 22, 1908), made an especially strong impression on Gruenberg.[15] On the cover of his score, Gruenberg wrote: "Wien: Heard Busoni play these twelve etudes magnificently in the classroom. It was horribly hot. June 22, 1908."[16] Following in the score are a number of penciled annotations, such as added accent or dynamic markings, in Gruenberg's hand—perhaps notes from lessons with Busoni or records of what Busoni did in performance. In addition, there were performances by rising stars, including José Vianna da Motta and Béla Bartók, who played his 14 Bagatelles, op. 6, for the class on June 29, 1908. Two-piano readings of symphonic literature by the students supplemented the performances.[17]

FIGURE 4.2. Prize pupils of the Vienna master class. From left to right: Leo Sirota, Ferruccio Busoni (seated), Ignaz Friedman, Louis Gruenberg (leaning forward), Louis Closson, and József Turczyński. Staatsbibliothek zu Berlin—Preussischer Kulturbesitz, Musikabteilung mit Mendelssohn Archiv, Staatsbibliothek zu Berlin, PI, 103.

Busoni considered Gruenberg to be one of the best pupils of the master class, and he was especially impressed with his interpretation of Liszt's piano sonata in B minor, S. 178, which he described in a letter to Egon Petri: "Pity you aren't here. My group of pupils is delightful—the men, at any rate—with many a fine head. Very able. One of them recently played the Liszt sonata so well that I struggled to restrain my tears. There is no rivalry amongst them, they are all good fellows. We carry on until mid-July."[18]

Gruenberg also performed Schumann's *Carnaval*, op. 9, in June.[19] At the end of the master class, Busoni reported to Ludwig von Bösendorfer the names of his most talented pupils. Even despite his late entry to the class, Gruenberg's name was included in the list: "Distinction was won by the pupils Sirota (Kiev), Gruenberg (New York), Closson (Liège), Turczynski (Warsaw), and Friedmann [sic] (Vienna). The company was cordial, convivial, and *unclouded* (see figure 4.2)."[20] Gruenberg, for his part, considered Busoni to be one of the greatest living pianists.[21]

That Busoni held high hopes for Gruenberg from the beginning is evident in his dedication of a new composition to him. As a tribute to several of his favorite students, including Gruenberg, Busoni dedicated a collection of pieces for piano, *An die Jugend*, BV 254, to them:

1. Preludietto, Fughetta, ed Esercizio, dedicated to Józef Turczyński (June 1909)
2. Preludio, Fuga, e Fuga figurata (study on J. S. Bach's *Well-Tempered Clavier*), dedicated to Louis Theodor Gruenberg (July 1909)
3. Giga, Bolero, e Variazione (Study after Mozart), dedicated to Leo Sirota (July 1909)
4. Introduzione, e Capriccio (Paganinesco, dedicated to Louis Closson August 1909)
5. Epilogo, dedicated to Émile R. Blanchet

The piece represents Busoni's vision of the future of music that he hoped his youthful students would bring to full maturity:[22] "My love belongs to the young and shall always belong to them. Their impossible plans, their open-minded questions, disarming criticisms, defiant contradictions and fast-beating hearts—they turn the earth over and sow new seed in it."[23]

It is fitting that the movement dedicated to Gruenberg is a Bach transcription. Gruenberg was in awe of Busoni's treatment of Bach, and his own recitals frequently featured Bach-Busoni transcriptions, especially the Bach-Busoni Chaconne in D Minor (BWV 1004), BV B24. The piece, dedicated to Gruenberg, superimposes a prelude and fugue by J. S. Bach. Although beginning with a near literal quotation of the Prelude and Fugue in D Major, BWV 850, from Busoni's own edition of *The Well-Tempered Clavier*, book I, a third part combines the prelude and fugue with virtuosic counterpoint.

Piano scores, which Gruenberg methodically dated and signed, provide evidence as to what he studied and heard with Busoni. The first page of his score for Liszt's Sonata in B Minor, S. 178, for instance, states: "Busoni-Wien Mai 1908."[24] A score of two organ toccatas (C Major and

D Minor, BWV 564–565), transcribed by Busoni, likewise contains the note: "L-T-Grünberg, May 11th 1908, Vienna."[25] In turn, Busoni presented Gruenberg with a score of Anton Rubinstein's Theme and 12 Variations in G Major, op. 88. Annotations reveal Busoni's free approach with the score, and his dedication and signature at the beginning indicates that the score was a gift to Gruenberg in memory of Vienna ("für erinnerung an Wien").[26] Several cuts are suggested in the score. One, stating "Variations VI and VIII to be omitted [sic]" appears to be in Busoni's hand.[27] Measures are also crossed out at the end of variation VII. During the fourth etude, a connection is made to Adolf von Henselt, while Chopin's name is crossed out.[28]

The longevity of the Busoni-Gruenberg relationship is evident, in part, by manuscripts given to Gruenberg throughout the years. Busoni gave him a copy of his experimental *Sonatina seconda*, BV 259, when on tour of the United States in 1915 (from January 1915 to August 28, 1915). Since Busoni used New York as a home base while in the United States, Gruenberg and Busoni still conversed about musical matters even after Gruenberg left Europe. The first page contains the dedication: "To my friend L. T. Gruenberg with all good feelings."[29] Gruenberg evidently studied the score, as page 4 contains finger markings indicating the redistribution of notes between hands. The two met again in Berlin in 1920, in London in 1921, in Paris in 1922, and in Berlin in 1923.[30] Busoni gave him a copy of his *Toccata: Preludio-Fantasia-Ciaccona*, BV 287, in 1921 with the dedication on the first page in English: "To Louis Theodor Grünberg London, 1921, F. Busoni."[31] Numerous letters between Gruenberg and Busoni also document the continued friendship. When he returned to Europe in 1923, he also played for Busoni.[32] Gruenberg reportedly tried to entice Busoni to stay in America, an offer Busoni did not even consider, in part because of his growing distaste for American capitalism and culture.[33]

COMPOSITION INSTRUCTION

Despite the fact that Gruenberg came to Vienna for a piano master class, he also received instruction in composition. This was one of the first times he had received composition instruction, and it had a major impact on his development.[34] Busoni's aesthetic ideas and compositional style were influential for Gruenberg, who only began to make headway professionally after studying with Busoni. Gruenberg claims that he composed for several hours per day in Vienna and it was there that the germinal seeds were laid for a number of compositions that would become important for his career, including his symphonic tone poem *The Hill of Dreams*, op. 10, which earned him the Flagler Prize in 1920 and the performance of the work with Walter Damrosch conducting.[35] He told an interviewer that the idea was conceived years before the competition, while he was studying in Vienna."[36]

Gruenberg brought scores to Busoni for critique, not just in Vienna, but also throughout his time in Europe. Even though the meetings were not regular, as Busoni and Gruenberg were both actively touring at that time, they were fruitful. During lessons, Busoni imparted a clear vision of the difference between high and low art. Gruenberg remembers that during one lengthy absence, he tried writing more popular music under the name of Teddy Gruenberg, just to make ends meet. When the two finally met after an absence of nine months, Busoni, who looked down upon art created for monetary purposes, was displeased: "After 8–9 months I went to see Busoni again. He invited me for dinner and I was telling him happily about the operetta which I called stomach music. Busoni remarked that I should not depend on anything so speculative to earn money and to write serious music."[37]

The piece in question was likely *Piccadillymädel*, an operetta in one act that he composed in 1913 with song texts by Jacques Burg after Erich Urban's play. Gruenberg persisted throughout his career in writing music for profit out of necessity under the pseudonym George Edwards, but he assumed a critical attitude, claiming in 1919 from America that he felt like a "musical whore" when he did so.[38]

Thus despite limited musical instruction, one of the first Americanist composers at last had begun to find his way, with Busoni as a guide. Busoni opened Gruenberg's eyes and ears to possibilities beyond the virtuosic piano pieces he knew so well.

GRUENBERG'S COMPOSITIONS AND AESTHETICS

Discussions about music aesthetics and Busoni's own compositions had a transformative impact on Gruenberg's compositional style. Busoni opened Gruenberg's mind to a realm of aesthetic ideas that transformed his compositional approach and musical ideals. Gruenberg's writings reveal a thorough awareness of Busoni's aesthetic texts, in particular, the *Entwurf einer neuen Ästhetik der Tonkunst* (1907): "Then again Busoni was the most imaginative writer about music of his age; witness his prophecies "A New Aesthetic of Music," wherein his accumulative summing-up of future possibilities of new scales will someday possibly bring forth a new color in music. A real fusion of old and new."[39]

On the inside of his copy of the English version, he wrote: "There is enough material suggested here to completely satisfy the demands of the composer for a century to come, and written in 1905 [sic]!!"[40] In the margins of the text, he placed a number next to every point he considered important, 117 in total. Many of these, he bracketed, boxed, and/or underlined as well.[41] The passages with the additional markings range from the abstract declaration that music was born free to the more concrete suggestion that the seven-tone scale could be expanded.

Some of Gruenberg's statements also gloss Busoni's text. For instance, in a reiteration of Busoni's views of Young Classicality, he stated his ideal was a fusion of the old and the new: "The majority of modernists—I don't say all, mind you, but the majority—strive for clever effects at the sacrifice of the beautiful. Cleverness has never been my creed. I believe in a combination of the old and the new."[42] It was Busoni who first wrote about an ideal of music in which music of the past would be fused with the innovations of the present: "By 'Young Classicism' I mean the mastery, the sifting and the turning to account of all the gains of previous experiments and their inclusion in strong and beautiful forms. This art will be old and new at the same time at first."[43] Gruenberg elaborated to some degree on how this combination worked in his estimation. He re-echoed Busoni's thought that there is nothing new, that everything is part of an evolutionary process. Originality does not refer to invention ex nihilo, but rather to the creative transformation of tradition.

Both men also envisioned unique musical structures inspired by architecture. While Busoni drew an image of gothic architecture to illustrate the formal structure in his two-piano version of the *Fantasia contrappuntistica*, BV 256, which Gruenberg would have heard performed in Salzburg in 1923, Gruenberg envisioned pyramids and temples as models for musical form: "The forms will become something else; architecture will be changed structurally, so that, built as the pyramids, skyscrapers, temples in external shape, there will be a counterpart in music."[44]

Gruenberg, like Busoni, also envisioned expanding the musical alphabet and new harmonic possibilities, including microtones, quartal chords, and chord clusters:[45] "The harmonic system which has heretofore been founded upon the technic of the piano will, in order to continue to function, have to be based upon the technic of the orchestra, where it really belongs. And after the harmonic possibilities of the orchestra have been exhausted, and that is still a way off, the new combinations will have to come with the new inventions of third and quarter notes which will have been incorporated in the new instruments.... It is now merely an educational step to an unbridled experimentation."[46]

He argued, like Busoni, that music's possibilities were limitless, and that they needed to be unfettered from the regulations taught in traditional settings: "Music possesses no rules. Its boundaries are as limitless as the universe itself." This is a gloss on Busoni's equation of music with the freedom found in nature: "This child [music]—it *floats on air!* It touches not the earth with its feet. It knows no law of gravitation. It is well-nigh incorporeal. Its material is transparent. It is sonorous air. It is almost Nature herself. It is—free."[47]

If Busoni's aesthetic ideas impacted Gruenberg, so did his music. An undated handwritten list, folded in Gruenberg's copy of a small bound concert book of Busoni's historical piano concerto programs, reveals the compositions with which he must have been familiar early in his career, possibly before beginning his studies with Busoni (see table 4.1).[48] Gruenberg's writings also mention familiarity with *Arlecchino*, BV 270, the Bach transcriptions, and the incomplete *Doktor Faust*, BV 303. He would have heard the two-piano version of the *Fantasia contrappuntistica,* BV 256b, in Salzburg in 1923, and he owned scores of Busoni's *Sonatina seconda*, BV 259, and *Toccata: Preludio-Fantasia-Ciaccona*, BV 287. In addition, Gruenberg performed the piano part in the American premiere of Busoni's Sonata in E Minor for Violin and Piano, BV 244, on April 2, 1922. Gruenberg also stated he was learning and hoped to perform the mammoth Concerto for Piano, Orchestra, and Male Chorus, BV 247.[49]

Gruenberg considered Busoni to be one of the greatest composers of his age, and his operas to be the pinnacle of achievement.[50] He also especially

TABLE 4.1 GRUENBERG'S LIST OF COMPOSITIONS BY BUSONI

BUSONI'S KOMPOSITIONEN*

Op. 1.	22. Variationen und fuge (nach Chopin)
2.	23.
3.	24.
4. Scherzo	25.
5. Prelude et Fuge	26. Zweites Quartet
6. Scene de Ballet	27.
7.	28.
8.	29.
9.	30. Zwei Klavierstücke
10.	31a. Konzertstücke
11.	32.
12.	33a. Vierte Ballet Scene
13.	34a. Zweite Orchester Suite
14.	35a. Konzert für Violine
15.	36.
16. Sechs Etüden	37.
17. 5 Variatione	38.
18.	39. Klavier Konzert mit chor
19.	40.
20. Zweite Balletscene	41.
21.	42.

Busoni's use of opus numbers is confusing, because he started assigning each composition a number when he wrote it. Beginning at op. 40, he began reassigning opus numbers from youthful works. He then started over again at opus 30 and used letters as additional indicators from op. 30 to op. 36.

Source: Louis Gruenberg Papers, Music Division, New York Public Library, Astor, Lenox, and Tilden Foundations, Box 14.

admired Busoni's orchestrations, which he considered witty, subtle, and transparent.[51]

Busoni's influence on Gruenberg's compositional style was marked. Gruenberg's earliest compositions, mainly for piano, display little personality and are written in extended late-Romantic chromatic tonal language. His Intermezzo, op. 13 no. 1 (1907), contains idiomatic improvisatory keyboard figures, but little formal or thematic sophistication.[52] In simple ABA

MUSIC EXAMPLE 4.1. Gruenberg, Intermezzo, op. 13 no. 1, mm. 1–20.

form, the primary interest resides in the harmonic colors and virtuosic passagework. In the key of G-sharp minor, temporary chromatic movement to B-flat major is unexpected in measure 4, as is the middle section modulation to D-flat major (see music example 4.1).

MUSIC EXAMPLE 4.2. Gruenberg, Scène de Ballet, mm. 1–20.

Gruenberg's *Scène de Ballet* (1910) shares the same key signature as the intermezzo (5 sharps) and also modulates to a flat key in the middle section (5 flats), but it is more sophisticated in its treatment of harmony, melody, and rhythm. Nisbett has argued that the piece is likely modeled after Busoni's *Kleine Ballet-Szene*, BV 235/2, and he has already noted Gruenberg's newly adopted use of quartal chords and unusual cadences.[53] Connections can also be drawn to the *Vierte Ballett-szene*, BV 238 (1894), which Busoni revised and republished in 1913 as BV 238a, and which Gruenberg noted in his early list of Busoni compositions. In addition to large-scale harmonic parallels there are also thematic similarities. Both begin with

MUSIC EXAMPLE 4.3. Busoni, Vierte Ballett-Szene, mm. 1–13.

single melody lines and on the dominant. Both feature chromatic voice leading and tonicization of the dominant, while evading cadences at the beginning, leading to tonal ambiguity (see music examples 4.2 and 4.3).

Marked changes can be observed in Gruenberg's style in comparison to the intermezzo, and this can be attributed to Busoni's influence. Of note is the sophisticated tonal ambiguity, thematic treatment, and structural approach. Beginning with a single unharmonized pitch, D-sharp, the opening hints at G-sharp minor and B major, but eluded cadences obscure the tonality. Instead of virtuosic figurework, Gruenberg develops themes. He starts with a lilting waltz melody which serves as germinal material that is developed in numerous ways, including through the redistribution of material between hands and registers, through fragmentation, and through transposition. Although in ABA' form, the final A represents culmination and development rather than a simple repetition. The initial tonally ambiguous sixteen bars are omitted in the final A section, and the tonally stable material from the beginning in G-sharp minor is destabilized.

Gruenberg worked on several compositions during the time that he studied with Busoni in Vienna and Berlin, branching out from piano music to orchestral, chamber, and vocal music (see table 4.2). Busoni, who

TABLE 4.2. GRUENBERG'S COMPOSITIONS, 1908–1914

DATE	TITLE
1904–1912	Eleven Songs for Voice and Piano, op. 4 (unpublished)[1]
1908–1920	*The Hill of Dreams*, op. 10 (unpublished)
1910	*Signor Formica* (unpublished)
1912	Suite for Violin and Piano, op. 3 (pub. 1914, G. Schirmer)
1912	*The Witch of Brocken*, op. 1 (published 1931, C. C. Birchard and Co.)
c. 1912	Thirteen Impressions for Piano (five published in 1922, Composers' Music Corp.)
1913/1915	*Die Götterbraut/The Bride of the Gods*, op. 2 (unpublished)

[1] Song no. 2 (August 10, 1904), no. 4 (1905), no. 5 (1912), no. 8 (August 23, 1912), no. 9 (February 1911), no. 10 (January 21, 1912), nos. 1, 3, 6, and 7 (undated). Nisbett, "Louis Gruenberg," 341.

was composing several operas at the time, including *Die Brautwahl*, BV 258 (1906–1911), *Arlecchino*, BV 270 (1914–1916), *Turandot*, BV 273 (1916–1917), and *Doktor Faust*, BV 303 (1910–1923), encouraged Gruenberg to write operas. He thought that ideal libretto subjects were those that invited music and were perfected by it. Gruenberg remembers: "Busoni said to me, 'A play that is complete needs no music. Therefore, they ought to welcome us. Their incomplete plays can be helped.'"[54] He idealized number operas even as he strove after polystylistic (almost cinematic) music that reflected the stylistically diverse musics called for in "musical" plots that invited diegetic and non-diegetic music. Busoni idealized Mozart's operas, especially *Die Zauberflöte*, K. 620, and drew upon puppet plays for his libretto of *Faust* and *Arlecchino II* (1918).[55]

Busoni encouraged Gruenberg to study Mozart's *Le Nozze di Figaro*, K. 492.[56] Busoni's well-loved score, which he gave to Gruenberg, contains annotations, cuts, and exclamations of adoration in English, such as "The finale is simply marvelous," "great!," and "What exquisite simplicity."[57] Annotations at the beginning of Susanna's aria "Venite, inginocchiatevi" provide specific notes related to his instruction: "Beautiful! Study this for almost everything a) the relationship between voice and orch. B) orchestration c) form (O, beautiful)."[58] Another note for scene 10 suggests updating Mozart's score, although no concrete suggestions are provided: "Could this be modernized?"[59]

TABLE 4.3. GRUENBERG'S OPERAS, OPERETTAS, AND OTHER WORKS FOR STAGE

DATE OF COMPOSITION	TITLE	LIBRETTIST
1910	*Signor Formica*	unknown (after E.T.A. Hoffmann)
1912	*The Witch of Brocken*, op. 1	Emil Ferdinand Malkowski
1913/1915	*Die Götterbraut*	Busoni (translated by Charles Henry Meltzer)
1913	*Piccadillymädel*	Jacques Burg and Erich Urban
1919	*Roly-Boly Eyes* (musical)	Edgar Allan Woolf
1923	*The Dumb Wife*, op. 12	unknown (after *The Man Who Married a Dumb Wife* by Anatole France)
c. 1925	*Hallo! Tommy!* (as "George Edwards")	(unknown)
c. 1927	*Lady X* (as "George Edwards")	Ludwig Herzer
1931	*Jack and the Beanstalk*, op. 35	John Erskine
1931	*The Emperor Jones*, op. 36	Gruenberg (after Eugene O'Neill)
1937	*Green Mansions*, op. 39 (radio opera)	Gruenberg (after William Henry Hudson)
1938	*Helena's Husband*, op. 38	Philip Moeller
1954	*The Miracle of Flanders: A Legend with Music in Three Scenes for a Narrator and Orchestra*, op. 65	Gruenberg
1955	*The Delicate King*, op. 67	Gruenberg (after Alexandre Dumas)
1958	*Volpone*, op. 57	Gruenberg (after Ben Jonson)
1958–1961	*Antony and Cleopatra*, op. 68	Gruenberg (after William Shakespeare)
n.d.	*One Night of Cleopatra*, op. 64	Gruenberg (after Théophile Gautier)
n.d.	*The Golden City of Iram: A Dance Legend for Speaker and Orchestra*, op. 55	unknown

Gruenberg began writing operas and operettas while studying with Busoni, and his approach is patterned after Busoni's opera aesthetics (see table 4.3). In terms of topics, most, if not all of Gruenberg's early operas are based on fairy tales or unrealistic, supernatural, or exotic themes.

Source material for libretti includes texts by E.T.A. Hoffmann, Busoni, Shakespeare, and Jonson, for instance. Gruenberg's propensity for fanciful themes or oriental topics is displayed throughout his works for stage, and in aborted projects as well. Undated music sketches indicate that he also had plans to set music for a puppet play.[60]

Gruenberg followed in Busoni's footsteps in writing libretti, some of which he eventually set to music. One unpublished and undated scenario bears similarity to Busoni's *Turandot*, BV 273. An oriental setting features an improbable plot in which human events are altered through interaction with a puppet. The hard-hearted Empress Mao-Tun ended a siege after becoming jealous of an attractive female puppet. The libretto synopsis alludes to a folk-like melody to be used for local color.[61]

Gruenberg shared Busoni's adoration of commedia dell'arte figures and number operas.[62] His incomplete *The Great Liar* (undated) includes the Doctor, Pantalone, Arlecchino, and Columbina. Set in Venice, it is a number opera based on older musical forms. The outline for act 1 is as follows:

1. Overture
2. Intermezzo
3. Serenade
4. A snatch of the overture
5. Lelio's song
6. Lelio's exit
7. Serenade
8. Lelio's song
9. Intermezzo
10. Intermezzo
11. Song of Ottavio
12. Intermezzo (March)
13. Sonnet
14. Duet
15. Delirious music[63]

Gruenberg's first attempts at opera were made in collaboration with Busoni, who reportedly suggested the topic of *Salvator Rosa* in 1908:

> Gruenberg has the idea for "Signor Formica" from me. I have a volume of Italian poems by S[alvator] Rosa in which is included a biography of the

painter (or poet in this case). The events in E.T.A. Hoffmann's tale—when compared with this account—are *historically exact* and it is almost baffling how the author, despite his pedantic accuracy, unfolds an aura of the fantastic and improbable over the events in a magic cloak. Gruenberg is a pleasant, talented fellow.... I am very fond of him and it is my wish that "Mr. Ant" should bring him good fortune.[64]

Based on a fictitious musician and playwright, Signor Formica, who successfully foils the amorous plans of an aged uncle for his beautiful niece through instructional plays, Hoffmann's plot blends commedia dell'arte characters with historical people in a series of improbable events that involve not only love and intrigue, but also music and moralizing.[65] Gruenberg described his setting as a "musical comedy in three acts after Hoffmann's novel of the same name."

Throughout the opera, which features extended tonality, Gruenberg associated musical themes with specific characters, and he notated the themes at the beginning of the score (see figure 4.3). Dreamy themes in $\frac{6}{8}$ for Antonio and Marianna contrast with Salvator Rosa's robust themes in simple duple meters. Capuzzi's themes, by contrast, are grotesque and exaggerated, featuring large clumsy leaps. A lengthy overture featuring a medley of the main themes begins in E major, but is tonally unstable with abrupt movements to remotely related key areas, including A-flat major and A minor. Overall, the vocal writing is simple and tuneful while the aria and recitative styles freely blend together. Salvator Rosa's entrance aria emerges without a break from an instrumental introduction to act 1. The vocal style alternates between arioso and recitative, and is rarely melismatic or lyrical. The only ensemble appears at the end of the third act, but instead of an incremental and dramatic buildup, all the characters suddenly appear at the end, largely in unison homophonic writing.

Gruenberg's second opera, *Die Götterbraut*, op. 2, was based on a libretto by Busoni. He reportedly planned to stage it in Europe in 1914, but the war disrupted the endeavor.[66] He revised the work in 1915 and provided it with English translation. His goal was to procure an American staging, especially with the Metropolitan Opera, of which Artur Bodansky had assumed the directorship at the recommendation of Busoni.[67] However, after he sent the score, Bodansky replied that although the work was interesting, it was not technically mature, especially in the treatment of the

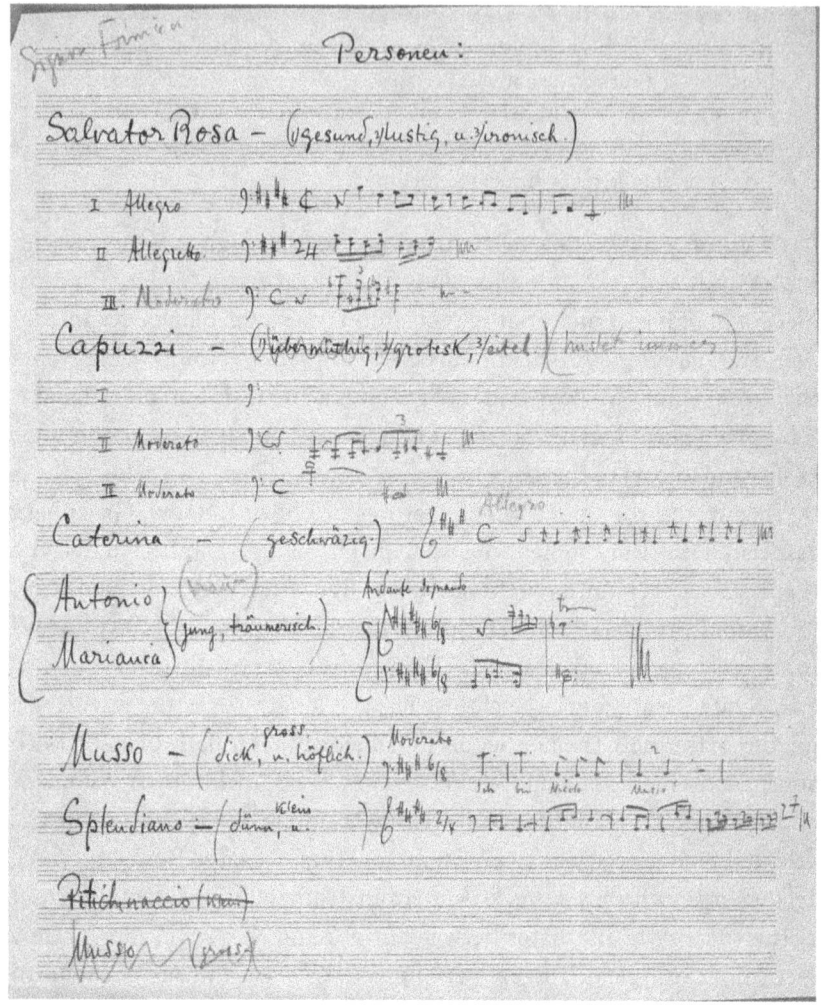

FIGURE 4.3. Gruenberg, *Signor Formica*. Main Themes Page, Louis Gruenberg Papers, Music Division, New York Public Library, Astor, Lenox, and Tilden Foundations, JPB 78–30.

voice.[68] He also had doubts about the suitability of the plot, which focuses on the plight of two Indian lovers, Nala and Damayanti, as originally told in the epic poem *Mahabharata*, for a US audience.[69]

Two extant versions of Gruenberg's musical settings exist in manuscript form. The first, a full orchestral scoring, nearly three hundred pages long, is dated June 15 to December 10, 1913. The second, a piano-vocal score with English translation of the libretto by Charles Henry Meltzer, is dated September 22, 1915, New York City. The orchestration in the first version is clearly the work of a student, with numerous alterations and notes about future revisions to better balance instruments. The second version, although predominantly a reduction of the orchestral version, does contain some minor revisions, especially in the beginning section. Like Gruenberg's *Salvator Rosa*, the music is nearly continuous and the vocal scoring is largely syllabic and speech-like. However, the organization is more sophisticated and unconventional. It is an opera in one act, but it features three scenes that are divided by brief interludes. One of the most significant interludes occurs just before the final scene and features a series of untexted dances. In addition, there are indications for spoken prose interspersed throughout the score and there is a pantomime performed by priests, dervishes, and warriors. This opera also features greater flexibility in the alternation of vocal ensembles, solos, and choruses than his earliest opera.

Gruenberg's approach reflects Busoni's ideas about opera. Busoni believed that the music should be preeminent in an opera. He dreamed of a composition in which the plot, staging, and scenery were secondary, where the music was independent and complete in and of itself: "It is, with the opera, a question of 'a musical work of the combined arts' as against the Bayreuth conception of it as 'a work of the combined arts.'"[70] Gruenberg likewise argued for prominence of the music in opera, viewing the genre as an abstract and absolute symphony with some suggestion of plot or situation added: "Possibly the most ideal form of opera could be to give the faintest outline of an idea, a mere suggestion of a situation, and allow the music to complete the picture in the imagination of the listener."[71] Busoni also idealized stylistic diversity in opera that was reflective of heterogeneous plots, and he favored pantomime, in which music and plot could be combined without the specificity of words: "Opera conceals, united in itself, all the means and forms which otherwise only come into practice singly in music. It allows them and requires them. It gives the opportunity for making use of them collectively or in groups. The domain of the opera extends over the simple song, march, and dance tunes, to the most complicated counterpoint, from the song to orchestra, from the 'worldly' to the 'spiritual'—and still further—the unlimited space over which it disposes qualifies it to take in every kind and style of music and to reflect every mood."[72]

Gruenberg's *Die Götterbraut* likewise features a pantomime and extended textless instrumental dance sections. He also aims for stylistic diversity in music. However, his vision was that music in opera would resemble music in film, a connection Busoni never made explicitly, even if scholars have claimed his operas are "cinematic."[73] In the following passage, he uses the term "music" to refer to instrumental music or instrumental music plus voice. As Gruenberg points out, there are many other textures, genres, and styles that can be employed in opera as well, including a capella choral music and rhythmic (unpitched) accompaniment. He envisioned opera in which the full variety of styles and types of music would follow in cinematic succession: "The opera will have the greatest range of change. There will be greater interplay between music and action, scenes without music at all (there is too much music in opera anyway), choral expression without music, only a rhythmic accompaniment to pantomime, possibly the film idea applied to stage, and possibly a total absence of scenery."[74]

In addition, Busoni viewed opera in nationalist terms. He had been preoccupied with establishing a new national form of opera in 1908, precisely when he was working with Gruenberg, and this informed Gruenberg's own quest to write nationalist American operas. It was in Verona in September 1908 that he began planning to create a national Italian form of opera.[75] He immersed himself in potential topics based on figures such as Leonardo da Vinci. His nationalist project, however, unlike Gruenberg's, never materialized in the way he envisioned it. His *Doktor Faust*, BV 303, ended up being a cosmopolitan blend of musical traits and figures.

Gruenberg likewise dreamed of creating a nationalistic form of opera in his own adopted country, America, and he did it in the polystylistic manner of Busoni's mature operas, especially *Doktor Faust*, BV 303, in which learned counterpoint, polychoral vocal writing and a Baroque instrumental suite coexist in response to the plot. However, he took Busoni's model in a new "American" direction. It was Gruenberg who made the connection between Busoni and his attempts at American opera. His plan was not to come up with a radically new art, but rather art that was modified to reflect the landscape in which he had been placed: "Busoni says the function of an artist is to CREATE laws, not to follow ready-made ones. This thought is of extreme importance when the subject of creating an American expression in opera is considered. Since the present continually receives material from the past, original matter simply does not exist. Some of it may be less familiar to our ears, as a landscape newly observed. But mountain, water, or plain are made up of the same materials everywhere and so are the ingredients of art the same throughout the ages."[76]

The Emperor Jones, op. 36 (1933), based on a 1920 play of the same title by Eugene O'Neill, was Gruenberg's most successful attempt at an American opera. It was only the eleventh American opera to premiere at the Metropolitan Opera and dealt with a topic that resonated with US ideals of unlimited possibilities as an African American ex-convict remakes himself and becomes a rich ruler. The music includes jazz and spirituals within a broader classical frame. However, his view of American opera extended beyond the incorporation of a style of indigenous music into a classical form. He realized that the American identity could not be reduced to any single style—"Bostonian accents," "polychromatic, perspiring human hash of New York," "the homely song of the frontiersmen of the North," or "the boisterous, uproarious, laughing westerners."[77] He instead identified distinctively American characteristics that he tried to incorporate into his music: "speed, restlessness, mystery, ballyhoo, display, and uplift quality."[78]

It was not only in opera that Busoni had a major impact on Gruenberg but also in symphonic music, which he began writing in Vienna while working with Busoni for the first time (see table 4.4). His influence can be observed in the manner of orchestration and in the approach toward form and extra-musical associations. His ideals of orchestration mirror Busoni's in their insistence on sustained sound and on melody: "The orchestra is a LEGATO instrument; that is to say that sustained notes are generally to be used; the rhythmic elements are not as a basis, but a contrast."[79] It was Busoni who first stated that orchestration should feature sustained sounds resembling those of the sustain pedal on the piano: "The orchestra, takes over the function of 'the pedals' in the pi-

TABLE 4.4. SYMPHONIC WORKS BY GRUENBERG

DATE	TITLE
1908–1920 (rev. 1960)	*The Hill of Dreams*, op. 10
1915	First Concerto for Piano and Orchestra, op. 8
1921–1930 (rev. 1957)	*Vagabondia*, op. 27
1929	Symphony no. 1, op. 17
1929	*Jazz-Suite for Orchestra*, op. 28
1929	Overture to *Jack and the Beanstalk*, WoO
1930	*The Enchanted Isle*, op. 11
1930	*Prairie Song for Orchestra*, op. 31
1931–1956	*Moods for Orchestra*, op. 29
1934	*Serenade to a Beauteous Lady*, op. 37
1940–1947 (rev. 1963)	*Kubla–Khan*: Symphonic Poem for Voice and Piano or Orchestra, op. 54
1941 (rev. 1963)	Symphony no. 2, op. 43
1941–1942 (rev. 1964)	Symphony no. 3, op. 44
1944	Concerto for Violin and Orchestra, op. 47
1945 (rev. 1964)	*Music to an Imaginary Ballet*, op. 46
1945 (rev. 1964)	*Americana Suite*, op. 48
1947	*Variations on a Pastorale Theme*, op. 51
1954 (rev. 1955)	*The Fight For Life: A Symphonic Synthesis*, WoO
1963	Concerto for Cello and Orchestra, op. 58
1953	*Harlem Rhapsody*, op. 62
n.d.	*Five Country Sketches*, op. 56
n.d.	*Music to a Festive Occasion*, op. 69
n.d.	Symphony no. 5, WoO
n.d.	Symphony no. 6, WoO

anoforte. At times one plays the pianoforte without pedal, yet the right foot is usually active, continually helpful, filling out and joining together, not to speak of the pronounced big pedal effects. This 'right foot' is also indispensable in the orchestra."[80] Additionally, Gruenberg's tendency to move quickly from one instrument group to the next mirrors Busoni's practice and ideals.

Gruenberg, like Busoni, also initially focused on symphonic works with extra-musical associations—Busoni, in fact, never published a "symphony" in the strictest sense of the word. However, he composed symphonic compositions, such as the *Nocturne symphonique*, BV 262 (1912), and the *Berceuse élégiaque*, BV 252 (1909), with descriptive titles and unique forms, yet without narrative programs, when Gruenberg was studying with him. Gruenberg, similarly, avoided explicit narrative, but used human ideas to shape the content and the form. Gruenberg, for instance, describes the ideas that shaped *The Hill of Dreams*, op. 10: "While writing it [*The Hill of Dreams*], I imagined myself once more on the top of my hill [in Vienna], and I tried to convey something of the atmosphere of the blue skies, warm sunshine, and keen upland air. I lived in a memory, which I tried to mirror. I did not seek to tell a story; it is not program music; I just dreamed my dreams, and I hoped that my listener would be inspired to dream his dreams, and if they were as beautiful as mine, I felt that my efforts would be repaid."[81]

Although never published, the composition still exists in the form of two holograph scores plus nine pages of sketches. The title page of the earlier manuscript states the full title on the cover: "The Hill (Isle) of Dreams: Symphonic Poem or Episode for Orchestra."[82] The first page alternatively states yet another possible title: "Symphonic Impression (or poem)."[83] The last page provides a date of completion: "7 days, N.Y., Feb. 13–1920." The draft is notated in short score and contains numerous corrections and crossed-out sections. Instruments are suggested in prose. The title page of the more developed manuscript listed only "The Hill of Dreams" (1920) as the title.[84] He apparently revisited the work again in 1960, although it is unclear which revisions took place then. He did leave the following ideas for the revision: "The tonal part should be retained with some modification (Take away Wagner!), and a new middle section should be added. The composition now to be called 'A Viennese Rhapsody.'"

In the composition, Gruenberg creates thin transparent textures that make the sonorous qualities of each instrument audible. Divisi strings begin with thirty-second note figures that gradually rise over the span of four and a half measures. Visually and aurally, the writing resembles the rising hill Gruenberg mentioned in his memoirs. Floating above this "hill," plucked harmonics on the harp also ascend registrally, featuring two prominent pitches, B and E, before the rustic sound of the bassoon begins a lyrical solo in measure 3. The oboes play a descending chromatic line in measure 4, and the flutes and piccolos punctuate the sound with

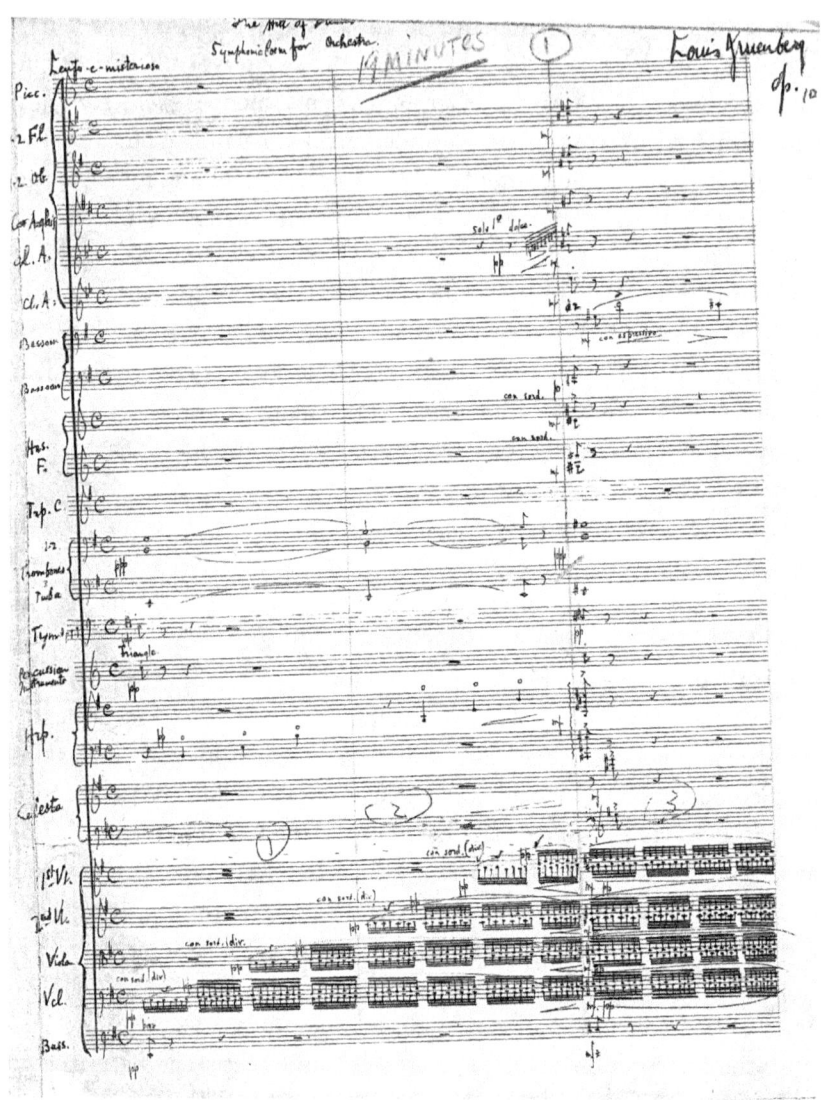

FIGURE 4.4.a, b, c (*above, facing, and the following page*) Gruenberg, The *Hill of Dreams*, mm. 1–9, mss. Louis Gruenberg Papers, Music Division, New York Public Library, Astor, Lenox, and Tilden Foundations, JPB 83–400.

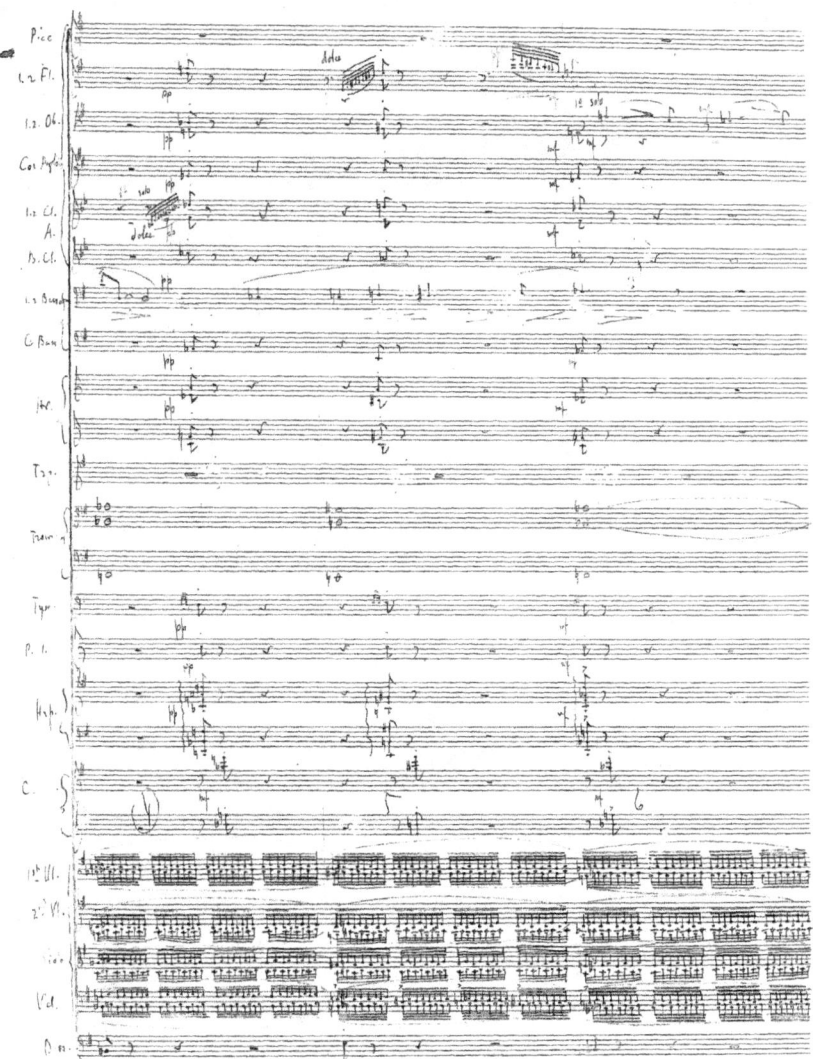

FIGURE 4.4.b

upward scalar interjections. The ensuing tranquillo section, beginning in measure 14, features arpeggios in the harp that support motives passed between instruments, such as a descending chromatic figure passed from oboe and clarinet to piccolo and flute (see figures 4.4a, b, c).

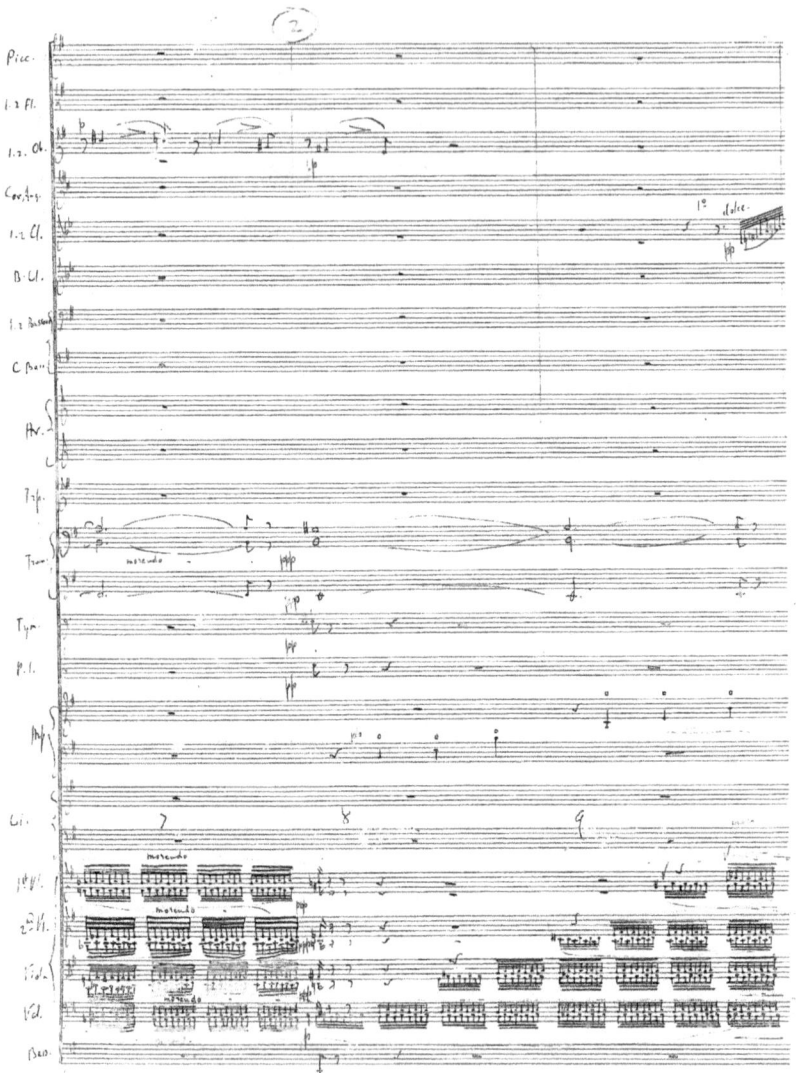

FIGURE 4.4.C

Busoni's influence can also be observed in Gruenberg's treatment of form. He taught that composers needed to be as original in form as in motivic idea.[85] The piece does not fall into any easily recognizable form from the *Formenlehre* tradition. A slow opening introduction in E minor that consists of the rising tremolo figures in the strings frames a harmonically unstable tranquillo section with harp arpeggiations:

Slow Introduction:
A. mm. 1–14, lento e misterioso, E Minor
B. mm. 15–38, tranquillo, harmonically unstable
A. mm. 39–45, E Minor

This slow introduction is repeated at the end of the composition at rehearsal 44 after a retransition section. The slow opening and closing sections, in turn, frame a middle section characterized by dramatic contrasts of key, motivic material, and increased speed. *Meno-mosso/tranquillo* sections centered on an E tonality form a refrain of sorts around *allegro agitato* sections. The *allegro agitato* sections, in turn, contain contrasting musical ideas, some of which derive from the opening section and that pass by in rapid succession. There are some resemblances to rondo form, but the structure is unique:

Formal Structure: *The Hill of Dreams*:
(ABA) CD (A'B') CD (ABA):
ABA. (See Above): mm. 1–44
C. Allegro Agitato: mm. 45–72, harmonically ambiguous (three flats), triplets in strings, rising scalar figures in winds
D. Un poco meno mosso/più mosso: mm. 73–134, dotted rhythms/triplets
A'/B' Andante semplice/Tranquillo: mm. 134–197, E major, undulating figures in strings from opening, but in diminution, and juxtaposed to material from other sections in the tone poem, mixed meters ($_8^6, _2^2, _4^4$)
C. Allegro Agitato: mm. 198–276, 3 flats, dotted rhythms and triplets
D. Un poco meno mosso/allegro: mm. 277–348, dotted rhythms/triplets
Retransition: mm. 352–360
ABA.: mm. 360-end, return of music from slow introduction in E minor

Gruenberg thus gradually developed his own voice in response to Busoni's esoteric ideas about music and expanded the genres in which he worked. New approaches toward form and orchestration were just two of the manifestations. However, this was just a beginning for Gruenberg's musical experimentation that eventually led to an interest in film music and technology.

NEW DIRECTIONS AND THE BURGEONING OF GRUENBERG'S CAREER

Although Busoni primarily focused on the art of composition, he was also concerned about the welfare of his students. Gruenberg achieved his first major successes in Europe, and Busoni's concert and career promotion was an important factor. Already by November 1909, he was able to announce to his mother that he had a full schedule of piano recitals: "I expect to come to America in January 1910. It is very possible that I will be engaged in twenty concerts. On December 10 I will play in Berlin with orchestra and Busoni will conduct. I expect to play November 20 in Bonn (the birthplace of Beethoven) on November 26 in Worpswede (an artist colony), and the first of December in Bremen. At last I am commencing to find my way. It was hard and is not yet finished but I have very good success every time I play."[86]

Throughout the time Gruenberg spent in Europe, Busoni was his advocate, conducting his orchestral premiere in Berlin and encouraging him to go on concert tours outside of Germany.[87] In 1913, he traveled as far as Finland and visited Sibelius by dog sled.

Busoni also helped launch Gruenberg's career as a composer. In 1909, one of his compositions placed second in a highly competitive competition. Busoni was one of three judges—the others were Gustav Hollaender (1855–1915) and Philipp Scharwenka (1847–1917).[88] The *Signale für die musikalische Welt* issued an announcement in May 1909 for a composition competition that attracted 874 entries. Of the entries, Gruenberg's ranked second. Monetary prizes ranged from 500 marks for first place to 100 marks for fifth through tenth place.[89]

When the results were announced on December 8, 1909, Émile Blanchet, Louis Gruenberg, Willy Renner, Gisella Selden-Goth were the top prizewinners, in that order.[90] All but Willy Renner were pupils of Busoni. Even though contributors were instructed to choose a motto for the composition that could be used in lieu of their name in order to preserve anonymity, it is hard to believe the assessment was unbiased given the number of Busoni pupils selected as winners. Regardless, the results of winning helped launch Gruenberg's compositional career.[91] The top ten piano compositions were subsequently published in a collected volume.[92]

Gruenberg's first full composition concert also took place in Berlin, and another of Busoni's pupils, Petri, participated in the performance. The concert included lied, pieces for solo piano, and a suite for violin and piano. Although Busoni was touring at the time and unable to attend, he was anxious to hear how it went. Writing to Petri from London, he stated: "About Gruenberg's Evening, I would gladly hear a report."[93]

Concert Program for Gruenberg's First Composition Concert
Klindworth-Scharwenka-Saal
Dienstag den. 1. Oktober 1912 abends 8 Uhr
Kompositionen
Von
L.T. Grünberg
Mitwirkende:
Die Herren Professor Carl Flesch (Violine),
Egon Petri (Klavier), Hermann Weisshorn (Bariton)
Und der Komponist.
Programm
1. Suite für Violine und Klavier, op. 3
1. Allegro scorrendo
2. Allegretto con civitteria
3. Andante con espressione
4. Presto giocoso
Professor Carl Flesch und Herr Egon Petri
2. Impressionen—Dreizehn Klavierstücke, op. 4
Prolog—Suleika—Trauerlied—Der Gaukler—Wolken—
    Tanz eines Somali-Weibes—Kobold—Idylle—Karawane—
    Haremstanz—Arabischer Tanz—Eine Traum-Burlesque
Der Komponist
3. Sechs Lieder, op. 5
1. Wellentanzlied (R. Dehmel)

2. Vision (T. von Schaeffer)
3. Ich schaute in den Garten (M. Dauthendey)
4. Hans, der Schuster (H. Benzmann)
5. Maimond aus "Reliquien" (M. Dauthendey)
6. Erfüllung (S. Zweig)
Hermann Weissenborn—am Klavier: Der Komponist[94]

Aspects of Gruenberg's personal style are already evident in these early Berlin pieces. The Suite for Violin and Piano, op. 3, features tonal ambiguity and unconventional formal structures.[95] Although the first movement begins and ends in E, the key is not established through traditional means, nor does it help define important structural moments. At the same time a striking new approach appears—harmonies derive from melodic and thematic material that is fragmented, augmented, or chromatically altered. Since the derivation of harmonies from melodic material was very much on Busoni's mind in 1913, it is likely that Gruenberg was applying a theory he had discussed with Busoni. In measure 1, for instance, the pitches in the violin suggest a pentatonic collection (E, F sharp, G sharp, A sharp, C sharp). Although the piano initially plays the pitches of an E major triad, the second chord in the piece is an unexpected F-sharp major ninth. When the C-sharp leads to a D, and then an arpeggiated C major triad in the violin part in measure 2, the harmony shifts to the flat submediant. It is the melodic and thematic material that drives the harmony forward through a plethora of chords that would otherwise seem unrelated in measures 1–9 and beyond: E, F-sharp9, C, A, B, E, A-sharp dim.7, G-sharp, D-sharp7, E-sharp, E, B-flat7, F7, E (see example 4.4).

Busoni not only promoted his young protégé in the concert world; he also helped him with more practical matters. Gruenberg struggled financially throughout his career, and Busoni did his best to help him find more regular employment. Letters in the private collection of Joan Gruenberg Cominos from 1911 provide records of two instances when Busoni recommended him for professional positions. The first position was offered by Franz Kaim, the son of a piano manufacturer and a known concert promoter in Munich. Writing from America, Busoni recommended Gruenberg to Kaim for a performance position, but nothing seems to have come of this:

MUSIC EXAMPLE 4.4. Gruenberg, Suite for Violin and Piano, mm. 1–17.

San Francisco, March 20, 1911

Dear Louis Theodor-Amadeus,

The Munich Councilor Dr. Kaim asked me about the name of an excellent soloist who also possesses intelligence for chamber music. This could (with a chamber music orientation) earn 4000 Marks in six winter months.

I received the letter dated 16 Feb. only now here in California, but I wrote today and immediately communicated your name (and address).

Best wishes and goodbye,

Your friendly and devoted
Ferruccio Busoni[96]

A second letter just one month later brought the sad news of the suicide of another of Busoni's pupils, but also the mention of another possibility of employment:

April 24, 1911

Dear Gruenberg,

Please let me know:
1) Whether you received the letter about court counselor Kaim;
2) Whether you would like to compete for the position in Montreal.

With heartfelt greetings to you.

Yours truly,
Ferruccio Busoni

P.S.
Perhaps you have already found out about the terrible news that my dear O'Neill Phillips shot himself![97]
I have directed today a series of inquiries related to his successorship in Montreal.
Here you could at least overcome shyness.
McGill University's Conservatory of Music in Montreal, Canada (Dr Peterson).[98]

Busoni also tried to help Gruenberg professionally by introducing him to other contemporary composers, including Edgard Varèse and Arnold Schoenberg (and his circle). This led to several important engagements, the first of which took place in Berlin in 1912 when he collaborated in concert with several of Schoenberg's pupils.[99]

Program of February 4, 1912, featuring Schoenberg's New Music:

Harmonium-Saal, Steglitzer Strasse 35
Sonntag, den. 4. Februar 1912, mittags 12 Uhr
Morgen-Konzert
Kompositionen von
Arnold Schönberg
Mitwirkende:
Martha Winternitz-Dorda (Sopran)
Opernsängerin am Hamburger Stadttheater
Louis Closson (Klavier und Celesta) L.T. Grünberg (Klavier)
Max Saal (Harfe) Eduard Steuermann (Klavier)
Dr. A. von Webern (Harmonium)
Vortragsfolge:
1. Gesänge mit Klavierbegleitung (ältere Kompositionen)
a) Verlassen b) Am Wegrand c) Mädchenlied d) Der Wanderer e) Waldsonne
Martha Winternitz-Dorda und Eduard Steuermann
2. Sechs Klavierstücke (komp. 1911)
Louis Closson
3. "Das Buch der hängenden Gärten," Liederzyklus (komp. 1908)
Martha Winternitz-Dorda and Eduard Steuermann
4. "Herzgewächse" für Sopran, Harmonium, Celesta und Harfe (komp. 1911)
Martha Winternitz-Dorda, Dr. A. von Webern, Louis Closson, und Max Saal
5. Drei Orchesterstücke (komp. 1909) für zwei Klaviere achthändig arrangiert von Kapellmeister Erwin Stein[100]

> Gruenberg left the following recollection of the event: "At the request of Busoni I offered to play a fourth piano part of Schoenberg's Three Orchestral Pieces, arranged for two pianos; my partner was von Webern. He was such a fanatic, that he pounded the piano so unmercifully, that Schoenberg himself protested at rehearsals saying that what he (Webern) was playing were muted trombones.[101]

Although Busoni did not perform in the concert, he was in the audience, and had been actively promoting Schoenberg in Berlin.[102] Busoni's review of the concert was mixed, although he praised the performance of Gruenberg and the other pianists: "Finally, three pieces on two pianos for eight hands. At the keyboards sit four young men with fine characteristic heads: to see them place their young intelligences, submissive and efficient, at the service of what is still an unsolved riddle, makes an almost impressive effect."[103]

Busoni continued to help Gruenberg professionally in the United States after his hasty return to the United States in 1914 due to the outbreak of World War I, where he struggled to make a living by working various odd jobs, including as theater director at the Garrick Theater (originally Harrigan's Theater) in New York.[104] He experienced constant disappointment with publishers and concert agents. In a letter to Busoni, Gruenberg mentioned that he had tried unsuccessfully to get pieces published by Breitkopf and Härtel and to earn money from Steinway for a concerto. He claimed in desperation that he earned enough through teaching only to buy cigars.[105] During these years, Gruenberg managed to have only one piece published, his Suite for Violin and Piano, op. 3, in 1914 by Schirmer, and was not able to give a major recital in New York until 1919 (February 14, 1919, in Aeolian Hall), when he played a Beethoven sonata, Busoni's arrangements of Bach's Toccata in D Minor (BWV 564), BV B29, and a *Mephisto Waltz* by Liszt as well as some of his own compositions.[106] His next break was a tour as accompanist for Enrico Caruso in 1920. Busoni, for his part, could not understand how Americans could so neglect their own artists.[107]

Busoni continued to promote Gruenberg whenever he could. For instance, in August 1915, he suggested that Harriet Lanier should consider scheduling a performance of Schoenberg's *Pierrot Lunaire* for her "Society of the Friends of Music."[108] In this context, he specifically mentioned Gruenberg and his familiarity with Schoenberg. Unfortunately, nothing seems to have transpired as a result of this recommendation.[109]

In addition, some of the connections Gruenberg had made through Busoni began to aid his career even in America in the 1920s, especially Varèse. Some of his compositions premiered in Varèse's International Composers' Guild (ICG), New York Branch, concerts. For instance, Gruenberg's *Polychromatics,* op. 16, appeared on the first program of the ICG in 1922 and a "Fantasy" appeared in a program in 1923.[110] At one of the early concerts of the ICG that took place on February 4, 1923, in Klaw Theater, Schoenberg's *Pierrot Lunaire*, op. 21, received its American premiere with Gruenberg conducting.[111]

Gruenberg soon followed in Busoni's and Varèse's footsteps in helping promote new music concerts. He helped found several societies, including the International Society for Contemporary Music, the American Music Guild, devoted to performances of American music, and the League of Composers, which was started by a group of composers splitting off from the ICG in 1923.[112] The American Music Guild wrote that its goal was to "encourage and give support to the production of new and significant works. It will effect cooperation between composers of all nations, and give well-planned performances of new music selected from every school. While first performances will be a feature of the League's concerts, they will not exclude such modern works as may have been given before and which are of sufficient importance to be given a re-hearing."[113]

Several of Gruenberg's works were performed by the society, including *The Daniel Jazz*, op. 21, and *The Creation*, op. 23. The initial concert featured the following works:

> Albert Stoessel, Sonata in G for Violin and Piano
> Frederick Jacobi, Charles M. Loeffler, and John Alden Carpenter, Songs for soprano
> Sandor Harmati, String Quartet (unfinished), two movements
> Louis Gruenberg, Concerto for piano in one movement[114]

Gruenberg's concert promotion activities soon reached an international scale. He returned to Europe as a delegate to the first International Society for Contemporary Music Festival that was held in Salzburg in August 1923 at the request of Busoni's friend and the current president, Edward Dent. Gruenberg subsequently attended every year until 1938 when Dent ceased to be president. From 1928 to 1932, he also served as president of the American branch of the International Society for Contemporary Music.[115]

EPILOGUE: FILM SCORES AND THE FUTURE OF MUSIC

Busoni was the most important composition teacher Gruenberg would ever have. Busoni, for his part, was deeply touched by Gruenberg and considered him an important student and friend. His letters to Gruenberg are filled with admiration and respect. Gruenberg's excursions into opera and symphonic music were informed by his lessons with Busoni, as were his music aesthetics. Moreover, it was through Busoni that he began to develop his own musical voice and to expand the genres in which he wrote. Yet even though he absorbed many of Busoni's ideas, he took them in new directions, especially in his development of American music, radio music, and film music, thereby helping to realize the future of music of which Busoni spoke.[116]

Building upon Busoni's predictions about music, Gruenberg also wrote down his own dreams about the future of music that melded opera and technology in ways Busoni did not even imagine. He envisioned that opera would soon be associated with film and new technologies, such as the radio. He predicted that opera would be listened to by people in the solitude of their homes in the future:

> Also Opera will not remain in the present state of existence, and it will not remain in the present state, it will be associated with film (as has been so often tried today with varying degrees of success) and must be supplied by radio delivered to the listener. That very thing that I said about the symphony is valid in a much stronger sense in relation to opera.... I see suddenly a strange vision before me: a city of millions, the streets eerily empty, one hears and sees nothing, but in every soundproof and closed room people are sitting, listening to their opera film or symphonic work in full enjoyment without anything else to interfere.[117]

During the 1940s, Gruenberg tried fulfilling his dreams in ways that Busoni could not have done in his own age. He sought to create art film scores based on principles of composition gleaned from Busoni (see table 4.5).[118] He applied many of the same techniques he had used in his operas, including episodic and polystylistic music in response to the plot coupled with underlying thematic development. He also paid close attention to the orchestrations. His projects were amply rewarded with three Oscar nominations in his own day, but have been largely forgotten in our time.

In *The Fight for Life* (1940), a documentary about maternal mortality rates among the lower class, Gruenberg aimed to create a score that contributed to the dramatic action and that conveyed meaning when words were inadequate. His description of the music glosses Busoni's own writing about opera aesthetics in terms of the interplay between the music and the action and in his insistence that what mattered was not the genre or

TABLE 4.5. FILM SCORES BY GRUENBERG

YEAR	TITLE
1940	*The Fight For Life* (Academy Award nominee for Best Score)
1941	*So Ends Our Night* (Academy Award nominee for Best Score)
1942	*Commandos Strike at Dawn* (Academy Award nominee for Best Score)
1944	*An American Romance*
1945	*Counter-Attack*
1947	*Gangster*
1948	*Arch of Triumph*
1948	*Smart Women*
1949	*All the King's Men* (Golden Globe nominee for Best Score)
1950	*Quicksand*

venue, but the quality of the music. According to Busoni, there was no difference between music written for church or theater or concert, between dance, fugue, or sonata—all music formed a oneness that was divided into categories only by mankind. What mattered was the quality. For Busoni, the ideal realization of this musical oneness was opera, because good plots invited stylistic diversity in the music.[119] Gruenberg's description of his compositional approach sounds like a near quotation of Busoni, yet applied to film sound tracks rather than opera:

> There are parts in "The Fight for Life" where music practically illuminates the inner thoughts of human beings on the screen, totally unaccompanied by dialogue or narration. In other words, music has the primary emphasis in its own right. There are, of course, times when music takes a secondary role, as it does also in opera. As in opera, there are times when human action is so important that no other form of expression is possible. It is generally accepted that serious music today has no place in the scheme of screen plays, again with rare exceptions. In this case I have made no attempt to write down to the level of usual screen music. The film itself is of such importance that anything trivial or light would be completely out of place. Therefore, I have written as good music as I am capable of writing and can find no difference in its quality from either my symphonic or operatic compositions.[120]

Gruenberg's score is organized around musical contrast and the formal structure is unique. Nisbett claims that there are twenty-four different sections that subdivide four larger ones. Connecting all the sections is a metric pulse imitating and signifying the varied heartbeats of mother and baby.[121] The diverse sections vary in relation to the plot and include two lullabies, a policeman's march in the street, and a night walk scene. In addition, there is jazz improvised by Joe Sullivan and the Café Society Band incorporated into the score, and music written in a classical Viennese style.

Gruenberg also dreamed about other ways opera and music could be melded with new technology. At the end of his life, Busoni watched silent films in his home while his students accompanied, as Gottfried Galston recorded in his diary.[122] Yet Busoni became increasingly disillusioned with and distanced from modern technology in his maturity, even while Gruenberg continued to embrace the newest developments to the end of his life. He dreamed about a future in which music and technology were melded in then unprecedented ways. Many of the ideas are now realized, but for Gruenberg, they were merely visions and dreams. A few include musical scores projected on a screen while music progresses in time, a way to type without changing sheets of paper, multi-media compositions, and electronic means of manipulating dynamics:

1. A laboratory for students where commentary and music on gramophone records are synchronized with a film which shows the page of the musical score as it is being discussed or heard.
2. A gramophone manual of orchestration
3. (August 15, 1931). An addition to a typewriter which will enable it to continue to type without the necessity of changing sheets of paper. At the back of the machine a roll of paper is placed which unfolds itself in connection with the moving part above. Near the top of the roll, paper moves through a bar under which a knife is placed so that any length can be cut at will. The roll could also be prepared with a duplicate. This would be an advantage to writers.
4. (September 29, 1931). Each composition should be published with the composer's comments throughout—regrets, appreciations, etc., in the margin. Possibly a new form of music work could be developed, something like a book with pictures. This could be a delightful help to the critics, who could forget all about the music and speak only of the comments.

5. Projection idea: two footlights, one running around the back of stage, illuminating the rear; the other in front, lighting up the actor. The rear light is in a machine which is capable of showing moveable scenes in colors (moving in a circle) which should enable the background to show various scenes at great speed. The two footlights (the rear one used to silhouette a figure) should make it possible for the actor to move about without being disturbed by the rear scenery.
6. When the electrification of instruments (all) has been developed to a point wherein the strength can be controlled either to a *pp* or to an extraordinary volume, a machine should be invented which can be attached to the desk of the conductor, enabling him to manipulate with a minimum of effort the various degrees of loudness at will. I can imagine an unearthly impression.
7. I visualize a new sort of musical concert entertainment, the entire program to be under a general idea. Something like this:
a. Introduction—nothing busy, but melodic, for example a concert version of a folk song as *Deep River.*
b. *A soloist—singer, violinist.*
c. *An orchestral number—a brilliant number.*

One of Gruenberg's more notable attempts to realize his dreams was his creation of a radio opera, *Green Mansions,* op. 39, which premiered on October 17, 1937, and was freely adapted from a novel by W. H. Hudson.[123] Gruenberg called the work a "non-visual opera" for the "imagination alone."[124] He stated that when the visual is eliminated, "the inner ear of imagination is substituted."[124] He envisioned it as a complete work—ideally suited for the format. Were it ever to be performed live, he believed it should be performed in complete darkness because the music alone was enough without any visual elements.[125] Although he claimed his approach was not unusual when it came to the musical structure, he did insist that voices be widely varied to make the drama clear, since characters could not be seen. Moreover, he suggested using prerecorded music for certain of the sounds, such as the animals, and amplified sound for others. This was novel in the 1930s. He left the following scenario describing the unseen voices:

The announcer explains the scope, the idea, and the outline of the story. Somewhat like a newspaper headline. Completely impersonal.
Unseen Voices:

1. The various characters
2. Poetic descriptions by a different voice in quality than the characters (or by the voices 3, 4, 5, 6, 7, 8, 9)
3. The winds (men's voices). The storm.
4. The sky (women's voices).
5. The flowers (children's voices).
6. The spirit of the jungle (spoken through a megaphone).
7. The animals of the jungle (voices imitating the various animals all expressing thought relative to the story and its characters). Humming birds.
8. The sobbing of the trees (complete chorus) expressing among themselves their reactions to events, descriptions of pantomime and actions of the characters.
9. The announcer again, this time relating the end of the story, again impersonal.[126]

Gruenberg sought to use the technology available to him in the production, including using microphones to bring into relief sounds that could not otherwise stand above the orchestra. In addition, he used the theremin for the voice of a half-human, half-animal character, Rima.[127] Bruno David Ussher, who interviewed Gruenberg while he was in the process of writing the libretto, describes his vision of channeling technology to create new sounds in this way:

> Gruenberg is conceiving also a specific employment of the microphone by means of which certain instruments can be singled out in unusual solo fashion. A particular instrument, to be brought into dynamic high relief, having reached its own maximum dynamics, will be reinforced by an individual microphone at minimum microphone amplification. As a dramatic situation requires and waxes, then a final and third dynamic sound strength can be achieved by "stepping up" the amplification range of the microphone. Inasmuch as the snakes will speak with the "sound of a whip" and the monkeys by use of phonographic records, quite extraordinary sonorities of every degree may be expected from the technically resourceful and imaginative Mr. Gruenberg.[128]

Just as Busoni's ideas lived on and evolved in the hands of his student, so Gruenberg's ideas were only fully realized after his death with the advent of new technology. Although widely remembered as one of the earliest to pioneer an American musical style, his contributions were also significant in the way he applied serious symphonic and operatic ideals to film and multi-media music as well.

To the end of his life, Gruenberg would look back to Busoni as his spiritual father and as the man who changed the course of his career and life. Busoni provided the stimulus and the foundation, and Gruenberg adapted the ideas to the geographic location in which he lived and to his own era. An exchange of compositions and aesthetic ideas led to the continuation of Busoni's dreams, embodied in Gruenberg's operas and film scores as composite musical works of art that embraced the new technology of a rapidly changing world. Gruenberg's own dreams started coming true on a green hill in Vienna and most have now been realized, either by Gruenberg himself or by his successors, even if he himself has been largely and unjustly forgotten.

NOTES

1. I am indebted to Neil Lerner (Professor, Davidson College) for drawing my attention to Louis Gruenberg, and to Joan Gruenberg Cominos, Jonathan Hiam (New York Public Library), Pam Juengling (University of Massachusetts Amherst), Laura Mills (Roosevelt University), Theresa Rowe (McGill University), and Bradley Short (Gaylord Music Library, Washington University in St. Louis) for their assistance in locating documents and scores. Joan Gruenberg Cominos and Robert Nisbett also commented on earlier versions of the chapter. The original German for the epigraph is as follows: "19 mal musste ich vorsprechen, bevor es mir gelang, bis zu dem Mann zu dringen, der für mich immer eine Idealgestalt bleiben wird—Ferruccio Busoni, der edelste Mensch und weitblickende Künstler, der Grösste, den ich auf meinem Lebensweg getroffen habe." Louis Gruenberg, "Vom Jazz und ander Dingen: Ruckblick und Ausblick," *25 Jahre neue Musik, Jahrbuch der 1926 Universal Edition* (Vienna: Universal Edition, 1926), 230.

2. Hans Heinz Stuckenschmidt, *Ferruccio Busoni: Chronicle of a European*, trans. Sandra Morris (New York: St. Martin's, 1970), 190.

3. Gruenberg to Busoni, April 1, 1915, Staatsbibliothek zu Berlin, Preußischer Kulturbesitz, Musikabteilung mit Mendelssohn-Archiv, Mus. Nachl. F. Busoni, BII, 1976.

4. Stuckenschmidt, *Ferruccio Busoni: Chronicle of a European*, 190.

5. Robert Franklin Nisbett, "Louis Gruenberg: His Life and Work" (PhD diss., Ohio State University, 1979).

6. See, for instance, the following articles: Rebecca B. Gauss, "O'Neill, Gruenberg and *The Emperor Jones*," *Eugene O'Neill Review* 18:1/2 (Spring/Fall 1994), 38–44; Robert F. Nisbett, "Louis Gruenberg's American Idiom," *American Music* 3:1 (Spring 1985), 25–41; Robin Freeman, "Three 'Years', and Louis Gruenberg," *Tempo* 180 (March 1992), 58–62.

7. Although Abraham Gruenberg was a violinist, he only taught piano, according to Joan Gruenberg Cominos in an email to the author, April 2, 2013. Margulies studied at the Vienna Conservatory and her New York orchestral debut in 1884 was well received. "Amusements: Miss Margulies' Concert," *New York Times*, February 24, 1884. However, her March solo recital was criticized as "mechanical' in interpretation. Margulies joined the faculty of the National Conservatory in 1888. Emanuel Rubin, "Jeannette Meyers Thurber and the National Conservatory of Music," *American Music* 8:3 (Autumn 1990), 300. According to Nisbett, Gruenberg was applying for a scholarship to the conservatory at the age of eight, but became "tongue tied" and did not receive it. Nisbett, "Gruenberg," 10.

8. Gruenberg, diary, quoted in Nisbett, "Gruenberg," 11. The name of the theory instructor was not recorded in Gruenberg's diary, and no other sources seem to have record of the information.

9. It had been over six years since Busoni had taught an official class, and he was hesitant at first to accept a post in an institution after frustrations in other traditional settings, such as the Helsinki Music Institute (1888–1890), the Moscow Conservatory (1890–1891), and the New England Conservatory (1891–1892). Teaching in a master class in Weimar during the summers of 1900–1901 had been rewarding, but it was at the invitation of the Grand Duke Carl Alexander of Saxe-Weimar, and was not subject to the normal requirements or supervision of a music institution. Busoni finally consented to conduct the class at the Vienna Conservatory for one year after securing permission to choose his own pupils and to have complete freedom with regard to the course of study. In addition, he received permission to take extended leaves for the purpose of concertizing, although his extended leave from mid-February to April ended up causing conflict with the administrators. Edward Dent, *Ferruccio Busoni: A Biography* (1933; London: Eulenberg Books, 1970), 158.

10. That Gruenberg took a job as a percussionist is mentioned by Joan Cominos, email to the author, April 13, 2013.

11. Albert M. Petrak, "Ferruccio Busoni: His Life and Times," http://www.rprf.org/PDF/Busoni_Bio.pdf, accessed April 9, 2013.

12. Nisbett, "Louis Gruenberg," 14.

13. Gruenberg, "Conversations," 1962, private collection of Joan Gruenberg Cominos. There is also a collection entitled "Conversations with Myself," Gruenberg Papers, Special Collections Research Center, Syracuse University Libraries, Box 1.

14. Dent, *Ferruccio Busoni*, 160.

15. Ibid., 166. Other pieces that evening included the Busoni-Bach Chaconne in D Minor (BWV 1004), BV B24, two Bach-Busoni chorale preludes, and his own recently composed *All'Italia! in modo napolitano* and *Turandots Frauengemach (Intermezzo)*, from his collection of piano elegies, BV 249 (1907).

16. Louis Gruenberg Papers, Box 8, Folder 3, New York Public Library, Special Collections.

17. Busoni summarized the class in a letter to Ludwig von Bösendorfer. Busoni to Ludwig von Bösendorfer, July 7, 1908, in Busoni, *Selected Letters*, trans. Antony Beaumont (New York: Columbia University Press, 1987), 91.

18. Busoni to Egon Petri, June 3, 1908, in Beaumont, *Selected Letters*, 90.

19. Busoni to Gerda Busoni, June 19, 1908, King's College Archive Centre, Cambridge, Papers of Edward Joseph Dent, EJD.
20. Gruenberg, "Conversations" (1962), Private Collection of Joan Gruenberg Cominos.
21. Bernard van Dieren, quoted in Beaumont, *Busoni the Composer* (Bloomington: Indiana University Press, 1985), 156.
22. Busoni, preface to *An die Jugend*, BV 254, 1909, reprinted in Busoni, *Von der Einheit der Musik: Von Dritteltönen und junger Klassizität, von Bühnen und Bauten und anschliessenden Bezirken*, ed. Martina Weindel, Quellenkataloge zur Musikgeschichte, ed. Richard Schaal, vol. 36 (Wilhelmshaven: Florian Noetzel Verlag, 2006), 39. Excerpt also reprinted in Beaumont, *Busoni the Composer*, 157.
23. Louis Gruenberg Papers, Box 8, Folder 6, New York Public Library, Special Collections.
24. Ibid., Box 7, Folder 6.
25. Ibid., Box 9, Folder 3.
26. Ibid., Box 9, Folder 3.
27. Ibid., Box 9, Folder 3.
28. "An Freund L.T. Gruenberg mit allen guten Gefühlen, New York 1915 F. Busoni." Ibid., Box 7, Folder 10.
29. Busoni was in London in February 1921 and in Paris in March 1922. Gruenberg wrote to Busoni in December 1920 about his impending visit to Europe and his desire to see him. Gruenberg to Busoni, December 5, 1920, Staatsbibliothek zu Berlin, Preußischer Kulturbesitz, Musikabteilung mit Mendelssohn-Archiv, Mus. Nachl. F. Busoni, BII, 1980. Gruenberg was in Salzburg for the Festival of the International Society for Contemporary Music, which met August 2–7, 1923. Even though Busoni's *Fantasia contrappuntistica* for two pianos was performed, Busoni was too ill to travel. Gruenberg must have visited him in Berlin. A letter discussing this possibility is preserved in the Staatsbibliothek zu Berlin, Preußischer Kulturbesitz, Musikabteilung mit Mendelssohn-Archiv, Mus. Nachl. F. Busoni, BI, 571.
30. Louis Gruenberg Papers, Box 14.
31. Tamara Levitz, "Teaching Young Classicality: Busoni's Master Class in Composition, 1921–1924" (PhD diss., Eastman School of Music, 1993), 123.
32. Ibid., 391.
33. The lessons continued afterward in Berlin as well.
34. In a letter to Busoni, Gruenberg claimed that the performance was only mediocre even though it was conducted by Walter Damrosch. Gruenberg to Busoni, January 26, 1922. Staatsbibliothek zu Berlin, Preußischer Kulturbesitz, Musikabteilung mit Mendelssohn-Archiv, Mus. Nachl. F. Busoni, BII 1981. Gruenberg's memoirs state the following about composition in Vienna: "I was a master pupil at the Vienna Conservatory at this time, studying with Busoni; it was at his insistence that I toured through Norway, Sweden, Russia, and Austria. My main ambition was to write all the time. I did find a few hours each day to devote to composition, and in collaboration with Busoni wrote an opera, which was to have its initial performance in the summer of 1914. The outbreak of the war, however, interrupted all my plans, and I had to leave my study and work in Europe at once." "Louis Gruenberg and the

Flagler Prize," *International Interpreter: The International News Weekly* (April 15, 1922), 18.

35. "Louis Gruenberg and the Flagler Prize," 18.

36. Gruenberg, diary, 10, quoted in Nisbett, "Louis Gruenberg," 21.

37. Gruenberg to Busoni, August 30, 1919, Staatsbibliothek zu Berlin, Preußischer Kulturbesitz, Musikabteilung mit Mendelssohn-Archiv, Mus. Nachl. F. Busoni, BII, 1979. The opus numbers listed here are not consistent with the order in which he composed the pieces or published them. A more current accepted numbering is found in the list of works in the New Grove Dictionary. Robert F. Nisbett, "Gruenberg, Louis," *Grove Music Online, Oxford Music Online*, http://www.oxfordmusiconline.com/subscriber/article/grove/music/11863, accessed April 29, 2014.

38. Gruenberg, "Conversations" (1962), Private Collection of Joan Gruenberg Cominos.

39. Busoni, Gruenberg's copy of Busoni, *Sketch of New Esthetic of Music*, trans. Th. Baker (New York: G. Schirmer, 1911), private collection of Joan Gruenberg Cominos.

40. These additional include the following:

Page 1. Gruenberg boxed the whole quotation beginning, "What seek you?" He also boxed the last paragraph beginning "it is true, that admirable works of genius arise in every period."

Page 2. Gruenberg boxed the first paragraph discussing "the spirit of an art-work." He also boxed the middle of paragraph 3: "There is nothing properly modern— only things which have come into being earlier or later; longer in bloom, or sooner withered. The Modern and the Old have always been."

Page 3. Gruenberg boxed the following "But all arts, resources, and forms ever aim at the one end, namely the imitation of nature and the interpretation of human feelings."

Page 4. He underlined the passage beginning with the following: "We have formulated rules, stated principles, laid down laws;—we apply laws made for maturity to a child that knows nothing of responsibility!"

Page 5. He underlined the passage beginning: "Music was born free; and to win freedom is its destiny. It will become the most complete of all reflexes of Nature by reason of its untrammeled immateriality."

Page 9. Gruenberg boxed the following: "Wagner, a Germanic Titan, who touched our earthly horizon in orchestral tone-effect, who intensified the form of expression, but fashioned it into a *system* (music drama, declamation, leading-motive), is on this account incapable of further intensification. His category begins and ends with himself."

Page 12. Gruenberg placed a big box from "Begin with the most self-evident of all, the debasement of Tone to noise" to the end of paragraph. In the middle, he underlined the following, "march-rhythm to signify measured strides, the chorale as vehicle for religious feeling. Add to the above the characterization of nationalities.—national instruments and airs —and we have the complete inventory of the arsenal of program-music." In the right margin he wrote, "Engel uses this."

Page 22. Gruenberg placed a big box around the section beginning: "The creator should take over. . . ." He underlined most things in the following passage: "For his individual case he should seek out and formulate a fitting individual law. . . . The function of the creative artist consists in making laws, not in following laws ready-made. . . . But an intentional avoidance of rules cannot masquerade as creative power, and still less engender it."

Page 29. Gruenberg boxed the following: "I have made an attempt to exhaust the possibilities of the arrangement of degrees within the seven-tone scale; and succeeded by raising and lowering the intervals, in establishing *one hundred and thirteen different scales.*"

Page 32. Gruenberg boxed Busoni's graph of microtones.

Page 42. He underlined the following: "One longs to exclaim, 'Avoid Routine!'"

41. "Louis Gruenberg and the Flagler Prize," 18.

42. Busoni, "Young Classicism" (Busoni to Paul Bekker, February 7, 1920), in *The Essence of Music and Other Papers*, 20.

43. "Auch die *Formen* werden sich ändern, die Architektur wird bildlich verwendet werden, so dass Bauten wie die Pyramiden, Wolkenkratzer, Tempel in ihrer äusseren Form ein Wiederspiel in der Musik finden werden." Gruenberg, "Vom Jazz und ander Dingen," 236.

44. Gruenberg, "Conversations with Myself," Gruenberg Papers, Special Collections Research Center, Syracuse University Libraries, 14.

45. Ibid., 9.

46. Busoni, *Sketch*, 4.

47. Busoni signed and gave him the small bound program book of his cycle of concerts in Berlin in which he performed concerti from Bach to Liszt in four programs (on October 29, November 5, November 12, and November 19, 1898), and this, no doubt, was an inspiration for Gruenberg's own recitals. Louis Gruenberg Papers, Box 7, Folder 6, New York Public Library, Special Collections. The meaning of the "Gs," some underlined and some not, after the titles of certain compositions, is not specified.

48. Gruenberg to Busoni, February 14, 1909, Staatsbibliothek zu Berlin, Preußischer Kulturbesitz, Musikabteilung mit Mendelssohn-Archiv, Mus. Nachl. F. Busoni, BII, 1975.

49. Gruenberg, "Conversations with Myself," January 15, 1938, Gruenberg Papers, Syracuse University Library, Special Collections, 35; Gruenberg, "Conversations" (1962), Private Collection of Joan Gruenberg Cominos.

50. Gruenberg, "Conversations" (1962), private collection of Joan Gruenberg Cominos.

51. Additional early sketches for a piano sonata and a cello sonata reside in the New York Public Library, Special Collections, Gruenberg Papers, Box 12, Folder 9.

52. Nisbett, "Louis Gruenberg," 87.

53. Gruenberg, "Interview for Recording Purposes Concerning the Federal Music Project," Gruenberg Papers, Special Collections Research Center, Syracuse University Libraries.

54. Busoni to Jarnach, March 28, 1916, quoted in Tamara Levitz, "Teaching New Classicality: Busoni's Master Class in Composition, 1921–24" (PhD diss., University of Rochester, 1993), 111.

55. "Dem lieber Freunde und unvergleichlichen Lehrer als kleines Zeichen der Dankbarkeit und Verehrung von Egon Petri, Weimar Juli 1901." Gruenberg's copy of Mozart's *Le Nozze di Figaro*, K. 492, Louis Gruenberg Papers, Box 8, Folder 8, New York Public Library, Special Collections.

56. Gruenberg's copy of Mozart's *Le Nozze di Figaro*, K. 492, Louis Gruenberg Papers, Box 8, Folder 8, New York Public Library, Special Collections, pp. 144, 227, and 245.

57. Ibid., 92.

58. Ibid., 227.

59. Louis Gruenberg Papers, Box 10, Folder 6, New York Public Library, Special Collections.

60. Ibid., Box 11, Folder 17.

61. Busoni wrote in a letter to his wife dated April 30, 1908, that he was pleased with Gruenberg and the extent of his literary knowledge. King's College Archive Centre, Cambridge, Papers of Edward Joseph Dent, EJD.

62. Louis Gruenberg Papers Box 11, Folders 19–22, New York Public Library, Special Collections.

63. Busoni to H. W. Draber, August 24, 1908, in Beaumont, *Selected Letters*, 99.

64. E.T.A. Hoffmann, *Signor Formica* (1820) (Adelaide: University of Adelaide, 2012), http://ebooks.adelaide.edu.au/h/hoffmann/eta/formica/complete.html, accessed April 14, 2013.

65. The *Witch of Brocken*, op. 1, composed in 1912, was an operetta. Busoni, *Die Götterbraut: Heroisch-heiteres Sagenspiel in 3 Bildern von Ferruccio Busoni*, http://www.rodoni.ch/busoni/Faust/gotterbraut.html, accessed April 17, 2013. The manuscript states that Gruenberg worked on the opera from June to December 1913. On the cover to the 1913 score, he wrote: "Poor baby wanted to write an opera so badly!—he did so oh, so badly!" Gruenberg, *Die Götterbraut*, New York Public Library, Special Collections, JPB 78–31.

66. Artur Bodansky (1877–1939) was an Austrian conductor who became head of the German repertory at the Met Opera under Arturo Toscanini in 1915 as a result of Busoni's recommendation.

67. Bodansky, quoted in Gruenberg to Busoni, January 31, 1916, Staatsbibliothek zu Berlin, Preußischer Kulturbesitz, Musikabteilung mit Mendelssohn-Archiv, Mus. Nachl. F. Busoni, BII, 1978.

68. The *Mahabharata* is an epic poem from ancient India that provides a narrative about the Kurukshetra War. The story of Damayanti is a placed within the larger narrative. Authorship is believed to be by Vyasa, a major character in the poem.

69. Busoni, "The Essence and Oneness of Music," in *The Essence of Music and Other Papers*, trans. Rosamond Ley (New York: Dover Publications, 1957), 7.

70. Gruenberg, "Conversations with Myself," Gruenberg Papers, Special Collections Research Center, Syracuse University Libraries, 30.

71. Busoni, "The Essence and Oneness of Music," in *The Essence of Music and Other Papers*, 5.

72. Several scholars and critics have claimed that Busoni's operatic style is cinematic. See, for instance, A. Brent-Smith, "Ferruccio Busoni," *Musical Times* 1 (February 1934), 113–116; Friederike Wissmann, *Faust im Musiktheater des zwanzigsten Jahrhunderts* (Berlin: Mensch und Buch Verlag, 2003), 55; Célestin Deliège,"Limiti razionali di un' estetica della libertà," in *Il Flusso del Tempo: Scritti su Ferruccio Busoni*, ed. S. Sablich and R. Dalmonte, Quaderni di Musica, 11 (Milan: Edizioni Unicopli, 1986), 272–281; Frank Hentschel, "Ferruccio Busonis *Doktor Faust*: Eine 'Oper, die keine Oper' ist," *Archiv für Musikwissenschaft* 62:4 (2005), 303–326.

73. Gruenberg, "Conversations with Myself," Gruenberg Papers, Special Collections Research Center, Syracuse University Libraries, 17.

74. Busoni to Gerda Busoni, September 9, 1908, quoted in Edward Dent, "Ferruccio Busoni," 177–178.

75. Gruenberg, "Conversations with Myself," Gruenberg Papers, Special Collections Research Center, Syracuse University Libraries, 32.

76. Gruenberg, "The Future of Opera in America," Gruenberg Papers, Special Collections Research Center, Syracuse University Libraries.

77. Ibid.

78. Louis Gruenberg Papers, Box 13, Folder 2, New York Public Library, Special Collections.

79. Busoni, "The Theory of Orchestration," in *The Essence of Music and Other Papers*, 36.

80. Gruenberg, quoted in "Louis Gruenberg and the Flagler Prize," 18.

81. Louis Gruenberg, "The Hill of Dreams," unpublished manuscript, New York Public Library, Special Collections, JPB 83–399.

82. Ibid.

83. Louis Gruenberg, "The Hill of Dreams," unpublished manuscript, New York Public Library, Special Collections, JPB 83–400.

84. Busoni, *Sketch of a New Esthetic of Music*, trans. Dr. Th. Baker (New York: G. Schirmer, 1911), 7.

85. Gruenberg, diary, 8, in Nisbett, "Louis Gruenberg," 14.

86. It did not hurt matters that Gruenberg also came under the concert direction of Praeger and Meier, Bremen, in 1909. Founded in 1864, it was a well-respected concert agency with a lengthy history.

87. Hollaender was a violinist, conductor, and composer. Scharwenka was a composer and he taught composition and theory at the Musical Academy in Berlin.

88. "Ein Preisausschreiben," *Signale für die musikalische Welt*, May 31, 1909.

89. Gisella-Selden-Goth (1884–1971) wrote a biography about Busoni. Blanchet (1877–1942) had been Busoni's pupil in Weimar and Berlin.

90. "Das Resultat unseres Preisausschreibens," *Signale für die musikalische Welt* 49 (December 8, 1909).

91. "Zehn Preiskompositionen für Klavier die beim Preisausschreiben der 'Signale' von den Preisrichtern Ferruccio Busoni, Gustav Hollaender, Philipp Scharwenka aus den eingesandten 874 Kompositionen mit zehn Preisen im Gesamtsbetrage von 2000 Mark ausgezeichnet worden sind". *Signale für die musikalische Welt* (1910), http://hdl.handle.net/1802/2419, accessed April 23, 2016.

92. "Über Grünberg's Abend würde ich gern berichten hören." Busoni to Egon Petri, October 6, 1912, in *Briefe an Henri, Katharina, und Egon Petri*, ed. Martina Weindel, Taschenbücher zur Musikwissenschaft 129 (Wilhelmshaven: Florian Noetzel, 1999) 193.

93. Program of October 1, 1912, reproduced in Nisbett, "Louis Gruenberg," 19.

94. Gruenberg, Suite for Violin and Piano, op. 3 (New York: G. Schirmer, 1914). Gruenberg also published five impressions for piano as his opus five, but the titles are different from those listed in this composition program. Gruenberg, Five Impressions for Piano, op. 5 (n.p.: Composer's Music Corporation, 1923).

95. S. Francisco den March 20, 1911

Lieber Louis Theodor-Amadeus,

Der Münchner Hofrath Dr. Kaim frägt mich über der Namen eines ausgezeichneter Leute namend voller Soloister, der sie nötige musical Intelligenz für Kammermusik besitz; "dieser könnte (mit einer Kammermusik orientierung) in 6 Wintermonaten 4000 Mk verdienen. Ich erhielt den Brief vom 16 Febr. erst getreu hier in Kalifornien; habe aber heute sofort geschrieben und Ihre Namen (u. Adresse) mitgeteilt. Beste wünsche u. auf wiedersehen.

Ihr herz. ergebener
Ferruccio Busoni

Busoni to Gruenberg, March 20, 1911, private collection of Joan Gruenberg Cominos.

96. O'Neill Phillips was one of Busoni's pupils in Berlin who had been recently living in Montreal. He was apparently imbalanced and shot himself in the head. Busoni was deeply affected by his death.

97. April 24, 1911

Lieber Grünberg,

Bitte lassen Sie mich freundlich wissen:
1) ob Sie den Brief über Hofrath Kaim hätte erhalten;
2) ob Sie Lust hätten, die Stellung in Montreal anzutreten.
Mit herzlichen Grüssen an Sie und treue.

Ihr
Ferruccio Busoni

P.S.
Vielleicht haben Sie schon die schlimmere Nachricht erfahren, das mein lieber O'Neill Phillips sich erschossen hat!
Ich habe heute Erkundigungen über Serie
Zweige Nachfolgerschaft nach Montreal adressiert.
Auch hier dürfte Ihrer allenfalls etwas offen Scheu.

McGill University's Conservatorium of Musik in Montreal, Canada (Dr. Peterson), Busoni to Gruenberg, April 24, 1911, private collection of Joan Gruenberg

Cominos. William Peterson was president of McGill University from 1895 to 1919. He was a Latinist and Classical scholar. The original letter from Busoni to Peterson appears to be missing. However, Theresa Rowe, director and university archivist of McGill University Libraries, located a letter of May 12, 1911, from C. H. Perrin to Peterson indicating that Busoni had written to Peterson on Gruenberg's behalf. Record group 2, c.24, file 77 File title: Music 1904–1911. C. H. Perrin was appointed Professor of Music at McGill University in 1907. The McGill Conservatory was founded in 1904, and Sir William Peterson was the principal of McGill University from 1895 to 1919.

98. Schoenberg had originally approached Busoni to perform in the concert, as Schoenberg explains in one letter, but Busoni passed the honor on to some of his most gifted pupils, Gruenberg, Eduard Steuermann, and Louis Closson. Schoenberg to Busoni, January 22, 1912, in Beaumont, *Selected Letters*, 414.

99. The performers are not listed for the final number, the one Gruenberg would have participated in. Concert Program of February 4, 1912, reproduced in Nisbett, "Louis Gruenberg,"18.

100. Gruenberg, biography, in Nisbett, "Louis Gruenberg," 15. While Gruenberg considered Webern unmusical and percussive, Schoenberg took an initial disliking to Gruenberg, stating that he was rhythmically challenged. It should be noted that Busoni had also been criticized for excessive rubato. Schoenberg was perhaps, in reality, reacting to a perceived attitude of indifference to his music, which was untrue, and his opinion would change over the years. Arnold Schoenberg, entry of January 23, 1912, *Berliner Tagebuch* (n.p.: Propyläen Verlag, n.d.), 11.

101. In addition, he had been seeking pupils for him. Busoni wrote a letter in *Pan* inviting potential pupils to submit names for composition study with Schoenberg. The letter was so successful that Schoenberg moved to Berlin in October 1911. Beaumont, *Busoni the Composer*, 178.

102. Busoni, "Schönberg Matinée," *Pan* 2 (February 1, 1912), 327–330.

103. It was taken over by the New York Theater Guild and burned down in 1932. Nisbett, "Louis Gruenberg," 22.

104. Gruenberg to Busoni, January 31, 1916, Staatsbibliothek zu Berlin, Preußischer Kulturbesitz, Musikabteilung mit Mendelssohn-Archiv, Mus. Nachl. F. Busoni, BII, 1978.

105. "Louis Gruenberg in Piano Recital," *New York Times*, February 15, 1919. The newspaper review lists the Beethoven sonata as op. 100. This must be a typographical error.

106. Busoni to Egon Petri, March 29, 1915, in Beaumont, *Selected Letters*, 195.

107. Harriet Lanier (1866–1931) was a co-founder of the "Society of Friends of Music" in 1913, patterned after "Die Freunde der Musik" in Germany, "L' amica della musica" in Italy, and "Les amis de la musique" in France. The society aimed to engage musicians to give pre-concert talks at the Metropolitan Opera, to promote new compositions by American and European composers, and to "arrange concerts of old music, both vocal and instrumental, including church music." Lanier was elected the first president of the society, but the advisory board consisted of

well-respected musicians, including Walter Damrosch, Rubin Goldmark, and Arturo Toscanini. "New Musical Club of Society Women," *New York Times*, November 30, 1913.

108. Busoni to Harriet Lanier, August 18, 1915, in Beaumont, *Selected Letters*, 212. At the end of World War I, Gruenberg prepared to return to Europe where he thought job prospects were brighter, until he won the Flagler Prize in 1920, and then his career began to take off in America. The prize was the decisive factor in Gruenberg's ultimate decision to pursue a professional career in composition (rather than performance) and to stay in America. It was not only prestigious, but it also carried a cash award in the amount of $1,000 for first place and $500 for second place. "Music News and Notes: Orchestra Programs," *New York Times*, March 27, 1921. The judges included Leopold Stokowski, John Alden Carpenter, George W. Chadwick, Franz Kneisel, and Walter Damrosch. "Merging Local Orchestras: Gruenberg's 'Hill of Dreams,'" *New York Times*, June 19, 1921. Another important prize was the RCA Victor Prize for an outstanding orchestral composition. The judges consisted of Leopold Stokowski, Serge Koussevitzky, Frederick Stock, Rudolph Ganz, and Olga Samaroff. Robert Russell Bennett, composer, *Abraham Lincoln / Sights and Sounds*, CD, Naxos 8.559004. Additional prizes included the Bispham Memorial Medal for *The Emperor Jones* (1933) and the Lake Placid Club Prize of $1,000 for his string quintet in 1937. This is not to mention two Juilliard Foundation Awards, including one in 1930 for his children's opera, *Jack and the Beanstalk*.

109. The fantasy appears to be without opus number, or else was later renamed.

110. Richard Aldrich, " 'Pierrot Lunaire' and Others," *New York Times*, February 5, 1923, 18.

111. Co-founders of the American Music Guild included Louis Gruenberg, Marion Bauer, Frederick Jacobi, Sandor Harmati, Charles Haubiel, A. Walter Kramer, Harold Morris, Albert Stoessel, and Deems Taylor in 1922. D. J., "A Guild for American Composers," *Musical Digest*, April 24, 1922. The article states that the society members originally gathered in each other's homes for private performances of new compositions.

112. For more information about Gruenberg's involvement with the League of Composers refer to Marion Bauer and Claire R. Reis, "Twenty-Five Years with the League of Composers," *Musical Quarterly* 34:1 (January 1948), 1–14. The premiere concert took place on November 23, 1923. The reason the members split from the ICG was because they disagreed about whether or not concerts should be limited to premiere performances: "League of Composer Circular," reprinted in Bauer and Reis, "Twenty Five Years," 1.

113. D. J., "A Guild for American Composers," *Musical Digest*, April 24, 1922. The organization reached its peak during the 1923–1924 concert season, sponsoring a total of six concerts in that year alone. Only three concerts took place the following year, and thereafter the Society ceased to sponsor public concerts.

114. In the midst of all this organizational activity, Gruenberg's career took off nationally and internationally, and his compositions reached a new level of maturity.

For instance, in a concert series in Venice, his "Daniel Jazz" was featured. "Concerts at Venice," *New York Times,* June 21, 1925. Gruenberg also had several works published by the Viennese publisher Universal Editions from 1924 to 1929, and Robin Freeman claims Busoni was responsible for putting him in touch with the publisher (although I have not been able to substantiate the claim). Robin Freeman, review of "The Music of Louis Gruenberg," *Tempo* 180 (March 1992), 61.

115. Gruenberg, "Vom Jazz und ander Dingen," 233.

116. "Auch die Oper wird nicht in dem heutigen Zustand Bestehen bleiben, auch sie wird in Verbindung mit dem Film (wie das ja heute schon öfters mit mehr oder weniger Erfolg versucht worden ist) per Radio an die Teilnehmer geliefert werden müssen. Denn alles, was von dem Symphonieorchester gesagt wurde, gilt in noch viel stärkerem Masse von der grossen Oper.... Ich sehe da plötzlich eine seltsame Vision vor mir: eine Millionenstadt, die Strassen unheimlich leer, man hört und sieht nichts, aber—in jedem schalldicht abgeschlossenen Zimmer sitzen Menschen, die ihren Opernfilm oder ihr symphonisches Werk voll Genuss anhören, ohne das seiner den andern dabei stört." Gruenberg, "Vom Jazz und ander Dingen," 235.

117. Although Gruenberg started composing film music as a way to make money, that does not preclude the artistic quality of the endeavors.

118. Busoni, *The Essence and Oneness of Music,* in *The Essence of Music and Other Papers,* 1–4.

119. Robert F. Nisbett, "Pare Lorentz, Louis Gruenberg, and *The Fight for Life*: The Making of a Film Score," *Musical Quarterly* 79:2 (Summer 1995), 251.

120. An examination of his score with the film shows that the music can be divided into twenty-four sections. Musically, the childbirth scenes found in sections 2, 10, and 19 divide the score into an introduction (sections 1–2), two large parts (sections 2–11 and 12–22), and a coda (sections 23–24). Nisbett, "Pare Lorentz," 237.

121. Gottfried Galston, diary entry dated April 29, 1924, in *Kalendarnotizen über Ferruccio Busoni,* ed. Martina Weindel, Taschenbücher zur Musikwissenschaft, ed. Richard Schaal, vol. 144 (Wilhelmshaven: Florian Noetzel, 2000), 66. The diary can also be read in Italian translation: *Busoni: Gli ultimi mesi di vita, Diario di Gottfried Galston,* ed. Martina Weindel (Rome: Ismez, 2002).

122. The Columbia Broadcasting System asked six composers per year (1937–1938) to compose pieces specifically for radio. However, handwritten notes in the New York Public Library indicate that Gruenberg conceived of the piece at least three years before receiving the commission. Gruenberg, notes for *Green Mansions,* March 20, 1934, Gruenberg Papers, New York Public Library, JPB 80–20. Gruenberg also completed libretti drafts in 1936.

123. Gruenberg, "Everybody's Music," Gruenberg Papers, Syracuse University Library, Special Collections.

124. Gruenberg, "Interview for Recording Purposes Concerning Federal Music Project," Gruenberg Papers, Special Collections Research Center, Syracuse University Libraries,

125. Ibid.

126. Gruenberg, "Notes for *Green Mansions* (c. 1936), an Opera for the Imagination," Gruenberg Papers, Special Collections Research Center, Syracuse University Libraries.

127. The score indicates the use of the musical saw, but the recording at the Library of Congress features a theremin. Gruenberg, *Green Mansions*, Library of Congress, Recorded Sound Reference Center, LWO 9485 (7:06).

128. Bruno David Ussher, "Gruenberg Radio Opera," *New York Times*, May 2, 1937.

5

New Sonic Landscapes

> My preoccupation with the possibilities of electronic sound began when I read in 1917 *Sketch of a New Esthetic of Music* by the famous Italian pianist and composer, Ferruccio Busoni, first published in 1907.
>
> Otto Luening, "Essay by Otto Luening"

LUENING'S BURGEONING MUSICAL IMPULSES

ALTHOUGH OTTO LUENING (1900–1996) created over 300 compositions in diverse styles, it is his electronic music that has been viewed as the most influential. He created the first piece using electronic tape and the first piece for electronic tape and live performers in the United States.[1] In total, he composed (by himself or in conjunction with his colleague at Columbia University, Vladimir Ussachevsky [1911–1990]) twenty compositions for synthesizer and tape—sometimes with acoustic instruments as well. He also helped found the Columbia-Princeton Electronic Music Center in 1959, the first facility of its kind in the United States, which would be utilized by Milton Babbitt (1916–2011) and other significant composers from around the world. He helped pave a new future of music characterized by a synthesis of science and art, even as he continued to try out novel approaches with traditional music as well. Luening's acoustic compositions, which are often overshadowed by his more radical electronic experiments, are varied and stylistically eclectic, motivated as they were by his capacious interest in exploring new musical possibilities. His students, including John Kander (b. 1927), Mario Davidovsky (b. 1934), and John Corigliano (b. 1938), would also embrace disparate genres from traditional symphonies to film music, electronic music, and beyond.

Luening's composition talent was nurtured by several teachers, including Philipp Jarnach (1892–1982), Volkmar Andreae (1879–1962), and Anton Beer-Walbrunn (1864–1929), who laid a solid technical foundation. Yet it was the aesthetic ideas of Ferruccio Busoni that motivated Luening's most daring musical experiments as well as the eclecticism of his traditionalist pieces. Although Luening did not start experimenting with electronic music until 1951, when he had access to the necessary equipment, the seeds were planted when Luening encountered Busoni in Zurich during World War I. Busoni proved to be influential in a number of other ways. For example, he influenced Luening's treatment of counterpoint, his approach toward opera, and his embracing of stylistic pluralism.

Luening has mentioned the importance of Busoni for his compositional development in numerous sources and interviews. These include his autobiography, *The Odyssey of an American Composer,* and his interviews with Bruce Duffie and Tim Page.[2] Yet scholarship has been virtually silent about the topic. A rare exception is Severine Neff's article about Busoni's enthusiasm for the theories of Bernhard Ziehn and its impact on Luening's compositions of the 1920s and beyond.[3] Even so, there is still no single source detailing the nature of the relationship between Busoni and Luening and its significance for Luening's development and interest in electronic music. Documenting the nature and scope of the relationship not only sheds light on Luening's career, but also enriches understanding about the evolution of electronic music in the United States.

Beginnings

Luening began studying composition with Busoni while both were seeking refuge in Zurich during World War I, and he was already a promising composer and gifted flautist. Yet few could have predicted, based on his songs with folk-like vocal settings and subordinate accompaniments and his miniature piano pieces, that he would one day become a pioneer in electronic music. His song for soprano and piano entitled *Requiescat,* W. 25, based on a text by Oscar Wilde about the premature death of a golden-

MUSIC EXAMPLE 5.1. Luening, "Requiescat," W. 25, mm. 1–4.

haired beauty (completed April 26, 1917), is a traditional song lasting a mere thirty-six bars.[4] The setting is syllabic and triadic (see music example 5.1). Although the vocal line suggests a G tonality, harmonic ambiguity also suggests C minor. The opening phrase, for instance, starts with a G major triad in root position and the vocal line starts on the third-scale degree with regular quarter-note pulsations corresponding to the text "tread lightly." However, the phrase ends sadly with a turn to C minor at a reference to a girl's body buried under the snow.

Luening received a solid foundation in performance, theoretical and historical subjects, and composition at the Zurich Conservatory. He states that his aim there "was to learn everything [he] possibly could, in breadth if not in depth."[5] He not only studied his main instrument, the flute, but also took lessons on other orchestral and percussion instruments just to gain a better understanding of how they worked. Jarnach, who was then Busoni's personal secretary and also a professor at the Zurich Conservatory, provided Luening with a theoretical foundation. In particular, Luening remembers Jarnach's advice about analysis: "As an analysis teacher, he [Jarnach] restricted himself to note-by-note, rhythm-by-rhythm study of the preludes and fugues of the first volume of *The Well-Tempered Clavier*. The harmonic and contrapuntal movement was studied in detail until the overall form became clear. The net result of this workout was that I really learned how to read and analyze a composition carefully and to study every note in any composition."[6]

Jarnach also taught a course in score playing that started with four-part choral works in old clefs and progressed to string quartets and symphonies. During private lessons with Jarnach, which consisted of daily afternoon discussions of works in progress, Luening was expected regularly to bring canons, part of an invention, or a fugal exposition.[7] Luening also remembers discussing his Sonata for Violin and Piano no. 1, W. 26, the Sextet, W. 32, the String Quartet no. 1, W. 38, numerous songs, and other chamber pieces.[8] What Jarnach communicated, above all else, was the importance of high craftsmanship.[9]

After studying with Jarnach, Luening began to earn a reputation as a promising young traditionalist composer. When his Sonata for Violin and Piano no. 1, W. 26, and a few songs were performed publicly in Zurich, reviews were full of praise: "Thoroughly modern feeling was peculiar to songs by Otto Luening, 'Mysterium' and 'At Christmas'; his forceful idiom was rewarded by vigorous applause. The most important work on the program was the same composer's sonata for violin and piano. The first two movements showed decidedly personal traits and a fine mastery of modern form while the Fugato-Finale showed an admirably developed technical proficiency."[10]

STUDYING WITH BUSONI

Yet while Jarnach provided a solid technical foundation, Busoni provided imaginative stimulation and aesthetic ideas that transformed Luening's compositional approach, leading it in new and innovative directions. Luening first consulted Busoni about his compositions in 1919 at the suggestion of Jarnach, even if he had already witnessed and had been entranced by Busoni's performances and compositions beginning in 1917. In particular, Luening remembers being present at the premiere of Busoni's *Arlecchino*, BV 270, and *Turandot*, BV 273, on May 11, 1917, at the Zurich Stadttheater, a performance that impressed him so much he claims he "came under Busoni's spell."[11] The music was lighter, briefer, and more transparent than the German music he had previously encountered in Munich. The stylistic contrasts, ranging from Mozartian ensembles to instrumental dances to exotic orientalisms, were striking.[12] Luening also heard Busoni perform Bach's "Goldberg Variations" and the complete

Chopin ballades. He described the ballades under Busoni's hands as resembling an aeolian harp and as transcending brilliant piano playing.[13] By 1919, Luening had become close to Busoni. When playing flute and percussion that year in the Zurich Tonhalle-Orchestra, Luening reportedly had the job of bringing Busoni a half-bottle of champagne before each performance in a series of five concerts demonstrating the evolution of the piano concerto.[14]

In 1920, Luening moved to Chicago and Busoni to Berlin. If there were any letters between the two documenting extended contact, they appear to have been lost. However, Luening never forgot Busoni's teachings. Busoni, for his part, reportedly predicted a bright future for the young composer but had doubts about his prospects in the United States. As Luening was preparing to return to the United States in 1920, Busoni's comment was reportedly: "Too Bad! You have real talent!"[15] He was well aware of how difficult it was to succeed as a classical composer in the United States at that time.

Lessons were free for Luening but sporadic, and consisted of score critique and aesthetic discussions. Beginning in 1919, Luening took scores to Busoni for critique, and he discussed aesthetic ideas with him. The two also met at cafés and restaurants from time to time. In particular, Luening remembers his first meeting with Busoni, and then later bringing his Sonata for Violin and Piano no. 1, W. 26, his Sextet, W. 32, and his String Quartet no. 1 with clarinet obbligato, W. 38, for him to study.[16] Busoni looked at the scores for the violin sonata and sextet in detail, and kept them for several weeks—he reportedly devoted two full days to them, yet few records exist as to his thoughts and comments.[17] Surviving letters between Jarnach and Busoni suggest that Busoni was impressed, but also had criticisms he hoped would not discourage the young Luening.[18] In his memoirs, Luening records that Busoni was impressed by the Sextet, W. 32, considering it one of the greatest compositions by a young composer. He offered to sponsor a reading of it in his home. Busoni later reportedly attended a performance of the Sextet, W. 32, conducted by Luening's student, Hans Zimmerman, and was pleased with the composition.[19] However, Busoni criticized his lack of attention to detail in the notation of the manuscripts, and, as a result, he doubted how seriously Luening took his own work.[20] For Busoni, the finest details mattered, and he expected that any self-respecting artist would take the time to record his vision as carefully as possible: "Jarnach reported to me that Busoni felt the editing was imprecise and that Busoni had some doubts about me if I thought so little of my ideas as to present them in such a casual way.... I refrained from advertising this experience, and Jarnach was discreet, but I began working with great care and cleaned up both the violin sonata and the sextet."[21]

Luening, who had received poor grades in penmanship as a child, never had the neatest handwriting, and the notation of his scores was not entirely clear and accurate.[22] In the opening of the manuscript of Sonata for Violin and Piano no. 1, W. 26, for instance, his sprawling handwriting is not always legible (see figure 5.1). Dynamic signs, which are not frequent, are sometimes placed between notes, creating a sense of ambiguity as to when the signs are to be observed. Busoni, however, was not just commenting on the quality of the penmanship. He noticed a lack of detail that he felt should be in any score of an artist who had thoroughly worked out a composition and had really heard how he wanted it to sound. This advice made a lasting impression upon Luening, who immediately set out to be more careful and more precise. Paul de Jong, Luening's personal assistant from 1993 to 1996, was responsible for preparing Luening's scores for performances (Luening's eyesight suffered in his maturity). He remembers that Luening meticulously went over every note, phrase mark, and dynamic marking, insisting that the editing be very precise; he mentioned that the encounter with Busoni in Zurich was the catalyst for this attitude.[23]

Conversations with Busoni made a major impact on Luening, who began to think more creatively about form, instrumentation, and expressivity after talking with Busoni. He worked much more slowly on his next composition, the String Quartet, no. 1, W. 38, taking about nine months to complete it. Dates in the manuscript indicate that he started composing it shortly after he had received Busoni's feedback on the other two pieces, and that he finished it on April 11, 1920. Extensive drafts and sketches testify to the care with which Luening worked and reworked the piece until the notation closely matched his vision for the piece (see figures 5.2 and 5.3).[24] In particular, he reworked the last movement, which contained a clarinet obbligato and advanced treatment of harmony, multiple times. Seemingly minor differences between an early draft and subsequent revisions, such as the incorporation of a sustained octave before the entrance

FIGURE 5.1. Luening, Sonata for Violin and Piano no. 1, W. 26, mvt. 1, mm. 1–14, mss. Otto Luening Papers, Music Division, New York Public Library, Astor, Lenox, and Tilden Foundations, JPB 94–7, Box 129.

FIGURE 5.2. Luening, String Quartet no. 1, W. 38, sketch, mvt. 3, clarinet obbligato entrance. Otto Luening Papers, Music Division, New York Public Library, Astor, Lenox, and Tilden Foundations, JPB 94–7, Box 126.

of the clarinet and the insertion of numerous additional dynamic markings, better delineate form and highlight the clarinet's timbre even while evoking greater expressivity.

Throughout the quartet, Luening aimed for greater independence of the individual parts, more specific notation of expression, and greater attention to overall form. He claims that these changes were inspired by contact with Busoni, for conversations with him went way beyond notation to many aesthetic matters. He left this account of how greatly contact with Busoni had impacted his compositional approach:

> The effect of Busoni's musical personality on my own composing was strong. I worked for nine months on my next work, my first string quartet with clarinet obbligato in the last movement. I composed much more slowly and carefully than I had in the past. My writing became much more contrapuntal and was tonal and polytonal at different times. Each of the

FIGURE 5.3. Luening, String Quartet no. 1, W. 38, mss., mvt. 3, clarinet obbligato entrance. Otto Luening Papers, Music Division, New York Public Library, Astor, Lenox, and Tilden Foundations, JPB 94–7, Box 126.

string parts had a melodic life that was quite independent of the others, but I had also worked out a type of motivated development that gave to the harmonies a contrapuntal touch, even when the harmonies were only accompanying chords. I was much more preoccupied with what the work was expressing, with the musical style and idea and the expressive content, than in earlier works. I let this ripen as I myself became more introspective and found wider horizons than I had imagined existed. Above all, the overall form or *gestalt* of the entire quartet concerned me and was slowly revealed to me. The work was in three movements and was forty-five minutes long.[25]

In comparison to Luening's early compositions, the String Quartet, no. 1, W. 38, reveals a more mature style. When it premiered in 1924, it received positive reviews. An author for the *The Musical Times* of London praised its musical structure: "Another work offered was a new string quartet by Otto Luening, a young American. . . . A solid musical structure." Hugo Leichtentritt's review in the *Musical Courier*, on the other hand, focused on the counterpoint:[26] "There was also a string quartet by a young American, Luening, which shows a real sense for polyphonic writing."[27] Adolf Weissmann concluded, "Otto Luening, judging by his quartet played by the Roth's quartet, is a sensitive contemporary. . . . He has a technique that is wedded to his fine sensibility."[28]

Luening's earlier Zurich compositions, such as the Sonata for Violin and Piano no. 1, W. 26, and the Sextet, W. 32, are characterized by rhythmic and metric fluidity—it is rare for his works to stay in the same tempo for very long. A dearth of cadences and the fluid tempi contribute to a sense of musical continuity. The second movement of the Sextet, W. 32, for instance, contains multiple tempo markings, each associated with motives and key areas.[29] An *allegro con fuoco* in C major alternates with an *andante* in A-flat major and an *allegro moderato* in B major. Luening's Sextet, W. 32, which was "a salute to the 'Back to Mozart' movement then in vogue," was also based on tonality, but it would be more accurate to state that this piece, like others by Luening, fluctuates chromatically through keys.[30] In Luening's early works, key relationships center on thirds, but movements and pieces begin and end in different keys.[31] The final movement of the Sonata for Violin and Piano no. 1, for instance, starts in C major and ends in F major. If Luening's treatment of meter and key is flexible, he tends to be more redundant with the instrumentation. There is quite a bit of overlap and parallel motion between instrument parts. For instance, even despite the decorative violin line, parallel motion between the soprano line in the piano part and the violin predominates during the opening measure of the Sonata for Violin and Piano, no. 1, W. 26.

Luening's String Quartet no. 1, W. 38, displays the same fluidity of tempo characteristic of his earlier Zurich compositions, but the piece contains more advanced treatment of harmony, more independence of instrumental parts, and more variety of texture (see figure 5.4). For instance, the first movement begins in A minor, *andante con moto*, with the parts in unison. After the first half cadence, the parts resume, and textures remain thin, but the parts move in contrary motion. The following *adagio molto* begins with rhythmic and melodic pairing in the first and second violin parts, and then motivic imitation between the viola and second violin, before parallel motion happens between violin one and the cello, revealing greater flexibility and independence of the instruments. These types of contrasts in texture and tempo pervade movements and the composition as a whole. At times, individual parts even function in independent tonal regions. This is evident, for instance, in the final movement, where the first violin and bass often play contrasting scales. The final movement features polytonality and fugal passages.

Jarnach, who was impressed with Luening's first string quartet and the maturation it exhibited, urged Luening to show it to Busoni and wrote to him in advance, as evident from a letter dated June 2–3, 1920: "P.S. my former pupil, Mr. Otto Luening brought me this day a new work, it is a string quartet (right at the end is added a clarinet). You would do me a great personal favor if you look at several places in the extensive manuscript."[32] Busoni, who reportedly studied the composition for one week, was impressed with the work, as he expressed in his response to Jarnach, and he considered the clarinet obbligato in the final movement inspired.[33]

THE IMPACT OF BUSONI'S AESTHETIC IDEAS

If Busoni's critique of Luening's scores made a strong impact on his development, conversations between the two that touched on numerous aesthetic topics played an even more vital role. Luening's first private meeting with him took place in 1919, just before giving him scores, and

FIGURE 5.4. Luening, String Quartet no. 1, W. 38, mss., mvt. 1, mm. 1–15. Otto Luening Papers, Music Division, New York Public Library, Astor, Lenox, and Tilden Foundations, JPB 94-7, Box 126.

he remembers in detail what the two discussed. In particular, he recalls Busoni's ideas about texture, which he indirectly related when he discussed the merits of various composers. Mozart and Berlioz were idealized, while Wagner and Beethoven were criticized:

> He had been enthusiastic about the transparent and transcendental or floating quality in Mozart's music and commented that Andreae's interpretation of the *Haffner* Symphony was too heavy-handed and too Beethovenian. He then proceeded, again indirectly, to point out that Beethoven had held back the progress of musical composition by overemphasizing the heroic and the forceful. He admitted the greatness of the last sonatas, particularly the *Hammerklavier* Sonata, the G Major and the *Emperor* concerti, and the *Eroica* Symphony. But he stated that Beethoven's followers had taken over the turgidity and heaviness of his works and that in doing so they had completely forgotten the superior musical virtues of lightness, transparency, and what I can only translate as a floating kind of transcendentalism that brought one into touch with a supernatural dimension, expressed fully in such works as Mozart's *Zauberflöte, Don Giovanni*, and his G- and C-minor piano concerti. Jarnach defended the very power of Beethoven that Busoni was trying to decry. As the conversation went on they made allusions to Wagner, who served as a horrible example of nineteenth-century composing; to Berlioz, the real path breaker; and to Strauss, admired by Busoni for his intelligence but criticized for his overcomposing and his bombast.[34]

Although Luening was busy with school and performances, and thus unable to attend Busoni's social hours in the afternoons on a regular basis, he maintained contact with him, meeting him in cafés and restaurants, and absorbed many of his aesthetic ideas through in-depth conversations. Luening remembers in particular that Busoni expected his students to possess or develop a vast knowledge of music repertoire in order to become acquainted with a wide variety of styles and to mix those together in their own works as he himself did: "He expected us to be familiar with different styles of music, and in his larger works like *Doktor Faust*, the early piano concerto with male chorus, the Second Violin Sonata, and even *Arlecchino*, he used various styles as part of his overall form."[35] In terms of instrumentation, Busoni taught Luening that the composer needed to be able to hear all of the instruments internally such that testing was unnecessary and that each part needed to be written with a specific instrument in mind.[36] Busoni taught that students must never put down a note they have not imagined, and that they needed to record what they heard in their inner ear. Busoni worked daily on counterpoint, and Luening remembers that he expected the same level of dedication from all of his students as well:[37] "He believed that the individuality of the composer and his real personality were expressed through the melodic-rhythmic line and, of course, in combinations of two or more of these lines that brought the contrapuntal principle into play."[38] Busoni also expected that his students would be self-motivated, and able to learn on their own; self-discovery was the key to individuality: "In his Zurich years Busoni assumed that composers who showed him scores would have mastered technical problems more or less by themselves. He expected experimentation and analysis; novelty for its own sake interested him no longer. He talked of form, not formula, and spoke, as he had written in the past, of taste, style, economy, temperament (human, not musical!), intelligence, and equipoise."[39]

According to Luening, Busoni was very kind to the young if he felt they had talent, but he did not "hold anyone's hand." He was preoccupied with helping students form their own ideas:[40] "Busoni's relationship to people he was coaching was mostly respectful, but he was demanding and acted as though they understood everything he was talking about. If they didn't, they would be quiet, disappear, practice, read, or study, until they felt more or less at ease with him. He expected students to know the important areas of old music and the standard repertory, but wanted them to be alert to contemporary trends. He expected composers to master the theory of music through self-study."[41]

Luening also remembers that Busoni encouraged well-roundedness as the key to artistic greatness. He made students feel like they had to do a lot of reading to educate themselves. He himself bought many scores and studied them, making others feel that they, too, needed to do that as well.[42] In addition, he encouraged his students to read fine literature: "He was sensitive to the other arts. He sometimes spoke of the spiritual values of the arts and the priest-like function of the true artist. Many people who knew him considered him the greatest genius of his time and a true Renaissance man."[43]

Luening claims that form was particularly important to Busoni. He stressed that each piece needed to be shaped according to internal organic laws and according to the nature of music: "He wrote that art forms last longer if they stay close to the essence of each individual species. He suggested that music is almost incorporeal (he called it 'sonorous air'), almost like Nature herself. He opposed formalism, systems, and routine, but asserted that each musical motive contains within itself its 'life germ,' the embryo of its fully developed form, each one different from all the others. He proclaimed that the creative artist did not follow laws already made; he made laws."[44]

Another particular Busonian teaching that made a major impact on Luening's compositional style and, especially, his development of electronic music was the idea that there was virtually no difference between the old and the new. Luening described Busoni as "a 19th-century artist who looked back to the classics in music and literature, but speculated and prophesized about the future with equanimity."[45] Luening, like Busoni, took a Janus-faced approach to composition, even in his experimental electronic works, believing that the future should build upon the past and not make a break with it. He made the following observations about the ways Busoni followed this idea in his own music, and he sought to emulate it in his own:

> Busoni's aesthetic had its roots in the past, but he had a vision of a future and prophesized many artistic events that happened in the early twenties and also the electronic sound production that developed in the 50's, in which both Varèse and I were deeply involved. As a composer Busoni was a master of many styles. His genius was to immerse himself in the great repertory of music and the arts from all periods. He was particularly sensitive to 17th century opera, puppet plays, Cervantes, Mark Twain, Goethe and the fantastic stories of E.T.A. Hoffmann and Edgar Allen Poe; Verdi's *Falstaff*, Mozart's music, and the music of Liszt, Chopin, J. S. Bach and Berlioz and the paintings of De Goya and Delacroix. In searching for new harmonic materials, he was strongly attracted by the theories of the German-American, Bernhard Ziehn, whom he met in Chicago in 1910. Ziehn's principle of symmetrical inversion as applied to harmonies and in canonical techniques contributed to Busoni's later works.[46]

Luening's vision, even in his electronic music, was to draw upon the accomplishments of the past, not to reject them, in order to contribute new ideas and to help build a future of music as yet unheard. He expressed this philosophy in his interview with Bruce Duffie, claiming that it stemmed from his own upbringing, which stressed respect for tradition, and that it was reinforced by Busoni and Jarnach, who were also committed to searching out new paths:

> BD: I read that you were called a "Janus." Do you feel that you look both backward and forward?
>
> OL: Oh yeah, definitely, because of my whole background. I come from the Middle West, as you know, from Milwaukee, and I've all that Milwaukee-Chicago background: German, middle nineteenth century, where they had an enormous respect for the traditions of the past and the values and so on. On the other hand, they were very forward-looking. They wanted to come because America was the land of freedom and opportunity. They were politically radical and culturally adventuresome. When I went back to Europe I felt the same thing. I was at the Academy in Munich, which has a very conservative background, but at the same time, in 1912, I read Schoenberg's harmony book. Then I came in touch with Ferruccio Busoni, and Philipp Jarnach. Both of them were the same way; they had a very strong traditional and romantic background, and demanded that of us, but at the same time they were way out, searching all the time. There was a combination of the traditional and this research and development and discovery. That was part of the way we were brought up—or the way I was brought up, anyhow. I think Varèse was, too. He was a very close friend of mine.[47]

Luening demanded that music should be up to date and reflect the complexities of the current age, but he demanded with equal emphasis that composers not reject the past.[48] He remembers Busoni's admonition in his *Entwurf einer neuen Ästhetik der Tonkunst*, which he had read in 1917, to expand the current musical vocabulary and the current set of instruments: "Busoni decried a too rigid adherence to existing notation and said that the terms consonance and dissonance were too confining. He suggested an expansion of the major-minor-chromatic scale and assembled one hundred thirteen other scale formations within the octave C-C.... Busoni predicted a revolution in the field of harmony. He was convinced that instrumental music had come to a dead end and that new instruments were needed, and he suggested a scale of thirty-six divisions within the octave as an interesting possibility for new music."[49]

In addition, there were Busoni's teachings about the expansion of musical instruments, in particular, using electronic means. For Luening, an electronic approach was simply like adding an instrument to the orchestral mix. Electronic music did not mean radically departing from the past, but rather building upon it and adding to it through experimentation. Luening stated it this way: "In Cahill's instrument Busoni saw a way out of the impasse which instrumental music had reached. However, he warned that a lengthy and careful series of experiments and further ear-training was necessary to make the unfamiliar material plastic and useful for coming generations."[50]

THE ZIEHN CONNECTION

Many of Busoni's ideas were abstract and esoteric. One of the most tangible tasks that Busoni encouraged Luening to do was to investigate and employ the theories of Bernhard Ziehn about melody, harmony, and counterpoint. Busoni first encountered Ziehn's theories in Chicago in 1910 on one of his United States concert tours, and the theories contributed to his views about the derivation of harmonies from melodies. In addition, it reinforced his interest in counterpoint. Luening leaves the following memory of Busoni's fascination with Ziehn's theories: "When I met Busoni in Zurich in 1917, his views about composition had changed since 1907. On tour he had seen the German-American theorist Bernhard Ziehn in Chicago. Ziehn had published in 1887 a remarkable harmony text which developed a system of symmetrical inversion based on the old Contrarium Reversum. When Busoni met him in 1910, he was engaged in developing a system of canonical techniques."[51]

Busoni, for his part, described the theories as the first step toward new harmonic paths, citing, in particular, Ziehn's theories of symmetrical inversion: "The present-day harmony and that of the future interest me as they relate to the musical world and with similar intensity. At present there is a searching and a groping but I see the roads. There are five in all and as yet no composer has walked up to the end of any of them. The first new harmonic system rests upon chord formations according to customary scales.... By the symmetrical inversion of the harmonic order Bernhard Ziehn shows me the second way."[52]

It was Busoni who suggested Luening read Ziehn's writings—especially about his contrapuntal techniques and his theory of symmetrical inversion.[53] When Busoni learned that Luening was planning on returning to the United States in 1920, he encouraged him to study with one of Ziehn's student, Wilhelm Middelschulte, to whom Busoni dedicated his *Fantasia contrappuntistica*, BWV 256: "One city is quite musical, and that is Chicago. Frederick Stock and Wilhelm Middelschulte live there, and you may use my name in introducing yourself."[54] Luening did indeed study with Middelschulte for six months and tried out the new theoretical approach, in which every chord tone becomes a fundamental. This is especially evident beginning with his monothematic *Symphonic Fantasia no. 1*, W. 56 (1922–1924), a symphonic poem without program, in which the opening five measures present germinal material for the entire composition that continually undergoes metamorphosis and transformation. Luening later studied Ziehn's theories on his own as well in his musical arts studio.[55]

Luening employed Ziehn's theories in several of his compositions from the 1920s and beyond, including his first *Symphonic Fantasia* no. 1, W. 56 (1922–1924), Sonata for Violin and Piano no. 2, W. 46 (1922), and *Sonata for Piano in Memoriam Ferruccio Busoni*, W. 162 (1966).[56] Ziehn taught about five methods of pitch and chord generation that he had observed in pre-tonal, tonal, and post-tonal music literature: diatonic and chromatic "plurisignificance," "irregular" cadence, order permutation, figuration, and symmetrical inversion.[57] Of these, Busoni was especially interested in the latter. The result of symmetrically invertible sound is triadic, but tonally ambiguous. Ziehn was interested in the multiple structural and functional significances of pitches in triads; an invariant pitch in different diatonic chords can have different functions and importance. Ziehn showed that diatonic chords not related in terms of key area could be associated through invariant structure—common pitches or intervals—and this fascinated Luening. Chromatically varied stacks of thirds can also be used to create unusual harmonies, or chromatically varied surface ornamentation that can alter harmonies through local dissonances. As Neff reveals, during the opening of the *Symphonic Fantasia* no. 1, W. 56, C and E-flat remain stationary in timpani and strings for eight measures, but all the other instrumental parts move through different chordal settings of the interval, including A-flat major, C diminished seventh, and F seventh. At the end of the work, Luening leaves a suspended A-flat unresolved in the flute and first violin at the final cadence as the music dies away.[58] Melodic material is constantly varied rhythmically and through chromatic alteration to surface ornamentation.

Busoni had already implemented some of Ziehn's theories when he wrote a symmetrical canon in mm. 81–93 of the *Berceuse élégiaque*, BV 262 (1910). This piece inspired Luening to begin the second movement of the *Sonata for Piano in Memoriam Ferruccio Busoni*, W. 162 with a chordal canon symmetrically inverted.[59] In the sonata each movement is a set of variations. Luening draws on Ziehn's harmonic theories, constantly varying the melodies.

OPERA AND PLURALISM

If Busoni influenced Luening's approach toward harmony and melody, his impact can also be observed in Luening's adoption of stylistic pluralism and veneration of Mozart in his dramatic works. Like Busoni, who idealized an all-encompassing "essence of music" that included all stylistic possibilities, Luening embraced a multi-stylistic approach in many of his compositions, including in his opera, *Evangeline*, W. 85.[60] It was Busoni who wrote that opera was ideal for this stylistic pluralism: "A composer, a creator, brings to a single opera all that moves him, all that swims before his eyes, all that is within his powers to achieve: he is a musical Dante, a musical Divine Comedy."[61]

In addition, he relied on models praised by Busoni, especially Mozart and Verdi: "My admiration for Mozart's *Figaro* made me want clarity in the sound and Verdi's *Falstaff* inspired me to make plain, direct orchestral statements."[62] Mozart's music was indeed an important model for Luening, as it had been for Busoni, who upheld *Die Zauberflöte*, K. 620, as his highest ideal of opera. Busoni praised it for its mixture of the didactic and the fantastic as well as the musicality of the libretto and its stylistic pluralism. When asked if there was "any kind of particular esthetic behind" his production of the one-act *School for Wives* by Molière on July 25, 1941, at the Green Mountain Festival of the Arts in Middlebury, Vermont, Luening replied "Mozart."[63] Although Luening never considered himself a dramatic composer, *Evangeline* won the Bispham Medal, and he was very active in promoting the creation of American operas.[64] His opera displays many characteristics reflective of Busoni's opera ideals. Like Busoni's operas, Luening's *Evangeline,* commissioned by the American Opera Company in 1931, is pluralistic and thin-textured. The libretto emphasizes fantastic events in the plot. Written by Luening, the libretto is based on a play by Henry Wadsworth Longfellow and contains ten contrasting scenes. The setting is 1755 and the prelude takes place in a primeval forest, while act 1 takes place in an Acadian land in Novia Scotia filled with wooden houses and farmers. Evangeline, the main character, is the daughter of the wealthiest farmer—she was the pride of the village. Yet in act 2, Evangeline's life is shattered when the British separate her from her new husband, Gabriel, and force the farmers into exile in New Orleans while burning their homes. The two are reunited only at the very end at a Quaker almshouse in Philadelphia after much searching, but only just before Gabriel dies. Although the tale itself is based loosely on historical events, the libretto capitalizes on the fantastic and the otherworldly, becoming increasingly dreamlike as the drama proceeds. There are comparisons between Evangeline and the Virgin Mary, which are reinforced by a quotation of Ave Maris Stella, even as the wedding festivities are accompanied by a very physical and rhythmic dance chorus with the text "swing your partner round and round just anyway you please."[65] In the third act, an Indian woman tells the legend of a phantom lover, just before Evangeline and Gabriel are reunited.

The music is pluralistic, reflecting the conflux of religious, political, and social events in different locales. Luening used Acadian folk songs that he discovered through personal research, as well as the Swedish song "So Softly Blooming," which emanates from an offstage church in the final act. When Evangeline's father prepares for the arrival of his future son-in-law, he sings a little ditty characterized by simple step-wise motion, rather than an elaborate entrance aria: "The Prince of Orange was a dashing fellow. When he went out in the morning, his hat was green and his coat was yellow when he went out in the morning. Tra-la la la la la la la la-la-la-la." (see music example 5.2)[66]

In contrast, Evangeline's entrance, in which she sings about a nightingale, resembles a lied setting with a folk-like syllabic vocal line placed over a rolling triplet accompaniment. The opera also features recitatives and choral numbers. Simple vocal settings are accompanied by largely tonal

MUSIC EXAMPLE 5.2. Luening, *Evangeline*, W. 85, act 1, scene 1, opening.

subsidiary orchestral accompaniments in which the winds, percussion, and harp play the most important roles. The end of act 1 contains numerous choruses in contrasting styles, including a dance chorus and a sailor's chorus. Choruses at the beginning of act 2, by contrast, feature chromatic glissandi as the Acadians realize they must go into exile. They then sing a simple hymn-like prayer in Latin based on Ave Maris Stella, a vespers hymn to Mary: "Virgo singularis inter omnes mitis, nos culpis solutos (see music example 5.3)." Although the music is largely tonal, plurisignificance (the multiple functional significances of the same tone in different chords) allows chromatic movement to remote regions. For instance, the opening prelude centers on C at the beginning, but quickly moves to A minor and the A-flat major using C as a pivot with multiple significances and roles in the different key areas, tonic and median, respectively.

Like Busoni, Luening was especially concerned about the quality of the libretti and organized workshops specifically designed to help composers understand and locate good libretti and to collaborate with experts in areas outside of music, as he mentioned in his interview with Bruce Duffie:

> BD: You said one time that American operas tend to have bad libretti. Is that still true?
>
> OL: It's improved a lot because of the workshops. In 1925, after I left Chicago, I was Executive Director of the Opera Department of the Eastman School and there weren't any workshops. Then we had ten years at Columbia where we did a lot. Now there are workshops all over the place. And they get talking to the guy in the English Department, they get talking to the fellow in the Drama Department, and to everybody else who's interested, and that stuff begins to shape up.

For his part, Luening selected a text by Longfellow that was well known to most Americans at the time and he spent months working it into a suitable libretto. In particular, he noted that he had to change the dactylic hexameters into something more suitable for an operatic setting.[67]

Evangeline, W. 85, premiered at Columbia University in 1948 with Luening conducting, and met with mixed reviews, largely due to the pluralistic stylistic approach, which was considered detrimental to dramatic advancement. Olin Downes, for instance, praised the instrumentation, but criticized the dramaturgy:

MUSIC EXAMPLE 5.3. Luening, *Evangeline*, W. 85, act 2, scene 1, excerpt from the conclusion.

It would be a pleasure to say that "Evangeline" is a new opera of pronounced promise or confirmed achievement. Unfortunately the present writer cannot so testify. He finds the libretto poorly conceived for the dramatic effect or characterization or emotional impulse. Nothing is convincingly communicated either by libretto or score. The principal interest of the work is the instrumentation. The passages which showed out most distinctly were the orchestral preludes and interludes, some of which melodies that have a folk-like character are developed in nostalgic mood. There are also incidental ditties, choral dance songs, and the like, in the early scenes, acceptable as entertainment, but having little dramatically to do with the case.[68]

Indeed, Busoni was a catalyst for characteristic features of Luening's mature style, including his exploration of Ziehn's theories about melodic and harmonic construction and polystylism in opera. Yet he was even more of an influence on his excursion into electronic music in the 1950s.

ELECTRONIC MUSIC

In his interview with Page, Luening stated, "The electronic thing was an episode that could not be missed because Busoni told us about electronic possibilities."[69] He was convinced that instrumental music had reached a dead end and that new instruments were needed even while he predicted a revolution in the field of harmony and suggested a scale of thirty-six divisions within the octave as an interesting possibility for new music. He was especially fascinated by the earliest experiments with electronic instruments and drew his students' attention to them:[70]

> I received from America direct and authentic intelligence which solves the problem in a simple manner. I refer to an invention by Dr. Thaddeus Cahill. He has constructed a comprehensive apparatus which makes it possible to transform an electrical current into a fixed and mathematically exact number of vibrations. As pitch depends on the number of vibrations and the apparatus which makes it possible to transform an electrical current into a fixed and mathematically exact number of vibrations and the apparatus may be "set" on any number desired, the infinite gradation of the octave may be accomplished by merely moving a lever corresponding to the pointer of a quadrant.[71]

Discussions with Busoni stimulated Luening's interest in electronic instruments as well as in acoustics and timbre. Beginning in the 1920s, he started to investigate new possibilities within traditional genres. In the 1950s, this experimentation took on new life as he explored new timbral possibilities through the electronic manipulation of traditional instrumental sounds through electronic means. Since tape music can be viewed as music that is composed directly with sound instead of being first written on paper and later transformed into sound, it dovetails well with Busoni's emphasis on sound and sonority: "This child [music]—*it floats on air!* It touches not the earth with its feet. It knows no law of gravitation. It is wellnigh incorporeal. Its material is transparent. It is sonorous air."[72] Neff remembers that Luening cited two passages in particular of Busoni's music that were specifically shaped by an understanding of acoustics: successions of augmented chords and the stark octaves appearing after thicker textures in the Sonatina no. 2, BV 259 and the opening of *Doktor Faust*, BV 203 in which Busoni creates a quasi-electronic aura based on combinations of pitches reflective of the overtone series.[73]

Since the 1920s, Luening's music had reflected his interest in acoustical harmony or the use of voicings and overtones for special coloristic effects, and this stemmed from his studies in Zurich. In an interview with Theresa Bowers, he claimed that it was there that he became interested in sonority and acoustics: "I was then [in the 1920s] studying a lot of sound, acoustics, and the use of sound in a very free way and new way which has now come out very much through the electronic thing. But I had the feeling with them that they thought I was possibly—well they couldn't say I was academic because I was too much of a good practical musician. I could play too well and conduct too well so I wasn't academic. Well, I wasn't conservative either."[74]

In particular, Luening was interested in using a segment of the overtone series as the basis for harmonic material. He also experimented with varying the spacing of chord tones to achieve differing sonorous effects.[75] Already in 1922, his Trio for Violin, Cello, and Piano, W. 42, for instance, features bitonality based on the harmonic series. In addition, he also tried tuning the piano differently than the tempered scale even as he was avidly reading up about acoustics, relying on texts such as Helmholtz's *Sensations of Tone*, Dayton Miller's *The Science of Musical Sound*, and articles about Mersenne, Pythagoras, and Ptolomy.[76] He came to the conclusion that a study of acoustics and sound was essential for any composer, even if not working in electronic music: "I have come to believe that it is an essential basis for the contemporary composer to know something about how sound works—whether he uses electronic sound production or not. Not only how it is produced but what effect it has and how it is perceived under varying conditions."[77]

By the mid-1930s at Hanya Halm's *Trend* productions, Luening encountered for the first time a playback machine, which fascinated him: "We also had a playback machine, a new kind of sound recording with a fellow named Paneyka so I got interested in projection of sound and it seemed to be very advanced and daring."[78] With regard to electronic music, he was particularly interested in exploring whether electronics could help him detect new relationships between a fundamental tone and its overtone series. He wanted to know what would happen if partials were displaced by transposing them toward the upper and lower threshold of hearing or if transposition beyond the normal range of an instrument would make the instrument sound new and different.[79]

In his electronic compositions, Luening took as his starting point acoustic musical sounds—often produced on the flute and played by himself. These acoustic sounds then underwent metamorphoses as the sounds were manipulated and distorted. Repeating and amplifying pitches make the sounds spiral out with continuous pulsations, whereas changing the speed of the tape alters the register, for instance. Concern with color and timbre was indeed an important motivating factor behind his earliest electronic works, *Fantasy in Space*, W. 148 (1952), and *Low Speed*, W. 150 (1952), which focus on the manipulation of natural acoustical sounds as primary formal components. Luening was principally interested in extending timbral possibilities using electronic means. The juxtaposition of acoustic and electronic sounds creates multiple textures, timbres, and styles, a plurality encouraged by Busoni and adopted by Luening in Zurich.

Luening's first experiments with tape music began in 1951, and at that time he worked largely in collaboration with his junior colleague at Columbia University, Vladimir Ussachevksy, who had more technical expertise. In the beginning, they worked with primitive equipment, an Ampex 400 tape recorder—71/3 and 15—a borrowed Magnacord, earphones, a microphone, and a box-like device designed by Peter Mauzey, to create feedback for mechanical reverberation.[80] The first presentation of the results took place at the Composers Forum at Columbia University on May 9, 1952, in the McMillan Theatre. Soon thereafter, the two presented their work at the first public concert of electronic music in the United States on October 28, 1952, at the Museum of Modern Art in New York with Leopold Stokowski conducting. The program included Ussachevsky's *Sonic Contours* and Luening's *Fantasy in Space*, W. 148.

Luening saw these new experiments as a type of variation procedure in which sound, rather than melody or harmony, was the variant. He was not rejecting the idea of formal coherence; he was instead coming up with new ways of achieving that coherence: "I was from the beginning of my experiments preoccupied with organic musical forms. Unlike the fixed, exact sounds of triads, intervals and chords that one speaks of in traditional music, in electronic music, a tone or group of tones with ordered or displaced partials becomes the *sonority form* or *sound object.* Variations of such sonority forms would be related in some fashion to the original sonority form, so giving the piece a unity inherent in the original sound."[81]

Luening's early experiments used minimal equipment as he was finding his way slowly. In *Fantasy in Space,* W. 148, *Low Speed,* W. 150, and *Invention in Twelve Tones,* W. 149, he used his own playing of the flute as the basic sound source before creating sonority and speed variations and the mixing of taped sounds. Luening explains that he first recorded on one tape and then recorded a second time on another while listening to the first recording. He would then repeat the process a third time, sometimes mixing the recordings. During the process, he transposed pitches using speed variation, which allowed for transpositions beyond the normal range of the flute. He also used Peter Mauzey's box to create feedback producing mechanical reverberation.[82] The notation depicts this layering in part through the use of two staves, each of which displays multiple parts (see music example 5.4). The basic pitches are mostly there; however, Luening did not capture the repetitions, reverberations, special effects, and register on paper—the new soundscape was created electronically. In one section, Luening simply marked "in contrapuntal runs and arpeggios," which were left up to the performer to be improvised during the taping process.[83]

In *Low Speed,* W. 150, Luening also emphasized certain upper partials. By keeping phrases a fifth or a twelfth apart, the upper partials belonging to D and A would combine to sound upper partials, not common to either one alone. This technique highlighted new sonorous characteristics that were not apparent in the natural flute sound. He also transposed the entire piece one octave below the normal flute range.[84]

MUSIC EXAMPLE 5.4. Luening, *Fantasy in Space*, W. 148, mm. 1–5.

Luening describes the importance timbre and color had when approaching tape music, especially in relation to *Rhapsodic Variations for Tape Recorder and Orchestra,* W. 159, a piece commissioned by the Louisville Orchestra in 1954. The piano and flute were the foundation and sound was manipulated through repetitions. The most distinctive aspect of the piece, however, was the fluid and organic way Luening and Ussachevsky blended tape and live music, as Luening describes:

> OL: Oh, yes. We used the electronic tape in the *Rhapsodic Variations*. It was the first piece of its kind, actually, that was performed publicly. We used piano and flute as a sound source. I played the flute myself, and we used the tape part like a section of the orchestra—percussion, tape, woodwinds, brass, and so on. But we used it somewhat differently than Varèse did it in his *Déserts*. We blended it with the other sections. Sometimes it would play with the strings, sometimes it would be solo or do a cadenza in and out, but not like a concerto grosso. It wasn't just the tape and then the orchestra and then the tape and then the orchestra, but it was blending it and mixing it with strings and sometimes the woodwinds.
>
> BD: So it was an integral part?
>
> OL: Yeah, an integral part, a new section of the orchestra. Incidentally, that idea has taken hold considerably in Hollywood where they mix a lot of the electronic sound with live sounds. They've also done it in the small chamber orchestra groupings.[85]

Although Luening was interested in new sonorous possibilities, he did not reject musical procedures from the past. *Invention in 12 Tones,* W. 149, originally entitled "Invention for Flute on Tape recorder," combines traditional compositional procedures with experimental ones. It is based on a 12-tone row presented by the flute that is varied using devices of canon, augmentation, diminution, and retrogradation. The varied versions of the row are superimposed into complex patterns evoking unusual sounds made possible only by the tape recorder. The notation itself for the piece is very vague. Although the row itself is notated in full, along with three variations, the text provides most of the directions:

> Ampex 14R-8, Switches down, Equalization 15
> Theme—Moderato-rubato (reverberated)
> Play through theme and variations I, II, and III free in tempo and in canon in free rhythm—entrances marked *.
> Repeat this entire pattern to end of piece.
> At 63 ⅕ seconds superimpose this pattern 2 octaves higher (in double diminution). At 1 minute 52 ½ seconds superimpose this pattern 2 octaves higher (in double diminution).
> At 1 minute 52 ½ seconds superimpose this pattern 1 octave higher (in simple diminution).
> At 2 min. 48 ½ seconds superimpose this pattern 1 octave higher (in simple diminution) and simultaneously superimpose 2 octaves higher (in double diminution).[86]

A mixing of the old and the new is also evident in Luening's *Fugue and Chorale Fantasy with Electronic Doubles for Organ and Tape*, W. 224 (1973), which conflates two different compositions, Luening's Fugue for Organ, W. 221 (1971), and *Chorale Fantasy for Organ*, W. 43 (1922). Luening created electronic doublings based on tape-recorded sections by Fred Titian in St. Mary's Cathedral in San Francisco.[87] Luening varied the timbre of the fragments using a Bode Frequency Shifter at the Columbia-Princeton Electronic Music Center. These timbrally varied fragments were reworked and eventually used to double (or echo) original material. The three-voice fugue taken by itself is written in a Baroque style, but using a chromatically extended tonal language, and each is echoed by its electronic double. The exposition is contrapuntal and chromatic. The second section symmetrically inverts the main subject and develops it contrapuntally while the third section features retrograde development of material. Section 4 is lyrical, while in the fifth, the organ solo presents the lyric material in a pastorale with two-voiced triplet rhythmic variations. The chorale fantasy, on the other hand, is in truncated ABA form, and begins with a majestic diatonic melodic line with C as a tonal center. The electronic doubling varies the timbres and includes bell-like sounds. A brilliant allegro and variation section is framed again at the end by the chordal section reminiscent of the beginning, to which Luening adds a quote from Wagner's *Tristan und Isolde*. Fast figurations for pedal and contrapuntal lines move freely in contrary motion with a full registration. The organ double sections frame organ solos and evolve ever more clearly into the sound of bell chimes/church bells.

To facilitate the creation of electronic music, Luening helped found a center for electronic music, the Columbia-Princeton Electronic Music Center. Established in 1959, the center was assisted by a grant from the Rockefeller Foundation and was a joint venture between Columbia University and Princeton University.[88] A very important component of the Center was the RCA Mark II synthesizer, the first programmable electronic synthesizer. Luening used this synthesizer for his composition "Synthesis for Orchestra and Electronic Sound," for live orchestra and recorded sound. The center also had tape recorder equipment, which was important for the work of Luening and Ussachevsky. The center became a nexus for composers from around the world interested in working in electronic media and enabled the creation of electronic compositions by Luening, Ussachevsky, Babbitt, Davidovsky, and others. The center stayed up to date with voltage-controlled synthesizers, digital computer music, and, eventually, commercial digital synthesizers with MIDI control.

LUENING'S MUSICAL HOMAGE TO BUSONI

Luening often acknowledged the impact Busoni had on his creative development, and he cemented his appreciation by writing a piano sonata in memory of his teacher, which he completed during the centennial of Busoni's year of birth, 1966. In the *Sonata for Piano in Memoriam Ferruccio Busoni*, W. 162, Luening tried to write a piece that reflected his teacher's brilliant pianism—yet avoided virtuosity for the sake of show. In addition, the sonata captures Busoni's love for the commedia dell'arte tradition in the Burlesque movement with hints of Harlequin and Columbine. In addition, the movement captures Busoni's love of dance and his predilection for counterpoint. Luening aimed for organic integration, balancing the phrases so that one leads into the other (a chain of musical phrases) with contrasting moods.[89]

The sonata is pluralistic, reflective of the diverse styles that fascinated Busoni, yet without direct quotations from his music. The piece contains four movements, the first and second of which are in a loose ABA form. The first movement begins majestically, and rhythmically resembles a French overture with dotted rhythm, mordents, and scalar passages. This is followed by a jaunty minuet. The French overture style returns at the end, but with richer block chords. In the first movement the ornaments and style harken back to the Baroque, but the tonal language belongs to the twentieth century (see music example 5.5). The second movement is a mysterious "dramatic scene," beginning and ending with homophonic block chords in a reverential chorale style that open up into a lyrical middle section with constant triplets and a soloistic line in the middle voice. This movement is an homage to Ziehn's principles of symmetric inversion—it begins with a chord canon in symmetrical inversion that is rhythmically as well as harmonically reminiscent of Busoni's *Berceuse élégiaque*, BV 252. The third movement depicts Busoni's wit and captures the spirit of the commedia dell'arte tradition with a modern twist. The idea of an Alberti Bass develops into a pseudo Boogie-Woogie bass that simulates a string bass in a pop combo. A stylized minuet at the end is reminiscent of Busoni's *Turandot*, BV 273. In addition, Luening paid homage to Busoni's command to try out new scalar and stylistic possibilities. The string of contrasting episodes depicts a dramatic scene through quick changes of pace and style. The final movement is a mysterious fantasia, which begins with improvisatory and chromatic rising figures in the bass.[90] The fantasia was a form idealized by Busoni as the freest and, hence, most natural. The piano writing is brilliant and Lisztian with double thirds descending octaves in both hands as well as chromatic figurations, but contains a mixture of virtuosity and vocal recitative writing. According to Luening, the use of only two contrasting rhythms was directly inspired by Busoni's piano concerto.[91] In addition, the music contains contrapuntal and imitative sections. Although predominantly atonal, the music passes through many key centers.

Despite all of the references to Busoni, Luening's own compositional voice can be heard prominently in the overall formal plan, which is based on relationships found in the overtone series. An introduction in G moves to B-flat and then back to G. The second and fourth movements center around A, which is the eighth overtone of G. In the first movement, the use of counterpoint also helps establish tonal areas through interval repetitions—in the first section, intervals of seconds, thirds, fourths, and their inversions and in the second, intervals of seconds, thirds, and sixths. This is followed by passages that lead into four-part rhythmic counterpoint. The third movement centers on F, but it develops polytonally with so many combinations that the impression is atonal until the F is reestablished at the end.[92]

In addition to the sonata, Luening also composed a Lyric Suite for Flute and Strings, W. 171, and five Suites for Flute Solo (W. 138, W. 156, W. 186, W. 196, W. 214) in memory of Busoni. These were pluralistic compositions that were meant to demonstrate the evolution of music. Luening stated it this way: "In the *Suites* I wished to build a bridge from the nineteenth century to the exciting new flute sounds of today. Each of the seven movements in *Suites III* and *IV* consists of a sonority from contrasting with all others. *Suite V* has four movements; Preamble, March Ceremony, Reception, and Conversations. The intervallic relations, integrated with tempo, rhythm, and dynamics bring out the certain acoustic characteristics of each movement. The contrasting sound images balance and give an impression of the flute's manifold possibilities."[93]

PROFESSIONAL CONNECTIONS

If Luening was impacted by Busoni's advocation to embrace stylistic pluralism and new sonorous and harmonic possibilities, he also benefitted professionally by contact with Busoni's other composition pupils—especially with Jarnach, with whom he corresponded to the end of Jarnach's life, and Edgard Varèse, who shared similar ideas about electronic music. Although Busoni did not introduce the two, as Varèse was already in the United States when Luening was studying with Busoni, Luening remembers Varèse as Busoni's protégé.[94] Luening did not hear Varèse's music until 1937 with Hanya Holm's *Trend* at Bennington College, even if he was familiar with some of his scores before that time. In an interview about his impressions of *Trend*, he summarized his familiarity with the music of Varèse:

MUSIC EXAMPLE 5.5. Luening, *Sonata for Piano in Memoriam Ferruccio Busoni*, W. 162, Introduction, mm. 1–12.

BOWERS: What do you remember about *Trend*?

LUENING: I remember mostly that it was the first time I heard Varèse's music. I knew his *Octandre* before but I heard that *Ionisation* was part of it and I was so impressed with it.[95]

The two soon met and socialized together after that, including at a bar in May 1937. Luening claims that Varèse became a close friend, and he eventually wrote a tribute in which he documented Varèse's views, his promotion of new music, his plans for new electronic instruments, and the relationship of his experimental music and music of the past.[96] Luening and Varèse shared an affinity for music of the past as well as new experimentation with electronic instruments. Luening also remembers a detail that is largely forgotten, or at least not mentioned in most sources—that Varèse loved to talk about masterworks of the past. In a lecture about new music at Bennington College, Luening maintained that Varèse shocked everyone by spending most of the time talking about classics: "To the astonishment of his listeners, he spent most of the time talking about the spacing in Beethoven's Symphonies, Berlioz's use of timbre as part of his musical form, and spoke of his favourite composers, Schütz and Monteverdi, for their expressive effects with utmost economy of means, and also of Obrecht's contrapuntal clarity."[97]

At the same time, he and Luening collaborated to promote new music. Both became active in the formation of the American Composers Alliance (founded in 1937), which aimed to help concert composers to make a living through their ventures in publishing and through promoting performances of American Composer Alliance publications.[98] In addition, the organization called for reforms in the way composers were compensated. From 1944 to 1952, Varèse also helped Luening with opera projects at Columbia University and was particularly interested in Luening's *Evangeline* because of its Acadian folksong background and choral writing. In addition, Varèse took over Luening's twentieth-century music seminar at Columbia in 1948. In the series he talked about modern music and included a description of the importance of Busoni's compositions. In addition, Varèse commissioned several works from Luening, including his *Alleluia,* W. 130, and an arrangement of the folk song "Poor Wayfaring Stranger" in 1943. Both also shared an affinity for the melding of science and art, which derived from Busoni. They built upon their teacher's ideas on this subject and took them in new directions. Luening wrote to Varèse about this very subject: "As in science where pure science and applied science go hand in hand, so I wish it were in music. Pure music is essential for the art even if understood by only a few; folk music is essential for the art even if understood by many. Humanly, I feel that music should in some way and for someone other than the composer animate or quiet the intelligence and awake or soothe the emotions, so helping man toward a greater realization of his nature and being and perhaps even toward a semblance of balance within himself."[99]

STUDENTS AND TEACHING METHODS

If Luening embraced a multiplicity of styles himself, it only made him a more tolerant teacher with a broad impact. Few composers have exerted a more wide-reaching influence on the next generation than Luening. Like Boulanger and Hindemith, he taught countless young composers, but, like few in similar positions, he insisted almost fanatically that they develop according to their own tastes rather than according to any predetermined method. Rather than dogmatically transmitting a set method, he, like Busoni, was open-minded, and encouraged students to follow their natural bents and propensities. His students, which included Ezra Laderman, Seymour Shifrin, Corigliano, Chou Wen-Chung, Charles Wuorinen, Davidovsky, and Kander, embraced a multiplicity of styles as well. Laderman wrote in an intensely romantic manner, Shifrin blended lyricism with rhythmic dislocation, and Chou mixed oriental and occidental influences. Chou specifically remembers that Luening was an individualistic composer and expected the same from his students: "As a composer he was highly individualistic and he believed in writing what he liked. Composing was a joy to him and his music reflects it. He encouraged young composers to pursue their own language. He urged his colleagues to continue to compose every day and never become disheartened by the lack of recognition or opportunity."[100]

Even so, he was diplomatic enough to launch the university's doctoral program in composition—he himself received an honorary degree in 1981. William Kraft, who studied with Luening at Columbia but ultimately pursued a more avant-garde path, remembers that Luening helped cultivate originality by teaching his students to avoid routine. On one occasion he did this with good humor as he improvised an ending to his student's composition, and it was a lesson that Kraft never forgot. He recounted the episode in an interview with Bruce Duffie:

WK: There was one little experience I had with Otto Luening, who was my teacher at Columbia in graduate school there. I was writing a violin-piano piece called *Sonata*, as one did in those days, and he was playing through my manuscript. He was a marvelous score reader, but he came to the end of what I had written and kept going on! I just was bowled over! It was wonderful what he was doing! It was exactly right; everything was just right and I listened intently. I watched his hands; I wanted to remember everything he did because it was so right. Finally he stopped and said, "Well, what do you think?" I said, "Well gee, Mr. Luening, that's really extraordinary! How did you do it?" And he said, "Don't you get it? It's routine." Well, that never left my mind! It's the same as another teacher saying look at every note. But I never forgot that.

BD: So have you stopped being routine?

WK: Yeah! Oh, I hope so! I find that something happens in my mind when I'm writing. I suddenly come to a block and I don't know what's wrong. I just can't figure out what should be next. That may last a few days, so I'll go out jogging; that's my way of thinking. I like to have something to think about when I'm jogging. I think about it and I generally come to a conclusion, something like, "It's time for a change, that's what it is. I'm not enjoying it." As you implied, the pencil was beginning to take over. That's the problem, and I go back and look at what the other possibilities are.[101]

Luening communicated to him, like Busoni had with his students, that the quality of the composition mattered more than style. For Kraft, as for Luening, this had to do with an awareness and assimilation of the craft of the past and of the present, coupled with the individuality of the composer.[102]

Like Busoni, Luening advocated self-study as the best way to develop individuality and personal style in art. This, coupled with artistic exchange with those outside the circle of composers—including musicologists, performers, authors, painters, etc.—enriches the human being and the art created.[103] Luening claimed that because people have different points of view, dialogue enriches art: "I believe that the musicologist, the performer, and the composer necessarily have different points of view of the art. Sometimes views converge, often they do not, but if they emanate from qualified and talented people they can all be useful in teaching. Sometimes in our universities the self-conscious search for novelty on the part of some is matched only by the withdrawal into archaic nebulae on the part of others. Neither attitude seems very productive to me, unless there coexists a balanced set of core activities that represents real artistic responsibilities."[104]

Luening also encouraged critical thinking, claiming that the purpose of teaching was not to fill students' heads with things they could discover for themselves through reading, but to invoke critical discussion. Also like Busoni, Luening maintained contact with his most gifted students and mentored them throughout their careers. John Corigliano remembered in 1999 that Luening became his friend and remained interested in his progress and career even after official studies had ended: "Otto Luening was my teacher and friend. He was not the sort of teacher who lost interest in his students after they left him. Rather, he always stayed very involved in their progress and musical growth. Quoting him is the best way to honor him. In 1995, in response to a birthday message, he wrote: 'Of course the best present you can give me is the career you carved out for yourself.' This quality of love and giving is irreplaceable."[105]

CONCLUSION

To the end of his life, Luening was grateful for the stimulating conversations and compositional guidance he received from Busoni during his formative years in Zurich. The process of assimilating the ideas was a life-long one, and Luening took those ideas in new directions according to his own personal talent. He also remained interested in the reception of Busoni's music. On February 26, 1962, Luening and Jarnach corresponded about a Düsseldorf performance of Busoni's *Doktor Faust*, BV 303.[106] In addition, he continued to collaborate with Busoni pupils. In a letter of June 25, 1938, Luening noted that he had collaborated with another Busoni pupil, Carlos Buhler, in a performance of Jarnach's flute sonata.[107] Moreover, he also corresponded with at least one of Busoni's sons even after moving to the United States. A letter from Rafaello Busoni of 1923 discusses Rafaello's artwork, which interested Luening greatly.

Yet of all the composers covered in this book, Luening's relationship with Busoni was the shortest. He did not visit him after moving away, and the two do not appear to have maintained active correspondence. Many of Luening's meetings with Busoni were suggested by Jarnach. Overall, Luening was closer to Jarnach, with whom he studied closely and with whom he corresponded to the end of his life. On October 5, 1952, Luening sent Jarnach an Aria for Cello and Piano, W. 124, with a dedication in celebration of the birth of his son, and he thanked Jarnach for helping him develop technique and to find his way professionally. Luening also invited Jarnach to America in the 1960s to give a series of talks, for which Jarnach prepared a lecture entitled "Electronic Music in the USA," in honor of the pioneering work of his pupil.[108]

Despite the brevity of the relationship between Luening and Busoni, it had a lasting impact on Luening, who was naturally drawn to the possibilities of musical sound. Busoni opened up his mind to new sonar possibilities that could only become realities during Luening's lifetime due to advances in technology. Busoni's mystical ideas about the freedom of music and its fluidity, its lightness and transparency, led Luening away from the Germanic tradition in which he had been trained to an all-encompassing pluralistic approach that eschewed routine and embraced a multiplicity of possibilities, including electronic music. Luening composed diatonic, serial, aleatoric, improvisatory, and electronic music, which opened up new soundscapes that were taken in new directions as technology advanced. Luening summed up his approach with a near quotation of Busoni: "Each one has its little plot in this great beautiful magical garden of music and he said that it's our privilege and our responsibility to cultivate that plot and to cultivate it as well as we can."[109]

NOTES

1. The pieces include *Fantasy in Space* for flute on tape (1951) and *Rhapsodic Variations* (1954, composed jointly with Vladimir Ussachevsky) for tape and live orchestra.

2. Otto Luening, *The Odyssey of an American Composer: The Autobiography of Otto Luening* (New York: Scribner, 1980); Otto Luening and Tim Page, *From the Archives: American Mavericks: Otto Luening Plugs America into Electronic Music (Otto Luening Speaks with Host Tim Page on Meet the Composer from 1985)*, http://www.wqxr.org/#!/story/194723-otto-luening-plugs-america-into-electronic-music/, accessed August 6, 2013; Otto Luening and Bruce Duffie, "Composer Otto Luening: A Conversation with Bruce Duffie," http://www.kcstudio.com/luening3.html, accessed August 6, 2013.

3. Severine Neff, "Otto Luening (1900–) and the Theories of Bernhard Ziehn (1845–1912)," *Current Musicology* 39 (1985), 39.

4. All work numbers (W.) come from the following source: Ralph Hartsock, *Otto Luening: A Bio-Bibliography*, Bio-Bibliographies in Music, no. 35, ed. Donald L. Hixon (New York: Greenwood Press, 1991). According to Hartsock, the work numbers are arranged chronologically and the list was prepared in conjunction with Luening and Emily Good.

5. Luening, *Odyssey*, 147.
6. Ibid., 154.
7. Neff, "Otto Luening," 21.
8. Luening, *Odyssey*, 154–155.
9. Ibid., 155.
10. Dr. Haeser, untitled and undated review, *Neue Zürcher Zeitung*, Luening Papers, New York Public Library, Special Collections, Box 48, no. 1. I have been unable to establish the exact date of the premiere performance. Hartsock's bibliography first lists a performance on December 9, 1921, in Chicago with Luening on the piano and Rudolph Mangold on the violin. No mention is made of the prior Zurich performance.
11. Luening, *Odyssey*, 168.
12. Ibid., 168.
13. Ibid., 169. Luening claims he heard the recital in 1917. Recital programs indicate that Busoni played those pieces on February 13 and February 15, 1918, in Basel as well. Ferruccio Busoni, *Briefe Busonis an Hans Huber*, ed. Edgar Refardt (Zurich: Hug and Co., 1939), 48.
14. Luening, *Odyssey*, 171.
15. Ibid., 184.
16. Ibid., 176–183.
17. Ibid., 179.
18. Busoni to Philipp Jarnach, May 3, 1919, Staatsbibliothek zu Berlin, Preußischer Kulturbesitz, Musikabteilung mit Mendelssohn-Archiv, Mus. Nachl. F. Busoni, N. Mus. Depos. 56.
19. Luening, *Odyssey*, 180. The performance took place on April 30, 1921. Hartsock, *Otto Luening*, 27.
20. Luening never followed up on the reading in Busoni's house. The first private performance took place in 1921 in Zurich with some success, and it was selected by the ICSM in American to go over to Europe, but it was not accepted for the Venice festival. Upon its revival in 1981, it was given an excellent review in the *New York Times*.
21. Luening, *Odyssey*, 180.
22. "My reports for third grade showed a yearly average of 'Excellent' in reading, spelling, language, and arithmetic; 'Poor' in penmanship; 'Poor' in drawing. I was excused from singing. Too advanced!" Luening, *Odyssey*, 52.
23. Paul de Jong, phone call with the author, September 11, 2013. De Jong also mentioned that Luening talked about Busoni's predictions about electronic music.
24. Drafts and sketches can be found in Otto Luening Papers, New York Public Library, Special Collections, JPB 94-7, Box 126.
25. Luening, *Odyssey*, 182.
26. "String Quartet, op. 4," *The Musical Times of London*, April 1924.
27. Hugo Leichtentritt, untitled article, *Musical Courier*, Berlin, March 11, 1924.

28. Adolf Weissmann, untitled review, *Die Musik*, Berlin, April 1924.
29. Luening, Sextet, Otto Luening Papers, New York Public Library, JPB 94–7, Box 148.
30. Luening, *Odyssey*, 192.
31. Luening, Sonata for Violin and Piano no. 1, Otto Luening Papers, New York Public Library, JPB 94–7, Box 129.
32. "P.S. mein ehemaliger Schüler, Herr Otto Luening hat mir diese Tage eine neue Arbeit gebracht; es ist ein Streichquartett (ganz am Schluss kommt eine Klarinette hinzu) Sie wurden mir persönliche einer grossen Gefallen ewigen, wenn Sie sich einige Stellen des umfangreichen manuskripts ansehen wollten." Philipp Jarnach to Busoni, June 2–3, 1920, Staatsbibliothek zu Berlin, Preußischer Kulturbesitz, Musikabteilung mit Mendelssohn-Archiv, Mus. Nachl. F. Busoni, 30.
33. Busoni to Philipp Jarnach, 1920 (unknown date), Staatsbibliothek zu Berlin, Preußischer Kulturbesitz, Musikabteilung mit Mendelssohn-Archiv, N. Mus. Depos., 56; Luening, *Odyssey*, 183.
34. Luening, *Odyssey*, 178–179.
35. Ibid., 181.
36. Ibid., 180–181.
37. Busoni studied in Leipzig with Salomon Jadassohn, a master contrapuntist who had been a student of Liszt.
38. Luening, *Odyssey*, 180.
39. Luening, "Some Random Remarks about Electronic Music," *Journal of Music Theory* 8:1 (Spring 1964), 93–94.
40. Luening, interview with Charles Amirkhanian, Other Minds Audio Archive, http://archive.org/details/AM_1981_03_31, accessed August 9, 2013.
41. Luening, *Odyssey*, 174.
42. Luening, interview with Charles Amirkhanian.
43. Luening, *Odyssey*, 174.
44. Luening, "Some Random Remarks about Electronic Music," 92.
45. Luening, untitled essay, Luening Papers, New York Public Library, Special Collections, Box 46, no. 8.
46. Otto Luening, program notes for the *Sonata for Piano in Memoriam Ferruccio Busoni*, http://www.newworldrecords.org/uploads/fileXuPcA.pdf, accessed August 10, 2013.
47. Luening, interview with Bruce Duffie.
48. Luening, quoted in "American Composers Alliance Bulletin", 1953, in *Otto Luening Centennial* (n.p.: Otto Luening Trust, 2000), 22.
49. Luening, "Some Random Remarks about Electronic Music," 92.
50. Ibid., 92.
51. Ibid., 93.
52. Busoni, "The New Harmony" (1911), in *The Essence of Music and Other Papers*, trans. Rosamund Ley (1922; London: Salisbury Square, 1957), 24. This essay was originally written in Chicago in January 1911 for *Signale*. The other harmonic "roads" include keeping the voices independent of each other in polyphonic compositions,

atonality, and a new key system in which all of the previously mentioned methods will be combined.

53. Neff, "Otto Luening," 21–22, based on an interview with Luening.

54. Luening, *Odyssey*, 184.

55. Neff, "Otto Luening," 22.

56. Neff has described in detail the process and its implementation into Luening's compositions after interviewing him in 1984 and analyzing his music. Neff, "Otto Luening (1900–) and the Theories of Bernhard Ziehn (1845–1912)."

57. An irregular cadence is a cadence in which a dissonant pitch is left unresolved; Ziehn was the first major theorist to classify such cadences.

58. Neff, "Otto Luening," 24–25.

59. Ibid., 31.

60. See the first chapter for an explanation of Busoni's aesthetic views. Busoni stated: "The time has come to recognize the whole phenomenon of music as a 'oneness' and no longer split it up according to its purpose, form, and sound-medium. It should be recognized from two premises exclusively, that of its content and that of its quality." Busoni, 'The Essence and Oneness of Music," in *The Essence of Music and Other Papers*, 1.

61. Busoni, "The Essence and Oneness of Music," in *The Essence of Music and Other Papers*, 6.

62. Luening, *Odyssey*, 309.

63. Luening, "Conversation with Theresa Bowers," Bennington Summer School of the Dance Project (New York: n.p., 1979), 41. For more about Luening's activities at Bennington College, see Elizabeth McPherson, *The Bennington School of the Dance: A History in Writings and Interviews* (Jefferson, NC: McFarland, 2013).

64. The Bispham Memorial Medal was awarded by the American Opera Society of Chicago from 1921 to 1932 for exceptional operas written in the English language on American subjects by an American composer. It was awarded in honor of David Bispham, a baritone.

65. Luening, *Evangeline: Opera in 3 Acts*, piano-vocal score (New York: C. F. Peters, n.d.), 39.

66. Ibid., 3.

67. Luening, *Odyssey*, 307. Luening also was active in promoting American opera. At Columbia he oversaw the performance of about forty new works, including Benjamin Britten's *Paul Bunyan*, and himself conducted Gian Carlo Menotti's *The Medium* (1946) and Virgil Thomson's *The Mother of Us All* (1947).

68. Olin Downs, "Opera by Luening at Its Premiere: *Evangeline*: Based on Poem by Longfellow Is Presented by Columbia University," *New York Times*, May 6, 1948, 31.

69. Luening, interview with Tim Page.

70. For better understanding Luening's theory about the evolution of electronic music consult Otto Luening, "Origins," in Jon H. Appleton and Ronald C. Perera, *The Development and Practice of Electronic Music* (Englewood Cliffs, NJ: Prentice-Hall, 1975).

71. Busoni, Sketch of a New Aesthetic of Music, trans. T. Baker (New York: Schirmer, 1911), 33.

72. Ibid., 4.

73. Severine Neff, phone interview with the author, May 22, 2014. Neff also noted that Busoni rewrote Schoenberg's Klavierstuck, op. 11, no. 2, because he didn't like the timbre.

74. Otto Luening, "Conversation with Theresa Bowers," 68.

75. Jack Beeson, "Otto Luening," *Bulletin of the American Composers Alliance* 3:3 (1954), 4.

76. Otto Luening, "Electronic Music—First Pieces: Analyses of Fantasy in Space, Low Speed, and Invention in 12 Tones," in *1952 Electronic Tape Music: The First Compositions* (New York: Highgate Press, 1977), 32.

77. Ibid.

78. Otto Luening, "Conversation with Theresa Bowers," 22. Holm was a dancer, choreographer, and dance instructor. She helped found the American Dance Festival, and her first major work, *Trend*, dealt with social criticism.

79. Otto Luening, "Electronic Music—First Pieces," 33.

80. Ibid.

81. Ibid., 34.

82. Ibid. He originally used minimal notation and improvised. However, copyright protection required notating ideas as specifically as possible. This required the use of some graphic notation and non-traditional symbols.

83. Luening, "Fantasy in Space," in *Electronic Tape Music*, 36–40.

84. Luening, ""Electronic Music—First Pieces," 35.

85. Luening, interview with Bruce Duffie.

86. Luening, "Invention for Flute and Tape Recorder," *in Electronic Tape Music*, 43.

87. The following observations are based partially on program notes by Otto Luening, http://www.newworldrecords.org/uploads/fileXuPcA.pdf., accessed August 10, 2013.

88. For a more detailed history of the center consult Nick Patterson, "The Archives of the Columbia-Princeton Music Center," *Notes* (March 2011), 483–502.

89. Luening, interview with Tim Page.

90. The following analysis relies on my own observations coupled with Luening's program notes for the sonata. Otto Luening, program notes for the *Sonata for Piano in Memoriam Ferruccio Busoni*, http://www.newworldrecords.org/uploads/fileXuPcA.pdf, accessed August 10, 2013,

91. Ibid.

92. Raymond Ericson, who wrote a review for the first public performance of the sonata by Ursula Oppens in the *New York Times*, described the piece in the highest terms: "The sonata is a first-rate work. Pianists looking for large-scale American pieces should look into it, no matter how they eventually react to it. It is not problematic, for Mr. Luening uses conventional material, although in unexpected and original ways, and its technical difficulties pay off in the virtuoso splash they make." Raymond Ericson, "Music: A First for Sonata by Luening," *New York Times*, November 20, 1975.

93. Luening, liner notes for the Suite for Flute solo no. 3, in *Flute Possibilities*, Harvey Sollberger, flute, Composers Recordings CRI 400 (1979).

94. Luening, interview with Charles Amirkhanian.

95. Otto Luening, "Conversation with Theresa Bowers," 22.

96. Luening, "Varèse and the Schola Cantorum, Busoni and New York," *Contemporary Music Review* 23:1 (March 2004).

97. Luening, "Varèse and the Schola Cantorum," 15.

98. This alliance was the brainchild of Roger Sessions, Aaron Copland, Virgil Thomson, and Edgard Varèse, but Luening was invited to the planning sessions. The association was designed to help young composers with the business of composing. Luening, *Odyssey*, 431. Luening became president of the organization in the late 1940s. He was also a co-founder in 1940 of the American Music Center, and in 1954 of Composers Recordings Inc.

99. Chou Wen-Chung, quoted in "Colleagues, Friends, and Students, a Tribute," in *Otto Luening Centennial*, 12.

100. William Kraft, "A Conversation with Bruce Duffie, http://www.bruceduffie.com/wm-kraft.html, accessed August 12, 2013.

101. Ibid.

102. "And most of all, I had to suggest self-study, which is how I learned. I didn't have an enormous amount of formal background in music. But I was, because of circumstances, booted around. I did have *some* formal musical training at the Academy in Munich and at the conservatory in Switzerland. But mostly people like my father, who had a very inquiring mind and was a fine musician, and Ferruccio Busoni, Philip Jarnach, and other people influenced me. . . . like James Joyce, whom I knew when I was in Zurich." Luening, "Conversations with American Composers: Ev Grimes, Interviews—Otto Luening," *Music Educators Journal* 72:5 (January 1986), 27.

103. "Teaching in our universities could be vastly improved if instructors would agree not to use class time to present materials that are readily accessible to students in books, on records, on record liners, on radio or TV programs, and on machines. Detailed reading and listening lists, and relevant outlines, are useful summaries of the necessary background material, but class time should be used to present material that is not readily accessible, to answer questions, and for discussion. Instructors should be encouraged to present their own opinions. Instructors should be encouraged to present their own opinions about contemporary and old music instead of trying, without much success, to represent an 'objective' wisdom that at best is most difficult to project." Luening, "Conversations with American Composers."

104. John Corigliano, quoted in "Colleagues, Friends, and Students: A Tribute," in *Otto Luening Centennial*, 13.

105. Jarnach to Luening, February 26, 1962, Luening Papers, New York Public Library, Special Collections.

106. Luening to Jarnach, June 25, 1938, ibid.

107. Jarnach to Luening, March 19, 1964, ibid.

108. Luening, interview with Tim Page.

6

New Music of the Weimar Republic

> By the way it seems to me that we have now forgotten, how much Zurich, already during the First World War, was the center of intellectual Europe. There I saw the author Jakob Wassermann, the poet Hermann Hesse, the wise world-observer Harry Graf Kessler, the composers Walter Braunfels and Stravinsky, and the architect van de Velde: spirits who were obsessed with completely new ideas. But one of them exercised a more decisive influence than all on me: Ferruccio Busoni.
>
> Philipp Jarnach, "Das Beispiel Busonis, 1963"

JARNACH'S BURGEONING COMPOSITION CAREER

PHILIPP JARNACH (1892–1982) was viewed as one of the most important young composers in Germany during the 1920s and early 1930s. In 1922, a reviewer stated: "Not merely hope, but already a fulfillment, Philipp Jarnach is for us one of the most pronounced leading figures of the young generation."[1] A performance of Jarnach's String Quintet, op. 10, at the Donaueschingen Festival on July 22, 1921 launched his career, and reviewers heaped praise on his compositions for about a decade.[2] As a member of the *Novembergruppe* along with Kurt Weill, Heinz Tiessen, Max Butting, Wladimir Vogel, Stefan Wolpe, Hans Heinz Stuckenschmidt, Felix Petyrek, Jascha Horenstein, Gustav Havemann, and Hanns Eisler, he was part of the avant-garde of the Weimar Republic, and his music is characterized by novel treatments of the musical language, form, and style, even if it is simultaneously described as intellectual, classy, spiritual, timeless, and noble.[3]

Jarnach attributed the formation of his personal style and his initial compositional success to Ferruccio Busoni, with whom he studied from 1915 to 1924. True, he also noted the importance of others for his development, including Richard Strauss (1864–1949) and Claude Debussy (1862–1918).[4] However, it was Busoni who laid the foundation for the most experimental aspects of Jarnach's style in the 1920s. Jarnach asserted he was most indebted to Busoni for his development: "Busoni's attitude about art, even more than his technical example, became the most important experience for me. Because, if I am considered his pupil, I have never obtained a single lesson. However, I feel that I owe him everything that I may have become."[5]

Busoni's influence was long lasting, and had as much to do with his attitude toward his pupil as the actual advice he gave. Jarnach notes that Busoni believed in him and expected great things: "Because he [Busoni] truly stuck by me and expected something from me—that is perhaps what decided for me the rest of my life."[6] He also helped him develop a vision of ideal art: "You came at a crucial moment in my artistic life, right when I came in possession of a secure compositional technique, but was rather clueless, swayed back and forth in the chaos of recent traditions. You taught me one thing above all: to recognize the immutable standard of art."[7]

Busoni's influence is evident from a marked change in Jarnach's style. Jarnach's early songs and instrumental compositions reveal the influence of French composers such as Debussy. They are largely tonal with some chromaticism and frequent textural shifts. After meeting Busoni, Jarnach's music became more experimental, displaying transparent, contrapuntal textures coupled with tendencies toward atonality, quartal harmonies, unique structures, and stylistic pluralism.

A brief comparison of works composed before and after Jarnach met Busoni in 1915 in Zurich reveals the depth of Busoni's influence. Jarnach's Sonata for Violin and Piano in E Major, op. 9 (1913), is tonal and features simple melodies over arpeggiated piano accompaniment (see music example 6.1). The traditional four-movement structure begins and ends in E major even if there is extended chromaticism throughout. French style

MUSIC EXAMPLE 6.1. Jarnach, Sonata in E Major for Violin and Piano, op. 9, mm. 1–9.

montage-like juxtapositions pervade the piece. By contrast, the Sonatine for Flute and Piano, op. 12 (1919), contains no key designations and a mixture of styles (e.g., recitative, cadenza, lament, lied, march, and dance) (see music example 6.2).[8] The juxtaposition of vocal and instrumental styles contributes to the overall structure of the piece, such as in measures 23–40, where rhythmic dance-like music in the piano alternates with free and improvisatory recitative passages in the flute. Contrapuntal textures create *gravitas* even while the single movement continuously unfolds like a developing fantasia coupled with variation form. The unusual and nearly symmetrical structure of ABCDC'B'D'A' in which each section displays contrasting textures and rhythms, is nonetheless consistently based on the opening motivic material that is varied through processes of augmentation, diminution, transposition, and variation.

MUSIC EXAMPLE 6.2. Jarnach, Sonatine for Flute and Piano, op. 12, mm. 1–11.

SUMMARY OF SCHOLARSHIP

Despite Busoni's significance for Jarnach's development, little scholarship (especially in the English language) discusses the Busoni-Jarnach connection. The most comprehensive source on Jarnach's life, works, and career, by Stefan Weiss, documents Jarnach's evolution as a composer. Weiss's book imparts valuable information about the Busoni-Jarnach connection. However, the information is scattered throughout the text, which is devoted to Jarnach's life and works, and thus must be pieced together by the reader. Weiss also focuses on the music and does not spend much time discussing the aesthetic ideas.[9] Tamara Levitz, by contrast, compares some of Jarnach's and Busoni's aesthetic ideas, focusing mainly on the concept of Young Classicality. However, her article does not aim to provide a comprehensive overview of the Jarnach-Busoni relationship, and does not discuss Jarnach's works or stylistic evolution in detail.[10] Levitz's dissertation also provides valuable information about Jarnach's years with Busoni in Berlin (1921–1924), but its main focus is Busoni's Berlin master class, of which Jarnach was not a member.[11] Nevertheless, it is one of the few English-language texts discussing Jarnach. In addition, Virgilio Bernardoni examines the scope and importance of Busoni's influence on Jarnach's aesthetic thought and musical influence.[12] The length of the article, however, precludes a thorough discussion of any of the topics. Other sources of information include Hans Jelmoli's and Laureto Rodoni's work on Busoni's activities in Zurich.[13]

Based on numerous letters and scores in the Jarnach and Busoni Nachlass collections in the Staatsbibliothek Berlin, the Otto Luening Papers at the New York Public Library, and the Edward Dent Collection at the Rowe Library in Cambridge, England, as well as published writings by Jarnach and Busoni, this chapter presents the first detailed exploration of the Jarnach-Busoni connection in English and reveals Busoni's importance for the development of the most experimental aspects of Jarnach's music.

BEGINNINGS OF THE JARNACH-BUSONI CONNECTION

The Jarnach-Busoni connection began in Zurich during World War I. Jarnach had already received sound musical instruction in piano and theory in Paris, and he had met Claude Debussy and Maurice Ravel.[14] Yet after moving to Zurich in August 1914, he floundered in composition, struggling to develop his own voice.[15] Contacting Busoni was a step toward realizing that goal.[16] Because Busoni received countless requests, he did not answer Jarnach's initial letter, but the two eventually met when Jarnach made an unannounced visit at his home.[17] The first meeting proved to be just the beginning of many lessons and discussions that lasted until Busoni's death in 1924.[18]

Jarnach's lessons with Busoni were hardly traditional. Technique was rarely discussed. Instead, according to Jarnach, Busoni tended to focus on the spiritual or aesthetic content of art:

> Busoni was no teacher in the strict sense of the word. He lacked any instructional inclination, as well as that which goes without saying—the dispassionate objectivity of the pedagogue. He had gone through a thorough study of theory, but did not believe in instruction systems. He said that only spiritual independence and insight could inform craftsmanship so that not routine but rather art would arise. Individual perception was for him the only possible force able to overcome the resistance of the material; moreover if he required the seamless appropriation of empirical experience to be essential, he demanded of the artist that he never rest on what he has learned, but rather deduce the means from the particular idea.[19]

Rather than discussing a method book, they focused on aesthetic concepts. For instance, they talked about Busoni's concept of the *Essence of Music*.[20] Like Busoni, Jarnach came to believe in an inaudible source that encompassed all styles of music and that provided a model for stylistically heterogeneous music. Jarnach called it "the infinite" in his writings.[21] They also discussed Busoni's theories of Young Classicality.[22] In particular, Jarnach learned about Busoni's idealization of linearity, objectivity, and the omnipresence of time, that is, the notion that music of all eras is equally valid. Jarnach described the ideals as refined and universal:[23] "A music that is rooted in the emotional, yet rejects a massively destructive amount of affect and does not provide conflict, but rather synthesis, a sonic image that disperses impressionistic polyphonic lines, yet still allows a spiritual background to shine through in the color, the ornamentation, and even the virtuoso element; such a universal yet at the same time such an austere art is not bound to the present."[24]

In embracing Young Classicality, Jarnach helped pioneer a broader cultural shift from Schoenbergian expressionism to *Neue Sachlichkeit* in the Weimar Republic in the 1920s. He called for a simplification and objectification of music:[25]

> While Schoenberg seeks to draw from his sonorous material a maximum of expression, Busoni, by contrast, reduces extreme means; he spiritualizes, you might say, the process, and transforms it, impregnating a central idea from which the technical elements of each work strictly depend. Sound, rhythm, and silences themselves take on a new and almost symbolic significance; the progressive momentum of each phrase, the violent dynamics of a feigned "culminating point"—commonly favored sections of neo-romanticism—are banished from a music which does not proceed from an accrual, but rather from a reduction of accents.[26]

The topic of absolute music also came up frequently in conversations. Busoni and Jarnach talked in particular about the adaptability of music—about the idea that music, when placed in diverse settings, could assume different functions. Part of Mozart's Requiem, K. 626, for instance, could be easily repositioned in a comic opera without seeming out of place. Music was music, Busoni argued, regardless of the setting or accompanying text, thereby allowing for its reworking in new settings. Galston recounts Busoni's teachings and Jarnach's reaction:

> This led us to the favorite theme—that music adapts itself to any situation as if transformed magically. The "Tuba mirum" from *Mozart's Requiem* could in the same form also be of the best effect in the genre of comic opera. At that, Philipp Jarnach, who was present, talked about what mattered to him about Schubert Lieder. Where the same music accompanies the most diverse strophes, each time the expression is more suitable and meaningful for the words. Earlier, he had described a special ingenuity of the composer, who had found a type of cheerful melody universally right for each particular case. Now he sees it with FBs eyes. The music always fits and transforms itself.[27]

If Jarnach adopted many of Busoni's aesthetic ideas, he was also particularly impressed by the composer's call to avoid routine. Busoni advocated exploring new scales, structures, and styles in every composition. For Jarnach, who was naturally systematic, this was one of the most difficult lessons he learned from Busoni—at the same time—it seemed to unlock

Jarnach's creativity: "The Busonian art, however, imparted the awareness of new problems and opportunities that could not be solved according to recipes. Here was no 'direction,' no manner or formula to be found that was reproducible, but the sacrosanct example of a creative power, which only served expression while at the same time provided the maximum discipline of expression."[28]

In addition to aesthetic ideas, they also talked about drama, film, literature, and architecture. Even though Jarnach never distinguished himself as an opera composer, he was impacted by Busoni's ideas about stylistic pluralism that arose from conversations about opera.[29] Busoni also often discussed opera libretti with his students to aid their sense of pacing and their aesthetic understanding of his ideals of opera. Students, for instance, had a chance to read the opera libretto that Busoni created for Louis Gruenberg, Die Götterbraut (1913–1915). He also discussed his own operatic compositions. In particular, he went into detail about progress on Dr. Faust, BV 303. In one letter to Jarnach, Busoni discussed the integration of contrasting instrumental and vocal styles in the work.[30]

Lessons also involved collaboration on composition projects and score critique. A notable pedagogical collaboration between Jarnach and Busoni was Das Wandbild (The Mural), an opera-pantomime that explores the ambiguity between reality and the dream world. It contains a plethora of styles suggested by the libretto: vocal parts, speaking, pantomime, as well as action accompanied by instrumental music and non-texted syllabic singing. Jarnach introduced Busoni to Martin Buber's Chinesische Geister- und Liebesgeschichten (1911) upon which Busoni based the libretto. Jarnach was to compose the music. Hoping to communicate his ideals of opera to Jarnach, Busoni left detailed suggestions for the musical setting, such as the recommendation to use antique oriental melodies for the religious singing and that the chorus of the maidens should begin and end vaguely. He also cautioned against incorporating descriptive ghost music into the score.[31]

Jarnach was pleased by the libretto and began to set it right away, even if he did not finish the first movement until January the following year.[32] However, he had a hard time setting the unconventional libretto, which featured solo singing, spoken text, pantomime, instrumental sections, and untexted singing. After setting the prologue and first scene, Jarnach abandoned the project in June 1918. Nevertheless, Jarnach's sketches remain a testament to his early lessons about dramaturgy and style with Busoni (see figure 6.1). Jarnach worked on the following movements:

I. Interludium
II. Gebet und Heiliger Tanz
III. Lyrische Szene

The interludium, a completely instrumental movement, is scored for bass clarinet in B, horns in F, cellos, contrabass, and percussion, contributing to an initially dark orchestral color well suited to the dark stage setting and lugubrious affect. Chromatic motives permeate the movement. In the second movement, which follows without break, a choir behind the stage joins the instruments singing "ah!" The stage is lighted as young women begin to dance and sing, and the scenery contain trees, colorful birds, and a temple in the background. During a *mädchenchor* section, the priests join in with unison lines before splitting into imitative counterpoint on the syllable "ah!" The second movement is unified with the first through the reuse use of the chromatic motives despite frequent shifts of meter, style, and tonality. The unfinished fragment of the third movement contains the first settings of a texted voice as a female choir sings about a child that has become a bride.

In addition to these less conventional methods of instruction, Busoni frequently critiqued Jarnach's scores. Letters between Busoni and Jarnach as well as surviving manuscripts document some of Busoni's advice. The manuscript for the String Quartet op. 16 is notated in Jarnach's neat hand, but there are a few annotations in the margins in what appears to be Busoni's more scrawling handwriting. The annotations focus on minor details such as phrasing and dynamic markings.[33]

By contrast, Busoni offered philosophical and aesthetic advice about Jarnach's *Sinfonia Brevis*, op. 14. He specifically urged Jarnach to strike out in a new direction: "Philippo . . . I expect more from you and something different from what I heard in your piece yesterday [*Sinfonia Brevis*]. . . . Are you so caught up in the joy of certain achievements that you don't express yourself, but rather what you have achieved? I dare tell you all this because I know that you already have new goals in sight. Finally (and

FIGURE 6.1. Jarnach, *Das Wandbild*, "Gebet und Heiliger Tanz," excerpt. Staatsbibliothek zu Berlin—Preussischer Kulturbesitz, Musikabteilung mit Mendelssohn Archiv, N. Mus. Depos. 56.17.

this will reveal to you the most important point I want to make), I think you will soon have to seek a new horizon. Your soul should experience something which is not realized here."[34]

Busoni also advised Jarnach about instrumental forces for the setting when he looked at the *Prolog zu einem Ritterspiel*.[35] However, Busoni was more than satisfied with the counterpoint and formal structure, stating that Jarnach was on his way to becoming a "master architect." For Busoni, this was high praise indeed: "Your 'Ritterspiel' has become a realistic construction, with a contrapuntal underpinning which is guided masterfully and... I do congratulate you on this new step on the way of the Champion Architects."[36]

Although Busoni did not typically talk about technical matters in a systematic way, he did frequently discuss form with Jarnach. Jarnach specifically remembers that Busoni taught that form should not be viewed as a mold according to which pitches were shaped, but rather as an individual exploration of the ways unique musical ideas could unfold. At the same time, he stressed the need for proportion and balance: "Form is not a scaffold but an experience to see how to evaluate precisely the measure of proportion and economy of expression. The task of the artist is to derive from the particular musical idea the means to shape its visible form."[37]

Jarnach's String Quintet, op. 10 displays his exploration of Busoni's ideas about form, polyphony, tonality, and stylistic diversity. Weiss maintains that this piece represents the first deep traces of Busonian influence.[38] A letter from Jarnach to Busoni documents that the formal structure was among the aspects of the piece that the two discussed in some detail: "I thank you for your kind letter of advice about the division of the Quintet. I had already intended to move in the direction of expanding the movements—some kind of paraphrase would lengthen the work by about two or three minutes of music."[39]

Jarnach described the form as a theme and seven free variants, which also serve as self-standing movements:[40]

Praeambulum (F Minor to D Major)
Thema (F Minor to D Major)
    I. Sinfonia (C Minor to D Minor)
    II. Melodram (G Minor)

III. Giga (D Minor)
IV. Aria (F Major to D Major)
V. Rezitativ (A Minor to D Major)
VI. Marsch (C Major)
VII. Choralvorspiel (C Minor to D Major)
VIII. Finale and Coda (Doppelfuge) (F Minor to D Major plus C major closing triad)

As Weiss has already noted, of these movements, only two (the Melodram and Gigue) begin and end in the same key.[41] At the same time, stylistic heterogeneity pervades the movements, thereby reflecting Busoni's theories of the Essence of Music. The polyphonic underpinning in the Sinfonia, Choralvospiel, and Finale, in addition to the suite-like succession of short movements, is reminiscent of the Baroque period. This is coupled with allusions to vocal styles. The work thus crosses genre boundaries. In particular, the designations "melodram" and "recitative" with the tempo marking of menuetto are unusual for a string composition. Also unexpected is beginning with a variation, as the theme is, in essence, a variation of the prelude. According to Jarnach, initial pitches and groups of notes grow into a motive and then a theme, which then serve as the basis for variations: "Two simple motifs of the Introduction (Praeambulum), which ... initially in the 'theme' obtain clear shape, form at the same time the melodic core of the whole; from these two main motives all the variation themes develop."[42] Variations of the main theme occur both rhythmically and intervallicaly (see music example 6.3). The interval of the ascending second, appearing prominently in the opening of the main theme (C, F, G-flat, F, G), forms main motivic material. During the opening bar of the Sinfonia (var. I), for instance, in the bass, the same m2, M2 motion occurs at the beginning and is followed by another m2, M2 progression, yet in alternating ascending and descending motion: C-C-D-flat-C-D-E-flat-D-C. In measure 17, the opening undulating second motion appears in the first violin part: C, D-flat, C, D, C, D, E-flat, F, G, A (see music example 6.4). The original rhythmic presentation of the intervals featuring a dotted quartered followed by eighth notes is also altered in subsequent variations In the Melodrama, similar motivic configurations appear with double dotted eighths and sixteenth notes. At the same time, Jarnach var-

MUSIC EXAMPLE 6.3. Jarnach, String Quintet, op. 10, Theme, mm. 1–9.

ies the style, from the lively dance-like giga to the lyrical song-like aria to the free recitative and rhythmic march and the turgid polyphony of the double fugue in the finale.

Busoni also worked with Jarnach on orchestration. Jarnach remembers that he believed timbre to be integral to a work.[43] In response to his reading of Jarnach's *Ballata für Orchester* (March 14–31, 1916), which Jarnach

MUSIC EXAMPLE 6.4. Jarnach, String Quintet, op. 10, Sinfonia, mm. 17–21.

sent as a present on Busoni's birthday (April 1, 1916), Busoni specifically advised the study of orchestration in Mozart's scores, especially *Le Nozze di Figaro*, K. 492, and *Die Zauberflöte*, K. 620.[44] Jarnach's annotated copy of *Die Zauberflöte* offers a glimpse into what the two must have discussed in their meetings about Mozart and orchestration.[45] It contains numerous annotations, the majority of which have to do with instrumentation. In particular, notes are made about unusual instrumentation, such as the use of the glockenspiel and of the importance of the bassoon in Sarastro's vocal parts.[46] In addition, the score contains changes to the printed instrumental parts. For instance, "corno di bassetto" is crossed out on page 112, and on page 147 the following numbers are notated next to the string parts: "4 v1, 4 v2, 3 viola, 4 celli and bass." Busoni stated to Jarnach that Mozart had a gift for placing instruments in registers that achieved the richest possible sonorities without requiring unnecessary doublings:[47]

> One of Mozart's secrets lies in his use of each instrument in its most natural register—for example in the doublings of a Tutti, where he assigns greater importance to this than to the equal strength in every octave. Thus each instrument is able to give its fullest sonority. Here the top octave is *single,* the next *doubled,* the third *trebled,* the last *single.* And yet this is the best way; contrary to the teaching of Wagner, he assigns three unison

FIGURE 6.2.a and b. Mozart, Piano Trio in G Major, K. 496, mvt. 2, mm. 9–23, copied in Jarnach's hand. Jarnach, letter of August 28, 1920, to Busoni, Staatsbibliothek zu Berlin—Preussischer Kulturbesitz, Musikabteilung mit Mendelssohn Archiv, N. Mus. Nachl. 30, 118.

voices to each octave, which is illusory, inasmuch as different instruments produce varying intensity on different notes; an oboe in its lowest register sounds disproportionately loud, a high bassoon weaker.[48]

Jarnach left his own record of discoveries about instrumentation in Mozart's music in his letters to Busoni. On one occasion, he mentioned being particularly impressed by the sonorous effects in Mozart's Piano Trio in G Major, K. 496.[49] Jarnach copied out the passage (mm. 9–23 of variation four) from the allegretto movement and included it in the letter (see figure 6.2a, b).

Jarnach tried out some of Busoni's ideas about orchestration in several of his works from the Zurich years, including the *Sinfonia Brevis*, op. 14 (1919). This piece, as Hugo Leichtentritt notes, represented another important shift in style. In particular, Leichtentritt notes Jarnach's movement away from thicker Straussian textures to more transparent ones:

> The "Sinfonia brevis," which one heard with the Dresden Orchestra under Fritz Busch in Berlin, is the work out of which the characteristic transformation of Jarnach's compositions started. His earlier works display fluid, memorable melodies; in orchestral writing the color and fullness of the Wagner-Strauss-manner appeared. Under the influence of Busoni, Jarnach came to a new style of writing, which may be described as unromantic objectivity. To all unnecessary, superfluous pomp of sound, he now bids farewell, concentrating instead on forming contours that provide a clear, spiritual, and soulful form; in short, he strives after that "Young Classicality" which Busoni establishes as an ideal, and which Jarnach seems to appropriate through a Romanesque, finely pronounced sense of form.[50]

The piece is scored for a fairly traditional collection of instruments (flutes, piccolo, oboes, English horn, clarinet in A, bass clarinet, bassoons, French horns, trumpets, trombones, tuba, percussion: triangle, tam tams, other drums, glockenspiel, celeste), harp, and strings (first violins—14, second violins—14, violas—8, cellos—8, basses—6). However Jarnach avoids thick textures by including polyphony in which instruments have their own individual lines, and by alternating smaller instrumental groupings.

In addition to providing feedback on Jarnach's compositions, Busoni insisted that Jarnach study the scores of other composers from Claudio Monteverdi, Giovanni Pierluigi da Palestrina, Johann Sebastian Bach, and Mozart to contemporary composers, such as Claude Debussy and Igor Stravinsky.[51] Part of Jarnach's education consisted of studying the Beethoven string quartets in detail as well. Busoni taught that it was the task of the artist to be knowledgeable about past works in order to evolve musically.[52] By combining line, form, and sonority, represented by Palestrina, Mozart, and Berlioz, respectively, music becomes classic, timeless, and great. Distinctions between past, present, and future dissolve and lead to new experiments: "The distinction between classical and romantic then disappears of its own accord: the two together—like Helena and Faust—should procreate a Euphorian strong enough not to perish in his adolescence. We must smooth the path for this genius to come (one always does come). And this we can do with insight and sense of purpose."[53]

Mozart, Liszt, and Bizet received frequent and special praise from Busoni. Even while he criticized Wagner and his followers,[54] Busoni specifically praised Berlioz's *Les Troyens* discussed *Roméo et Juliette*, H. 79, and claimed that Berlioz was "the only composer who always works toward inventiveness and that every page reveals something new and surprising." At a loss for words to explain why the French praised Wagner over their own countryman, Busoni sarcastically concluded that perhaps the latter's music was not erotic enough. Jarnach shared Busoni's enthusiasm, working on a set of Berlioz variations.[55] He also expressed his admiration for Berlioz's music in a number of his letters to Busoni, including one in which he provided a detailed analysis of Berlioz's *Roméo et Juliette*, H. 79.[56]

Busoni's music was also a frequent topic of conversation, and Jarnach studied several of his scores in detail. Unlike some of Busoni's other pupils, Jarnach maintained profound respect for Busoni's compositions. His personal copy of *Die Brautwahl*, BV 258, contains handwritten performance times and notes from Busoni, as well as indications of alternate versions/cuts.[57] Jarnach also studied his Sonatina no. 3, "Ad usum infantis," BV 268. The title page is signed "Philipp Jarnach 1916" on the front cover in blue pencil and an accidental is marked in red on page 3. Jarnach also wrote an essay about the piece in which he praised its "most subtle, sense for contrast and movement, and youthful inspiration."[58] Jarnach knew *Arlecchino*, BV 270, and *Turandot*, BV 273, intimately, not to mention Busoni's incomplete *Doktor Faust*, BV 303.[59] He was involved with all of the rehearsal details for *Turandot*, including overseeing the copying of parts, scheduling rehearsals, and dealing with musicians who left much to be desired in sight-reading skills. In March 1917, Jarnach called *Turandot* an extra-special composition: "Bravo my dear master. I got home from the new theater piece. I mark the day with a white stone. Long live the beautiful and expansive *Turandot*! Cheers grand and dear Busoni!"[60] In addition, Jarnach evidently studied Busoni's Violin Concerto, BV 243, in some detail. His copy is well loved with a hand-made cover and contains performance markings. Additionally, Jarnach appears to have studied the orchestration, dynamics, and tempo markings. Tempo and affective markings are boxed or circled. In his introductory words (1949) to Busoni's Sonatina 1910, BV 257, he called the piece one of the most important compositions of the age because it exhibited elements of a new *Tonsprache* and new approach to form.[61]

Truly, Busoni was Jarnach's musical father, teaching him through his ideals and music to follow after a spiritual and experimental art characterized by new instrumental combinations, new forms, stylistic heterogeneity, and new treatments of the tonal language. It was shortly after Busoni's death (1924) that he most closely approached his ideals.

MENTORSHIP, POLITICS, AND BUSONI'S LASTING INFLUENCE ON JARNACH AFTER BUSONI'S DEATH

After Busoni's death, Busoni and his teachings were never far from Jarnach's mind. Jarnach not only completed Busoni's *Doktor Faust* as a final act of loyalty, but he also created an orchestral edition of Busoni's *Lied des Brander*, BV 299, in 1938.[62] In his version, which he described as a "free orchestral transcription," Jarnach transposed the piece one half-step and added an introductory measure (see figure 6.3).[63] Jarnach's scoring is for winds and strings plus baritone. Jarnach also added expression markings, such as crescendo signs in measure 5, and in measure 16 he added a run in the violin passage. There are extra grace notes in the clarinet part beginning in measure 23 as well as triplets in the strings and trills in the oboe part beginning in measure 27. The orchestra arrangement becomes increasingly complex as the piece progresses, with triplets passed between instruments and the grouping of instruments into high and low winds, thereby creating captivating instrumental colors.

FIGURE 6.3. Jarnach's orchestral transcription of Busoni's *Lied des Brander* (1938), Staatsbibliothek zu Berlin, Preussischer Kulturbesitz, Musikabteilung mit Mendelssohn Archiv, N. Mus. ms. 12, pg. 1.

In the 1920s, as Jarnach saw a meteoric rise in his compositional career as well as the burgeoning of his pedagogical career, he reached his most experimental in terms of the expansion of the tonal language, the creation of unique forms, and the blending of diverse styles, as he followed Busoni's ideals in his own way. As a member of the *Novembergruppe*, he was part of a group of artistic "rebels." Surrounded by a small circle of innovative artists, architects, and composers, Jarnach invented his own atonal approach even as his music became increasingly dissonant and innovative. As Tamara Levitz has noted, much of Jarnach's music of the 1920s was organized unconventionally—it does not feature twelve equal tones, but uses hard and mild dissonances in connection with tritones along with an interchange between major and minor.[64] He does not follow a system but explores new ways of treating the musical language in each of the pieces.

In following Busoni's ideals, Jarnach discovered his own voice and his career took off. Numerous premieres and performances of his works took place throughout Germany, including his Sonatina for Piano (*Romanzero I*), op. 18, on April 3, 1925, in Berlin during an evening concert of the *Novembergruppe* and then again at the Donaueschingen Festival on July 26, 1925. Wilhelm Furtwängler directed the *Morgenklangspiel* (*Romanzero II*), op. 19, in 1926 in a Leipzig Gewandhaus concert. Premieres continued throughout Jarnach's time in Cologne as well, beginning with his Sarabande from the *Drei Klavierstücke*, op. 17, in January 1927.[65] His Konzertstück für Orgel (*Romanzero III*), op. 21, premiered in Baden Baden in 1928. Weiss documented nine performances of Jarnach's music in Germany alone from October 1929 to June 1930.[66] The *Clown Songs*, op. 24, premiered in London in 1930.

As Jarnach's career peaked, his music became increasingly experimental. He followed Busoni's suggestions to seek new ways of organizing music and to search for new sounds and harmonies. Jarnach's structures became less connected to traditional forms and his approach increasingly polyharmonic with quartal harmonies. Three of the pieces from 1924 to 1928 bearing the subtitle *Romanzero* (for piano, orchestra, and organ, respectively) represent Jarnach's experimentalism. Of these, Weiss has suggested that the Sonatina for Piano, op. 18, was a direct tribute and homage to Busoni, who had been occupied with composing six sonatinas during

MUSIC EXAMPLE 6.5. Jarnach, Konzertstück für Orgel (*Romanzero III*), op. 21, mm. 1–11.

the last two decades of his life (not to mention its Romanesque title and Italian tempo markings).⁶⁷ Yet it is the Konzertstück für Orgel (*Romanzero III*), op. 21, that represents Jarnach at his most experimental (see music example 6.5). The piece is characterized by fragmented melodic lines, polytonality, free form, and diverse rhythms. The $\frac{5}{8}$ meter lends the piece a narrative quality in keeping with the subtitle *Romanzero*. A purely secular and abstract work, it has no known religious ties, even despite the fact that it is written for organ, and it sought to make a break with Romantic and Baroque organ traditions. The treatment of the musical language ranges from atonal to polytonal. The first few measures begin with crisp staccato alternations between E-flat and B-flat in the pedals. When the manuals are heard for the first time in measure 3, a chromatically saturated right hand in addition to quartal chords in both hands beginning in measures 3–4 in the treble complicate the suggested straightforward E-flat harmony in the bass. During the final measures of the piece, the pedals revert to alternating E-flat and B-flat pitches even while the bass moves chromatically by step from a D-sharp ninth chord to a perfect fourth interval featuring the pitches C and F—a major second removed from the bass pedal motion.

Jarnach was seen as a leader of Weimar's avant-garde, but because he did not follow a set system, few could imitate his approach. Moreover, his position as an experimental composer was short lived, even if he was considered influential in his own time. He discovered his own voice and means of organizing the musical language, but perhaps too late. Unlike Paul Hindemith, he chose to stay in Germany, and there he was suddenly forgotten. Politics changed everything artistic.

As Weiss has demonstrated, Jarnach was not supportive of the National Socialist government or their ideals in the 1930s, calling it, at least in retrospect in 1951 in a letter to Schoenberg, "a fearful regime for which he had no sympathy."[68] Even if his passive resistance was not detected, Jarnach suffered psychologically, creatively, and financially. As an emigrant, Jarnach's "Germanness" was constantly called into question. In addition, his most avant-garde works could not be performed. Whether his works were banned simply because of his associations with the avant-garde in the 1920s or whether he was trying to avoid direct conflict with the regime is not entirely clear.[69] As an "exile" in his own homeland, Jarnach was not free to create and have performed the type of sounds he idealized in the 1920s.[70] His previous involvement with the *Novembergruppe* and the Donaueschingen Festivals, at the very least, made him suspect, and it did not help matters that he had written increasingly abstract and atonal music in the 1920s. Jarnach's music was viewed as a symbol of decay and decadence by the National Socialists.[71] Weiss has documented that Jarnach was investigated by the police in 1932 and that performances of his music were banned. From 1932 to 1935, only a single performance of his music took place—that of the string quintet, at the Berlin Singakademie in 1934. His last premiere of a piece was the *Vier Orchesterlieder*, op. 15a, in December 1930.[72]

Jarnach had to renounce experimentation with the musical language to survive, but he once again drew upon Busoni's flexible aesthetic ideals to regain footing. This time, he embraced Busoni's ideals of Young Classicality. Previously, Jarnach had created a sense of atemporality through the blending of old and new techniques, but now he looked to earlier music as direct inspiration for new creations, including more obscure composers he had studied with Busoni. Not long before his death, Busoni was discussing Giovanni Benedetto Platti with Jarnach. In 1923, Jarnach arranged two of Platti's sonatas for violin and piano, mainly updating the keyboard part. Jarnach wrote to Busoni on January 16, 1924, thanking him for biographical details about Platti: "Many thanks for your friendly investigation of particular details relating to Platti, and even more for the musical; the sonatas of our still questionable Venetian wander to Mainz [Schott's Sons]."[73]

Jarnach continued to adapt Platti's music after Busoni's death, reworking his music into a *Nachdichtung* written in the style of Platti, but with a new structure. Jarnach's *Concertino nach Giovanni Platti in E moll nach alten Vorlagen des Giovanni Platti (um 1759) mit Streichorchester mit zwei obligaten Sologeigen*, op. 31 (1942), contains four movements, all with Baroque titles: Ouverture, Arietta, Menuetto, and Giga. The last three movement designations are borrowed directly from Platti, and the material in all four movements of the concertino is based heavily on Platti's four-movement flute sonata in E minor, yet reworked into a concerto format. Contrary to its title, "ouverture," supplied by Jarnach, the first movement is largely an Italianate ritornello form with the opening section of the flute sonata serving as the basis for the ritornello material that appears at the beginning and in fragments throughout the movement. The first nine measures are nearly an exact quotation of soloist material, even if the music is rescored for string orchestra and two solo violins. However, Jarnach reworked the formal structures to create alternating tutti and soloist sections. Subsequent soloist sections, although based on motives from the Platti, are largely newly composed. The second movement is a free elaboration on motivic material from the second movement of the Platti flute sonata and the third, a minuet, is done in the spirit of Platti, but with only fragments of borrowed motivic material. The fourth movement once again quotes heavily from the Platti, but Jarnach plays with textural and instrumental combinations even while reworking and elongating the musical material to bring the piece to a more brilliant conclusion. Although Weiss claims Stravinsky's *Pulcinella* was Jarnach's main model for his *Nachdichtungen*, the claim is unsubstantiated.[74] More similar and likely models were Busoni's *Nachdichtungen*, since Jarnach tended to be critical of Stravinsky's music, and he recognized that Stravinsky's approach was more stylistically homogeneous than his own.[75] Moreover, Jarnach was well aware of Busoni's reuse of material in *Doktor Faust* and acquainted with his *Nachdichtungen*—especially—the Piano Sonatina no. 5: *Sonatina in Brevis "In Signo Joannis Sebastiani Magni,"* BV 280, and the Sonatina no. 6 ("Super Carmen"), BV 284. Busoni gave a score of the Piano Sonatina no. 5 to Philipp Jarnach on August 18, 1918, which Jarnach studied in some detail.[76] It is based on material from Bach's Fantasy and Fugue in D Minor, BWV 905, even if the formal structure, some of the motives, and working out of the piece was Busoni's own. The opening section resembles Bach's Fantasy and the second is based on the fugal section, but it features Busonian harmonies and adventurous counterpoint. In the third section, thematic material from both sections is combined, and the fourth is a coda based mainly on completely new material.

Mozart also played a central role in Jarnach's activities. He became Jarnach's model for reconquering joyfulness and serenity and helped him escape from weighty German romanticism to lightness.[77] In addition, he liked the older aristocratic Mozartian world and lamented its loss.[78] He created a fairly literal transcription of a set of theme and variations for piano and violin based on the second movement of Mozart's Divertimento in D Major, KV 334. Mozart's original was scored for two violins, viola, bass, and horn in D. Jarnach copied the violin part and reduced the other parts for piano. His main alterations were to dynamics and phrasing. He claimed rescoring the work allowed for more performance opportunities and to create as perfect as possible a composition of its kind.[79]

In addition, he composed *Musik mit Mozart* in 1936. In a radio interview in 1977, Jarnach retrospectively claimed he had dreamed for years of creating a piece with Mozart's harmonic language, yet still in a free modern style—*Musik mit Mozart* was the realization of that inspiration.[80] Although some might argue it is not "modern" in the sense of Jarnach's compositions of the late 1920s, that is, in terms of musical language and harmonies, it displays the same approach toward thematic material and form that Jarnach sought to pioneer in works in which he had free creative rein.⁸¹ Of all the elements in the composition, the formal structure is the most unique. Jarnach explained his approach in the 1942 program: "The variations here are not treated in the traditional sense, but rather, as a great cyclic form, in which the four sections are organized and developed independently."⁸² The four movements are suggestive of a four-movement symphony, therefore alluding back to the classical age in which Mozart lived and worked:

   I. thema—canzone
   II. menuetto
   II. siciliano
   IV. rondo

However, at the same time, Jarnach creates motivic variations. They are not melodic and rhythmic variations, not harmonic variations, but modern reflections on Mozart by Jarnach using mixed techniques.

Jarnach's approach to thematic material is intimately linked to the form. The piece is also filled with quotations. The Siciliano comes from the middle movement of Mozart's Piano Concerto in A Major, KV 488, and the Rondo theme comes from the finale of the Mozart String Quintet, KV 593. The lyrical theme of the middle movement of Mozart's piano trio in E-major, KV 542, is also quoted and varied throughout the first movement, forming the basis for the main melodic material (see music examples 6.6 and 6.7). Yet Jarnach transforms the material to suit his own creative purposes. For instance, he uses the thematic material from Mozart's Piano Trio in E Major, KV 542, as the basis for the themes for his first movement. He then varies the rhythmic and melodic material, especially beginning at measure 37, when rhythms and intervals from Mozart are altered and recombined to form the basis for Jarnach's own creative working out of the piece.

Musik mit Mozart, op. 25, was a piece of public rehabilitation for Jarnach, yet one that led on a pathway of renunciation of the increasingly dissonant musical path he had taken in the 1920s.⁸³ In a series of lectures and writings during the post–World War II period, Jarnach articulated his continued reverence for Mozart and the clarified the aspects of his music that he considered to be most notable. In his "Portrait of a Master," Jarnach praised Mozart for excelling in a diversity of forms and genres.⁸⁴ In addition, like

MUSIC EXAMPLE 6.6. Mozart, Piano Trio in E-major, KV 542, mvt. 2, mm. 1–16.

Busoni, he idealized him for mixing genres and forms.[85] He saw in him a classic and timeless mixing of the old and new that he attempted in his own compositions.[86] Jarnach also idealized Mozart's approach to form, calling it complex, involved, and well reasoned, even though it sounds simple on

MUSIC EXAMPLE 6.7. Jarnach, *Musik mit Mozart*, op. 25, mvt. 1, mm. 1–15.

the surface.[87] He also glorified Mozart's polyphony, which he considered hardly less complex than Bach's. Both, he claimed, functioned independently of external and artificial rules.[88] Yet no composer before Mozart had achieved this blend of naturalness, clarity, and maturity of form.[89]

NEW MUSIC PROMOTION

Despite his curtailed career, Jarnach promoted the new music he dreamed of before and after the Nazi regime. Initially, Jarnach worked together with members of the Busoni circle to promote new music. Together with Heinz Tiessen and Hermann Scherchen, he founded the Melos Konzerten für Neue Musik. He also collaborated with the Internationale Componisten-Gilde in 1922 with Edgard Varèse and then the Internationale Gesellschaft für neue Musik (IGNM) beginning in October 1922. He participated in the Allgemeiner Deutschen Musikverein (ADMV) in 1926 and the Tonkunstlerfeste in 1933, on which he served on several national and international juries, including with Alban Berg (1885–1935).

Jarnach's new music promotion activities were cut short during the war years, as were some of his connections with others of the Busoni circle for political reasons. Despite his continued reverence for Busoni, Jarnach intentionally distanced himself from some of Busoni's circle. Jarnach survived in the Nazi regime without supporting it by avoiding open and direct challenge, by curtailing his creative activities, and by avoiding direct and obvious contact with Jews. Although his avoidance of some members of the Busoni circle, Kurt Weill included, might seem reprehensible, it can also be seen as a desperate attempt to survive in a difficult political climate.[90] However, as a teacher, he continued to discreetly promote the music of Jews and "musical bolshevists," such as Hindemith and Schoenberg, to some of his composition pupils.[91] The following memoir, recorded by his pupil Otto Luening, fully reveals Jarnach's fears and attempts to remain true to art, even despite restrictions: "After meeting us at the station he suggested a walk through the fields. He stopped in the center of some pastureland. 'Now we can talk, but look around! We're not near a tree, are we?' He told me teaching at the conservatory in Cologne was difficult, but not impossible. A Nazi student had confronted him in class with 'You always talk about Mozart, but Max Reger was *ein grösserer* composer, and he's German, not Austrian.' Jarnach answered, 'Quite possibly true, depending on what you mean when you say great.' The fellow looked puzzled, but he backed off."[92]

Jarnach's promotion of Busoni's music and new music resumed soon after the war. He directed Busoni's *Turandot* in 1946 in Hamburg and from 1947 to 1948 he created the Godesberger Musiktagen for contemporary music in Cologne, with which several of his students were involved, including Jürg Bauer, Bernd Alois Zimmermann, and Rudolf Petzold.[93] The concerts featured the newest music, as well as historical pieces by composers such as Monteverdi, Purcell, Bach, and Mozart, as Busoni had done in his historic concert of November 1921 in Berlin.[94] Also in 1948, Jarnach joined the Neue Gesellschaft für Musik, which brought Schoenberg's music to the Hamburg Hochschule on June 27, 1952. He also became a juror for the NWDR composition prize and came up with a plan to transform the Schule für Musik und Theater der Hansestadt Hamburg into a Staatlichen Musikhochschule. He was on the jury of the Arbeitsgemeinschaft der öffentlich-rechtlichen Rundfunkanstalten der Bundesrepublik Deutschland (ARD) in Munich from 1953 to 1958. In 1951 he served on the jury at the Luxemburg International Klavierwettbewerb "Maurice Ravel" and in March of that year launched the composition prize for students in Hamburg.

CONCLUSION

Although Jarnach was honored and respected as a teacher and juror after World War II, his compositional career largely ended during the Nazi period.[95] He was allowed to continue teaching in Germany, as Everett Helm has noted, but his experimental music was not performed in the 1930s, and his reputation as a composer never completely recovered after World War II, even if he sought to exonerate himself and to distance himself from National Socialist ideologies and activities:

> Those who were familiar with German music before 1936 will be shocked not to find the name of Phillip [sic] Jarnach in the list of well-known composers. This is one of the tragedies of contemporary German music. Jarnach is possibly the most gifted composer after Hindemith, but today

he is scarcely ever performed. During the Nazi regime he fell under the same kind of cultural ban as was promulgated against Hindemith: he was not directly persecuted as a non-Nazi; he was allowed to go on teaching, performances of his works were forbidden. Whereas Hindemith left Germany, Jarnach chose rather to stay, however much he disliked the Nazis. For nearly ten years his works disappeared from concert and opera programs; he was forgotten, and since the war he has not been remembered as a composer.[96]

Unlike many of Busoni's other pre-Berlin masterclass pupils, Jarnach never fully embraced new electronic instruments, even if he experimented with new scales, new styles of musical organization, and a proto-postmodernist mixing of styles in the short time he could. Yet he was considered a cutting-edge composer in the Weimar Republic. His experiments with atonality, form, and polystylism were viewed as forward thinking. The question as to what trajectory his career would have taken if unhindered by the political situation will have to remain unanswered, including whether or not he would have embraced electronic instruments had he obtained access to them. In an essay entitled "Mechanische Musik" of 1926, Jarnach stated that the current technology left much to hope for and that only future experiments would show whether or not they would be fulfilled.[97] Living in Germany during the Nazi regime precisely when new technology became accessible in the West made personal experiments with those tools impossible for Jarnach. However, he was enthusiastic when introduced to the electronic music of his pupil, Luening. For instance, he heard a piece played by nineteen loudspeakers at Columbia University and believed it to be an important form of expression, even while realizing significant material and spiritual consequences of electronic instrument use.[98] He also spoke of the developments in electronics as having a positive influence on music in a speech of 1957.[99]

Busoni considered Jarnach to be one of his most gifted students, and he could never have predicted the sudden decline in Jarnach's career in the 1930s. He found in him a great musician and friend whom he missed when away. In London, he wrote: "I'm starving for the companionship of a man like Jarnach, for instance."[100] A piece that he especially revered and promoted was the String Quintet, op. 10, which he considered to be quite innovative.[101] That Busoni maintained his affection for and friendship with

FIGURE 6.4. Ferruccio Busoni (seated, center) and Philipp Jarnach (rear center), with the Amar Quartet (Paul Hindemith, Maurits Frank, Licco Amar, Walther Caspar). Photo by John Graudenz. Ullstein Bild, Getty Images.

Jarnach even throughout the Berlin years is evidenced by a dedication from March 1924 in *Zigeunerlied*, op. 55, no. 2: "To Philip Jarnach in loving appreciation (see figure 6.4)."[102]

During his lifetime, Busoni promoted Jarnach endlessly with publishing companies, concert organizations, and conservatories. Although Jarnach had published several pieces with A. Durand & Fils in Paris, and one with Ferdinand Zierfuss in Munich, he had not yet made much progress with German publishers.[103] In 1916, Busoni recommended Jarnach to Breitkopf und Härtel in the warmest terms both for creating transcriptions and for his personal compositions: "A young Philip Jarnach Spaniard by birth, (a 'relative' of R. Strauss) has just prepared the piano reduction of my completed opera and in that capacity expressed so much understanding and skill that I want to highly recommend him to you for the time being for this kind of work; then also I want to attract your attention to his compositional talent."[104] Two years later, Busoni specifically urged them to publish his String Quintet, op. 10.[105] When that did not work out, he suggested contacting Hug music publishers in Switzerland, but the terms ended up being unfavorable for Jarnach.[106] The work was finally published by Schlesinger in 1920, a publishing firm with which Busoni had established ties in 1909 with the publication of his four-volume *An die Jugend*, BV 254.[107]

Busoni also used his connections to secure performances of Jarnach's compositions. By late 1916, Jarnach still had not managed to make his way in Zurich concert life. Weiss notes that the performance of three of his compositions during the 1916–1917 concert season at the Tonhalle would have been unthinkable without Busoni's influence.[108] This launched Jarnach's career in Zurich and led to subsequent performances of the *Sinfonia Brevis*, op. 14, and the String Quintet, op. 10. Busoni promoted Jarnach in Berlin as well. He was largely responsible for the performance of Jarnach's String Quintet, op. 10, at the Donaueschingen Festival in 1921.[109] Having made the acquaintance of Heinrich Burkhardt, who was the director, he suggested compositions by three of his pupils: Reinhold Laquai, Luc Balmer, and Jarnach. Of these, only Jarnach's composition was selected and the performance was a great success, leading to numerous additional engagements and the attention of the publisher B. Schott's Son.[110]

In addition, Busoni recommended him for several jobs, including as a composition professor at the Lisbon National Conservatory:

> It is not easy to suggest a composition teacher. But, should an opportunity present itself, I would like to draw your attention to my 25-year-old assistant *Philipp Jarnach*. A Spaniard by birth, educated in France, German in outlook, he has a very rapid mind and great clarity in understanding and planning. He has helped me, prepared the vocal scores of both operas, which he is also going to rehearse with the singers; as, at my instigation, he has been engaged by the Zurich Stadt-Theater. A string quartet and a violin sonata of his have been played, an orchestral work is on the programme for the next symphony concert—He is also very fond of "theory" and often elucidates my own works to me. He speaks perfect French and cultivated German.—Voilà Philipp! (Is a skillful pianist.)[111]

Although that job never materialized, largely due to the language barrier, political issues (Portugal and Germany were at odds), and Jarnach's reluctance to leave Switzerland, Jarnach did become Kapellmeister of the Stadttheater in Zurich at the recommendation of Busoni, from 1917 to 1918.[112] Busoni also privately marketed him as a composition and counterpoint teacher. Beyond this, Jarnach also quickly assumed the role of Busoni's assistant, and in that capacity aided him with editorial work for the collected Liszt edition and the revision of Liszt's *Totentanz*, S. 126, for piano and orchestra. Until 1918, he accompanied *Turandot* and *Arlecchino* at rehearsals, reduced the orchestral part, collaborated in writing some of the parts, secured copyists, and taught the work to the singers.

In Berlin, Busoni continued to promote Jarnach and often referred students for technical advice in counterpoint and composition. From October 1921 to April 1927, Jarnach worked as a teacher of theory and piano and also as a music critic. His most gifted Berlin student, Weill, whom he taught for free from 1921 to 1925, came almost every day and studied counterpoint.[113] Although Jarnach communicated many Busonian ideas to his pupils, such as contrapuntal transparency, his teaching was more technical and systematic than Busoni's, and he frequently referred to Ernst Kurth's *Grundlagen des linearen Kontrapunkts* during lessons.[114] In addition, he also concentrated on the composition of lieder and introduced Weill to the newest music and the avant-garde of Berlin as well as to important young composers of whom Busoni was skeptical, such as Hindemith.[115]

Busoni had occasionally criticized Jarnach for failing to break free from previous accomplishments, and he tried to guide him past his writing blocks. Yet he still held Jarnach in the highest regard. Jarnach, for his part, talked about Busoni frequently with his students, describing what he felt to be his most important compositional traits. He claimed it was almost impossible to capture with words the essence of Busoni's creativity. He was also one of Busoni's few composition pupils who truly appreciated Busoni's compositions and considered them underestimated. In 1924, Jarnach had predicted that Schoenberg and Busoni would be the leaders in new but different strands of modernism in Germany—and he considered himself a follower of Busoni and his experimental ideas:[116]

> Busoni, no less bold in treading unknown ways, has received a more wary assessment. Simply different than Schoenberg, Busoni wanted to secure the continuity of tradition; he did not want to relinquish it, but to enrich it. Everything different appeared to him comparable, because it

was time-bound. In everything that has been created in music, he hunted down the oneness of the spiritual will, of a sense of humanity. Therefore for him atonality was a pure new means of expression that had come—not (as for Schoenberg) a new language that excludes everything else. What motivated him is the overcoming of all physical material in music, the synthesis of a form that is no longer bound by a pattern, but only the mind. All Busoni's late works are based on this central idea, and their importance lies in the fact that they have initiated the renewal of musical classicism in a specifically modern sense.[117]

For all the veneration, there was occasional friction between the two, including jealousy and a struggle for individuality. In Zurich, Jarnach felt that Busoni was too overpowering in his ideas and had to push back to find his own way: "It seems to you ... perhaps a little strange that I do not completely submit myself to your influence after I learned to have so much love and respect. No, I'm not a Petri of composition, I do not want to copy, and I will better honor, understand and interpret your high personality, and I am trying to follow your example, the example of the independent strictly self-thinking artist, and if I succeed, I will, with more authority than anyone, ennoble myself with the title of being your student."[118]

Notwithstanding Busoni's respect for Jarnach, he was concerned that his creativity was hampered by his intellect, and he wasn't one to mince words. This caused Jarnach pain on more than one occasion: "You, my dear master, have no confidence in me; I mean, you doubt my character, my mental strength. ... I beg you not to believe in pettiness on my part. I love you too much to feel offended, but you can wound me. Despite my talkativeness I do not have the ability to exhibit my feelings. Is my coldness or businesslike manner evidence that I feel less full of life than others?"[119]

Jarnach became irritated and stopped visiting or corresponding with Busoni for a few months, beginning around March 1923, accusing him of being too egotistical.[120] It is possible that the friendship gradually also deteriorated due to misunderstandings and Jarnach's growing independence as an artist.[121] Busoni needed adoration, and Jarnach's sudden fame and independence might have been threatening for him. In addition, by the 1920s Busoni had turned from the experimentalism he espoused in the 1910s and was consequently upset that Jarnach had become too involved with the avant-garde in Berlin. At that time, he was trying to forge a middle ground between the conservatives and liberals as he focused on his theories of Young Classicality. His late style made him wary of the experiments of the avant-garde. Weiss also documents harsh words between the two regarding a performance of Jarnach's *Sinfonia Brevis*, in 1920, but these differences were not enough to permanently tear the friendship asunder.[122] Indeed, Jarnach was present at the end of Busoni's life.[123]

Despite a curtailed career and a few clashes with his teacher, Jarnach not only helped establish his own brand of atonality, but helped pioneer a leaner and more objective style of writing in the 1920s before such had become popular with Weill, Krenek, Schoenberg, and other German composers of the Weimar Republic. He pioneered new formal approaches that broke away from traditional formal molds even within motivically unified compositions. He helped forge a proto-postmodernist way of writing that blended diverse styles (old and new, vocal and instrumental, etc.). Although many of his ideas came from Busoni, the exact working out was his own and represents a significant contribution to serious concert music in Germany in an age of great change and turmoil. He went beyond Busoni in his experimentation with the tonal language in the late 1920s. In addition, Jarnach offered an alternative form of modernism, based on Busonian ideals, that was rooted in classic ideals of the past even if it looked forward to a new and unknown future. Jarnach, like Busoni, sought to stand beyond any system, showing that great music does not need to be valued based on its application of a system of any kind—whether tonality or atonality, expressionism, *Neue sachlichkeit*, neoclassicism, pointillism, or serialism. Nor is it to be found in the material of music, but within the artist as he or she discovers that which is new and untried, that which is true to his or her nature.[124]

NOTES

1. "Nicht blosse Hoffnung, sondern bereits eine Erfüllung ist uns Philipp Jarnach [*sich*], einer der ausgeprägtesten Charakterköpfe der jungen Generation." Manfred Paulson, untitled article, *Allgemeine Musikzeitung* 49:19 (May 12, 1922), 404.

2. The festival for new music takes place annually in October, and the inaugural year was 1921. Busoni, Hans Pfitzner, Richard Strauss, and Arthur Nikisch were on the original planning committee. For additional information about the festival, con-

sult Josef Häusler, *Spiegel der Neuen Music: Donaueschingen* (Stuttgart: J. B. Metzler, 1996).

3. Weiss has documented the frequent use of these (and similar terms) in relation to the music of Jarnach throughout his book. Stefan Weiss, *Die Musik Philipp Jarnachs* (Cologne: Christoph Dohr, 1996). For more information consult Helga Kliemann, *Die Novembergruppe* (Berlin: Mann Verlag, 1969), 39.

4. Philipp Jarnach, "Neue Klassizität" (1949), in *Schriften zur Musik*, ed. Norbert Jers, Beiträge zur Rheinischen Musikgeschichte, vol. 153 (Berlin: Merseburger, 1994), 46–47.

5. "Busonis Einstellung zur Kunst ist für mich das entscheidende Erlebnis geworden, mehr noch als das fachliche Beispiel. Denn wenn ich auch als sein Schüler gelte, so habe ich doch nie an einer einzigen Unterrichtsstunde teilgehabt. Indessen habe ich das Gefühl, dass ich ihm alles verdanke, was ich geworden sein mag." Jarnach, "Das Beispiel Busonis" (1963), in Jarnach, *Scriften zur Musik*, 192.

6. "Dass er wirklich von mir etwas hielt und von mir auch etwas erwartete—das ist vielleicht für den Rest meines Lebens dann doch entscheidend geworden." Jarnach, Rundfunkinterview with Reinhold Schuberts, July 20, 1977, in Eschenburg, quoted in Weiss, *Die Musik Philipp Jarnachs*, 76.

7. "Sie traten im entscheidenden Moment in mein künstlerischen Leben, im Augenblick wo ich, im Besitze einer gewissen Kompositionstechnik gelangt, ziemlich ratlos im Chaos jüngsten Überlieferungen hin und her schwankte. Sie lehrten mich vor allem das Eine: die unabänderlichen Wertmesser der Kunst zu erkennen." Jarnach to Busoni, June 23, 1917, Staatsbibliothek zu Berlin, Preußischer Kulturbesitz, Musikabteilung mit Mendelssohn-Archiv, N. Mus. Dep. 56, 92.

8. Jarnach, Sonatine for Flute and Piano, op. 12 (Zurich: A. Biolley, 1920).

9. Weiss, *Die Musik Philipp Jarnachs*.

10. Tamara Levitz,"'Junge Klassizität': Zwischen Fortschritt und Reaktion: Ferruccio Busoni, Philipp Jarnach und die Deutsche Weill-Rezeption," *Kurt Weill-Studien*, ed. Nils Grosch, Joachim Lucchesi, and Jürgen Schebera Kurt-Weill, Gesellschaft, vol. 1 (Dessau: M &P, 1996), 9–37.

11. Tamara Levitz, "Teaching New Classicality: Busoni's Master Class in Composition, 1921–1924" (PhD diss., University of Rochester, 1994).

12. Virgilio Bernardoni, "Jarnach e Busoni," in *Ferruccio Busoni e la sua scuola*, ed. Gianmario Borio, Mauro Casadei, and Turroni Monti, Nuovi percorsi musicali (Lucca: Una cosa rara, 1999), 37–48.

13. Laureto Rodoni, "Die gerade Linie ist unterbrochen: L'esilio di Busoni a Zurigo (1915–1920)," in *La Svizzera: Terra s'Asilo* (Atti—Kongressbericht-Ascona, 1998) (Bern: P. Lang, 2000), 27–106; Hans Jelmoli, *Ferruccio Busonis Zürcherjahre* (Zürich: Orell Füssli, 1929).

14. Jarnach studied piano with Edouard Risler and theory with Albert Lavignac.

15. He moved to Zurich by August 25, 1914, at the latest. Weiss, *Die Musik*, 51. Pieces produced in Zurich immediately predating studies with Busoni include *Quatre humoresques pour le piano* (May 1914), *Rondel* (May 1914), *Schilflieder* (September 1914), *Jasmin* (1914), *Zwei Balladen* (March 1915), *La résurrection d'Adonis* (July 1915), *Vorspiel zu "Prometheus"* (1915), and *Vier Lieder*, op. 6, *Das mitleidige Mädel* (1915).

16. Jarnach to Busoni, December 8, 1915, Jarnach Nachlass, Staatsbibliothek zu Berlin, Preußischer Kulturbesitz, Musikabteilung mit Mendelssohn-Archiv, N. Mus. Depos. 56, 85.

17. Philipp Jarnach, "Das Beispiel Busonis" (1963) in Jarnach, *Schriften zur Musik*, 192.

18. For additional information about the Berlin years, consult Tamara Levitz, "Ferruccio Busoni and His European Circle in Berlin in the Early Weimar Republic," *Revista de Musicología* 16:6 (1993), 3705–3721. As Levitz notes, two scholarships, from the McCormick Rockefeller Foundation and the Infante Don Alfonso of Spain, enabled Jarnach to leave his position in Zurich and move to Berlin without a secure position. Levitz, "Ferruccio Busoni and his European Circle," 3710. Jarnach followed Busoni to Berlin in April 1921. A letter from Paris in 1920 indicates that Jarnach was still sending Busoni scores for critique. Jarnach to Busoni, March 10, 1920, in Busoni, *Selected Letters*, ed. Antony Beaumont (New York: Columbia University Press, 1987), 305. Although Jarnach was not a participant in Busoni's Berlin master class (1921–1924), he maintained close contact with Busoni and provided fundamental technical training to several of Busoni's pupils. During this time, Jarnach stayed up to date with Busoni's compositions, seeing a fragment of *Doktor Faust* performed on June 22–23, 1921. Busoni and Jarnach also continued to dialogue about Jarnach's pieces and about publishers.

19. "Busoni war kein Lehrer im engen Sinne des Wortes. Ihm fehlte jede erzieherische Neigung, wie auch—was sich von selbst versteht—die leidenschaftslose Unparteilichkeit des Pädagogen. Er war durch eine umständliche Schule der Theorie gegangen, glaubte aber nicht in Unterrichtssysteme. Er meinte, nur geistige Selbständigkeit und Einsicht könne das Handwerkliche so durchdringen, dass nicht Routine, sondern Kunst entstünde. Individuelle Empfindung war ihm die einzig taugliche Kraft, die Widerstände des Materials zu überwinden; und wenn er lückenloses Aneignen der empirischen Erfahrung als unerlässlich voraussetzte, so forderte er vom Künstler, dass er sich niemals auf ein Erlerntes stütze, vielmehr aus der jeweiligen Idee die Mittel herleite, sie zu formulieren." Jarnach, "Ferruccio Busoni," in Jarnach, *Schriften zur Musik*, 39–40.

20. Gottfried Galston, diary entry of June 4, 1924, *Kalendarnotizen über Ferruccio Busoni*, ed. Martina Weindel, Taschenbücher zur Musikwissenschaft, ed. Richard Schaal, vol. 144 (Wilhelmshaven: Florian Noetzel, 2000), 121–122. Busoni completed the article on June 8, 1924.

21. See also Jarnach, "Bemerkungen zur Kunst Busonis" (1932), in Jarnach, *Schriften zur Musik*, 45. For a description of Busoni's views of the Essence of Music, consult Busoni's essay "The Essence and Oneness of Music," in *The Essence and Oneness of Music and Other Papers*, trans. Rosamund Ley 1922; (London: Salisbury Square, 1956), 1–16.

22. Jarnach, "Das Stilproblem der neuen Klassizität im Werke Busonis" (1921)," in Jarnach, *Schriften zur Musick*, 35–38.

23. Ibid., 36.

24. "Eine Musik, die, im Gefühlsmässigen verwurzelt, dennoch die masszerstörende Form des Affekts ablehnt und nicht Konflikte, sondern Synthesen geben will; ein Klangbild, das die polyphonie Linienführung impressionistisch auflockert, aber noch in der Farbe, in der Ornamentik, ja selbst im virtuosen Element einen geis-

tigen Hintergrund durchschimmern lässt; eine so universall gerichtete und zugleich so strenge Kunst ist nicht gegenswartsgebunden." Jarnach, "Bemerkungen zur Kunst Busonis," 43.

25. Jarnach, *La Musica Contemporanea in Europa: Saggi Critici di G.M. Gatti, Henry Pruniers, Edward J. Dent, Philipp Jarnach, Boris de Schlözer, Guido Pannain* (Milan: Bottega di Poesia, 1925), 62.

26. "Mentre Schönberg mira a trarre dal suo materiale sonoro un Massimo di espressione, Busoni al contrario reduce all'estremo i mezzi di cui si serve; egli spiritualizza, si potrebbe dire, il procedimento, e lo trasforma impregnando di un'idea motrice dalla quale rigorosamente dipendono gli elementi tecnici di ciascuna opera. Suono, ritmo, i silenzi medesimi assumono un significato nuovo e quasi simbolico; lo slancio progressive d'ogni frase, la violenza dinamica dei sedicenti 'punto culminate'—luoghi comuni favorite del neo-romanticismo—sono banditi da una musica la quale non procede per accumulazione, ma per riduzione di accenti." Ibid., 63.

27. "Das führte auf das Lieblingsthema—dass Musik sich jeder Situation fügt— jede Situation magisch transformierend. Das Tuba mirum aus Moz.[arts] Requiem könnte in gleicher Gestalt in einer buffo Oper von bester Wirkung sein. Dazu bemerkte der anwesende Philipp Jarnach, wie es ihm mit bedeut.[enden] Liedern Schuberts ergangen sei. Wo die gleiche Musik die verschiedentlichsten Strophen begleitet und jedesmal, als der charakterische Ausdruck der Worte erschien. Früher hätte er das einer besonderen Genialität des Tonsetzers zugeschrieben, der Art glückliche Universalmelodie für den bes.[onderen] Fall erfunden hätte. Jetzt sieht er mit FBs Augen. Die Musik fügt sich immer und verwandelt alles." Galston, diary entry of March 9, 1924, 18.

28. "Die Busonische Kunst dagegen vermittelte das Bewusstsein neuer Probleme und Möglichkeiten, die nicht zue Rezepte zu lösen waren. Hier war keine 'Richtung,' keine Manier oder Formel zu finden, die man hätte nachbilden können, sondern das unverlierbare Beispiel einer Gestaltungskraft, die nur dem Ausdruck diente und zugleich höchste Disziplin des Ausdrucks war." Jarnach, "Bemerkungen zur Kunst Busonis" (1932), in Jarnach, *Schriften zur Musik*, 43.

29. Busoni to Jarnach, January 1, 1920, Staatsbibliothek zu Berlin, Preußischer Kulturbesitz, Musikabteilung mit Mendelssohn-Archiv, N. Mus. Depos. 56, 89, quoted in Levitz, "Teaching New Classicality," 184.

30. Busoni to Jarnach, October 30, 1920, in Beaumont, *Selected Letters*, 326–327.

31. Busoni to Jarnach, June 21, 1917, in Beaumont, *Selected Letters*, 262.

32. Busoni to Jarnach, July 16, 1917, in Beaumont, *Selected Letters*, 263–264.

33. Jarnach, Manuscript for the String Quartet, op. 16, Staatsbibliothek zu Berlin, Preußischer Kulturbesitz, Musikabteilung mit Mendelssohn-Archiv, N. Mus. Depos. 56, 10.

34. Busoni to Jarnach, June 1, 1920, quoted in Levitz, "Teaching New Classicality," 149.

35. Jarnach to Busoni, October 24, 1917, Staatsbibliothek zu Berlin, Preußischer Kulturbesitz, Musikabteilung mit Mendelssohn-Archiv, N. Mus. Nachl. 30, 96.

36. Busoni to Jarnach, November 26, 1917, Staatsbibliothek zu Berlin, Preußischer Kulturbesitz, Musikabteilung mit Mendelssohn-Archiv, N. Mus. Nachl. 30, 24.

37. "... die Form nicht als Gerüst, sondern als Erlebnis zu sehen, Ebenmass der Proportion und Oekonomie im Ausdruck als Gefühl zu werten. Die Aufgabe des Künstlers ist: aus der jeweiligen Idee die Mittel herzuleiten, ihre sichtbare Gestalt zu prägen." Jarnach, "Bemerkungen zur Kunst Busonis" (1932), in Jarnach, *Schriften zur Musik*, 44.

38. Weiss, *Die Musik*, 100.

39. "Je viens vous remercier de votre bonne lettre du conseil qu'elle contient an sujet de la péroraison du Quintette; j'avais déjà formé le projet d'un remaniement dans le sens d'un élargissement du movement—une espêce de paraphrase qui allongeait l'ouvrage de deux ou trois minutes de musique." Jarnach to Busoni, October 29, 1918, Staatsbibliothek zu Berlin, Preußischer Kulturbesitz, Musikabteilung mit Mendelssohn-Archiv, N. Mus. Nachl. 30, 104.

40. Jarnach, "Thematische Analyse," *Neue Musikzeitung* 42:20 (July 21, 1921), 317.

41. Weiss, *Die Musik*, 95–96.

42. "Zwei einfache Motive der Einleitung (Präambulum), welche... erst im 'Thema' klare Gestalt gewinnen, bilden gleichsam den melodischen Kern des Ganzen; aus diesen zwei Hauptmotiven entwickeln sich sämtliche Variationenthemen." Ibid., 101.

43. Jarnach, "Über Ferruccio Busoni" (1954), in Jarnach, *Schriften zur Musik*, 53.

44. Busoni to Jarnach, April 2, 1916, quoted in Weiss, *Die Musik*, 57.

45. Jarnach's copy of Mozart's *Die Zauberflöte*, Staatsbibliothek zu Berlin, Preußischer Kulturbesitz, Musikabteilung mit Mendelssohn-Archiv, N. Mus. Nachl. 30, 113.

46. Ibid., 90, 97.

47. Orchestration was such a frequently discussed topic between the two that Busoni even asked Jarnach to collaborate together on a treatise on orchestration. An unfinished draft of Busoni's planned treatise on orchestration in Jarnach's handwriting is preserved in the Staatsbibliothek zu Berlin, Preußischer Kulturbesitz, Musikabteilung mit Mendelssohn-Archiv, Mus. Nachl. F. Busoni, CI-135. A letter from December 1919 reveals that Busoni asked about Jarnach's ideals, but also supplied his own based on Mozart.

48. Busoni to Jarnach, December 1, 1919, in Beaumont, *Selected Letters*, 299–300.

49. "Ich tische habe da die Empfindung vollkommener Schönheit—Vom 5 Takt an spielt das Klavier die Rolle der Viola und 2 Geige im Striechquartett—und hat, diese gegenüber den Vorzug des Klangkontrastes. Eher könnte man an Holzbläser denken." Jarnach to Busoni, August 28, 1920, Staatsbibliothek zu Berlin, Preußischer Kulturbesitz, Musikabteilung mit Mendelssohn-Archiv, N. Mus. Nachl. 30, 118.

50. "Die 'Sinfonia brevis,' die man in Berlin vom Dresdner Orchester unter Fritz Buschs Leitung hörte, ist das Werk, von dem aus die charakteris Wendung in Jarnachs Schaffen ihren Ausgang nahm. Seine früheren Arbeiten zeigen eine leichtflüssige, eingängliche Melodik, im Orchestersatz den Glanz und die üppige Fülle der Wagner-Strauss-Manier. Unter dem Einfluss Busonis kam Jarnach zu einer neuen Schreibweise, die man unromantischsachlich nennen kann. Allem unnötigen, überflüssigen Pomp des Klanges gibt er nun Abschied, sorgt sich um die feinste Durchbildung der Konturen, um eine klare, durchgeistigt, beseelte Form, kurz, er strebt bewusst jene 'neue Klassizität' an, die Busoni als Ideal aufstellt, und die dem romanischen,

fein ausgeprägten Formgefühl eines Jarnach sehr gemäss erscheint. Über dieser Gefolgschaft an Busonis Ideen verlor er keineswegs seine Selbständigkeit." Hugo Leichtentritt, "Philipp Jarnach," *Musikblätter des Anbruch* 5:9 (1923), 259.

51. Busoni to Jarnach, September 3, 1921, Staatsbibliothek zu Berlin, Preußischer Kulturbesitz, Musikabteilung mit Mendelssohn-Archiv, N. Mus. Nachl. 30, 128, and Busoni to Jarnach, July 20, 1923, Staatsbibliothek zu Berlin, Preußischer Kulturbesitz, Musikabteilung mit Mendelssohn-Archiv, N. Mus. Nachl. 30, 77. Busoni asks if Jarnach has studied Stravinsky's *L'Histoire du soldat*.

52. Busoni to Jarnach, August 13, 1920, in Beaumont, *Selected Letters*, 320–321.

53. Busoni to Jarnach, December 2, 1919, in ibid., 301–302.

54. Busoni to Jarnach, March 22, 1920, in ibid., 305–306.

55. Jarnach, Sketches for Berlioz Variations, Staatsbibliothek zu Berlin, Preußischer Kulturbesitz, Musikabteilung mit Mendelssohn-Archiv, N. Mus. Depos. 56, 58.

56. Jarnach to Busoni, August 10, 1920, Staatsbibliothek zu Berlin, Preußischer Kulturbesitz, Musikabteilung mit Mendelssohn-Archiv, N. Mus. Nachl. 30, 117.

57. Jarnach's score of Busoni's *Die Brautwahl*, BV 261, Staatsbibliothek zu Berlin, Preußischer Kulturbesitz, Musikabteilung mit Mendelssohn-Archiv, N. Mus. Depos. 56, 94.

58. Jarnach, "Zur Partitur der "Brautwahl," in Jarnach, *Schriften zur Musik*, 56.

59. Busoni completed the Intermezzo on December 13, 1917, the Vorspiel II in 1918, and the Sarabande and Cortège movements in 1919. In addition, Busoni busied himself with several piano compositions, including his sonatinas. He finished the Sonatina no. 4 ("In diem nativitatis Christi"), BV 274, in 1917, and the Sonatina no. 6 ("Super Carmen") in 1920, for instance. Other pieces include: Divertimento for Flute and Orchestra, BV 285, and the *Lied des Unmuts*, BV 281a, among others.

60. "Bravo, mon cher maître! Je reçois la nouvelle en rentrant du théâtre. Je marque le jour d'une pierre blanc[he]. Vive la belle et généreuse partition de Turandot! Vive grand et cher Busoni." Jarnach to Busoni, March 6, 1917, Staatsbibliothek zu Berlin, Preußischer Kulturbesitz, Musikabteilung mit Mendelssohn-Archiv, N. Mus. Depos. 56.

61. Jarnach, "Einführende Worte zu Busonis 'Sonatine 1910,'" (1949) in Jarnach, *Schriften zur Musik*, 61.

62. Antony Beaumont has already discussed the details of Jarnach's completion of *Doktor Faust* so that it could premiere at the Dresdner Staatsoper on May 21, 1925. Beaumont, "Busoni's 'Doctor Faust': A Reconstruction and Its Problems," *Musical Times*, 127:1718 (April 1986), 196–199. See also Johanna Keller, "Trying to Put a Proper End to 'Doktor Faust,'" *New York Times* (January 7, 2001), 40. As Beaumont notes, two scenes were left incomplete, the Helen of Troy vision in the second tableau and the ending, which breaks off during Faust's closing monologue.

63. Jarnach, arr., *Lied des Brander aus Goethe's Faust*, by Busoni, Staatsbibliothek zu Berlin, Preußischer Kulturbesitz, Musikabteilung mit Mendelssohn-Archiv, N. Mus. Ms. 12.

64. Tamara Levitz, "Jarnach, Philipp," *Grove Music Online, Oxford Music Online*, Oxford University Press, http://www.oxfordmusiconline.com/subscriber/article/grove/music/14193, accessed January 15, 2014.

65. Weiss, *Die Musik*, 172–173.
66. Ibid., 176–177.
67. Ibid., 250.
68. "Von jedem anderen hätte ich dies als Beleidigung empfunden, von Ihnen aber macht es mich nur traurig, dass Sie auch nur einen Augenblick denken konnten, dass ich in irgendeiner Weise und zu irgendeinem Zeitpunkt mit dem furchtbaren Regime des dritten Reiches sympathisiert hätte" (From anyone else I would have considered this as an insult, but from you it simply makes me sad that you could think for even a moment that I in any way would have sympathized at any time with the terrible regime of the Third Reich). Jarnach to Schoenberg, May 11, 1951, in Weiss, *Die Musik*, 268.
69. "[Nach 1927] bestanden natürlich die alten Bindungen mit Berlin weiter, bis ich 1933 von den Nationalsozialisten aus meinen sämtlichen Ehrenämtern entfernt wurde. Meine Werke durften nicht aufgeführt werden, und das dauerte, bis Hermann Abendroth den Mut hatte, eine Uraufführung von mir im Leipziger Gewandhaus herauszubringen" ([After 1927], of course, the old ties with Berlin persisted until 1933, when I was removed by the Nazis from my all honorary offices. My works were not to be performed, and that lasted until Hermann Abendroth had the courage, to launch a world premiere by me with the Leipzig Gewandhaus Orchestra). Jarnach, broadcast with NDR as part of the series "Das musikalische Selbstporträt," quoted in Weiss, *Die Musik*, 269.
70. "Daneben bestanden die alten Bindungen an Berlin weiter, bis ich dort 1933 von den Nationalsozialisten aus allen meinen Ehrenämtern entfernt wurde. Meine Werke durften nicht aufgefürht werden. Und das dauerte lange Zeit. Bis Hermann Abendroth den Mut hatte, eine Urafführung von mi rim Leipziger Gewandhaus herauszubringen. Und dies war auch nur deshalb möglich, weil es sich um ein besonderes Werk handelte, nämlich meine *Musik mit Mozart*, die durch die Bindung an die Klassik vielleicht keinen so exponierten Charakter hatte wie das übrige, was ich geschrieben habe." Jarnach, "Das Beispiel Busonis" (1963), in Jarnach, *Schriften zur Musik*, 196.
71. Weiss has uncovered documents naming Jarnach on a list of musical bolshevists by the Nazis and condemning the activities of the November Group. Weiss, *Die Musik*, 272.
72. Ibid., 274.
73. "Vielen Dank für die freundliche Untersuchung über Plattis Personalien, u. noch mehr für die musikalische Art der Auskunft; die Sonaten unseres—jetzo unzweifelhaften—Venezianers wander nach Mainz [Schotts Söhne]." Jarnach to Busoni, January 16, 1924, Staatsbibliothek zu Berlin, Preußischer Kulturbesitz, Musikabteilung mit Mendelssohn-Archiv, N. Mus. Nachl., 30, 138. Jarnach performed Platti's G major sonata with Alfred Lichtenstein on May 12, 1923, in a private concert in the home of Herbert Graf. Weiss, *Die Musik*, 419.
74. Weiss, *Die Musik*, 279.
75. "Strawinsky hat sich intensiv beschäftigt mit den musikalischen Formen und Stilen vergangener Zeiten und daraus Anregungen geschöpft, deren Spuren man in vielen seiner Werke wiederfindet—wie z.B. in 'Oedipus rex' und 'Apollon musagète.' Es fällt aber in solchen Fällen auf, dass diese Einflüsse stets vollständig assimiliert

und gleichsam als Bestandteil seines eigenen Stils erscheinen, so das kein Bruch entsteht und sie nicht als Fremdkörper wirken." Jarnach, "Igor Strawinsky" (1971), in Jarnach, *Schriften zur Musik*, 123.

76. The score itself contains a few corrections, including measure 6, eighth notes beats 1–2 and accidentals measures 9–10. In measure 11, notes are crossed out, and an 8ve sign is crossed out in measure 12 as well as an inner voice added, suggesting that it was a piece Jarnach knew well and performed.

77. See Jarnach's essays "Wolfgang Amadeus Mozart: Portrait eines Meisters," "W. A. Mozart: 1756–1956," and "Mozart nach zweihundert Jahren [1973]," in Jarnach, *Schriften zur Musik*, 69–84.

78. See Jarnach, "W. A. Mozart: 1756–1956," in ibid., 73.

79. Jarnach, nachwort to *W. A. Mozart; Thema und Variationen für Violine und Klavier*, arr. Ph. Jarnach (Mainz: Schott, 1936), 8.

80. Jarnach, Rundfunk interview of July 20, 1977, with Reinhold Schuberts in Eschenberg, quoted in Weiss, *Die Musik*, 297.

81. Ibid.

82. "Handelte es sich hier *nicht* um Variationen im üblichen Sinne des Wortes, sondern um eine zyklische Grossform, deren vier Sätze selbständig gegliedert und entwickelt sind." Jarnach, "Über die *Musik mit Mozart*," *Berliner Philharmonisches Orchester*, Spielzeit VIII (February 15, 1942).

83. The piece premiered under the baton of Gustav Havemann on May 24, 1935, in a concert of the Berufsstandes der deutschen Komponisten (a division of the *Reichsmusikkammer*) in Leipzig. The chief National Socialist music critic was impressed: "Philipp Jarnachs 'Musik mit Mozart' fesselt bei Verzicht auf auffällige archaisierende Elemente durch die Klarheit und Reinheit des Stils" (Philipp Jarnachs 'Music with Mozart' captivates with a renunciation of striking archaic elements by the clarity and purity of style). Fritz Stege, "Die Berliner Kunstwochen," in *Zeitschrift für Musik* (July 1935), 763.

84. Jarnach, "Wolfgang Amadeus Mozart: Portrait eines Meisters," in Jarnach, *Schriften zur Musik*, 69.

85. Jarnach, "Die Musik und die Oper" (1930), in ibid., 162.

86. Jarnach, "W. A. Mozart: 1756–1956" (1956), in ibid., 73.

87. Ibid., 75.

88. Ibid., 75.

89. Ibid., 76.

90. See Levitz, "Teaching New Classicality," 432.

91. Weiss, *Die Musik*, 286.

92. Otto Luening, *The Odyssey of an American Composer* (New York: Scribner, 1980), 371. During the post–World War II period, Jarnach might have been able to relaunch his compositional career. However, he was not particularly industrious as a composer then. He was mainly writing piano pieces, such as the *Marsch, Wiegenlied, und Pastorale*, op. 32. He also transformed the ninth of his ten short piano pieces into the Siciliano for piano (1947) and created a four-voice choral piece on the volklied *Wach auf, meins Herzens schöne* (1947). Yet none of these works played a major role in concert life in postwar Germany.

93. Weiss, *Die Musik*, 326. Reportedly, seven concerts took place in thirty-two days in which thirty-two works were performed.

94. Ibid., 326.

95. He became a member of the Akademie der Künste in Berlin and was awarded the Berliner Kunstpreis (1955), the Hamburg Bach Prize (1957, with Blacher), the Hamburg Brahms Medal (1958), and the Grosses Verdienstkreuz der Bundesrepublik Deutschland (1959).

96. Everett Helm, "Current Chronicle," *Musical Quarterly* 36:4 (October 1950), 602. See also Albrecht Dümling, "What Is Internal Exile in Music?" http://orelfoundation.org/index.php/journal/journalArticle/what_is_internal_exile_in_music/#fn19, accessed February 14, 2014.

97. Jarnach, "Mechanische Music" [1926], in Jarnach, *Schriften zur Musik*, 176. Similar sentiments are expressed in "Das Problem des Musikapparates," in Jarnach, *Schriften zur Musik*, 174–176.

98. Jarnach, "Elektronische Musik in U.S.A.," Staatsbibliothek zu Berlin, Preußischer Kulturbesitz, Musikabteilung mit Mendelssohn-Archiv, N. Mus. Depos. 56, 270.

99. "Die heutige Situation der Musik und die Musikerziehung," in Jarnach, *Schriften zur Musik*, 182.

100. Busoni to Jarnach, October 5, 1919, in Beaumont, *Selected Letters*, 270.

101. Busoni to Jarnach, August 22, 1921, in ibid., *Selected Letters*, 345.

102. "An Philipp Jarnach in liebender Hochschätzung." Busoni, *Ziguenerlied*, op. 55 no. 2, Staatsbibliothek zu Berlin, Preußischer Kulturbesitz, Musikabteilung mit Mendelssohn-Archiv, N. Mus. Depos. 56.

103. Jarnach published his Sonate für Violine allein, op. 8, with Zierfuss in 1913.

104. "Ein junger Philipp Jarnach, Spanier von Geburt, (ein Verwandter R. Strauss') hat so eben den Klavierausz. meiner Oper fertiggestellt u. dabei so viel Verständnis u. Geschick bekundet, dass ich ihn Ihnen vorerst für Arbeiten dieser Art waermstens emphfehlen möchte; sodann auch Ihre Aufmerksamkeit auf seine selbständige Komponisten—Begabung ziehen." Busoni to Breitkopf und Härtel, December 20, 1916, in *Ferruccio Busoni im Briefwechsel mit seinem Verlag Breitkopf und Härtel*, ed. Eva Hanau, vol. 2, Busoni ed., ed. Albrecht Riethmüller (Wiesbaden: Breitkopf und Härtel, 2012), 174.

105. "Inzwischen ist ein Brief des Herrn Ph. Jarnach mit Ihren freundlichen, empfehlenden Zeilen bei uns eingegangen. Wir haben Herrn Jarnach gebeten, uns sein Streichquintett zu senden, damit wir uns näher mit ihm beschäftigen können." Bretikopf and Härtel to Busoni, August 16, 1918, in *Ferruccio Busoni im Briefwechsel*, vol. 2, 382.

106. Busoni to Jarnach, May 3, 1919, Staatsbibliothek zu Berlin, Preußischer Kulturbesitz, Musikabteilung mit Mendelssohn-Archiv, N. Mus. Nachl. 30, 51, and Jarnach to Busoni, October 10, 1919, Staatsbibliothek zu Berlin, Preußischer Kulturbesitz, Musikabteilung mit Mendelssohn-Archiv, N. Mus. Nachl. 30, 109.

107. That Busoni had something to do with the publication is suggested by a letter from Jarnach to Busoni in which he notes that Busoni received a copy of the String Quintet before Jarnach even knew it had been published: "Lienau überraschte mich

dadurch, dass er Ihnen das Quintett schickte, bevor ich wusste, dass es endlich erscheinen war" (Lienau surprised me in that he sent you the quintet before I knew it was finally published). Jarnach to Busoni, November 26–30, 1920, Staatsbibliothek zu Berlin, Preußischer Kulturbesitz, Musikabteilung mit Mendelssohn-Archiv, N. Mus. Nachl. 30, 122. Correspondence with the publishing company has shown that only the original manuscript and contract remain in the archives (i.e., no additional letters). Judith Picard, emails to the author, March 18/25, 2014.

108. Weiss, *Die Musik*, 64. He gave a piano-violin recital together with Lidus Klein on November 16, 1916, in which his sonata for violin and piano was programmed, and on February 8, 1917, the Tonhalle Quartet performed his String Quartet, op. 22. On March 26–27, 1917, his *Ballata für Orchester* and "Das leise Lied" from *Winterbilder*, op. 15, were performed.

109. Burkhard to Busoni, May 18, 1921, quoted in Weiss, *Die Musik*, 133. Other performances include his sonata for violin and piano at the Beethovensaal in April 1921. The performance is reviewed in the *Signale* 79:16 (April 20, 1921, 434.)

110. Weiss, *Die Musik*, 133.

111. Busoni to José Vianna da Motta, March 21, 1917, in Beaumont, *Selected Letters*, 255–256.

112. Weiss has provided a breakdown of the subjects Jarnach taught by years:

1917–1918, score reading, conducting, and counterpoint
1918–1919, score reading, conducting, counterpoint, theory, and composition
1919–1920, score reading, conducting, counterpoint, and composition
1920–1921, counterpoint

Weiss, *Die Musik*, 80.

113. Levitz, "Teaching New Classicality," 358. He also instructed Wilhelm Maler (1923), Adolf Brunner (1921–1925), Robert Oboussier (c. 1922), and Nikos Skalkottas (1925–1927).

114. Brunner left a brief memory of studies with Jarnach in Berlin. He specifically remembers writing many canons and studying counterpoint with him. Chris Walton, ed., *Adolf Brunner: Erinnerungen eines Schweizers Komponisten aus der Schule Philipp Jarnachs und Franz Schrekers* (Zurich: Hug and Co., 1997), 41.

115. Weill dedicated his *Fantasia, Passacaglia, und Hymnus*, op. 6 (1922), to Jarnach, but the friendship was unfortunately broken in the second half of the 1920s even if Jarnach kept up with his developments, and was appalled at his turn toward *Trivialmusik*. Weill and Jarnach eventually had a falling out and Weill cut off contact with Gerda Busoni as well. Levitz, "Teaching New Classicality," 429. In July 1927 *Mahagonny-Songspiel* premiered in Baden-Baden, and *Die Dreigroschenoper* on August 31, 1928, in Berlin. Blum, Vogel, and Jarnach rejected the latter work as "honky tonk." Levitz, "Teaching New Classicality," 21.

116. Jarnach, "Die zeitgenössische Musik in Deutschland und Österreich" (1924), in Jarnach *Schriften zur Musik*, 138.

117. "Busoni, nicht minder kühn im Beschreiten unbegangener Wege, ist in der Auswertung seiner Erkenntnisse behutsamer. Eben anders als Schönberg wollte Busoni die Kontinuität der Zusammenhänge sichern, er wollte nicht preisgeben,

sondern bereichern. Alles Andere erschien ihm relative, weil zeitgebunden. In allem, was in der Musik von je geschaffen wurde, spürt er der Einheit eines geistigen Willens, eines Menschensinnes nach. Deshalb war für ihn die Atonalität rein neues Ausdrucksmittel, das hinugekommen ist,—nicht aber (wie für Schönberg) eine neue Sprache überhaupt, die alles andere ausschliesst. Was ihm vorschwebt, ist die Überwindung alles materiell Stofflichen in der Musik, die Synthese einer Form, die nicht mehr einem Schema, sondern nur dem Gedanken verpflichtet ist. Alle Spätwerke Busonis sind von dieser zentralen Idee getragen, und ihre geschichtliche Bedeutung liegt darin, dass sie die Erneuerung des musikalischen Klassizismus in einem *spezifisch modernen* Sinne eingeleitet haben." Jarnach, "Über Ferruccio Busoni" (1954), in *Schriften zur Musik*, 52–53.

118. "Es ist Ihnen . . . vielleicht etwas befremdend, dass ich mich Ihrem Einfluss nicht restlos unterwerfe, nachdem ich durch Sie so vieles begriffen, lieben oder ablehnen gelernt.—Nein, ich werde kein Petri der Komposition; ich will Sie nicht kopieren; ich will Ihre hohe Persönlichkeit besser ehren, verstehen und deuten; ich bemühe mich, Ihrem Beispiel zu folgen, dem Beispiel des unabhängigen, streng eigendenkenden Künstlers—und wenn mir das gelingt, so werde ich, mit mehr Berechtigung als irgend jemand, mich mit dem Titel *Ihres Schülers* adeln können." Jarnach to Busoni, March 3–4, 1918, Staatsbibliothek zu Berlin, Preußischer Kulturbesitz, Musikabteilung mit Mendelssohn-Archiv, N, Mus. Nachl. 30, 102.

119. "Sie, mein lieber Meister, haben kein Vertrauen zu mir; ich meine, Sie zweifeln meinen Charakter, meine seelische Festigkeit an . . . Ich bitte Sie, nicht an Empfindlichkeit meinerseits zu glauben; ich liebe Sie zu sehr, um mich von Ihnen gekränkt zu fühlen—Aber verwunden können Sie mich.—Trotz meiner Geschwätzigkeit besitze ich nicht die Fähigkeit, meine Gefühle zur Schau zu tragen. Ist Ihnen mein kaltes oder allzu sachliches Benehmen ein Beweis dass ich weniger lebhaft empfinde als andere?" Jarnach to Busoni, March 3–4, 1918, quoted in Weiss, *Die Musik*, 74.

120. Jarnach to Busoni, May 3, 1923, uncatalogued, Staatsbibliothek zu Berlin, Preußischer Kulturbesitz, Musikabteilung mit Mendelssohn-Archiv, and Jarnach to Busoni, August 2, 1923, Staatsbibliothek zu Berlin, Preußischer Kulturbesitz, Musikabteilung mit Mendelssohn-Archiv, N. Mus. Nachl. 30, 135.

121. See Levitz's "Teaching New Classicalty," 224, for a fuller description of the conflicts, including the idea that Jarnach was becoming too nationalistic by composing too many German lieder and the fact that Jarnach failed to invite Busoni to rehearsals of his own compositions. A letter from Jarnach to Busoni from July 1923, however, gives no hint of the breach of friendship.

122. Weiss, *Die Musik*, 74–75.

123. Despite the revival of the friendship, Busoni apparently continued to criticize even his favorite pupils, including Petri, Zadora, and Jarnach. In particular, he never quite got over Jarnach's inability to set *Das Wandbild* to music. Galston, diary entry of March 29, 1924, 28.

124. Jarnach, "Die heutige Situation der Musik und die Musikerziehung (1957)," in Jarnach, *Schriften zur Musik*, 183–184.

7

Conclusions: "Passing the Torch"

He was a very individualistic composer who wanted this same kind of search for the "real self" to be lived by his students. He did not try to organize us into a school. Although accused by conservative German composers of being a futurist, he was actually trying to bridge the gap between the old and the new by accepting traditions but transforming them into music for the future.

Otto Luening, *The Odyssey of an American Composer:*
The Autobiography of Otto Luening

A BUSONI SCHOOL?

AS A COMPOSITION teacher, Ferruccio Busoni sought to reveal new musical vistas to his students.[1] His pedagogical strategy consisted mainly of inspiring his disciples with new ideas. He dialogued and critiqued; he talked about literature, art, history, philology, and music, but he did not focus on specific methodologies or techniques. Nor did he impart knowledge in an authoritarian sense. He believed that natural talent would bridge the gap between a vision of ideal music and the treatment of tones, harmonies, and rhythms.

Busoni's composition mentees found his teaching inspiring and embraced his ideals of music. They gloss them in letters, interviews, and writings when explaining their own composition philosophies. Yet the scope of Busoni's impact as a composition mentor is difficult to measure, because the individual styles of his students are so dissimilar. That the compositions by his disciples also fail to resemble his own music is unusual, as Gianmario Borio has already pointed out.[2]

To speak of a Busoni composition school in the most paradigmatic sense—that is, as a group of students and a teacher sharing a similar technique or style—is difficult. Attempts to find a unifying technical approach have been largely unsuccessful so far, and this is caused not only by Busoni's avoidance of methods and routines, but also by his evolution as a composer and thinker. Borio's suggestion of post-tonal counterpoint as a unifying feature, for instance, fails to be comprehensive enough.[3] It applies mainly to Busoni's Berlin master class pupils.[4] Moreover, Busoni was not the only teacher stressing non-tonal counterpoint at the time, Hindemith and Schoenberg being notable examples. Additionally, Busoni did not mandate a radically new method of counterpoint, and post-tonal counterpoint does not account for other characteristic aspects of his students' works, including pluralism, an emphasis on sonority, and experimentation with new forms, scales, and instruments.

What unites Busoni's students is his aesthetic ideals, even if each student applied them individualistically.[5] Busoni communicated his vision of great music (in *The Essence of Music*), and of the future direction of music, expecting his students to translate the visions into audible sound.

Busoni's teachings were intentionally suggestive, and they were also constantly evolving. His enthusiasm for the unexplored and the new colored most of his ideas about music in the 1900s and early 1910s, and it also informed the ideas that he imparted to and emphasized with his composition mentees at that time. Prior to World War I, he was full of optimism about future musical developments, calling music a "child that has learned to walk, but must still be led. It is a virgin art, without experiences in life and suffering. It is all unconscious as yet of what garb is becoming, of its own advantages, its unawakened capacities."[6] By contrast, his later teachings were tinged with a degree of cynicism about the future even as he sought to forge a middle ground between the conservative and the avant-garde. Composition pupils that attended his Berlin master class at the end of his life, as Tamara Levitz has documented, were most heavily influenced by his ideals of Young Classicality.[7]

Busoni's pre-Berlin masterclass composition pupils therefore experienced his ideas at a time when he focused on musical experimentation, and their compositions reflect that. His earlier pupils experimented with new sounds, styles, and forms, embracing his enthusiasm for new technology and new instruments. Some examined ways sonority could become an integral material of music, and others explored proto-postmodernist stylistic pluralism. Examining Busoni's pre-Berlin masterclass pupils thereby enriches understanding about the breadth of Busoni's influence as a composition teacher and the genealogy of experimental music in the early twentieth century.[8]

Connections and Summaries: Sonority and Instrumentation

Even if the works of Busoni's early composition pupils sound radically different from one another, that does not preclude similar underlying aesthetic premises and ideals. Busoni's early- and mid-career composition pupils were interested in the new sounds, new scales, new technology, and new combinations of styles. Many of his composition pupils, for instance, explored timbral variety in their compositions.[9] In his tone poem *The Hill of Dreams*, op. 10, Gruenberg, for instance, relied on thin textures to highlight contrasting colors and timbres, including harmonics on the harp and a lyrical bassoon solo. Jarnach likewise gave instruments individual motives and characters in his compositions, such as the *Sinfonia Brevis*, op. 14, to draw attention to each distinct timbre. Others explored ways overtones could expand instrumental color. While studying in Zurich with Busoni, Luening developed an interest in acoustics, and that became a catalyst for his experimentation with acoustical harmonies. He was a pioneer in the use of voicings and overtones for special coloristic effects. Luening was also interested in using electronic technology, such as the tape recorder, to expand the timbral possibilities of acoustic instruments. In *Fantasy in Space*, W. 148 (1952), what makes the music interesting is not the motivic combinations, but the timbral colors made possible through electronic manipulation of acoustic sounds. In *Low Speed*, W. 150 (1952), Luening used overtones to derive harmonies and intervals. Sibelius and Varèse took Busoni's teachings to yet another level when they used overtones, timbres, and sonorities to generate harmonies and forms. In particular, Varèse and Sibelius created sound masses characterized by collections of specific instruments, rhythms, motives, and textures. Sibelius not only audibly highlighted instrumental timbre and color through his choice of instruments in specific registers with unique musical material, as Gruenberg and Luening had done. He also used sound on a structural level, pioneering an approach commonly used later in electronic music. His pieces feature alternating textures, or sheets of sound. Timbre and chord spacing are not just superficial features, but primary structural elements, thereby foreshadowing electronic and textural music. In many cases, Sibelius's textures span a wide registral range, allowing for greater timbral variety, or else are presented in a very constricted range, creating compressed sound, thus drawing attention to any timbral movement.[10] In Varèse's music, variation and renewal stem from continuous metamorphosis of sound material.[11] Chou Wen-Chung has also noted that Varèse paid special attention to instrument groupings according to timbre.[12] Timbres, in turn, generate germinal ideas, define texture, enhance linear elaboration, and delineate phrases and sections.

A fascination with timbre and sonority led some of Busoni's students to investigate new electronic resources when this possibility was hardly considered in serious art circles.[13] Although Busoni did not utilize electronic instruments in his own compositions, he instilled in his early composition pupils a sense of wonderment, excitement, and curiosity not only about using traditional instruments in new ways, but also about exploring the ways music could be enriched through technology. Varèse, in particular, felt a longing to work with electronic instruments even before it was technically feasible.[14] His works from the 1920s feature traditional instruments but combine them in manners foreshadowing approaches used with electronic music in later decades. In his attempts to fulfill his artistic vision, Varèse commissioned two instruments from Léon Theremin that he hoped would possess an "infinite gradation of pitch, intensity, and timbre."[15] His *Ecuatorial* (1934) was the first known composition for electronic and acoustic instruments. After receiving an Ampex tape recorder, in *Déserts* (1954) he was able to include organized sound on tape, which appears together with an ensemble of winds, percussion, and piano. The use of electronics in *Déserts* is somewhat disappointing, largely due to the fact that Varèse did not have access to the equipment until he had nearly finished the composition. Thus the three interpolated tape-music segments are ancillary. *Poème électronique* (1958), on the other hand, is widely acknowledged as one of the first great electronic compositions. Featuring four hundred loudspeakers in eight rows, it represents a brilliant spatialization of sound and was synchronized to black and white images by Le Corbusier during its first performance.

Varèse was not the only Busoni student experimenting with electronic music. Gabrielle Buffett, who studied with Busoni in Berlin, also tried her hand at creating machines to realize his ideas about the possibilities of electronic music, claiming: "With the help of and through improvements to these sound-machines, an objective reconstitution of the life of sound could be possible. We would be discovering sound-forms independently of musical conventions."[16] Buffett and her husband, Francis Picabia, were soon caught up in the Dada movement, in which the visual and musical were synthesized together.[17] Percy Grainger, who studied piano with Busoni briefly in 1903 and who maintained contact with Busoni for over a decade after that, likewise composed for unusual instruments and created his own homemade music machines from industrial materials. How many of these ideas were inspired or informed, at least in part, by Busoni's radical thoughts, remains difficult to establish, as Grainger was not one to speak often of those who influenced him.[18] Although he is not as widely remembered as Pierre Schaeffer in France or Varèse and Milton Babbitt in America, Luening was one of the earliest to write electronic music, and he did it in his own way. In his first piece for electronic tape and live performers, *Rhapsodic Variations for Tape Recorder and Orchestra*, W. 159 (1954), he aimed for an organic synthesis of tape and live music, as opposed to a juxtaposition of opposing forces in the style of a concerto grosso, as is more true of Varèse's *Déserts* (1954).[19]

Other pupils of Busoni that did not write tape music still embraced the melding of music and technology. Gruenberg, for instance, never liked the sound of tape or synthesized music. He was also heavily critical of certain electronic compositions, such as one he heard by Boulez: "I have just heard music by Henry Brant and Boulez; a concocted piece for a recording machine and orchestra and this had been heralded as electronic music, the music of the atomic age—My personal impression of this music, is the monotony of it—After the initial impact the subject matter is terribly mediocre—and continuous being so, no matter what strange electrical sounds are added, they remain monotonous. The dominant impression is faceless and dissonant."[20]

Even so, he was fascinated by ways technology could be melded with acoustic sounds and he dreamed about ways in which new technologies could revolutionize composition and the reception of music. In particular, he imagined ways in which technology could privatize the listening experience by allowing people to listen to music in the solitude of their own homes.[21] Gruenberg also dreamed about new and alternative ways opera and music could be melded with technology.[22] In his radio opera, *Green Mansions,* op. 39 (1937), he suggested using prerecorded music for certain sounds, such as the animals (see figure 7.1). He wanted other sounds amplified and played with spatial effects.[23] For instance, in his notes, he wrote that the characters of "Abel and Rima should be represented by speakers stationed at both ends of the stage."[24] He also called for the use of a "musical saw," noting that one of the bird melodies should be played on it,[25] and he used a megaphone for the "voice of the jungle."[26] In addition, there are some elements left up to the performer, and he used the theremin for Rima's voice. He notes in one passage for Abel that "the following regardless of musical pitch, should start rather slowly, and gradually rise to an uncontrollable outburst."[27] In addition, he applied symphonic and operatic ideals to film and multi-media music as well, aiming for large-scale structural continuity even despite surface heterogeneity in response to the plot.

Pluralism

If Busoni's early composition pupils experimented with new sounds, many also embraced proto-postmodernist pluralistic stylistic approaches. He expected his students to develop a broad knowledge of music repertoire in order to become acquainted with a variety of musical styles.[28] He called for a distillation of musical styles into an aurally heterogeneous whole.

While stylistic heterogeneity was not uncommon in the 1920s, with Ives, Stravinsky, and even Schoenberg melding diverse elements, Busoni's approach was idiosyncratic. Schoenberg combined Baroque forms and serialism, Stravinsky blended Baroque mannerisms with pungent dissonances, and Ives blended allusions to hymnody and popular music

FIGURE 7.1. Gruenberg, *Green Mansions*, mss., indication to insert prerecorded bird sounds. Louis Gruenberg Papers, Music Division, New York Public Library, Astor, Lenox, and Tilden Foundations, JPB 80–18.

with bitonality and dissonant chord clusters even while including numerous quotations. Yet overall, these composers utilized a more consistently modern treatment of the musical language. Busoni, by contrast, audibly juxtaposed musics and scales from different eras as well as folk songs, syncretically drawing upon a wealth of traditions.

Busoni's students shared his appreciation of stylistic heterogeneity. Sibelius approached music ahistorically. He drew upon Lisztian innovations of form, Mozartian proportion and equilibrium, and Bachian counterpoint, quoting from composers of different time periods, including Chopin, Wagner, Beethoven, and earlier composers such as Monteverdi.[29] Although predominantly tonal, his music also contains moments of dissonance and modality. Jarnach similarly combined Mozartian orchestration, Bachian counterpoint, and atonal treatments of the musical language. Although Varèse rejected juxtaposing the old and the new, he combined timbres, textures, tunes, and scales from around the world. In *Ecuatorial*, incantatory lines are juxtaposed to polyphony. His music is filled with the sounds of Chinese blocks, gongs, and percussion from around the world, as well as sounds from city life in New York, including the siren, but presented in a Western concert idiom. Luening's *Fugue and Chorale Fantasy with Electronic Doubles for Organ and Tape*, W. 224 (1973), which conflates two different compositions, his own *Fugue for Organ*, W. 221 (1971) and *Chorale Fantasy for Organ*, W. 43 (1922), also demonstrates stylistic pluralism. The three-voice fugue is written in a Baroque style, but with chromatically extended tonality. Each section of the fugue included in the *Fugue and Chorale Fantasy* is echoed by its electronic double in which sound is manipulated. For his part, Gruenberg blended jazz scales and rhythms with classical forms, genres, and instruments. In *The Daniel Jazz*, op. 21, a piece for voice and chamber orchestra, three themes bear similarities to spirituals and one to folk songs. The syncopated rhythms of ragtime and the flatted pitches of the blues scale alternate with traditional diatonic ones and vocal chanting. In the first movement of *Jazzberries*, op. 25, "Foxtrot," Gruenberg blends classical imitation, chromaticism, and repetitions with foxtrot rhythms. In the second number, "Blues," Gruenberg juxtaposes unstable and chromatic tonal material as well as polychords with a contrasting tonal section characterized by flatted blues pitches. Pluralism in the Busonian sense is particularly noticeable in his works for stage and film. In *The Emperor Jones,* op. 36 (1933), jazz, spirituals, and Broadway styles appear side by side with chanting, recitative, and aria-like vocal writing in addition to atonal and tonal passages. This is not to mention his film scores, such as *The Fight for Life,* in which lullabies, marches, and jazz appear next to music written in a classical Viennese style.

This stylistic pluralism was aided by an expansion of the tonal language. Busoni was only one of many experimenting with harmony in the early 1900s, when it seemed that tonality had run its course. Yet he was unusual in that he never rejected tonality's continued possibilities even while he sought out new ways of organizing music. He was not searching for a new *system,* as Schoenberg was—he simply hoped for an expansion of possibilities. His students likewise did not reject tonality but actively pursued ways to expand upon or enrich the tonal system, particularly through the use of non-conventional or microtonal scales, through polytonality, or through the coloristic use of harmony. Gruenberg, like Busoni, was fascinated by the possibility of microtones, even if he was not actively employing them in his compositions. He also wrote about expanding the musical alphabet and exploring new harmonies that moved beyond diatonicism.[30] His own compositions use harmonies, scales, and key areas coloristically, even if his pieces remain largely rooted in tonality. For instance, "Syncopep" from *Jazzberries,* op. 25, features sections in which one hand plays white keys and the other black ones, leading to temporary tonal ambiguity even if the overall key is A-flat major. Luening, for his part, although writing primarily tonal music, experimented with alternative tuning systems and with bitonality, polytonality, and protoserialism.[31] Varèse wrote extensively about the need for new scales, paraphrasing Busoni frequently in this context, and he tried out microtones as early as *Amériques* (1918–1921), which features quarter tones in the viola parts. Although he wrote almost entirely in an atonal idiom, it is possible to discover moments of tonality or serialism as well. Sibelius's music, by contrast, remains largely rooted in tonality, although he expanded the tonal palette by moving through keys for coloristic purposes. Jarnach, for his part, experimented with combining different modes, such as the church modes with diatonicism, polytonality, a mixing of major and minor modes with tritones, and with differing levels of dissonance. He viewed atonality as one means of organization to add to the spectrum of possibilities.

Form

Another characteristic of Busoni's early pupils is that they sought to create unique musical structures. Above all, Busoni stressed the need to avoid fitting material into prescribed forms or according to external programs. He called for formal originality in compositions related to the natural unfolding of the content, and, as a result, he preferred the fantasy or the free prelude over more traditional sonata-allegro forms: "Indeed, all composers have drawn closest to the true nature of music in preparatory and intermediary passages (preludes and transitions) where they felt at liberty to disregard symmetrical proportions, and unconsciously drew breath."[32] In Sibelius's music, for instance, references to traditional forms are often secondary, not primary.[33] James Hepokoski argues that the term sonata deformation is not even adequate to describe the formal processes. Hepokoski claims that Sibelius conflates sonata principles and rotational or folk-like forms when insistent repetition of a short melodic phrase or set of phrases combines with the forward motion of the sonata. Sibelius's fifth symphony is based on fragments with a rotational structure that gradually become more complex. Motivic hints grow in later reiterations until fully unfurled. Luening, for his part, maintains that Busoni stressed the need for unique structures intimately related to the content of the piece.[34] When describing his first attempts at composing after personally meeting Busoni for compositional advice, he stated: "Above all, the overall form or *gestalt* of the entire quartet concerned me and was slowly revealed to me."[35] In a later letter to Varèse, Luening elaborated on this: "I feel that the composer must take from this world of tone those materials which are most meaningful to him and fashion them into new forms and tonal relationships which are inherent in their nature."[36] Busoni's teachings about form likewise made a major impact on Jarnach, who juxtaposed diverse forms to create unique structures. In the String Quintet, op. 10, for instance, he blends elements of dance and vocal forms with variation form and large-scale tonal and motivic coherence to create a one-of-a-kind structure.

Although many composers in the early twentieth century were seeking new ways of organizing music in response to the changing tonal language, Busoni's teachings about how to do this were idiosyncratic and are reflected in his students' approaches. He believed in the abstract and non-representative nature of musical tones even while suggesting that the tones could be shaped according to human ideas. The thought of Gothic architecture, for instance, could be translated into musical ideas, suggesting a structural shape characterized by main musical pillars separated by transitions, contrapuntal and grandiose textures, and musical allusions to Baroque music. The approach is not narrative in the sense of much New German School music, nor is it absolutist like Schoenberg's music—he thought of ideas as musical motives that develop into appropriate forms.

Several of Busoni's pupils, Gruenberg and Varèse included, used human ideas as sources of structural inspiration. Gruenberg, for instance, envisioned unique musical structures inspired by architecture around the world. Gruenberg specifically envisioned pyramids and temples as models for musical form.[37] He, like Busoni, avoided explicit narrative, but used ideas derived from human experiences to shape the content and the form, such as in his *The Hill of Dreams*, op. 10, a tone poem, inspired by the sights in Vienna. The music is descriptive but not narrative, and the descriptive ideas provide a unique structure apart from the *Formenlehre* tradition.[38]

When discussing form, Varèse also explicitly acknowledged his indebtedness to Busoni, especially in relation to a quest for structural originality and a synthesis of form and content.[39] With his background in science and math, Varèse attributed the working out of his formal structure to human ideas—especially scientific ones. These, he claimed, were not programmatic, merely important conceptually in relation to the ways he chose to combine the pitches and rhythms and unfold them into larger structures. Extra-musical thoughts that inspired his formal structures included crystallography (*Hyperprism*) plants (*Octandre*), and mathematics (*Intégrales*).

Busoni's pupils thus acted upon a nexus of ideals espoused by Busoni, but the specific working out of those ideals was highly individualistic. True, Busoni and his pupils were surrounded by a *Zeitgeist* characterized by musical experimentation. The opening chapter of this book details just a few of the trends that informed the *Zeitgeist* inhabited by Busoni and his pupils, including *Jugendstil*, German romanticism, Italian futurism, and more. There was also plenty of compositional experimentation resulting in structural originality, atonality, and a new play with color. It was Schoenberg who came up with the idea of the *Klangfarbenmelodie*, associating tones and colors. As Hugill has noted, the third of his *Fünf Orchesterstücke*, op. 16 (1909), also contained a section featuring a chord that changed timbre.[40] He and his students were also interested in new musical structures. Busoni's students were also not the only contemporaneous composers experimenting with new instruments—Harry Partch and the Italian futurists being notable examples as well. Busoni's mentees thus participated in this general spirit of experimentation that surrounded them and were doubtless influenced by it. Yet this in no way diminishes the fact that Busoni was the most seminal influence on the development of the figures covered in this book. His teachings shaped their thought processes, ideals, and career trajectories. They, in turn, transmitted Busoni's ideas to their own students and colleagues, disseminating his ideas far and wide.

BUSONI'S GRAND PUPILS AND BEYOND

> Ferruccio Busoni's aesthetic philosophy inspired artists in many disciplines, but his role as progenitor of a particular stream of modernism is notably absent from the master narrative of twentieth-century music.
>
> Austin Clarkson, "Wolpe, Varèse, and the Busoni Effect"

Busoni's ideas did not die out with his students. They were passed down to his grand pupils, thus contributing to a significant and lasting composition legacy. As Clarkson has noted, Busoni's impact on subsequent generations of composers, especially experimentalist ones, was significant even when considering the transmission of his ideas to the pupils and followers of Varèse and Wolpe alone: "The seeds that Varèse and Wolpe had sown bore fruit in a generation of composers that looked up to them as mentors: Lucia Dlugoszewski, Ralph Shapey, Chou Wen-Chung, Earle Brown, Morton Feldman, Mario Davidovsky, James Tenney, Ursula Mamlok, Charles Wuorinen and Eric Salzman, to name a few. Though each of these composers became a lawgiver unto him- or herself, it is possible to discern features of their work that epitomized Busoni's vision for modern music and that were so richly realized and transmitted by Varèse and Wolpe."[41]

This is not to mention Arthur Lourié as well, who pioneered microtones and Russian futuristic music.[42] Lourié met Busoni in St. Petersburg in 1909 and interacted with him on a regular basis in Berlin in the 1920s. It was there that he also met Varèse. However, the contributions are even wider if one takes into consideration the grand pupils of those studied in detail in this book. Busoni's students passed down many of his ideas to their pupils, who absorbed and adopted them in idiosyncratic ways.[43]

Jean Sibelius and His Students

During lessons, Sibelius communicated Busoni's ideas about orchestration and sonority.[44] Student memoirs are few and brief, yet they reveal that Sibelius taught the way Busoni did in many respects. In his recollections of Sibelius as teacher, Leevi Madetoja (1887–1947) claimed that Sibelius was an unconventional teacher—the kind "one does not find in conservatories."[45] Sibelius focused on ideas rather than technical methods. Madetoja remembers bringing a five-voice fugue to Sibelius for advice.[46] Yet Sibelius offered only terse aesthetic comments, such as "There is no dead sheet music! Each note keeps living!"[47]

If Sibelius stressed any musical parameter with his students, it was that of orchestration, and some of his ideas are distillations of Busoni's teachings. Bengt de Törne, who met Sibelius at a rehearsal for his fourth symphony, left one of the most vivid portraits of what it was like to study orchestration privately with Sibelius. He related this conversation in which Sibelius shared his secrets of orchestration:[48] "You know, I could talk to you about the orchestra every day for a year, without exhausting the subject. There are different ways of treating this vast ensemble. Everybody can learn the average conservatoire orchestration, but that is still very far from real instrumentation. It has become a fashion of late to make the orchestra purvey for the successful tradesman and earn his applause."[49]

Sibelius transmitted several orchestration principles borrowed directly from Busoni, including the idea that there always needs to be a sustaining instrument, the idea that a composer must always know how something will sound in his own mind before writing it down, and an idealization of Mozartian orchestration along with a distaste for unison orchestrations in the style of Wagner.[50] Accordingly, both of Sibelius's most important pupils, Madetoja and Toivo Kuula (1883–1918), display an interest in instrumental color.

Despite the brevity of Madetoja's studies with Sibelius, Sibelius was his most important and influential teacher, and the two continued to meet and correspond from the beginning of Madetoja's studies with Sibelius in 1909 until at least 1929.[51] Madetoja eventually distinguished himself in his orchestral music, choral music, and songs, which are characterized by careful attention to color and unique structures, as well as unusual harmonies. Madetoja's symphonies, for instance, display the influence of Sibelius and the distillation of Busoni's ideas about orchestration in their clarity and play with instrumental color.[52] His first successful orchestral work, the Symphonic Suite, op. 4 (1910), contains moments of brilliant orchestration. Even though Madetoja was writing for a traditional ensemble of instruments, he combined them in unusual ways, capitalizing on small ensembles and transparent textures to display a wide palette of orchestral color. The third movement, a pastorale, is largely a duet between the English and French horns while the finale opens with a dramatic timpani solo. His Symphony no. 3 in A Major, op. 55, a groundbreaking and classically inspired work (1922–1926), although written more than a decade later, displays many of the same approaches toward instrumentation, and it was written while Madetoja was still in contact with Sibelius (see music example 7.1). Although composed for a full orchestra, the piece features solos and small chamber ensembles throughout, thereby allowing the colors of individual instruments to be readily heard. In the first movement, for instance, clarinets and bassoons in duet alternate with flutes and oboes in imitation on the dominant during the opening bars while first and second violins interject the tonic pitch on the off beats. This is followed by pizzicato pitches in the contrabass accompanied by sustained tones acting as a pedal in the horns. Beginning in measure 14, melodies in the high winds and strings are superimposed on top of the sustained brass and pizzicato bass. Every instrument group is fully audible, and the contrast in colors and musical materials is on display—especially when the melody is passed between the instruments. In the winds, the oboe and bassoon begin in measure 14 in unison, and the flute and clarinet offer countermelodies in imitation beginning in measure 16. While oboes and bassoons descend, first violins play a rising line, also beginning in measure 14, meeting the two winds momentarily with the same pitches in

MUSIC EXAMPLE 7.1. Madetoja, Symphony no. 3 in A Major, op. 55, mm. 1–5.

measure 16 before continuing higher and crossing the wind instruments' lines, then dissolving into sustained notes as the first violin's line is passed to the second violin in measure 18.

Kuula, like Madetoja, only officially studied with Sibelius for a short time (from 1907–1908), before moving on to study in Bologna. His music, like Madetoja's, is notable for richness of harmony and a play with orchestral color even as he upheld Bach as a source of inspiration as well. Kuula was a master at evoking divergent colors even out of limited instrumental ensembles. Even though his music is tonally centered, his voicings and chord choices are unusual, creating interesting colors. This is evident in his Piano Trio, op. 7, on which he worked with Sibelius, where there is movement from V7 to I7, for instance. Sibelius was evidently quite impressed with the piece, writing the following in a letter of January 1908 to Kuula: "The world abounds with pianists as with gray cats, but your trio is a rarity among compositions."[53]

Varèse and His Students

Varèse, who taught composition privately, chose not to follow a specific methodology, but to focus on ideas, some of which represent his assimilation of Busonian aesthetics.[54] In addition to inciting curiosity about new instruments and the possibilities of electronic sound, Varèse spoke of the chromatic scale as a restricting element. Roger Reynolds described Varèse's discussion of sound and form: "Varèse was talking about the problem of how to describe, metaphorically, the listening to of agglomerations of carefully controlled sound and fused timbres."[55] Although Varèse did not often speak about his own music with his students, many who heard it, including those outside his direct circle, were impressed by the new treatment of timbre, sound, form, and the tonal system. According to Earle Brown, who often met with Varèse after 1952 whenever he went to New York, Varèse frequently talked about the structuring of sound. Without Varèse he would not have known how to construct his open-form pieces where sound blocks, masses, and self-contained units "combined in any conceivable way."[56]

Busonian ideals transmitted via Varèse had a lasting impact on his pupils.[57] Although each developed their own compositional style and voice, an emphasis on sound, acoustics, electronics, expansion of the tonal language, and pluralism remain evident traces of the distillation of Busonian aesthetics. This will be demonstrated through more detailed explorations of the music of three of his significant pupils, Chou Wen-Chung, William Grant Still, and André Jolivet.

Chou Wen-Chung (b. 1923) distinguished himself through a play with sound characterized by a blending of Eastern and Western ideals. Chou came to the United States in 1946 and studied composition with both Luening and Varèse, the latter being the more influential. Luening introduced him to electronic music and Varèse talked about sculpting with sound. Before working with Varèse, he sought a stylistic fusion; after Varèse, he thought of ways Eastern and Western styles could coexist. The common denominator and the unifying factor was sonority.[58] Chou's first orchestral compositions after beginning studies with Varèse reveal a new exploration of sound; line masses interact together with articulation, duration, intensity, and timbre. All are organized into bodies of sound that ebb and flow in space through changing textures and sonorities. *All in the Spring Wind* (1953) and *And the Fallen Petals* (1954), in particular, display a marked change in the use of instrumental resources. In *All in the Spring Wind*, there is structural interplay between layers of sound, including solo lines in flute and oboe, sustained notes on the high strings with harmonics and quartal harmonies, and sparse short punctuating notes(see music example 7.2a, b). These layers are varied through juxtaposition, linear elaboration, and verticalization. *And the Fallen Petals* (1955), a short tone poem for orchestra, demonstrates Chou's play with sonority, timbre, and a syncretic combining of diverse scales and harmonies, including pentatonic scales and quartal harmonies. The piece is a study in timbres; it is a musical rhapsody revealing a new sound cosmos, as Chou describes: "The characteristic successions of transparent intervals used in Chinese music are freely embroidered with opulent dissonances serving as the palette from which the composer paints in orchestral sonority, timbre, texture and dynamics. The changing mood and the emotional content of the work are thus projected by means of a tonal brushwork extending over the entire orchestral spectrum."[59]

Sonority and timbre were also key to the style of another student of Varèse, William Grant Still (1895–1978). Even though Still eventually

MUSIC EXAMPLE 7.2.a and b. (*above and facing*) Chou, *All in the Spring Wind*, example of timbral layering.

MUSIC EXAMPLE 7.2.b

shed the atonal, dissonant language he learned from Varèse, he embraced many of the aesthetic ideas distilled from Busoni about sound, form, and instrumentation.[60]

Still's lessons with Varèse began the summer of 1923 and continued for about two years.[61] However, Varèse's mentorship lasted until at least 1950.[62] After only the second meeting, Still expressed to a friend the impact Varèse's ideas had made on him:[63] "Although I have been with him but twice I have felt a change within myself. A broadening of vision, a more thorough comprehension of the possibilities of modern composition and the realization that he has those things I need and desire are the results of our short associations."[64]

After working with Varèse, Still began to create unique forms that do not readily fall into any traditional form or the popular music traditions he knew. His structures were informed by African American subjects, which Still studied avidly in his spare time.[65] In Still's essay "The Art of Musical Creation," Still's description of form bears striking similarities to Busoni's own writings. He said that each piece begins as a musical germ arising from something extraneous to music and then in turn becomes internalized as a melody. Then "the motive he deals with must be developed in a manner suited to its individuality, and it must dictate its development."[66] One of the first pieces Still completed with Varèse, *Darker America* (1924), exemplifies Still's new approach. The opening theme, introduced in unison by the strings, appears throughout the entire work. Still presented the three principal themes, all symbolically connected to the black tradition, in counterpoint in the final movement, juxtaposing them with pungent dissonances.[67] Carol Oja has shown that the music alternates between blues-derived harmonies and moments of "intense chromaticism." These are combined only in the finale where dense polyphony prevails.[68] At times, the music is polytonal, at times tonal, and blocks of sound are juxtaposed in a Varèsian fashion, building sonorous architectonics. Still's formal experimentation based on the blending of cultures continued even after he renounced Varèsian dissonances, returning to melodically based tonal writing. In the *Afro-American Symphony* (1930), for instance, Still combines elements of blues form and sonata form in the first movement to create a blended structure (ABCBA). Overall, the major divisions can be observed in measures 1–67, 68–104, and 104 until the end. However, the themes are presented in reverse order in the recapitulation. The first theme follows twelve-bar blues structure—AAB (trumpet, mm. 7–18—after introduction by English horn) and the second theme is written in the manner of a spiritual tune. Although it is in G, it has a pentatonic contour.

In addition to the experimental treatment of form, Still began to display an interest in sonority and instrumental color after studying with Varèse. Having arranged music for several bands, including those of W. C. Handy and Paul Whiteman, Still was not new to instrumental possibilities. However, Varèse expanded Still's vision of instrumental combinations. In Still's early sketchbook that bears the label "Material for Rashana" on the cover and is stamped with the date 1926, there are not only sketches for an aborted opera project, but also notes on orchestration that likely stem from his studies with Varèse. The notes include experimental groups of instruments that he hoped would portray specific moods. Although Still would later call many of these ideas "impossible and far-fetched," the experimentation with color stayed with him even when he began to aim for leaner, more transparent sonorities and colors reminiscent of Busoni's more Mozartian orchestrations.[69] He describes that when he orchestrates, he hears abstract tone colors and then tries to approximate them with acoustic instruments.[70] *From the Land of Dreams* (1924) represents Still's first piece experimenting with timbre and new sonorous combinations. Paul Rosenfeld was particularly struck by Still's use of register and instruments in this piece:[71] "Still has learned much from Edgard Varèse, his instructor, although he has not yet quite learned to speak out freely, a certain absence of freedom in the use of his ideas limits one's enjoyment, and the material of the first two sections of his composition is insufficiently contrasted. But Mr. Still has a very sensuous approach to music. His employment of his instruments is at once rich and nude and decided. The upper ranges of his high soprano have an original penetrating colour."[72]

The instrumentation was indeed unusual: flute, oboe, clarinet, bassoon, horn, viola, cello, double bass, bells, triangle and three voices. Gayle Murchison and Catherine Parsons Smith describe it as containing "a diatonic blues melody serves as the subordinate theme, embedded within a framework of startlingly original timbres and chromaticism."[73]

In *Darker America* (1924), one of the first pieces in which Still began to exhibit his own voice, Still associated themes with colors.[74] An opening theme of "the American Negro" appears in the strings, a "sorrow theme" in the English horn, a theme of "hope" in the muted brass, and a prayer "of numbed rather than anguished souls" in the oboe. Still incorporates the pentatonic and blues scales with modern dissonances. Still proudly noted in a letter from 1932 to Varèse that critics had noted Varèsian influence in the composition:[75] "I will never forget how pitiable were my efforts before you helped me. I will never forget that no one payed [*sic*] me any attention until after you had taught me and brought me to the front. And I will never forget that the things they complement me for are things I have learned from you. When they say that 'Darker America' shows I am under your influence they tell the truth and, what is more, leave much unsaid. If they knew me better they would learn that your broad-mindedness has influenced my character."[76]

Although Still would soon abandon some of the most experimental aspects of his writing, toning down dissonance, polytonality, and experimental chords and harmonies, in an attempt to escape the Varèsian shadow, he retained a long-lasting interest in sonority and unusual structures throughout the rest of his career. If he moved toward an emphasis on melody and tonality, rejecting the specific sound world of Varèse, he retained some of the aesthetic underpinnings of Varèse's music, melding them in his own way.[77]

André Jolivet (1905–1974) likewise embraced Varèse's ideas about new sounds.[78] Jolivet studied with Varèse from 1929 to 1933, spending time with him and his acquaintances almost daily. The two also remained friends even after Varèse's return to the United States.[79] Varèse communicated to Jolivet his passion for new sounds and instruments, especially electronic ones.[80] He talked about acoustics, orchestration, diverse treatments of the tonal language, and diverse ways of organizing music according to sound and texture/style, ideas that were distilled from Busoni.[81] Jolivet reiterated many of the ideas, including those about expanding the tempered system:[82] "The essential points that I retained from my contact with Varèse from 1929 to 1933 concern acoustics, rhythm, and orchestration. By acoustics, I mean the instrumental dispositions giving the best sound results, music being above all a sound phenomenon."[83]

Jolivet talked at length with his own students about what he learned from Varèse, especially orchestration. Marc Bleuse, for instance, remembers that Jolivet talked about how to voice chords so that the higher partials would be audible, and he generally advocated wider spacing in the bass and closer spacing in the treble (mirroring spacing in the overtone series). Philippe Hersant maintains that Jolivet also "showed us how Varèse managed to make a work sound detempered, outside of the tempered system. . . . By using the twelve tones of the tempered scale, he [Varèse] managed, by a very special orchestration, with extreme lows and highs, etc. to give us the impression of leaving the tempered system."[84]

After meeting Varèse, Jolivet composed several pieces for electronic instruments, in particular, the Ondes Martenot, for which he was one of the first composers to write serious music:[85]

1. *Overture en rondeau* (1938 version for four Ondes Martenot, 2 pianos and percussion, or for small orchestra—it is an amplified version of *Trois temps* for piano, 1930)
2. *Danse incantatoire* (1935 for 2 Ondes Martenot)
3. *Concerto pour Ondes Martenot et orchestra* (1947)
4. *Chant d'oppression* (1935 for alto and piano, transcription pour Ondes Martenot)

Jolivet also experimented with using overtones as a way of organizing the tonal language. This, as he noted, was in direct contrast to the procedures used by the serialists: "From a technical point of view, I forced myself, in these works, to free myself from the tonal system. I did this not by adopting the theory of twelve semitones, artificial in my own opinion, because it neglects the natural phenomena of resonance, but on the contrary by using these [the twelve tones] with all their harmonics and above all the most distant ones."[86]

In particular, he achieved changes in sound density by choosing upper harmonics common to several low tones, and then varying the low tones, something he learned from Varèse. In addition, he applied variation principles to sound—not just to thematic or harmonic material. This approach is exhibited, for instance, in his *Concerto pour Ondes Martenot* (1947), which Jolivet describes thus:

Regarding my first symphonic works, I spoke of "transmutation of sound matter." To this expression borrowed from Varèse, I prefer today ... the following definition, to add to the classical notion of musical development a new element *the variation of orchestral density*. In other words, development is no longer only linear (thematic) or harmonic, but variations of the sound intensity of the orchestra may also participate in the development of the discourse. From which it follows that the technique of "musical variation" can apply not just to melodic, harmonic, or rhythmic elements, but also to sound intensities. Thus development no longer takes place only in time, but also in space.[87]

Louis Gruenberg and His Students

Of the composers covered in detail in this book, Gruenberg appears to have had the least significant impact from a pedagogical standpoint. Although he did have private students beginning in Berlin and continuing throughout his time in America, the names of those students remain a mystery.[88] In 1922 he also opened a studio in New York where he taught piano, composition, and orchestration, and also coached opera singers.[89] At the invitation of Rudolph Ganz, another Busoni pupil, he became a faculty member at the Chicago Musical College (now part of Roosevelt University) from 1933 to 1936. College catalogs indicate that he was on the composition faculty from 1934 to 1935, a member of the theory faculty from 1935 to 1936, and the chair of the theory department from 1936 to 1937.[90] The catalogs also show that from 1935 to 1936 Gruenberg was responsible for teaching Form, Analysis and Composition; Composition (two hours weekly); Composition and Orchestration; Composition and Orchestration; and a course entitled "Experimental Studies in Composition," where students listened to great works and brought their own compositions to class for critique. He taught basic harmony to sophomores and composition to juniors. However, there are no extant records indicating the names of his students, and Gruenberg never mentions any names in particular as especially significant.

Teaching notes indicate that Gruenberg's lessons emphasized melody and textual clarity, and some of these ideas probably derived from Busoni's writings. In his composition classes, he covered variation form (especially passacaglia and chaconne) and rondo form, using musical examples from the repertoire, such as Schumann's *Symphonic Etudes*, op. 13, as models. His senior class covered orchestration and the larger forms, such as sonata form. Gruenberg defined the foundations of composition thus, placing melody in a place of great importance, just like Busoni:

1. Melody
2. Countermelody
3. Foundation
4. Embellishment[91]

However, he was expected to explain the entire history of theory and history to a class of forty pupils, and the gradual feeling of drudgery grated on his sense of purpose, so he left for California to focus on composition.

Perhaps the most meaningful pedagogical collaboration was Gruenberg's exchange of scores with Marion Bauer in the 1920s and 1930s, which, like his other teaching activities, is little documented. Gruenberg's daughter Joan Gruenberg Cominos remembers Bauer as Gruenberg's pupil.[92] However, if that was the case, by the 1930s it had turned into a collegial friendship that included the mutual exchange of scores for compositional advice. Bauer ended up dedicating *Turbulence*, op. 17, no. 2 (1924, pub. 1942) to Gruenberg. Gruenberg also performed Bauer's Sonata for Violin and Piano, op. 14 on April 1922 at the American Music Guild at MacDowell Gallery with Albert Stoessel on violin and dedicated his collection of short piano pieces, *Jazzberries*, op. 25 (1925), to her.[93] The few extant letters between them reveal Bauer's advice to Gruenberg rather than the other way around. In one exchange, Bauer praised Gruenberg's quartet: "I can't begin to tell you how thrilled I was with your quartet. I wanted to let you know immediately how much I thought of it. I had a curious reaction in listening to it. I had the impression of a heavy perfume, like the Black Tulip. This particularly interested me as I am not given to any outside associations with music. The workmanship was exquisite and it sounded wonderful."[94]

The following spring, she asked him to simplify the music to make it more accessible.[95] However, no extant record seems to exist indicating Gruenberg's suggestions to Bauer.[96]

Otto Luening and His Students

Luening also passed down a distillation of Busoni's ideas to his own students. Andrew Violette, who studied composition privately with him at the Juilliard School in the early 1970s when Roger Sessions was on sabbatical, remembers that Busoni was a frequent topic of conversation: "Luening often spoke of Busoni. It was because of Luening that I read Busoni's writings and learned some of his pieces."[97] One of Luening's lesser-known pupils wrote to him from Munich, thanking him for the introduction to Busoni in December 1966: "One hears and reads much of Busoni here in München. I thank you for the introduction. Warmly, Suzanne Bartel."[98]

Luening taught a wide array of students at the University of Arizona, Bennington College, The Juilliard School, and Columbia University. These include Charles Wuorinen, William Kraft, John Corigliano, Walter Carlos, Harvey Sollberger, Faye-Ellen Silverman, Malcolm Goldstein, John Herbert McDowell, Philip Corner, Daniel Goode, Sol Berkowitz, Elliott Schwartz, and Karl Korte. In addition, he also met privately and in social gatherings with a network of students and friends, such as Joel Feigin, many of whom absorbed Luening's ideas. Like Busoni, Luening encouraged experimentation with sonority, electronic music, and stylistic pluralism. Violette notes that the embracing of a multiplicity of styles required going against the compositional fads of Luening's generation, including total serialism:

> Luening said to me again and again that though Busoni respected Schoenberg's system he didn't agree with him that music had to move forward and that the entire tonal system had become anachronistic. Luening agreed with Busoni but I didn't agree with Luening at the time. Looking back I realize that Luening and Busoni were right. The faculty and the students were all so enamored of the Darmstadt Group at that time that we all formed a closed community of people who agreed with one another that the 12-tone system was the right and only way to go. (I'm told this still happens in some universities.) Only Luening disagreed. Now I see Luening was right. My own work has become triadic just like Luening's, though not functionally so, but coloristically, yes. So I see that in many ways Luening was a great individualist in that Juilliard crowd. And I think he learned that individualism from Busoni.[99]

Luening also had students examine obscure repertoire from throughout history and study Busoni's *Entwurf einer neuen Ästhetik der Tonkunst*.[100] Violette remembers that when he studied with Luening, he branched out a lot in terms of what he read and listened to:

> Luening placed great emphasis on a well-rounded education—something he said Busoni emphasized. Luening was always making me read things, listen to everything. I read all the articles in *Der Reihe*, the Boulez book, Carter's book, Babbitt's articles, Helmholtz's *On the Sensation of Tone (Sound?)* during that counterpoint term with Luening's encouragement. I spent many hours in the library listening to everything because Luening by way of Busoni encouraged me. Luening always said "Listen to everything." He said that's what Busoni told him. To this day I make sure I listen to all the new CDs that come out. I listen to them multiple times—particularly the ones I don't like.[101]

Luening also talked constantly with his students about the possibilities of electronic music. In this way he not only inspired many of them to create their own electronic music, but he sought to make Busoni's dream a reality for them by equipping his students and other composers to create electronic music through the establishment of the first electronic music center in the United States, the Columbia-Princeton Electronic Music Center.[102] One of the most important early pieces of equipment in the center was the RCA Mark II synthesizer. It was the first programmable electronic synthesizer, and it allowed for unprecedented experimentation with sound. By the mid-1960s, the center also had voltage-controlled synthesizers. A commercial digital synthesizer with MIDI control (MIDI [Musical Instrument Digital Interface] was then introduced in the 1980s. The center became a locus of composition for Luening, Ussachevsky, Babbitt, Davidovsky, Halim El-Dabh, Bülent Arel, Charles Dodge, Jacob Druckman, Charles Wuorinen, and many others.

Luening also talked frequently about orchestration and encouraged thin transparent textures. Some of his ideas were informed by acoustical theories. He specifically encouraged students, such as Fred Beyer, to reduce doublings, for instance: "The first movement of the piece seems to have unnecessary doublings in a number of spots. This makes it heavy without adding resonances and I think it will make the first movement overbalance the other two. I suggest that you go through it and take out those doublings unless they are an essential part of your idea."[103]

Violette also looked to Luening's own sparse orchestrations as models:[104] "I'm starting the piano concerto again. Your work gave me so many new ideas. Your orchestration is so intense and pure—and so few notes."[105] Joel Feigin, who met Luening at a party after a new music concert shortly after he had graduated from the Juilliard School, remembers that Luening shared ideas about acoustics and orchestration when looking at his compositions.[106] In particular, Feigin remembers that Luening talked about understanding and utilizing overtones to achieve greater resonance when he showed him his first opera, *Mysteries of Eleusis* (1986). Severine Neff likewise remembers that Luening demonstrated the possibilities of overtones by holding down a C triad in root position and striking a D triad one octave below, a combination producing a wealth of overtones that the ear could be trained to identify.[107]

Although skeptical of Luening's importance as a composer and impact as a teacher, in part because of his rootedness in a tonal tradition, Charles Wuorinen (b. 1938) nevertheless benefited from Luening's discussions about the potential for new resources in music.[108] Wuorinen claimed that Luening allowed him to develop on his own rather than imposing a set method. At the same time, Luening talked a great deal about philosophy, including the writings of Busoni detailing the new resources of music. He talked incessantly about the possibilities of the future of music, but rarely alluded to the practical working out of those ideas in concrete ways. In particular, Luening glorified the possibilities of electronic music, and his ideas were supplemented through contact with a dynamic nexus of composers including Elliott Carter, Babbitt, John Cage, and Ussachevsky.

Wuorinen is not primarily an electronic music composer—his approximately 270 compositions feature many styles and genres—but he did make some important contributions in that area. Studying with Luening in the 1960s, he was able to take advantage of the Columbia-Princeton Electronic Music Center and the excitement surrounding the possibilities of electronic music. Wuorinen's first electro-acoustic composition, *Consort from Instruments and Voices* (1960), stems from his student years at Columbia.[109] In 1965, he composed *Orchestral and Electronic Exchanges,* and in 1968 Wuorinen began *Time's Encomium,* his first major electronic work utilizing the RCA electronic synthesizer. It was awarded a Pulitzer Prize in 1970.[110] In *Time's Encomium*, he explores absolute time values. In the first half, he selected pure synthesized tones and in the second half featured reworked and recorded patterns from the first half.[111] Although he never again composed a completely electronic piece, he experimented with ways electronic and traditional instruments could intersect, including in *Arabia Felix* (1973), which features an electric guitar, in addition to a flute, violin, vibraphone, and piano. One version of *New York Notes* (1982) also contains digitally synthesized sound. Although the score for flute, clarinet in A, violin, cello, percussion, and piano is fully written out, it also lists cues for the optional tape part, which is inserted a total of ten times throughout the course of the composition (five times each in the first and third movements).[112] *Bamboula Squared* (1984) is scored for orchestra and four-channel tape. During performance, the tape, aired by two speakers, on either side of the stage, is played by an operator, who starts and stops the small fragments of electronic sounds produced by computer synthesizer.[113] Wuorinen used timbral modeling for the electronic portions, based on numbers derived from a system based on a plucked string. Wuorinen likened the process to "artificial intelligence."[114] The notation for the tape parts is non-traditional, in many cases, consisting of wavy lines that rise or fall from expansive chords to single pitches.

Wuorinen did not imitate Luening's approach—he struck out on his own path—even if Luening passed down Busoni's interest in new electronic resources. Wuorinen focused on electro-acoustic interactions in which there is the possibility for spontaneity in performance. This is the result of his concern about the human performative element and the fixity of purely electronic pieces.[115] He was especially wary of the fixity of an electronic work in which composers were forced to make compositional compromises as a result of the limitations of the equipment.[116]

In the 1960s, there was no question in Wuorinen's mind that electronic resources would be important for the development of the music of the future. He was interested in Luening's discussions of the new musical possibilities of electronic music. However, he could not predict the exact course it would take, and he was personally intent upon forging a new path by blending serial technique with electronic music. Additionally, he wanted to blend electronic and acoustic resources as he experimented with ways to make the music more spontaneous and performance-based by having operators "play" the electronic segments during an otherwise live acoustic performance. However, by 2007, he had become disappointed that there had not been more developments in the electronic realm.[117] He expressed the opinion that electronic music had ended up becoming more limiting in some respects than acoustic music.

John Corigliano (b. 1938), who also studied with Luening at Columbia University in the late 1950s and early 1960s, found a long-lasting friend in Luening and received foundational ideas from him, some of which were distillations of Busonian ideals that he developed in his own way after his graduation.[118] Luening, for his part, described Corigliano as "a very lively undergraduate," and considered him to be one of the most talented students, as he described in a letter to Hans Heinsheimer of Schirmer Publishers:[119] "I'm also quite impressed that you have taken on John Corigliano. I've always considered him a real talent and one who has the courage to go his own way. It's nice to see a house like Schirmer introducing a person like Corigliano."[120]

Corigliano's music and aesthetic ideals reflect a distillation of Busoni's ideas about sonority and pluralism transmitted via Luening, as well as any number of other contemporaneous influences. Corigliano began to forge a pluralistic style during his studies with Luening, which he continued to develop in his own way as he matured—his compositions today often juxtapose the unexpected in audible ways. This involves not only the use of diverse treatments of the musical language, including tonality, atonality, and serialism, but also a juxtaposing of diverse textures into a Busonian-type collage. His early works are largely tonal, although they incorporate polychords, serialism, and polytonality at times. *Kaleidoscope* (1959), completed while Corigliano was working with Luening at Columbia (and dedicated to him), combines a twelve-tone row and C-major music in the style of ragtime. A central lyrical section treats a folk-like theme contrapuntally to help create a "kaleidoscope" of styles (see music example 7.3).

Corigliano further developed this play with scales and styles in his own way as he matured, increasingly drawing from scales, styles, and time periods, mixing them in atemporal manners. Labeling him as a syncretist, Mark Adamo states: "Corigliano is neither a tonal nor an atonal composer,

MUSIC EXAMPLE 7.3. Corigliano, *Kaleidoscope*, mm. 1–12.

neither romantic nor neo-Romantic, neither modernist nor post-modernist, though his music has partaken of materials fairly described by these labels."[121] His symphony no.1 (1988), for instance, draws on avant-garde aleatoricism, dodecaphony, and romanticism (i.e. cello cantilena in the third movement).[122] *The Ghosts of Versailles* (1980) is, as Corigliano describes it, a grand opera buffa. It contains memorable Mozartian themes and Rossini quotations. Although the text is predominantly in English, it has a section written in a chant-like syllabic unison vocal style with Latin texts (e.g., "Ave maria, gratia plena. Benedictus fructus ventris"). At the same time, it contains large choral numbers and special effects characteristic of French grand opera. Juxtaposed to this are ghost scenes characterized by quarter-tone dissonances, chord clusters, twelve-tone rows, and string glissandi as Queen Marie Antoinette initially seeks to recreate history by escaping the guillotine before finally coming to terms with her death.[123] As Colleen Renihan argues, it is the music's ability to navigate the realm of atemporality (espoused by Busoni already at the beginning of the century) that allows Queen Marie Antoinette's transformation of historical engagement with the past and present as she comes to grips with historical reality.[124] As Renihan also notes, the dramatic atonal and aleatoric interruptions by strings and winds to Marie Antoinette's act 1 aria, "Ah! There was a Golden Bird," are not present when the aria returns in act 3 during a reenactment of Marie Antoinette's trial, and dominant and diminished seventh chords lead to a much hoped for tonal resolution.[125]

Luening also transmitted a distillation of Busoni's ideas about sonority and acoustics. Corigliano specifically noted Luening's activities with electronic frequencies as being especially impactful on his own understanding of creating climaxes through sonorous means:[126]

> If you want the kind of climax that shatters—and I certainly do—you have to know that it's doing that physically to somebody. Physical sound can do that, and also sub-audio frequencies. I haven't talked about that, but that's rather a peculiar little problem that is below the threshold of sound. They can produce tension, agitation and all sorts of very serious emotional problems. My old teacher, Otto Luening, who is in his nineties now and is still a very active guy, worked with Vladimir Ussachevsky on electronic music. Orson Welles had them do the first electronic score ever for *King Lear* at the City Center in the fifties. Welles asked them to produce a reel of sub-audio frequencies that had nothing to do with their music. He then had two huge speakers placed out in the audience, and whenever he was doing his mad scenes he played that. The audience started perspiring and just feeling terribly agitated, and thought this was the most incredible acting in the world; it was really 1984! I mean, THE *1984*. It was mind control by using sub-audio frequencies to agitate to produce an audience reaction.

Corigliano's compositions display a play with sonority to achieve special effects, to impact the audience, and to contribute to dramatic climaxes. He used sonority in a structural sense when he created a timbral fugue in *The Ghosts of Versailles,* when eight or nine instruments were given the same notes, but they were told to finger them silently rather than play them. This created a pointillistic halo of sound. Sound substituted for pitches in the traditional fugue.[127] An especially wide array of percussion instruments (including, among others, a ratchet, wind machine, glockenspiel played with a bow, bell tree, dumbec drums, and temple blocks) plus synthesizer and the usual array of orchestral instruments also allowed for a wide array of special sonorous effects. The opening prologue conveys the ghostly setting with the ethereal sound of bowed vibraphone and strings featuring chord clusters and tremolos as well as aleatoric movement to wide registral extremes. In Marie Antoinette's act 1 aria, mentioned above, windows breaking and throngs pushing are accompanied by fist clusters and chromatics in the string parts. Corigliano writes: "Fast, chromatic scampering, to be engulfed by the resounded fist clusters so that aura, not pitch, is important."[128] Most recently, he has been experimenting with the possibilities of voice amplification.[129]

Philipp Jarnach and His Students

Jarnach began his pedagogical career in 1918 at the Konservatorium für Musik in Zurich, spent six years as a private teacher of piano and theory in Berlin (1921–1927), and beginning in 1927 taught at the Kölner Musikhochschule. In 1950, he became director of the Hamburg Musikhochschule.[130] In these traditional institutional settings, Jarnach transmitted Busoni's ideas about sonority and stylistic pluralism. In Jarnach's lectures, Busoni was a frequent topic of conversation, and Jarnach discussed Busoni's compositions in some detail, including Busoni's *Doktor Faust*, BV 303, and *Turandot*, BV 273, the latter of which he taught to his composition students as early as Zurich in 1919.[131] Jarnach taught a number of students who would eventually have successful careers in composition, including Busoni pupils Kurt Weill and Otto Luening, as well as Nikos Skalkottas (1904–1949) and Bernd Alois Zimmermann (1918–1970).

Private lessons consisted of score critique of student compositions or analyses of his own pieces. Yet he never insisted that his students compose in a set style. Walter Steffens (b. 1934), from Jarnach's 1960 Hamburg composition class, remembers: "What immediately fascinated me about

Jarnach's teaching method, was his great tolerance, which left each of his students the right to stylistic individuality. Conscientiously he read note-by-note, spoke little, limited criticism on technical defects, let himself rarely be carried away by ideas and demanded searching the music—ultimately, music and only music was able to convince him."[132]

Aside from Weill and Luening, Bernd Alois Zimmermann (1918–1970) was one of Jarnach's most talented pupils, and Jarnach transmitted to him an ideal of stylistic heterogeneity.[133] He also emphasized the need to explore new sonorities. Zimmermann gradually developed a personal style in which quotations merge in and out of an atonal framework.[134] Wulf Konold describes Jarnach as Zimmermann's most important teacher and claims many of the ideas were distilled from Busoni, even if Jarnach was decidedly more focused on technique: "Philip Jarnach, probably Zimmermann's most influential compositional mentor, once noted in a conversation the immense pleasure and dynamic force that drove Zimmermann to compose and that it endowed him with exceptional diligence and great attention to detail.... Already Zimmermann traced the basis of his composition to the objective and form-based style of Young Classicality the Busoni pupil Jarnach had taught him he must also expand. This style, which came against Zimmermann's tendency to adopt repressive tendencies, at the same time, influenced his manner of expressiveness."[135]

Although few records indicate specific stylistic and formal details the two talked about, Jarnach did offer score critique on pieces he submitted nearly weekly.[136] One entry in Zimmermann's diary (dated July 25, 1945) provides a record of a lesson, thus offering a general glimpse into some of the ideas Jarnach emphasized with his pupil, including sonority and form. In particular, Jarnach talked about the need for a central and well-developed *idee* that helped determine the unfolding of the musical content. He also stressed the importance of sonority and a need for a use of instruments intimately related to the musical material—this was passed down from Busoni:[137]

> I was yesterday at Jarnach's and Schneider's. Jarnach very sharply criticized the trio. [He said it had] "no *Idee*." Well done and proper growth etc., but idle music. In addition to Schneider, he also sees the problem of the trio in the sonority, but Jarnach also calls for more substance, more *Idee*. Both judge the symphony favorably.... Certainly operating with

new sonorities is not an experiment; it should be there anyway, and the sound is secondary; it is conditionally a manifestation of the melody, and the melody is the primary sound formation, however paradoxical it appears.[138]

According to Konold, Jarnach also communicated to his disciple Busoni's notions of Young Classicality, which included, in addition to an emphasis on form and objectivity, a non-linear notion of time, a notion of time as omnipresent.[139] His vision of ideal music was one in which there was the "mastery, the sifting and the turning to account of all the gains of previous experiments and their inclusion in strong and beautiful forms."[140] This predates Zimmermann's notion of the "Kugelgestalt der Zeit," or the spherical shape of time, which was a gradually developing philosophy of time that he put in writing in 1957 in an essay entitled "Intervall und Zeit" and that served as the philosophical underpinning for his own pluralistic musical style of composition.[141] In his essay, he argued for a unity of time in terms of past, present, and future: "From this viewpoint, the idea of the unity of time is preserved as a unit of present, past and future, as Augustine has established it in the essence of the human soul, which overlaps the fleeting moment in a spiritual expansion as the ephemeral moment in time overlaps with the past and future in a permanent presence—this is so modern and at the same time an immemorial thought, a new perspective in music as 'time art,' as the art of temporal order within the constant present, a dominant fact in modern literature no less than in modern painting."[142] The theory manifested itself musically in quotations from multiple time periods and in the juxtapositions of plots from different time periods in his theatrical works, leading to brilliant pluralism.

The foundations for this approach were already in evidence in his works of the 1940s, although the extensive use of quotations would come later. In his Trio for Violin, Viola, and Cello, which he worked on with Jarnach (1944), neo-Baroque and modernist elements intermingle. The overall treatment of the language is tonal (even despite moments of polytonality). The twenty-eight-bar introduction teems with references to the Baroque overture, especially in terms of the contrapuntal lines and homophonic cadences, even if the tempo is flexible, moving from *sostenuto molto* to *ein klein wenig schneller*. The final movement displays elements of ritornello form mixed with sonata form and is in the perpetuum mobile character of a virtuosic toccata, yet with chromaticism characteristic of Jarnach's age. Pluralism reached its zenith in Zimmermann's *Die Soldaten* (1965), which featured not only a dramatic mixing of styles, including a serial treatment of the language and Baroque forms, but also multiple quotations of pieces, among them the Gregorian Dies Irae, the Bach choral prelude, *Wenn ich einmal soll scheiden,* and Wagner's *Lohengrin.*

BEYOND BUSONI'S "GRAND PUPILS"

The distillation of Busoni's ideas extended beyond his immediate circle of pupils and grand pupils, with many composers looking to the works of Sibelius and Varèse as models for spectral, textural, and avant-garde compositions. In spectral composition, an interest in sonority is taken to an unprecedented level of importance. Sound and texture are intimately related as the music alternates between washes of sound and timbre and more traditional musical textures with standard instrumental groupings. Acoustical properties of any given sound can generate the basic musical materials. Computer technology has only made it easier to analyze the acoustical data from any given tone. Composers create their own themes, harmonies, and textures based on the data.

Spectral Composers

Gérard Grisey (1946–1998) and Tristan Murail (b. 1947) cite Sibelius and Varèse as "grandfathers" of the spectral movement. Grisey specifically expressed his admiration for the music of Sibelius even while writing about the importance of Varèse's views about new instruments, acoustics, sound textures, and microtones:[143] "Varèse is our great ancestor and his intuition was incredibly ahead of the sound tools and methods of composition of his time. *Arcana* in particular features complex sound—what he called harmonic timbre—that can only be explained by a spectral analysis of the components. Varèse knew the acoustics of Helmholtz, which was rare in his time."[144]

Although Magnus Lindberg (b. 1958) never studied directly with Sibelius, he has been called his heir and was influenced by his emphasis on color and sound.[145] He admired Sibelius above all for his attention to sonority, and arguably treated chords like a group of partials issued from one fundamental, approaching them, as he sometimes did, from the point of view of color, as opposed to harmonic function:

> While Varèse is credited with opening the way for new sonorities, Sibelius himself perused a profound reassessment of the formal and structural problems of composition. I do not think it is fair that he has been considered as a conservative, even if the surface of his music remains highly dependent on traditional tonal thinking.... His harmonies, while tonal, have a resonant, almost spectral quality. You find an attention to sonority in Sibelius works which is actually not so far removed from that which would appear long after in the work of Gerard Grisey or Tristan Murail, who were both interested in Sibelius' music ten years ago.[146]

Lindberg's music, whether for electronic or acoustic instruments, is all about sound, and he was especially interested in sonic textures.[147] While working recently at IRCAM, which develops spectral harmony based on acoustical phenomenon, Lindberg attempted to forge his own unique approach, combining spectralism and serialism in *Kinetics*.[148] As he stated, "I wanted to let the acoustics—overtone harmonies, analyses of different sound objects, instrumentation—create a background harmony. The foreground should be made out of the type of harmony I worked with in earlier works, like for example *Kraft*."[149]

Textural Composers

It was Varèse's approach to sound and sound textures that also left a lasting impression on Iannis Xenakis and other textural composers,[150] such as Penderecki and Stockhausen. Xenakis described what he considered to be the extraordinary aspects of Varèse's music thus:

> Varèse was a man who felt the sound in an extraordinary way. He also tried to get rid of tonality, or melodic patterns. His method was the crashing of sounds and a kind of immobility, of continuity [connected notes]. For some reason he didn't apply discontinuity [jumps of notes]. I don't know why not—perhaps he simply didn't think of it. Continuity would have entailed the danger of reviving melodic patterns, which would have been tonal in the way Stravinsky was tonal.... What does change with him is rhythm, timbre, intensity, and a specific mixture of these.[151]

Xenakis's breakthrough work was *Metastasis* (1953–1954), completed just after hearing Varèse's *Déserts*. In *Metastasis*, a single pitch on the violin branches out gradually into twelve separate lines, before forming a sound cluster in a manner quite different than the avant-garde experimentation with pointillistic sounds dispersed throughout registers and tonal space. *Pithoprakta* (1955–1956) was considered by many to be Xenakis's first mature orchestral piece—it takes the notion of sound mass a step farther—based on clouds of points or percussive attacks.

Polystylistic Composers

Sibelius was also held as a model for stylistic pluralism in the music of several British composers, including Peter Maxwell Davies (1934–2016), who became acquainted with the Sibelius symphonies as a youth when he attended Hallé Orchestra concerts conducted by John Barbirolli.[152] Davies's pluralistic imagination is evident from some his earliest works, such as his Sinfonia for Chamber Orchestra (1962), which combines serial techniques with Renaissance ones.[153] However, Sibelius's notion of time and timelessness provided models for fusing older treatments of form, harmony, and theme with newer ones beginning in the 1970s, when there was a marked change in Davies's compositional style. He moved away from isorhythmic designs toward rotational designs that pay homage to classical forms modeled after Sibelius.

Julian Anderson has noted that Davies was fascinated by Sibelius's thematic treatment in the fifth symphony, after which he patterned his own rotational transformation of the Ave Maris Stella theme in his own first symphony (1976).[154] Richard McGregor describes it thus: "While overall there is 'play' at the surface level with 'classical' musical form, background layers of slow, independent transformations, sometimes suddenly are exposed. This evolution in his formal thinking clearly owes much to the tangible influence of Sibelius."[155] In an interview from 1996, during a run of concerts in which Davies was conducting Sibelius's Symphony no. 6 in D Minor, op. 104, and *The Tempest*, op. 109, Davies also specifically cited reverence for Sibelius's stylistic allusions to the past, praising him for the clever ways he interwove early dance forms and counterpoint into quasi-minimalist musical textures. He concluded by stating: "I think these two works today, they prove so much how he was looking into the past but also into the future far beyond his own lifetime." Davies's attempts to blend the past and present were directly influenced by Sibelius, with Davies citing a connection to the form and thematic treatment in his own Symphony no. 1 (1973–1976).[156] Davies's Symphony no. 5 also illustrates some of Sibelius's influence. The piece is specifically indebted to Sibelius's Symphony no. 7 for its formal structure, and Davies's use and transformation of two plainchants from the Liber Usualis, the "Haec dies" and the "Domine audivi," was also informed by Sibelius's treatments of thematic metamorphosis. In his program notes, Davies stated: "The music of Sibelius, in particular its possibilities of self-generating form, was also central to my thinking, having recently studied and conducted Sibelius's Symphonies 6 and 7 with several orchestras."[157] Davies's contrapuntal approach has also been linked to Sibelius's Symphony no. 6, op. 104. But Davies combines the counterpoint with a post-tonal treatment of the musical language.

Michael Finnissy (b. 1946), whose music references a wide range of styles and time periods, was directly inspired by Busoni, even if he never studied with him.[158] Finnissy discovered Busoni's music as a young teenager when he heard the *Sonatina seconda*, the piano score of *Doktor Faust*, and a 78 rpm record of the Glyndebourne performance of *Arlecchino*.[159] He also studied with a Busoni enthusiast at the Royal College of Music, Bernard Stevens (1916–1983), who suggested that he read Busoni's aesthetic texts.[160] Finnissy's music is richly filled with allusions to folk songs and classical music of diverse eras as well as the complexity of contemporary musical expression. He states that he thinks of his "'processes' as forms of editing, as types of assemblage and montage."[161] His music is a blending of associated styles throughout the centuries, alluding to Busoni's teachings about the connectedness of past, present, and future music. In addition, Finnissy's music contains clear references to Busoni's compositions. In particular, the *Verdi Transcriptions* allude to the *Fantasia Contrappuntistica* in the *Falstaff* transcription and the *Indianisches Tagebuch* in the *Alzira* transcription. His *History of Photography* also alludes to Busoni's Piano Concerto, op. 39.

Alistair Hinton (b. 1950) is likewise a composer who brings together diverse styles in his music, and who was influenced by Busoni's ideas and piano compositions. His music, which explores a spectrum of possibilities, tonal, atonal, and serial, frequently alludes to others' music as he creates elaborate *Nachdictungen* that unite styles and musics of diverse time periods, an aspect that he observed and admired in Busoni's music:

> I was particularly curious that, at a time of stylistic turmoil in the years immediately preceding WWI in which some composers might be seen as stretching tonality to and beyond its breaking point, Busoni seemed to be enhancing and expanding its use yet without sounding any less "modern"; I could sense an independence of mind and an individuality that cared neither for musical fads and fashions nor for modernist revolution *per se* in his compositions but whose mature works were by no means easily reflective of existing compositional traditions—indeed, he struck me as subconsciously drawing the future and the past together in the present, an observation that I later heard Ronald Stevenson make.[162]

Although—as Hinton claims—Busoni's influence is felt in subtle and subconscious ways throughout much of his music, it is more overtly referenced in his *Sieben Charakterstücke* (1998–2003), a piece that is largely autobiographical.[163] The first piece is entitled "Doktor Busoni," and the third, "Malvern Air," quotes from Busoni's Piano Concerto, op. 39, in addition to music and ideas by Schoenberg and Edward Elgar.[164] By contrast, the second piece, *?Naissance / Espérance / Découvrance?*, references Chopin's Ballade no. 4, op. 52 (1842), Ravel's Piano Trio in A Minor (1914), and two of his own first piano sonatas, and the sixth, *Étude for Elliott*, in which Elliott Carter's string textures served as points of inspiration for a four-voiced opening section and the final section mixes serial techniques with a quotation of Elgar's "Enigma" Variations.

Ronald Stevenson (1928–2015), who studied orchestration with Guido Guerrini in Rome, and who has written extensively about Busoni, has composed in many genres, but most often for solo piano, solo song, or chorus.[165] Stevenson's compositions display admiration for Busoni throughout his career, from his early polyphonic works based on the theories of Bernhard Ziehn to the folk song settings of the 1960s to experimentation with non-retrogradable rhythms, serialism, and bitonality. Like Busoni, he often uses preexisting works in his compositions and features a blending of musical styles. While some, such as his *Fantasy on Doktor Faust* (1949), pay homage to composers, others are a more eclectic blending of styles. One example is his *Motus Perpetuus Temporibus Fatalibus* (1988) about the threat of nuclear disaster, which blends a twelve-tone row with themes based on the monograms BACH, DSCH (Shostakovich), FB (Ferruccio Busoni), and ASCH (Schoenberg). In fact, most of Stevenson's mature works display a stylistic pluralism based on Busoni's vision of the plurality found in the *Essence of Music,* in conjunction with his own love for global musics. His Piano Concerto no. 2 (1972), for instance, combines Chinese pentatony, Indian rāga, blues, Vietnamese song, and classical variation structure.

Avant-Garde and Experimental Composers

Varèse was also hailed as a model by several non-serialist avant-garde composers[166] and called their forefather.[167] Varèse's composition course at Columbia University was attended by Luigi Nono and Dieter Schnebel, and Pierre Boulez became interested in his work because of conversations with Jolivet. Messiaen was also introduced to the music of Varèse via Jolivet and subsequently had his students analyze *Ionisation*. Varèse's sketch for the distribution of loudspeakers in *Poème électronique* is similar to Nono's work with live electronics of the 1980s. Nono also studied Varèse's scores and made annotations in them. Both were interested in industrial noises and the possibility of merging ambient noise and the human voice.

While Morton Feldman officially studied with Stefan Wolpe, Varèse would have the strongest impact.[168] He called him the greatest influence on his life, citing his teaching about sound as most influential.[169] Sibelius was also a minor influence.[170] Feldman stated that he believed Varèse's impact to be as profound in the United States as Webern's had been in Europe: "Well, don't you think that, for example, like Varèse was to us here in New York, perhaps what Webern was to them in Europe?"[171] Varèse's influence is more mysterious, since he had no set method, Feldman claims: "He changed my mind without putting any thoughts into it."[172] The seventeen-year-old Feldman took one orchestration lesson with Varèse in which he learned about the spatialization of sound: "Make sure you think about the time it takes the instrument to speak from the stage to out there."[173] In a Darmstadt lecture from 1984, Feldman also claimed he met with Varèse at least once per week beginning at age eighteen, even if he wasn't officially a student. In a near gloss of Varèse and Busoni, Feldman, for whom sound quality became very important, claimed that orchestration was so important to a piece's identity that it should be called composition:

> Orchestration is composition. All other musical ideas eventually become unimportant—swallowed whole or pounded into sediments like the ground beneath us. Orchestration is the life of music without "taking thought." ... And this is something that I know my most sophisticated students never talk about, no one ever thinks about. They feel it's an ad hoc thing, any instruments, it's the notes given to them from God, the ideas in a sense that give the work a certain distinction, naturally. You see, I feel that orchestration is another gift. And Varèse once said to me, 'orchestrators are born.' He never said composers are born. And I really feel it's another gift and very few people have that gift. Maybe that's why it's not considered another parameter.[174]

What most dramatically impacted Feldman, however, was the way Varèse played with pitches to explore registers and timbre.[175]

John Cage, for his part, was impacted by Varèse's writings about organized sound, which would later become central to his own notions of noise music, as well his ideas about electronic music:

> I've read your article, Organized Sound for the Sound Film, which was published in the Commonweal. I think it's the best and most exciting article about music that I've ever read. I hope that your work is established in some laboratory. It certainly should be. The general lack of audacity, desire to explore, on the part of the heads of companies having sound laboratories is increasingly understandable. I have not yet had any actual success in my attempts to establish a center of experimental music. Several institutions are interested, but don't seem to have any finds. They complain too of having no background for something so new, which is silly, because they are surrounded by the background.[176]

The two shared an interest in similar experimental ideas and in their movement away from traditional harmony toward sonority and timbre.[177] Salzman has also made the fascinating connection between Busoni's unfinished *Doktor Faust,* Varèse's incomplete *Astronome,* and Cage's performance art:

> As a pianist working in the German tradition, Busoni was tied up with (mostly) neo-classical ideas but as an Italian he did show some interest in theater and opera, which were then and now in bad shape and in need of renovation. Varese's one idea in this line (after an earlier work or two

which have disappeared) was *Astronome* which he conceived with Artaud and which was definitely in the Busoni line (the Mephistopheles character and the Astronomer are clearly related). Alas, it was never finished. Ives never wrote any theater pieces and Weill's notion of theater took elements from popular theater mixed in with ideas from Busoni, Brecht and the Zeitoper of the time. The most original creator of new theatrical forms was, of course, Cage, who more or less invented performance art—a notion that stills goes on and expands the Busonian/Varèsian idea of the New Esthetic much further than Busoni imagined it into a kind of theatrical domain.[178]

Larry Sitsky (b. 1934), a pianist-composer, has likewise found Busoni's aesthetics to be catalysts for musical experimentation. He originally encountered the music and ideas of Busoni via two of Busoni's piano pupils, Winifred Burston (1889–1976) in Australia and Egon Petri (1881–1962) in the United States. Sitsky states that Busoni's "presence has loomed large in [his] entire life." Additionally, he maintains that Busoni "provided a clear direction for [his] artistic endeavours."[179] Although some of Sitsky's compositions bear homage to Busoni's works, with his own completion of Busoni's *Doktor Faust* (2007), his *Sonatina Seconda in Extremis* (2012), which references Busoni's *Sonatina seconda,* his violin concerto, which responds to Busoni's Piano Concerto, his opera *The Golem,* which responds to the symbology and mysticism in Busoni's *Doktor Faust,* his many fantasias, and at least seven transcriptions of Busoni compositions, Sitsky claims that it was Busoni's ideas that had the greatest impact on his compositional career.[180] Crispin has specifically noted the impact of Busoni's thoughts of Young Classicality.[181] Sitsky also cites his ideas about the role of the composer and the mystical role of music as impacting his outlook.[182] Although Busoni's ideas influenced Sitsky, his pieces, written for both electronic and acoustic instruments, experiment with new sounds, instruments, and new treatments of the musical language that Busoni could only have dreamed about. His *Sonatina Seconda in Extremis* utilizes only the highest and lowest registers of the piano, for instance. He has also composed for the theremin. Sitsky, who was deeply influenced by Busoni's vision of a mystical Faust, is now embarking on his own experimental Faust project, a digital opera for computer based on Thomas Mann's *Doktor Faustus.* The piece features virtual orchestral and vocal forces and it will be viewed/available through the computer—hopefully, as Sitsky notes, in a three-dimensional version.[183]

CODA: BUSONI TODAY

> In music one cannot teach composition, but one can cultivate it.
> —Busoni, *Maximen und Aphorismen*

Busoni's impact as a composition teacher was far reaching, but it has largely remained unexplored.[184] This neglect has many logical explanations, not least that many of his pedagogical activities took place outside of institutional settings. In addition, it was his aesthetic ideas rather than his compositions that had the greatest impact on his students. In the traditional sense, he never "taught" students how to compose music. He never embraced or taught a specific methodology and he never developed his own system. Instead, he talked endlessly about compositional possibilities and new resources. That Busoni's students responded in different ways to his ideas makes a Busonian lineage difficult to trace, and some rejected his compositions as insignificant. This is not to mention the obvious difficulties in understanding how a man who produced so many conservative compositions could have contributed to trend-setting students. In addition, Busoni never subscribed wholeheartedly to the Schoenbergian and Stravinskian strands of composition that would dominate the musical scene until the 1960s. He stood on the periphery, but in doing so anticipated much of what was to come.

Despite these apparent contradictions and despite difficulties in tracing a stylistic lineage that began with Busoni, it is possible to reconstruct a Busonian composition legacy that made a major impact on the development of modernist streams of composition in the twentieth century. Busoni's pupils, grand pupils, and admirers helped usher in a dynamic new age of music characterized by pluralism, ahistoricity, experimental scales, new sounds, and new sonorities.

One reason for Busoni's diverse results as a teacher was his centrifugal pedagogical approach. His approach to teaching was similar to his approach to composition. It was inclusive and open to possibilities, rather than focused and methodical. It was dialogic and inquisitive rather than dogmatic. It was problem-based rather than lecture-based. Busoni wanted his students to learn through doing projects and exploring concepts on their own. He wanted them to read, explore, and think for themselves.

Creation, he believed, could only be the by-product of the rich mind and soul, and it would take place when the time was right. There was no use in forcing productivity. It was not mandated by course requirements and rigid deadlines. It did not need to meet certain technical or ideological considerations.

Busoni believed that teaching composition was like gardening—it was his job to plant ideological seeds, water them by encouraging a fertile imagination, continue to cultivate the "seeds" as they grew, and wait for the plants to mature and produce previously unimaginable and original pieces of *Tonkunst*. However, the soil of the mind had to be naturally receptive to the ideas. For some, Busoni was the best of teachers, but his pedagogical approach was not suitable for everyone. He talked about new resources but rarely mentioned practical ways to use those resources. He eschewed systems, but rarely helped his students navigate the pragmatic difficulties of composing when traditional parameters were removed. In its focus on lofty ideas as opposed to pragmatic realities, Busoni's teaching could be seen as out of touch with reality. He had no patience for explaining the basics. Someone needed to lay a foundation, and Busoni was not that person. For some, he seemed egotistical, haughty, and intimidating. Petri has stated that "Busoni intimidated people, simply by being a mental giant, and people would sometimes give up—just through the sheer force of talking to him, the force of his personality, and the loftiness of his ideas and ideals."[185] Moreover, even despite the longevity of the mentorship in most cases, Busoni's approach was hands off. He was there for consultation and discussion, but he would not push his students to produce and achieve. They had to have initiative, be self-directed, and know what they wanted to avoid being overwhelmed by the magnitude of the ideas and ideals.

This book has focused mainly on success stories, on the early students who were inspired by Busoni's ideas. Yet even these were riddled by some contradictions and moments of doubt. Sibelius underwent bouts of jealousy, not understanding how Busoni's music, which he considered more traditional and inferior to his own, could be better received. Varèse wondered why such a radical thinker could produce such conservative compositions. The fact that each of Busoni's students had to be independent thinkers and strong personalities to benefit from Busoni's teaching also led to a few clashes. Jarnach and Busoni had a falling out in the 1920s, but were ultimately reconciled before Busoni's death. Gruenberg also had a few conflicts with Busoni just as he was developing his own voice as a composer. These resolved by the time Gruenberg moved back to the United States. In 1909, for instance, he argued with Busoni about the idea that routine was detrimental to the artist. In particular, he claimed that certain ways of playing can have universal application. To this, Busoni replied with such a convincing answer that Gruenberg would later go on to write about eschewing routine on his own:

> You said that there are three or four ways to play the piano, and one of these is suitable for any piece. This is correct to a certain point. But in each piece is one page, which does not fit in any category and belongs only to this one piece. Each time there arises a new problem. The same applies to composing. If you neglect this one page, the exceptional page, and play and compose according to categories, you will become a routinier, which means the opposite of an artist. If you do not try new problems, you will always direct your ideas according to existing knowledge. You said that you wrote enough fugues already. If you would tell yourself: I want to write a fugue which shall be in form, art, and emotion completely different from all I know, you would have the sensation of having never written a fugue before.[186]

In 1912, Gruenberg became resentful at the force of Busoni's ideas, writing that he believed Busoni was disappointed because he would not imitate him. In reality, Busoni delighted when students developed a personal voice: "Busoni cannot forgive me the fact, that I do not flatter him by imitation. But what use is this for me—L.T.G., if I am but a copy of someone else?"[187] On their next meeting, on December 27, 1913, Gruenberg showed Busoni some of his "stomach music": written for profit, and Busoni suggested he write a piano concerto instead. Gruenberg was less than happy about the suggestion, even though he did eventually write the suggested concerto. He initially stated

> I replied that I would consider this an unartistic category, because with the exception of the old masters (Mozart) this treated either:
> 1) piano or orchestra by itself
> 2) piano with orchestra accompaniment
> 3) if each of them would be treated independently it would give the impression of a double-headed person

Busoni's only answer was "Thank you!" First he talked to me like to a creative artist, then he judged me as audience! Am I obliged to agree with everything that Busoni ever composed, to be able to sit with him quietly at the table?[188]

This could only have been perceived as a direct insult by Busoni, who had presented a copy of his concerto to Gruenberg in Vienna in 1908 with the dedication: "To his dear, highly talented young friend L.T. Gruenberg."[189] However by 1953, Gruenberg had changed his assessment and responded: "This [Busoni's piano concerto] is a great work—a few cut[s] are necessary, and the last part should be eliminated. I feel sure that the future will judge this concerto as the greatest concerto written in our generation."[190]

Overall, many of Busoni's talented students recognized the merits of Busoni's teachings and melded them with their own ideas, leading to diverse and dynamic musical compositions at the forefront of twentieth-century streams of musical composition. As Violette notes, many of Busoni's ideas would only be adopted and implemented more widely in the latter part of the twentieth century—some of this was due to Busoni's influence, and some simply to the changing *Zeitgeist*: "Of course now everyone uses everything. Everyone is writing in all different styles and all different tonalities. But who knew at that time that Busoni and Luening would be right? It's all so easy in retrospect."[191] The musical world was unalterably impacted by Busoni's ideas even as his disciples and his grand pupils "passed the torch" and pioneered new musical ideals that contributed to major twentieth-century strands of composition, including electronic, textural, spectral, and pluralistic styles of music. This nearly forgotten mentor left a lasting composition legacy, the breadth of which is only now beginning to be comprehended.

NOTES

1. Special thanks are due the following people for their help locating archival sources for this chapter: Laura Mills (Roosevelt University), Joan Gruenberg, Cominos, Judith Grant Still, Leo Mononen (Sibelius Academy), and Jerry McBride (Stanford University). I am also grateful to Andrew Violette, Harvey Sollberger, Charles Wuorinen, Joel Feigin, Richard Taruskin, and Severine Neff for sharing their memories of Otto Luening, to Eric Salzman for sharing his memories of Luening and Edgard Varèse, and to Emiliano Ricciardi for commenting on a rough draft of the chapter.

Larry Sitsky used the phrase "passing the torch" in an interview with Judith Crispin and claimed that Egon Petri used the phrase as well. Crispin asked Sitsky: "When you finished studying with Petri, how did he articulate his wish for you to carry forward the Busoni tradition?" Sitsky responded: "Oh that was very clear and I remember the precise words. He said to me—I remember coming to say goodbye to him and he had provided a reference for my first job in Australia which was at the Queensland Conservatorium—and he said to me 'you are now a member of this club and it's your duty to pass the torch on.'" Judith Michelle Crispin, "Transcript of an Interview with Larry Sitsky," in *The Esoteric Musical Tradition of Ferruccio Busoni and Its Reinvigoration in the Music of Larry Sitsky: The Operas "Doktor Faust and "The Golem"* (Lewiston, ME: Edwin Mellen Press, 2007), 174. The epigraph comes from the following source: Otto Luening, *The Odyssey of an American Composer: The Autobiography of Otto Luening* (New York: Charles Scribner's Sons, 1980), 180.

2. Gianmario Borio, "Sul concetto di scuola nella musica del Novecento e sulla scuola di Busoni in particolare," in *Ferruccio Busoni e la sua Scuola*, ed. Gianmario Borio and Mauro Casadei (Lucca: Una Cosa Rara, 1999), 8–9.

3. Ibid., 9.

4. Borio, "Introduzione," in Borio, *Ferruccio Busoni e la sua Scuola*, n.p.

5. H. H. Stuckenschmidt, *Ferruccio Busoni: "Chronicle of a European,"* trans. Sandra Morris (New York: St. Martin's, 1970), 178.

6. Busoni, *Sketch of New Esthetic of Music*, trans. Th. Baker (New York: G. Schirmer, 1911), 3.

7. Tamara Levitz, "Teaching New Classicality: Busoni's Master Class in Composition, 1921–1924" (PhD diss., University of Rochester, 1994), 65. This would certainly not be the first school characterized by unity of thought rather than practice or style. As Borio has noted, the paradigm of the Schoenberg school, in which followers were united by similar technical procedures, however personalized the application, was not the only paradigm. As he points out, other schools, such as the so-called "New German School," or *Les Six*, also shared common ideologies. Borio, "Sul concetto di scuola nella musica del Novecento e la sua scuola di Busoni in particolare," in Borio, *Ferruccio Busoni e la sua Scuola*, 3–18. Yet aspects of his developing theory were present throughout the 1910s, as Austin Clarkson has already noted. Austin Clarkson, "Wolpe, Varèse, and the Busoni Effect," *Contemporary Music Review* 27:2/3 (April/June 2008), 263. Clarkson has also discussed the connection in "Varèses *Déserts*, Wolpes Symphony und Busonischer Modernismus," trans. Caroline Kliemt and Thomas Phelps, *Stefan Wolpe II* 152/153 (2011), 136–157.

8. Levitz and Borio, for instance, have focused on the Berlin masterclass pupils.

9. From as early as 1893, one of Busoni's main interests had been to explore the ways new treatments of traditional instruments could transform composition. In an open letter of 1893 addressed to the editor of *Musikalisches Wochenblatt*, Busoni stated:

Even if the ideas of most living composers do not exceed the limits of the possible, and even if our *masters* scarcely know how to handle the existing materials, it is nevertheless undeniable that:

1. the imperfections of the individual orchestral instruments as well as the arrangement of the orchestra as a whole hinder imagination and creativity;
2. the musical intelligence can, and presumably will, demand sounds [*Klangwirkung*], which are far beyond borders currently stretched to their limits.

Busoni, "Insufficiency of the Means for Musical Expression," open letter to the editor, *Musikalisches Wochenblatt* (1893), quoted in *Orchestration: An Anthology of Writings*, ed. Paul Mathews (New York: Routledge, 2006), 120. In the same letter Busoni called for experimentation with unusual instruments, such as the saxophone or zither, the expansion of more traditional instruments, such as the creation of a family of flutes and the use of chromatic harps, and the creation of brand new instruments, such as a bell instrument with a keyboard spanning a range of six octaves.

10. Julian Anderson, "Sibelius and Contemporary Music," in *The Cambridge Companion to Sibelius*, ed. Daniel M. Grimley (Cambridge: Cambridge University Press, 2004), 198.

11. Robert P. Morgan, "Notes on Varèse's Rhythm," in *The New Worlds of Edgard Varèse: A Symposium with Papers by Elliott Carter, Chou Wen-Chung Robert P. Morgan*, ed. Sherman van Solkema, ISAM Monographs, no. 11 (Albany: State University of New York Press, 1979), 9–26.

12. Chou Wen-Chung, "*Ionisation:* The Function of Timbre in Its Formal and Temporal Organization," in ibid., 28–29.

13. Jarnach was not initially interested in electronic sounds, largely because of insufficient technology at the time, but he became impressed after seeing Luening's experiments. Although electronic instruments had been imagined and talked about beforehand, the first electronic instrument was probably the singing arc invented by William Duddell in 1899. Andrew Hugill, "The Origins of Electronic Music," *The Cambridge Companion to Electronic Music*, ed. Nick Collins and Julio d'Escriván (Cambridge: Cambridge University Press, 2007), 15.

14. Caroline Rae, "Jolivet on Jolivet: An Interview with the Composer's Daughter," *Musical Times* (Spring 2006), 21.

15. Alfred Frankenstein, "Varèse, Worker in Intensities," *San Francisco Chronicle*, November 28, 1937, "This World Section," 13.

16. Buffet, quoted in Hugill, "The Origins of Electronic Music," 16. The original quotation is found in Gabrielle Buffet, "Musique d'aujourd'hui," in *Les soirées de Paris*, vol. 2, Slatkine Reprints (Geneva: n.p., 1971 [reprinted from the Paris edition, 1912–1914]), 183.

17. In March 1917, Buffet also wrote about the possibilities and powers of cinema. Buffet, "Cinematography" (1917), trans. Michelle Owoo, in *The Dada Reader*, ed. Dawn Ades (Chicago: University of Chicago Press, 2006), 111–113.

18. Grainger studied piano with Busoni in Germany from June 22 to July 16, 1903. Correspondence between the two survives in archival sources, such as the Busoni Nachlass at the Staatsbibliothek zu Berlin and in published collections such *The Farthest North of Humanness: Letters of Percy Grainger, 1901–1914*, ed. Kay Dreyfus (South

Melbourne: MMB Music, 1985). Curtis, another of Busoni's pupils, records that the two had a meeting as late as February 19, 1915, in New York while Busoni was on tour: "In the empty hall we sat at the morning rehearsal (February 19, 1915 Philadelphia, Stokowski), just a handful of friends, Madame Busoni on one side of me and on the other Percy Grainger, the young English composer who has done so much for interest in the folk song of America." Natalie Curtis, "Busoni's Indian Fantasy," *Southern Workman* (October 1915).

19. Otto Luening was a friend of Varèse, and was also undeniably influenced by Busoni's ideas about electronic music. In his many essays about the history of electronic music, Busoni is always mentioned. In his program notes to the *Sonata in Memoriam Ferruccio Busoni*, he made the explicit connection between Busoni's radical ideas and his electronic compositions: "Busoni's aesthetic had its roots in the past, but he had a vision of a future and prophesized many artistic events that happened in the early twenties and also the electronic sound production that developed in the 50's, in which both Varèse and I were deeply involved." Otto Luening, program notes for Sonata for Piano in Memoriam Ferruccio Busoni, http://www.newworldrecords.org/uploads/fileXuPcA.pdf, accessed August 10, 2013. Although Jarnach did not have access to the technology to create electronic pieces, he was impressed by Luening's electronic pieces.

20. Gruenberg, diary, January 1, 1960, private collection of Joan Gruenberg Cominos.

21. Gruenberg, "Vom Jazz und anderen Dingen; Rückblick und Ausblick," *25 Jahre neue Musik, Jahrbuch der 1926 Universal Edition* (Vienna: Universal Edition, 1926), 235.

22. Gruenberg, "Conversation with Myself," Gruenberg Papers, Syracuse University Library, Special Collections, 5–6.

23. Gruenberg, "Everybody's Music," in ibid.

24. Gruenberg, Notes for *Green Mansions*, Gruenberg Papers, Special Collections, New York Public Library, JPB 80-21.

25. Gruenberg, *Green Mansions*, in ibid, JPB 80-18, 28.

26. Gruenberg, *Green Mansions*, in ibid., JPB 80-18.

27. Gruenberg, *Green Mansions*, in ibid., JPB 80-18, 109.

28. Luening, *Odyssey*, 181.

29. For more detail about Sibelius quotations consult Tomi Mäkelä, "The Wings of a Butterfly," in *Jean Sibelius and His World*, ed. Daniel Grimley (Princeton, NJ: Princeton University Press, 2011), 89–125.

30. Gruenberg, "Conversations with Myself," Gruenberg Papers, Syracuse University Library, Special Collections, 9.

31. Otto Luening, "Electronic Music—First Pieces, Analyses of Fantasy in Space, Low Speed, and Invention in 12 Tones," in Otto Luening and Vladimir Ussachevky, *1952 Electronic Tape Music: The First Compositions* (New York: Highgate Press, 1977), 32.

32. Busoni, *Sketch*, 8.

33. James A. Hepokoski, *Sibelius: Symphony No. 5*, Cambridge Music Handbooks, ed. Julian Rushton (Cambridge: Cambridge University Press, 1993), 60.

34. Luening, "Some Random Remarks about Electronic Music," *Journal of Music Theory* 8:1 (Spring 1964), 92.
35. Luening, *Odyssey*, 182.
36. Luening to Varèse, June 9, 1946, Varèse Collection, Paul Sacher Stiftung, Basel.
37. Louis Gruenberg, "Vom Jazz und ander Dingen," 230.
38. Gruenberg quoted in "Louis Gruenberg and the Flagler Prize," *International Interpreter: The International News Weekly*, April 15, 1922, 18.
39. Varèse, "Autobiographical Remarks," dedicated to the memory of Ferruccio Busoni, from a talk given at Princeton University, September 4, 1959, reprinted in Christine Flechtner, "Die Schriften von Edgard Varèse (1883–1965)" (PhD diss., Universität Freiburg, 1983), 345–346. Busoni not only called for formal originality, as Varèse notes. He also insisted on congruence between content and form. Using a common analogy from nature, Busoni described this perfect congruence thus: "Every motive—so it seems to me—contains, like a seed, its life-germ within itself. From the different plant-seeds come different families of plants, dissimilar in form, foliage, blossom, fruit, growth and color. Even each individual plant belonging to one and the same species assumes, in size, form and strength a growth peculiar to itself. And so, in each motive, there lies the embryo of its fully developed form; each one must unfold itself differently." Busoni, *Sketch*, 10–11.
40. Hugill, "The Origins of Electronic Music," 15.
41. Clarkson, "Wolpe, Varèse, and the Busoni Effect," 379.
42. For more information about Lourié's life and works, see Klára Moricz, *Funeral Games in Honor of Arthur Vincent Lourié* (New York: Oxford University Press, 2014); Larry Sitsky, *Music of the Twentieth-Century Avant-Garde: A Biocritical Sourcebook* (Westport, CT: Greenwood Press, 2012).
43. Like Busoni before him, Varèse taught mainly outside of conventional institutions and he eschewed communicating specific methodologies. "Edgard Varèse: An Oral History Project, Some Preliminary Conclusions by Ruth Julius," *Current Musicology* (1978), 38–49. This project includes data from fourteen taped interviews with composers living in the Manhattan area. When speaking of Varèse's influence, it is important to remember that there were no live performances of his works between 1933 and 1947 in New York. Many composers just heard his works on recordings. See also Austin Clarkson, "The Varèse Effect: New York City in the 1950s and 1960s," in *Edgard Varèse: Composer, Sound Sculptor, Visionary*, ed. Felix Meyer and Heidy Zimmermann (Woodbridge: Paul Sacher Stiftung, 2006), 371–382.
44. Sibelius taught harmony, counterpoint, and violin sporadically from 1892 to 1910 at the Helsinki Music Institute, up to thirty hours per week at times. He usually taught out of financial necessity and avoided teaching when possible, yet also took on a few private pupils on rare occasions. Tomi Mäkelä, *Jean Sibelius*, trans. Steven Lindberg (Woodbridge: Suffolk, Boydell Press, 2011), 70. Following is a list of many of Sibelius's theory and composition students provided courtesy of Leo Mononen, Sibelius Academy. Mononen, email to the author, November 19, 2013:

1894
Miss Slöör, Miss Nappa, Mr. Lehtonen, Mr Kruskopf, Mr Soinne, Mr Tommila
(Theory class Ia)
Miss Gustafsson, Miss Heurlin, Miss Rapola, Miss Forssell, Mr. Vidgren
(Theory class IIIa)
Miss Corell, Miss Thesleff, Miss W. Tilgmann (Theory II)
1895
Miss Kauppinen, Mr. Sjöholm, Mr. Åhman, Mr. Lindell, Mr. Kaupelin,
Mr. Holmgren (Theory Ia)
Miss Haverinen, Mr. Jernberg, Mr. Laurén, Mr. Lindroos, Mr. Äyräs, Mr.
Kotilainen (Theory IIIa)
Miss Snygg, Miss Lindroos, Miss Gammal, Miss Tolpo, Miss Baltscheffsky
(Theory II)
1896
Miss Erwast, Miss Sckroderus, Miss Ehnqvist, Miss v. Schrowe (Theory Ia)
Miss Lindroos, Miss Gammal, (Theory IIa)
Miss Haverinen, Mr. Lauren, Mr. Lindroos, Mr. Kaupelin, Mr. Vidgren,
Mr. Äyräs (Theory X)
1897
Miss Gammal, Miss Ölander (Theory II)
Miss Haverinen, Miss Lindroos, Mr. Laurén, Mr. Vidgren, Mr. Kaupelin,
Mr. Äyräs (Theory X).

45. Madetoja, "Jean Sibelius Opettajana," in Lauri Ikonen, *Säveltaiteellis-Kirjallinen Julkaisu. 1925, Omistettu Suomen Säveltaiteen Suurelle Mestarille, Professori Jean Sibeliukselle Hänen 60-vuotispäiväkseen* (Helsinki: Suomen musiikkilehti, 1925), (Lahti : Suomen musiikkilehti, 1925), 40. Sibelius's pupils did not form a unified school, even if several, including Madetoja and Kuula, eventually became successful in Finland. Sibelius, who had jealous tendencies, taught his most talented pupils, Madetoja and Kuula, only briefly, Kuula in the winter of 1907–1908 and Madetoja from 1908 to 1909. He suggested that they study abroad soon thereafter. In particular, Sibelius recommended Vincent d'Indy and Robert Fuchs for Madetoja and Marco Enrico Bossi for Kuula. That said, notes in Sibelius's diary indicate that they stayed in contact until at least 1919. For more information about Madetoja, consult Erkki Salmenhaara, *Leevi Madetoja* (Helsinki: Kustannusosakeyhtio Tammi, 1987). Kuula switched teachers from Armas Järnefelt to Sibelius. Sources differ as to the exact dates/years of study. The dates provided here are from Madetoja's recollections. Madetoja claims it was the winter of 1907–1908 when Toivo Kuula studied with Sibelius. Leevi Madetoja, "Jean Sibelius Opettajana," in Lauri Ikonen, *Säveltaiteellis-Kirjallinen Julkaisu*, 40. One of the first pieces he critiqued was the Piano Trio in A Major. Erik Tawaststjerna, *Jean Sibelius*, vol. 2, 1904–1914, trans. Robert Layton (Berkeley: University of California Press, 1986), 133. See also Jean Sibelius, *Dagbok: 1909–1944*, ed. Fabian Dahlström, Skrifter utgivna av Svenska litteratursällskapet i Finland, nr. 681 (Helsinki: Svenska litteratursällskapet i Finland, 2005), 8.

46. Madetoja, "Jean Sibelius Opettajana," in Lauri Ikonen, Säveltaiteellis-Kirjallinen Julkaisu. 1925, 40.
47. Ibid., 40.
48. Sibelius considered Madetoja to be a rising new star in Finland: "I see how the youths are raising their heads—Madetoja higher than the others." Sibelius quoted in Mäkelä, *Jean Sibelius*, 256.
49. Törne, *Sibelius: A Close Up*, 29.
50. Ibid., 50–51.
51. Madetoja studied with Armas Järnefelt and Erik Furuhjelm. He studied with Jean Sibelius only during his final year of undergraduate education. Although there is very little English-language scholarship on the composer, a brief biography by Erkki Salmenhaara can be read here: http://www.fennicagehrman.fi/composers/madetoja-leevi/. Another source is Seija Lappalainen and Erkki Salmenhaara, *Leevi Madetojan Teokset* (Helsinki: Suomen Säveltäjät, 1987). Madetoja to Sibelius, January 19, 1929, Sibelius Collection, National Archives, Finland.
52. Diederik de Jong, "Madetoja: Comedy Overture, Symphony 3, Okon Fuoko Suite and Ostrobothnians Suite," *American Record Guide* (January/February 1993), 114.
53. "Pianisteja on maailmassa kuin 'harmaita kissoja' mutta Teidän trionne kaltaisia sävellyksiä on harvassa—siss." Jean Sibelius to Kuula, January 1908, Helsinki University Library, transcription and translation by UMass Translation Services.
54. Varèse did not teach many pupils. A few of the more prominent include Colin McPhee, André Jolivet, William Grant Still, Charles Wuorinen, and Chou Wen-Chung. James Tenney was influenced by Varèse's interest in technology and film. Ann Macmillan and Lucia Dlugoszewski also studied with him. Eric Salzman studied with Luening at Columbia but considered Varèse his most important mentor. For a more detailed survey of Busoni's students consult Clarkson, "The Varèse Effect." Varèse's friends were not just composers, but also sculptors, scientists, visual artists, and more. According to Clarkson, Alfred Lewin Copley (1910–1992), a medical scientist, was one of his closest friends in his maturity. He helped found the Eighth Street Club together with twenty artists, including Varèse, in 1949. Varèse gave a lecture to the club on November 10, 1950, and John Cage, Stefan Wolpe, and Morton Feldman were in the audience. Clarkson, "The Varèse Effect," 371–372. As with Busoni, Varèse assumed that students already knew the basics of composition, had a vast knowledge of literature, and were acquainted with the other arts. Chou Wen-Chung, "Varèse: Who Is He?" *Crossing the Line* (Winter 1998), 106.
55. Roger Reynolds, quoted in "Edgard Varèse: An Oral History Project, Some Preliminary Conclusions by Ruth Julius," *Current Musicology* (1978), 42.
56. Clarkson, "The Varèse Effect," 374.
57. Varèse reportedly dialogued with his students as Busoni had done, questioning his students' every decision, even while surrounding them with a network of artists, musicians, and thinkers to stimulate creativity. See the following source for a description of Varèse's teaching style: Don Gillespie, "Chou Wen-Chung on Varèse: An Interview," *American Music* 27:4 (Winter 2009), 441–460.

58. Chou Wen-Chung, "Independent Is the Key Word," *World New Music Magazine* 4 (1994), 35. Reprinted in Eric C. Lai, *The Music of Chou Wen-Chung* (Burlington, VT: Ashgate, 2009), 1. Sound sculpting would become a key characteristic of his music. Varèse rarely told Chou what to do to fix something when it was wrong. He also rarely made corrections in his works. Instead, he would inspire Wen-Chung by suggesting new ideas.

59. Chou Wen-Chung, "And the Fallen Petals," http://www.chouwenchung.org, accessed October 31, 2013. In the 1960s, Chou abandoned the direct use of Chinese melody and the experimentation of Chinese musical sound with Western instruments and replaced them with his interpretation of the Varèse concept of sound with the aesthetic principles of Chinese visual, literary, and musical arts. Chou's letters to Varèse reflect their conversations and philosophies about orchestration and stylistic pluralism, with Chou in one letter decrying the absurdity of requiring traditional instrumentations in his age. Chou to Varèse, August 20 (year unknown), Varèse Collection, Paul Sacher Stiftung, Basel.

60. Eileen Southern claims, for instance, based on obvious stylistic differences that "the influence of Edgard Varèse is negligible in Still's music, but Still credited the avant-garde composer with having opened new horizons for him and having loosened up his music." Eileen Southern, "America's Black Composers of Classical Music," *Music Educators Journal* 62 (November 1975), 46–59. See also Karen Monson, "Still Has Lived through Musical Changes," *Los Angeles Herald-Examiner* (January 24, 1970), B5.

61. Varèse nevertheless asked Still for help with his manuscripts as late as November 1926. Varèse to Still, November 4, [c. 1926], William Grant Still and Verna Arvey Papers, University of Arkansas. Since the piece premiered on November 22, 1926, the year is most likely 1926.

62. Varèse stayed in contact with Still throughout the end of his life and promoted him in a number of ways, including programming his music and making recordings of it. In a letter of 1944, Still thanked Varèse for a recording of a Slave song, claiming it sounded just as he wanted it to. Varèse collection, Paul Sacher Stiftung, Basel. Still claims that Varèse's efforts to have "From the Island of Dreams" performed made a lasting impression. Still to Varèse, September 9, 1924, Varèse Collection, Paul Sacher Stiftung, Basel. In addition, he introduced him to people who promoted his career, including Howard Hanson. Still, "A Vital Factor in America's Racial Problem," in *The William Grant Still Reader: Essays on American Music*, vol. 6, no. 2, ed. Jon Michael Spencer (Durham, NC: Duke University Press, 1992), 170. A letter of February 1, 1944, also indicates Varèse's continued attempts to program Still's music and his strong support of Still's style of composition. William Grant Still and Verna Arvey Papers, University of Arkansas.

63. Varèse's daybook includes the dates of some of their meetings:

July 3, 1923, 2 p.m.
July 10, 1923, 5 p.m.
July 17, 5 p.m.
September 18, 5 p.m.
October 9, 5 p.m.

Varèse, daybook, Varèse Collection, Paul Sacher Stiftung, Basel.

64. Varèse to Daisy B. King, July 11, 1923, Varèse Collection, Paul Sacher Stiftung, Basel.

65. Denise von Glahn, *The Sounds of Place: Music and the American Cultural Landscape* (Boston: Northeastern University Press, 2003). See also Varèse to King, July 11, 1923, Varèse Collection, Paul Sacher Stiftung, Basel.

66. Still, "The Art of Musical Creation," in *The William Grant Still Reader*, ed. Jon Michael Spencer, A Special Issue of Black Sacred Music: A Journal of Theomusicology 6:2 (Fall 1992), 84.

67. Gayle Murchison, "Dean of Afro-American Composers" or "Harlem Renaissance Man: The New Negro and the Musical Poetics of William Grant Still," http://publishing.cdlib.org/ucpressebooks/view?docId=ft1h4nbogo&chunk.id=d0e1427&toc.depth=1&toc.id=d0e1427&brand=ucpress;query=darker%20america#1, accessed November 6, 2013.

68. Carol J. Oja, "'New Music' and the 'New Negro': The Background of William Grant Still's *Afro-American Symphony*," *Black Music Research Journal* 12:2 (Fall 1992), 145–169.

69. Still, "On Orchestration," in *The William Grant Still Reader*, 255.

70. Still, "The Art of Musical Creation," in ibid., 84.

71. Varèse to Still, March 10, 1929, William Grant Still and Verna Arvey Papers, University of Arkansas. *From the Land of Dreams* (1924) is a composition for three voices and chamber orchestra in three movements and is dedicated to Varèse. In Still's notes for the composition, he stated: "In the first two movements I have sought to depict, or rather to suggest, the flimsiness of dreams which fade before they have taken definite form. The varying moods of these movements may be construed as suggestions of the ever-changing scenes which dreams unfold to the dreamer's vision. Some may contend that the last movement is too vigorous to be a past of the composition, but there are vivid dreams with clearly defined outlines. From these we often awake abruptly dwelling, as it were, on the borders of both the realm of fancy and of reality." Judith Anne Still, Michael J. Dabrishus, and Carolyn L. Quinn, *William Grant Still: A Bio-Bibliography*, Bio-bibliographies in Music, no. 61 (Westport, CT: Greenwood Press, 1996), 106.

72. Paul Rosenfeld, critique of 1925, http://publishing.cdlib.org/ucpressebooks/view?docId=ft1h4nbogo&chunk.id=d0e7410&toc.depth=1&toc.id=&brand=ucpress&query=forsyth., accessed November 6, 1913.

73. Gayle Murchison and Catherine Parsons Smith, "Still, William Grant," *Grove Music Online. Oxford Music Online*, Oxford University Press, http://www.oxfordmusiconline.com/subscriber/article/grove/music/26776, accessed November 5, 2013.

74. Catherine Parsons Smith has mentioned this piece in connection with Still's developing compositional voice in *William Grant Still: A Study in Contradictions* (Berkeley: University of California Press, 2000), 291.

75. Still's own views of Varèse's music were conflicted, as reflected by his assessment of *Ionisation* to Henry Cowell, which he found to be gripping on the one hand and grotesque on the other. Still to Henry Cowell, 1932, Varèse Collection, Paul Sacher Stiftung, Basel.

76. Still to Varèse, 1932, Varèse Collection, Paul Sacher Stiftung, Basel.

77. Still, "Horizons Unlimited," in *William Grant Still Reader*, 235.//
78. Caroline Rae, "Jolivet on Jolivet," 1–22.
79. Jolivet met Varèse on May 30, 1929. "A longtime friend of Varèse, Paul le Flem, with whom I was then studying harmony and counterpoint, sent me to Varèse on the afternoon of the famous May 30, 1929, to ask him to obtain seats for me for the concert of the same evening at which Gaston Poulet was directing *Amériques*." Hilda Jolivet, *Varèse, Musiciens de notre temps* (Paris: Hachette Littérature, 1973), 147–148.
80. Although Jolivet studied with and discussed music with a number of composers, Debussy, Dukas, Ravel, and le Flem included, Varèse made the most lasting impression.
81. Lucie Kayas, *André Jolivet* (n.p.: Fayard, 2005), 106. See also Bridget F. Conrad, "The Sources of Jolivet's Musical Language and His Relationship with Varèse" (PhD diss., City University of New York, 1994), 398. When Jolivet began rewriting the trio for a larger ensemble, Varèse advised about the instrumentation: "Your combination seems good to me—except that instead of the tuba, I would prefer a bass clarinet with the instruments I had chosen for you. It seems more homogeneous to me, and easier to blend. Be careful however of the potential for doubling in the piano and harp. Avoid monotony and imagine the contrasts you will get." Varèse quoted in Conrad, "The Sources of Jolivet's Musical Language and His Relationship with Varèse," 399.
82. Jolivet, in turn, communicated many of these ideas to other members of Le jeune France, including Olivier Messiaen. The other members included Yves Baudrier and Daniel-Lesur. For more details on the group, consult Serge Gut, *Le Groupe Jeune France* (Paris: Honoré Champion, 1977). His composition pupils included Marc Bleuse, Philippe Drogoz, Philippe Hersant, Jean-Paul Holstein, Edith Lejet, Pierre Yves Levalle, Jean-Claude Risset, Yoshihisa Taira, and Akira Tamba.
83. Jolivet, quoted in Bridget F. Conrad, "The Sources of Jolivet's Musical Language," 94.
84. Ibid., 269.
85. A list of Jolivet's music can be found in Association des amis d'André Jolivet, *André Jolivet: Guide des œuvres* (Paris: Association des amis d'André Jolivet, 2006).
86. Jolivet, "Reponse a un enquete," *Counterpoints* 1 (1946), reprinted in special double number of *La Revue musicale le musicien dans la cité* (1977), 19–22.
87. Jolivet, "Concerto pour Ondes Martenot" (1951), quoted in Conrad, "The Sources of Jolivet's Musical Language," 392. An important source of information is a lecture: Jolivet "La Musique: plaid pour le vif," *la Nouvelle Saison* 2/7 (July 1939), 400–406. In later lectures of the 1960s and 1970s he was trying to explain the philosophy behind his earlier works. His combination of interests is strikingly similar to that of the surrealists. He knew several surrealists, including Antonin Artaud, because of his association with Varèse. For more detail consult Barbara L. Kelly, ed., *French Music, Culture, and National Identity 1870–1939*, Eastman Studies in Music, ed. Ralph P. Locke (Rochester: University of Rochester Press, 2008); Martine Cadieu and André Jolivet, "A Conversation with André Jolivet," *Tempo* 59 (Autumn 1961), 2–4. See also Varèse and Jolivet, *Correspondence: 1931–1965*, ed. Christine Jolivet-Erlih (Geneva: Contrechamps, 2002).

88. Gruenberg mentions private pupils in his diary but not by name. Gruenberg, diary, private collection of Joan Gruenberg Cominos.

89. The name of even one student from these years has yet to be established.

90. Laura Mills, archivist at Roosevelt University, email to the author, September 17, 2013.

91. Louis Gruenberg, "Teaching Materials," Louis Gruenberg Papers, New York Public Library, Special Collections, Box 13, Folder 6.

92. Joan Cominos Gruenberg, personal communications with the author, August 2013.

93. Carol Oja, *Making Music Modern: New York in the 1920s* (New York: Oxford University Press, 2000), 368–369.

94. Marion Bauer to Louis Gruenberg, November 23, 1938, Louis Gruenberg Papers, New York Public Library, Special Collections, Box 12, Folder 16. It is unclear which piece they were discussing—perhaps *Four Diversions for String Quartet* (1930) or another lost composition.

95. Marion Bauer to Louis Gruenberg, March 29, 1939, in ibid.

96. Archival collections at Mount Holyoke College, the Library of Congress, and the New York Public Library contain mainly manuscripts. I have been unable to locate additional troves of letters between the two.

97. Andrew Violette, email to the author, May 13, 2014.

98. Suzanne Bartel (1945–2011) to Otto Luening, December 1966, Otto Luening Papers, New York Public Library, Special Collections, Box 70, Folder 6. After graduating from Columbia University, Bartel studied musicology at the University of Munich from 1966 to 1968 and subsequently earned her PhD in musicology from Stanford University. She subsequently became a lecturer at the University of Maryland.

99. Violette, email to the author, May 13, 2014.

100. Luening, *Odyssey*, 475.

101. Violette, email to the author, May 13, 2014.

102. See the following source for more detailed information about the center: Nick Patterson, "The Archives of the Columbia-Princeton Electronic Music Center," *Notes* 67:3 (March 2011), 483–502.

103. Luening to Fred Beyer, October 4, 1955, Otto Luening Papers, New York Public Library, Special Collections, Box 70.

104. Luening taught Roger Sessions's students when Sessions was on sabbatical.

105. Andrew Violette to Luening, undated, Otto Luening Papers, New York Public Library, Box 73, Folder 16. Violette is an American composer who remembers doing Fuxian counterpoint with Luening. More biographical information is available on his website, http://www.andrewviolette.com/bio.htm, accessed May 13, 2014.

106. Joel Feigin, phone interview with the author, May 22, 2014. Feigin is currently professor of composition at the University of California, Santa Barbara. He studied with Nadia Boulanger in Fontainebleau, at Columbia University, and at the Juilliard School, where he received his DMA in composition. He taught previously at Cornell University. Feigin met Luening while a faculty member at Cornell University.

107. Severine Neff, phone interview with the author, May 22, 2014. Neff is currently the Eugene Falk Distinguished Professor of Music Theory at the University of

North Carolina, Chapel Hill. She previously studied at Columbia University, Yale University, and Princeton University, and has taught at Bates College, Barnard College, and the Cincinnati College-Conservatory of Music. Neff is the author of "Otto Luening and the Theories of Bernhard Ziehn," *Current Musicology* 39 (1985), 21–41. Neff is also Feigin's wife; together they enjoyed many hours in Luening's company.

108. Charles Wuorinen is probably the student who worked with Luening the longest at Columbia University, entering his composition class as a sophomore and continuing until he graduated with a master's degree in 1963. Charles Wuorinen, phone interview with the author, November 18, 2013. Although Columbia University verified that Wuorinen completed his undergraduate degree in 1961 and his graduate degree in 1963, they would not release information about courses he took and from which instructors. Most of the information provided in this section derives from a phone interview between Wuorinen and the author, conducted on November 18, 2013.

109. A complete list of the electronic works created by Wuorinen at Columbia University through 1970 are found in the "Columbia Princeton Electronic Music Concert Tenth Anniversary Celebration Booklet." The pieces include *Consort from Instruments and Voices* (1960), *Symphonia Sacra*, for three voices, five instruments, and tape (1960–61), *Orchestral and Electronic Exchanges*, for orchestra and tape (1965), *Time's Encomium* for synthesized and processed synthesized sound (1969), Otto Luening Papers, New York Public Library, Special Collections, Box 14, Folder 2. In 1964, he returned to Columbia as a lecturer, as an instructor from 1965 to 1969, and as an assistant professor from 1969 to 1971.

110. Richard D. Burbank, *Charles Wuorinen: A Bio-Bibliography*, Bio-bibliographies in Music, no. 49 (Westport, CT: Greenwood Press, 1994).

111. Thom Holmes, *Electronic and Experimental Music: Technology, Music, and Culture*, 3rd ed. (New York: Routledge, 2008), 98.

112. Charles Wuorinen, *New York Notes* (New York: C.F. Peters, 1998). There are some similarities to Varèse's *Déserts* in that the electronic sections are interpolated. However, acoustic instruments continue playing (and do not just alternate with the electronic segments as is the case with Varèse's *Déserts*).

113. For a detailed analysis of the composition, see Lee Ray, "On Developing the Electronic Tracks for Bamboula Squared," http://www.charleswuorinen.com/Writings/Lee_Ray/Lee_Ray.pdf, accessed November 15, 2013.

114. Charles Wuorinen, "Bamboula Squared," http://www.charleswuorinen.com/audio.php., accessed December 5, 2013.

115. "And I found, myself, even very early on, a kind of anxiety developing as I contemplated the electronic medium, at whatever stage it was—of course, computers were far in the future at that time—wondering whether people were paying proper attention to the role of live human beings in the dynamic of performance and in the influence that the fact of live performance had on every composer since the beginning of time. This was also fluffed off and dismissed as unimportant, but it seemed critically important to me, and that's one of the reasons why I have never pursued the development of the electronic medium more aggressively than I have, which isn't aggressively at all." Frank J. Oteri, "Charles Wuorinen: Art and Entertainment," *New Music Box* (July 1, 2007),

http://www.newmusicbox.org/articles/charles-wuorinen-art-and-entertainment/3/, accessed November 13, 2013.

116. "I am thus led to be concerned about the unavoidable aspect of electronic music in which it represents a 'freezing' of a composer's one-time intentions, producing something that is presumed to be 'definitive' but is usually the result of compromises forced by the practicalities involving equipment.... That's why I believe it should always be possible to reinterpret compositions, and why the kind of electronic piece that interests me most is one that can be resynthesized in successive 'runs,' a possibility which seems most available in computer synthesis, which therefore seems to me to offer the most interesting prospect in the field of electronic music." Benjamin Boretz, "Conversation with Charles Wuorinen," *Contemporary Music Newsletter* 3:7–8 (1969), 5.

117. "I have to say that at this stage in the development of electronic music and my own thoughts on music, that it's about time something interesting happened." Oteri, "Charles Wuorinen: Art and Entertainment."

118. Corigliano graduated in 1959. His earliest published compositions predate his graduation from Columbia University (1959), a song cyclette for voice and piano and *Kaleidoscope* for two pianos (1959). The sonata for violin and piano (1963) launched his career. See Corigliano (1999), quoted in *Otto Luening Centennial* (n.p.: Otto Luening Trust, 2000), 13. For additional information about Corigliano, consult Mark Adamo, *John Corigliano: A Monograph* (Todmorden, Lancs: Arc Music, 2000).

119. Hans Heinsheimer (1900–1993) became vice president of Schirmer in 1972.

120. Luening, *Odyssey*, 476. Luening to Heinsheimer, January 6, 1967, Otto Luening Papers, New York Public Library, Special Collections, Box 70, Folder 9.

121. Adamo, *John Corigliano*, 49.

122. Ibid., 12.

123. Corigliano describes his approach thus: "I tend to think of style as a variable. I do have stylistic things that come back—certain intervals, certain kinds of progressions, certain sonorities that I use because they're part of me. That is an unconscious style. But as far as the idea of style as it exists in music today, in which one associates a sonority or a sound or a total piece with somebody, and he writes the next piece in that style and the next piece in that style, as Brahms did, I don't feel I'm that kind of composer." Bruce Duffie, "Interview with John Corigliano,"
http://www.bruceduffie.com/corigliano.html, accessed October 24, 2013.

124. Colleen Renihan, "'History as It Should Have Been': Haunts of the Historical Sublime in John Corigliano's and William Hoffman's *The Ghosts of Versailles*," *Twentieth-Century Music* 10:2 (September 2013), 249–272.

125. Ibid., 265–267.

126. Duffie, "Interview with John Corigliano."

127. Corigliano, quoted in Ann McCutchan, *The Muse That Sings: Composers Speak about the Creative Process* (New York: Oxford University Press, 1999), 36.

128. John Corigliano, *The Ghosts of Versailles: A Grand Opera Buffa in Two Acts*, piano-vocal score (New York: G. Schirmer, 2010), 24–25.

129. McCutchan, *The Muse That Sings*, 39.

130. For more information about Jarnach's activities at the Hochschule, consult Stefan Weiss, "Die Gründung der Hamburger Musikhochschule und ihr erster Direktor Philipp Jarnach," in Hanns-Werner Heister and Wolfgang Hochstein, ed. Kunsträume Studium Innenansichten (Hamburger: Bockel Verlag, 2000), 158–169.

131. Jarnach, lecture about *Doktor Faust*, Staatsbibliothek zu Berlin, Preußischer Kulturbesitz, Musikabteilung mit Mendelssohn-Archiv, Mus. Nachl. F. Busoni., N. Mus. Depos. 56, 248, and Jarnach to Busoni, October 10, 1919, Staatsbibliothek zu Berlin, Preußischer Kulturbesitz, Musikabteilung mit Mendelssohn-Archiv, Mus. Nachl. F. Busoni, N. Mus. Depos. 30, 109.

132. "Was mich sofort an Jarnachs Unterrichtsmethode begeisterte, war seine grossartige Toleranz, die jedem seiner Studenten das Recht auf stilistische Eigenart beliess. Gewissenhaft las er Note für Note durch, redete wenig, beschränkte sich in der Kritik auf technische Mängel liess sich kaum von 'Ideen'; mitreissen, forderte suchend Musik, und nur Musik vermochte ihn letzlich zu überzeugen." Walter Steffens to Uwe Kraemer, February 12, 1971, quoted in Stefan Weiss, *Die Musik Philipp Jarnachs* (Köln: Christoph Dohr, 1996), 78.

133. For more information consult Wulf Konold, ed., *Bernd Alois Zimmermann: Dokumente und Interpretationen* (Köln: Wienand Verlag, n.d.); Carl Dahlhaus, ed., *Festschrift für eine Verleger Ludwig Strecker zum 90. Geburtstag* (Mainz: B. Schott's Sohne, 1973); Christof Bitter, ed., *Intervall und Zeit: Bernd Alois Zimmermann Aufsatze und Schriften zum Werk* (Mainz: B. Schott's Sohne, 1974); Wulf Konold, *Bernd Alois Zimmermann: Der Komponist und sein Werk* (Köln: Dumont, 1986). Zimmermann underwent a steady evolution as a composer, although there was a pluralistic phrase and a dodecaphonic phase. Over the years he absorbed Hindemith, Stravinsky, Bartók, Schoenberg, Webern, Varèse, Messiaen, and Boulez. In 1950 he composed his first twelve-tone piece, and by 1954 he was incorporating jazz elements (e.g., in the trumpet concerto). *Die Soldaten* was the crowning work of his serial phase. *Tratti I* (1966) was his first purely electronic work, and his last great orchestral work was *Photoptosis*.

134. For a more detailed description of Zimmermann's studies, consult Konold, *Bernd Alois Zimmermann*.

135. "Philipp Jarnach, wohl Zimmermanns entscheidender kompositorischer Mentor, wies einmal in einem Gespräch auf die immense Lust und dynamische Kraft hin, die Zimmermann zum komponieren trieb, wobei ihm aussergewöhnlicher Fleiss und die Fähigkeit zu mikroskopischer Detailarbeit ausgezeichnet habe.... Schon bald spurte Zimmermann, dass er die Basis seines Komponierens uber den formstreng sachlichen Stil einer jungen Klassizität wie ihn der Busoni-Schuler Jarnach vertrat, hinaus erweitern musste. Dieser Stil, der Zimmermanns Tendenz zur formellen Bändigung entgegen kam, verstellte zugleich seiner Expressivität den Weg." Ibid., 16.

136. Weiss, *Die Musik Philipp Jarnachs*, 323.

137. Konold has already noted Jarnach's passing down of "klanglichen Elementen" from Busoni. Konold, "Zimmermanns kompositorische Entwicklung von den Anfängen bis zu den *Soldaten*," in *Bernd Alois Zimmermann: Dokumente und Interpretationen*, 101–107.

Conclusions 337

138. "Gestern bei Jarnach und Schneider gewesen. Jarnach kritisiert sehr scharf das Trio. Keine Idee; gut gemacht und richtige Steigerungen etc., aber Leerlaufmusik. Auch er sieht im Klanglichen, wie Schneider, das Problem des Trios, allerdings fordert Jarnach mehr Substanz, mehr Idee. Beide beurteilen die Symphonie günstiger.... Gewiss ist das Operieren mit neuen Klängen kein Experiment; es soll es jedenfalls nicht sein, und der Klängen ist ja zuletzt sekundar, er ist mit Vorbehalt ein Ausfluss der Melodie, und die Melodie ist primäre Klangbilderin, so paradox es erscheinen mag." Bernd Alois Zimmermann, *"Du und Ich und Ich und die Welt:" Dokumente aus den Jahren 1940 bis 1950*, Archive zu Musik des 20. Jahrhunderts, Band 4 (Berlin: Stiftung Archiv der Akademie der Künste, 1998), 29. Jarnach is mentioned as early as January 2, 1941.

139. Konold, *Bernd Alois Zimmermann*, 16.

140. Busoni, "Young Classicism," in Busoni, *The Essence of Music and Other Papers*, trans. Rosamund Ley (1920; London: Salisbury Square, 1956), 20.

141. Bernd Alois Zimmermann, "Intervall und Zeit (1957)," in *Bernd Alois Zimmermann: Dokumente und Interpretationen*, 37–41.

142. "Von dieser Seite gesehen, erhält der Gedanke der Einheit der Zeit als Einheit von Gegenwart, Vergangenheit und Zukunft—so wie sie Augustinus im Wesen der menschlichen Seele begründet hat, die in einem geistigen Sichausdehnen den flüchtigen Augenblick übergreift und Vergangenheit und Zukunft in eine ständige Gegenwart hineinbezieht—,dieser so modern und zugleich uralte Gedanke, eine neue Perspektive in der Musik als 'Zeitkunst,' als Kunst der zeitlichen Ordnung innerhalb der ständigen Gegenwart, ein beherrschender in der modernen Dichtung nicht weniger als in der modernen Malerei." Ibid., 37–38.

143. Robert Erickson, *Sound Structure in Music* (Berkeley: University of California Press, 1975), 20–21; Claude Ledoux, *From the Philosophical to the Practical: An Imaginary Proposition Concerning the Music of Tristan Murail*, trans. Joshua Fineberg, *Contemporary Music Review* 19:3 (2000), 41–65. Murail studied composition with Messiaen at the Conservatoire de Paris from 1967 to 1972 and he taught composition at IRCAM in Paris. Guy Lelong, *Écrits, ou, L'invention de la musique spectrale edition* (n.p.: Repercussions, 2008). Although Grisey studied with Messiaen, György Ligeti, Karlheinz Stockhausen, and Iannis Xenakis in 1972, as well as acoustics with Émile Leipp, he was deeply impacted by the music of Varèse and Sibelius. His compositions *Dérives, Périodes*, and *Partiels* were among the first pieces of spectral music.

144. "Varèse est notre ancêtre génial dont l'intuition était formidablement en avance sur les outils sonores et les méthodes de composition de son époque. Dans *Arcana* notamment, se trouvent des complexes sonores—ce qu'il appelait harmonictimbre—qui ne s'explique que par une analyse spectrale de leur composantes. Varèse—phénomène rare en son temps—connaissait l'acoustique de Helmholtz." Grisey and Guy Lelong, *Écrits*, 2008), 266. In a letter of April 7, 1995, to Sylvain Cambreilung. Grisey also urged students to study Sibelius's *Tapiola*. Grisey and Guy Lelong, *Ecrits*, 207.

145. See *Magnus Lindberg*, "A New World of Sound," in *Voice of Music: Conversations with Composers of Our Time*, ed. Anders Beyer and Jean Christiensen (Burlington, VT: Ashgate, 2000). Magnus Lindberg (b. 1958) studied with Rautavaara and Paavo

Heininen beginning with piano. He also studied with Brian Ferneyhough and Grisey. Peter Szendy and Risto Nieminen, *Magnus Lindberg*, trans. Nick Le Quesne (Helsinki: n.p., 1996).

146. Szendy and Nieminen, *Magnus Lindberg*, 13–14.

147. Ibid., 14–15.

148. For an analysis of *Kinetics*, consult Martin Eybl and Tomi Mäkelä, "Exploring the Perception of Magnus Lindberg's *Kinetics*: An Analytical Dialogue," in *Topics, Texts, Tensions: Essays in Music Theory*, ed. Tomi Mäkelä (Magdeburg: Otto-von-Guericke Universität, 1999), 64–75. The authors draw clear connections to Varèse's music on page 64: "1. In both cases the interplay of surfaces and prominent linear gestures is important. 2. A clear discernable traditional formal principle (symmetry, tripartition, etc.) is not discernable. 3. The composition's surface has an uncommonly profound influence on its structures." They also draw connections between Varèse's and Lindberg's use of sonority in a structural sense.

149. Ibid., 282.

150. Ivan Hewett et al., *Iannis Xenakis: Composer, Architect, Visionary* (n.p.: Fleet Center at RISD, n.d.). Xenakis was also influenced by Varèse's ideas about form. Balint Varga, *Conversations with Xenakis* (London: Faber and Faber, 1996), 127.

151. Xenakis, quoted in Hewett et al., *Iannis Xenakis: Composer, Architect, Visionary*, 56. See also Gianmario Borio, "'A Strange Phenomenon': Varèse's Influence on the European Avant-Garde," in *Edgard Varèse: Composer, Sound Sculptor, Visionary*, ed. Felix Meyer and Heidy Zimmermann (Woodbridge: Boydell Press, 2006).

152. "Peter Maxwell Davies Introduces and Conducts Sibelius: Symphony No. 6" (November 10, 1996: Vredenburg, Utrecht), https://www.youtube.com/watch?v=X3LL_zFAoBM, accessed November 2, 2015. Barbirolli conducted the Hallé Orchestra from 1936 to 1943. Davies makes the connection in his interview with Richard Dufallo, *Trackings: Composers Speak with Richard Dufallo* (New York: Oxford University Press), 153–154.

153. Paul Griffiths, *Peter Maxwell Davies* (London: Robson House, 1982), 103–104.

154. Julian Anderson, "Sibelius and Contemporary Music," *The Cambridge Companion to Sibelius*, ed. Daniel Grimley (Cambridge: Cambridge University Press, 2004), 211–214.

155. Richard McGregor, "Max the Symphonist," in *Perspectives on Peter Maxwell Davies*, ed. Richard McGregor (Burlington, VT: Ashgate, 2000), 116.

156. Anderson, "Sibelius and Contemporary Music," 211.

157. Peter Maxwell Davies, "Composer's Notes," http://www.boosey.com/cr/music/Peter-Maxwell-Davies-Symphony-No-5/3656, accessed November 2, 2015.

158. Other composers inspired by Busoni include Larry Sitsky (b. 1934) and his pupil, Judith Crispin (b. 1970). Crispin has detailed Busoni's direct influence on the compositional style of Sitsky. Crispin, *The Esoteric Musical Tradition of Ferruccio Busoni and Its Reinvigoration in the Music of Larry Sitsky: The Operas "Doktor Faust" and "The Golem"* (Lewiston, ME: Edwin Mellen Press, 2007). As a composer, Crispin paid direct homage to Busoni through her opera, *Leonardo: The Italian Faust*, which is based on an incomplete libretto fragment by Busoni.

159. Michael Finnissy, email to the author, March 16, 2016.

160. Stevens studied with E. J. Dent at the University of Cambridge.

161. Andrew Palmer, *Encounters with British Composers* (Rochester: Boydell Press, 2015), 178.

162. Alistair Hinton, email to the author, March 16, 2016.

163. Ibid. For more information about Hinton's life and works, see "The Music and Literature of Alistair Hinton," http://www.sorabji-archive.co.uk/hinton/hinton_brochure.pdf, *The Sorabji Archive*, March 19, 2016.

164. Alistair Hinton, email to the author, March 19, 2016.

165. See, for instance, Stevenson, "Busoni and Mozart," *The Score* 13 (September 1955), 25–38; "Busoni: The Legend of a Prodigal," *The Score* 15 (March 1956), 15–30; "Busoni's Great Fugue *The Listener* 87:2238 (February 3, 1972), 157; "Busoni: Doktor Faust of the Keyboard," *EPTA Piano Journal* 1:1 (1980), 14–15. For more information about Stevenson, see *Comrades in Art: The Correspondence of Ronald Stevenson and Percy Grainger 1957–1961*, comp. Teresa Balough, Musicians in Letters no. 2, Musicians on Music, no. 8 (n.p.: Toccata Press, 2010); Malcolm MacDonald, *Ronald Stevenson: A Musical Biography* (Edinburgh: National Library of Scotland, 1989).

166. For more information, see Giovanni Guanti, "Busoni e la nuova musica Americana," in *Ferruccio Busoni e la sua Scuola*, ed. Gianmario Borio and Mauro Casadei (Lucca: Una Cosa Rara, 1999).

167. See Walter Zimmermann, ed., *Morton Feldman Essays* (Koln: Beginner Press, 1985), and Robert Kyr, *Between the Mind and the Ear: Finding the Perfect Balance* (Boston: League-ISCM, 1990).

168. Morton Feldman was born in New York on January 12, 1926. He studied piano with Vera Maurina Press, who had been a pupil of Busoni at the age of twelve and also composed short Scriabinesque pieces. In 1949 Feldman met John Cage. See also Morton Feldman, *Morton Feldman Says: Selected Interviews and Lectures 1964–1987*, ed. Chris Villars (London: Hyphen Press, n.d.).

169. Morton Feldman, "In Memoriam: Edgard Varèse," in Zimmermann, *Morton Feldman Essays*.

170. Feldman praised him in his 1984 Darmstadt lecture.

171. John Cage and Morton Feldman, *Radio Happenings: Conversations—Gespräche* Edition Musik-Texte I, ed. Gisela Gronemeyer and Reinhard Oehlschlägel (Cologne: Musiktexte, 1993), 99. Based on a radio conversation of December 28, 1966. It is also quoted in Kyle Gann, "'Magnificent—in a Mysterious Way': Varèse's Impact on American Music," in *Edgard Varèse: Sound Sculptor*, 426.

172. John Cage and Morton Feldman, *Radio Happenings*, 116.

173. Morton Feldman, "Anecdotes and Drawings," in Zimmermann, *Morton Feldman Essays*, 156.

174. Feldman, "Notes on Orchestration," in *Orchestration: An Anthology of Writings*, ed. Paul Mathews (New York: Routledge, 2006), 202–203.

175. See Feldman, "Sound, Noise, Varèse, Boulez," *A Magazine for Abstract Art* (Autumn 1958).

176. John Cage to Varèse, January 3, 1941, Varèse Collection, Paul Sacher Stiftung, Basel. Varèse later chose to include Cage's music in his class at Columbia.

177. Richard Dufallo, *Trackings*, 226.

178. Salzman, email to the author, May 15, 2014. Salzman is a composer working in new-music theater and a writer about twentieth-century music.

179. Sitsky, email to the author, May 4, 2016.

180. For a list, see Crispin, *The Esoteric Musical Tradition of Ferruccio Busoni*, 78.

181. Ibid., 9–36.

182. Sitsky, email to the author, May 4, 2016.

183. Ibid.

184. Epigraph: "In der Musik kann man nicht Komposition lehren, aber man kann sie üben." Ferruccio Busoni, *Maximen und Aphorismen*, ed. Martina Weindel, Taschenbücher zur Musikwissenschaft 147 (Wilhelmshaven: Florian Noetzel Verlag, 2004), 57.

185. Egon Petri, quoted by Sitsky in "Transcript of an Interview with Larry Sitsky," by Judith Crispin, *The Esoteric Musical Tradition*, 181.

186. Busoni to Gruenberg, 1909, private collection of Joan Gruenberg Cominos.

187. Gruenberg, diary entry of July 6, 1912, private collection of Joan Gruenberg Cominos.

188. Gruenberg, diary entry of December 27, 1913, private collection of Joan Gruenberg Cominos.

189. Busoni, inscription (1908) to his piano concerto, private collection of Joan Gruenberg Cominos.

190. Gruenberg, diary entry of October 4, 1953, private collection of Joan Gruenberg Cominos.

191. Violette, email to the author, of May 13, 2014.

SELECTED BIBLIOGRAPHY

ARCHIVAL SOURCES

Busoni, Ferruccio. Collection. Gottfried Galston-Busoni Archive, University of Tennessee Libraries. Knoxville, TN.
———. Nachlass. Staatsbibliothek zu Berlin. Preussischer Kulturbesitz. Musikabteilung mit Mendelssohn Archiv. Berlin.
Dent, Edward Joseph. Papers. King's College Archive Centre. Cambridge.
Gruenberg, Louis. Papers. New York Public Library. New York.
———. Papers. Syracuse University Library. Syracuse, NY.
———. Private Collection. Home of Joan Gruenberg Cominos. Martinez, CA.
Jarnach, Philipp. Nachlass. Staatsbibliothek zu Berlin. Preussischer Kulturbesitz. Musikabteilung mit Mendelssohn Archiv. Berlin.
Luening, Otto. Papers. New York Public Library. New York.
Sibelius, Jean. Collection. Åbo Akademi Archive. Åbo.
———. Collection. Helsinki University Library. Helsinki.
———. Collection. National Archives of Finland. Helsinki.
———. Collection. National Library of Finland. Helsinki.
———. Collection. Sibelius Academy. Helsinki.
Still, William Grant, and Verna Arvey. Papers. University of Arkansas. Fayetteville, AR.
Varèse, Edgard. Collection. Harry Ransom Humanities Research Center. University of Texas at Austin.
———. Collection. Paul Sacher Stiftung. Basel.
Varése, Louise. Papers. Sophia Smith Collection. Smith College. Northampton, MA.

PERIODICAL ARTICLES

Aldrich, Richard. "'Pierrot Lunaire' and Others." *New York Times*, February 5, 1923.
Allgemeine Musikzeitung. Untitled article. February 23, 1912.
"Amusements: Miss Margulies' Concert." *New York Times*, February 24, 1884.
"Amusements: Miss Margulies' Concert." *New York Times*, March 28, 1884.

"Berliner Konzert." *Vossische Zeitung*, December 14, 1909.
"Composers form Guild to Bring New Works to Public Hearing." *Musical America* 34:13, July 23, 1921.
"Concerts at Venice," *New York Times*, June 21, 1925.
"Das Resultat unseres Preisausschreiberns." *Signale für die musikalische Welt* 49, December 8, 1909.
D. J. "A Guild for American Composers." *Musical Digest*, April 24, 1922.
Downes, Olin. "Music in the Future: Edgard Varèse Attacks Neo-Classicism and Suggests Electronics." *New York Times*, July 25, 1948.
———. "Opera by Luening at Its Premiere: *Evangeline:* Based on Poem by Longfellow Is Presented by Columbia University." *New York Times*, May 6, 1948.
"Ein Konzert in der Worpsweder Kunsthalle: Klavierabend des Pianisten L. T. Grünberg." *Berliner Tageblatt*, Oct. 14, 1909.
"Ein Preisausschreiben." *Signale für die musikalische Welt*, May 31, 1909.
Ericson, Raymond. "Music: A First for Sonata by Luening." *New York Times*, November 20, 1975.
"Ferruccio Benvenuto Busoni." *Musical Times* 65:979. September 1, 1924.
Frankenstein, Alfred. "Varèse, Worker in Intensities." *San Francisco Chronicle*, November 28, 1937.
Haeser, Dr. Untitled review. *Neue Zürcher Zeitung*, n.d. Luening Papers, New York Public Library, Special Collections, Box 48, no. 1.
Jarnach, Philipp. "Über die *Musik mit Mozart.*" *Berliner Philharmonisches Orchester, Spielzeit* 8, February 15, 1942.
Leichtentritt, Hugo. "Philipp Jarnach." *Musikblätter des Anbruch* 5:9, 1923.
———. Untitled article. *Musical Courier*. Berlin. March 11, 1924.
"Les sept jugements d'Edgard Varèse." *Le nouveau Candide*, 238, November 1965.
"Louis Gruenberg and the Flagler Prize." *International Interpreter: The International News Weekly*, April 15, 1922.
"Louis Gruenberg in Piano Recital." *New York Times*, February 15, 1919.
"Merging Local Orchestras: Gruenberg's "Hill of Dreams." *New York Times*. June 19, 1921.
Monson, Karen. "Still Has Lived through Musical Changes." *Los Angeles Herald-Examiner*, January 24, 1970.
"Music News and Notes: Orchestra Programs." *New York Times*, March 27, 1921.
"New Musical Club of Society Women." *New York Times*, November 30, 1913.
Oteri, Frank J. "Charles Wuorinen: Art and Entertainment." *NewMusicBox*, July 1, 2007.
G. P. "Klavier-Abend in Wordswede." *Bremer Tageblatt*, January 26, 1910.
Paulson, Manfred. Untitled article. *Allgemeine Musikzeitung* 49:19, May 12, 1922.
"Philipp Jarnach: Quartett Op. 16." *Allgemeine Musikzeitung* 51:22/23, June 6, 1924.
Schwers, Paul. "Aus dem Berliner Musikleben." *Allgemeine Musikzeitung* 62:42, October 18, 1935.
Stege, Fritz. "Die Berliner Kunstwochen." *Zeitschrift für Musik*, July 1935.
"String Quartet, Op. 4." *London Musical Times*, April 1924.

Tommasini, Anthony. "Renaissance and Medieval Hues in a Modernist Work." *New York Times*, January 26, 2009.
"Theater und Musik." *Vossische Zeitung*, December 17, 1910.
Ussher, Bruno David. "Gruenberg Radio Opera." *New York Times*, May 2, 1937.
Varèse, Edgard. "Performer's Choices—A Symposium." *Listen*, June 1946.
———. "The Music of Tomorrow." *Evening News*, June 14, 1924.
———. Untitled article. *Evening Bulletin*, Philadelphia, April 12, 1926.
"Varèse Envisions 'Space' Symphonies." *New York Times*, December 6, 1936.
Weissmann, Adolf. Untitled review. *Die Musik*. Berlin, April 1924.
Würz, Richard. Untitled review. *Neue Musikzeitung* September 1919.
"Zehn Preiskompositionen für Klavier die beim Preisausschreiben der 'Signale' von den Preisrichtern Ferruccio Busoni, Gustav Hollaender, Philipp Scharwenka aus den eingesandten 874 Kompositionen mit zehn Preisen im Gesamtsbetrage von 2000 Mark ausgezeichnet worden sind." *Signale für die musikalische Welt*, 1910. Accessed April 22, 2016.

PUBLISHED SCORES

Bach, J. S. *Das wohltemperierte Klavier*. Vol. 2. Edited by Ferruccio Busoni. Leipzig: Breitkopf und Härtel, 1916.
Busoni, Ferruccio. *Berceuse élégiaque: Des Mannes Wiegenlied am Sarge seiner Mutter*, BV 252. Leipzig: Breitkopf und Härtel, 1910.
———. Zweiter Orchester-Suite ["Geharnischte-Suite"], BV 242. Leipzig: Breitkopf und Härtel, 1905.
Corigliano, John. *The Ghosts of Versailles: A Grand Opera Buffa in Two Acts*. New York: G. Schirmer, 2010.
Gruenberg, Louis. *Five Impressions for Piano*, op. 5. N.p.: Composer's Music Corporation, 1923.
———. Suite for Violin and Piano, op. 3. New York: G. Schirmer, 1914.
———. *The Witch of Brocken*. N.p.: C. C. Birchard & Co., 1931.
Jarnach, Philipp. Sonate in Mi Majeur for Violin and Piano. Paris: Durand and Co., 1915.
———. Sonatine for Flute and Piano, op. 12. Zurich: A. Biolley, 1920
Luening, Otto. *Evangeline: Opera in 3 Acts*. Piano-Vocal Score. New York: C. F. Peters, n.d.
Sibelius, Jean. *Jean Sibelius: Complete Works*. The National Library of Finland and the Sibelius Society of Finland. 28 vols. Leipzig: Breitkopf und Härtel, 1996–Present.
Varèse, Edgard. *Déserts*. New York: Ricordi, 1959.
Wuorinen, Charles. *Josquiniana: Six Secular Works of Josquin des Prez in 3, 4, and 5 Voices*. New York: Peters, 2001.
———. *The Magic Art: An Instrumental Masque Drawn from the Works of Henry Purcell*. New York: C. F. Peters, n.d.
———. *Times's Encomium*. N.p.: Peter's, 1969.
———. *New York Notes*. New York: C. F. Peters, 1998.

PUBLISHED PRIMARY SOURCES BY BUSONI

Busoni, Ferruccio. *Briefe Busonis an Hans Huber,* edited by Edgar Refardt. Zurich: Hug and Co., 1939.

———. *Briefe an Henri, Katharina und Egon Petri.* Edited by Martina Weindel. Taschenbücher zur Musikwissenschaft. Edited by Richard Schaal. Wilhelmshaven: Florian Noetzel, 1999.

———. *Die Götterbraut: Heroisch-heiteres Sagenspiel in 3 Bildern von Ferruccio Busoni.* http://www.rodoni.ch/busoni/Faust/gotterbraut.html. Accessed April 17, 2013.

———. *The Essence of Music and Other Papers* [1922]. Translated by Rosamund Ley. London: Salisbury Square, 1957.

———. *Ferruccio Busoni: Selected Letters,* Translated and edited by Antony Beaumont. New York: Columbia University Press, 1987.

———. *Ferruccio Busoni im Briefwechsel mit seinem Verlag Breitkopf und Härtel.* Edited by Eva Hanau. 2 vols. Busoni-Editionen. Edited by Albrecht Riethmüller. Wiesbaden: Breitkopf und Härtel, 2012.

———. *Maximen und Aphorismen.* Edited by Martina Weindel. Taschenbücher zur Musikwissenschaft 147. Wilhelmshaven: Florian Noetzel Verlag, 2004.

———. "Routine." *Pan* 1:20 (August 16, 1911), 654–655.

———. "Schönberg Matinée." *Pan* 2 (February 1, 1912), 327–330.

———. *Sketch of a New Esthetic of Music* [1907]. Translated by Dr. Th. Baker. New York: Schirmer, 1911.

———. "Unsentimentaler Rückblick." *Die Gartenlaube* 35 (August 28, 1924), 688–689.

———. *Von der Einheit der Musik: Von Dritteltönen und junger Klassizität von Bühnen und Bauten und anschliessenden Bezirken.* Edited by Martina Weindel. Quellenkataloge zur Musikgeschichte. Edited by Richard Schaal. Vol. 36. Wilhelmshaven: Florian Noetzel Verlag, 2006.

———. *Wesen und Einheit der Musik.* Edited by Joachim Herrmann. Berlin: Max Hesses Verlag, 1956.

Weindel, Martina, ed. "Busonis 'Berlin Orchesterabende:' Eine Nachlese Unveröffentlichter Briefe von Schönberg, Mahler, Bartók und Sibelius." *Schweizer Jahrbuch für Musikwissenschaft* 23 (2003).

PUBLISHED PRIMARY SOURCES BY OTHER AUTHORS AND MEMOIRS BY BUSONI PUPILS, GRAND PUPILS, ACQUAINTANCES, CONTEMPORARIES, AND FOLLOWERS

Ades, Dawn, ed. *The Dada Reader.* Chicago: University of Chicago Press, 2006.

Balough, Teresa, comp. *Comrades in Art: The Correspondence of Ronald Stevenson and Percy Grainger, 1957–1961.* Musicians in Letters, no. 2. Musicians on Music, no. 8. N.p.: Toccata Press, 2010.

Bauer, Marion, and Claire R. Reis. "Twenty Five Years with the League of Composers." *Musical Quarterly* 34:1 (January 1948), 1–14.

Bitter, Christof. ed., *Intervall und Zeit: Bernard Alois Zimmermann Aufsatze und Schriften zum Werk.* Mainz: B. Schott's Sohne, 1974.

Boretz, Benjamin. "Conversation with Charles Wuorinen." *Contemporary Music Newsletter* 3:7–8 (1969), 5.
Buffet, Gabrielle. "Cinematography [1917]." Translated by Michelle Owoo. In *The Dada Reader*, edited by Dawn Ades, 111–113. Chicago: University of Chicago Press, 2006.
———. "Musique d'aujourd'hui. [1912–1914]." In *Les Soirées de Paris*. Vol. 2, Slatkine Reprints. Geneva: n.p., 1971.
———. *Rencontres avec Picabia, Apollinaire, Cravan, Duchamp, Arp, Calder*. Paris: Belfond, 1977.
Cadieu, Martine, and Andrè Jolivet. "A Conversation with Andrè Jolivet." *Tempo* 59 (Autumn 1961), 2–4.
Cage, John, and Morton Feldman. *Radio Happenings: Conversations—Gesprache Edition Musik-Texte I*. Edited by Gisela Gronemeyer and Reinhard Oehlschlagel. Cologne: Musiktexte, 1993.
Carter, Elliott, and Jonathan W. Bernhard. "An Interview with Elliott Carter." *Perspectives of New Music* 28:2 (Summer 1990), 180–214.
Cottlow, Augusta. "My Years with Busoni." *Musical Observer* 24:6 (June 1925), 11/ 28.
Dallapiccola, Luigi. "In Memoriam: Edgard Varèse (1883–1965): Encounters with Edgard Varèse." *Perspectives of New Music* 4:2 (Spring-Summer 1966), 1–13.
Daude, Dr. *Die Königl. Friedrich-Wilhelms-Universität zu Berlin: Systematische Zusammenstellung der für dieselbe bestehenden gesetzlichen statutarischen und reglementarischen Bestimmungen*. Berlin: H.B. Müller, 1887.
Davies, Peter Maxwell. "Composer's Notes." http://www.boosey.com/cr/music/Peter-Maxwell-Davies-Symphony-No-5/3656. Accessed November 2, 2015.
Dent, Edward. *Ferruccio Busoni: A Biography* [1933]. London: Eulenberg Books, 1974.
Dreyfus, Kay, ed. *The Farthest North of Humanness: Letters of Percy Grainger, 1901–1914*. South Melbourne: MMB Music, 1985.
Duffie, Bruce. "Interview with John Corigliano." http://www.bruceduffie.com/corigliano.html. Accessed October 24, 2013.
Feldman, Morton. *Morton Feldman Says: Selected Interviews and Lectures 1964–1987*. Edited by Chris Villars. London: Hyphen Press, n.d.
Flechtner, Christine. "Die Schriften von Edgard Varèse (1883–1965)." PhD diss., Universität Freiburg, 1983.
Galston, Gottfried. *Kalendarnotizen über Ferruccio Busoni*. Edited by Martina Weindel. Taschenbücher zur Musikwissenschaft. Edited by Richard Schaal, vol. 144. Wilhelmshaven: Florian Noetzel, 2000.
Gillespie, Don. "Chou Wen-Chung on Varèse: An Interview." *American Music* 27:4 (Winter 2009), 441–460.
Goss, Glenda Dawn, ed. *Jean Sibelius: The Hämeenlinna Letters: Scenes from a Musical Life 1874–1895*. Helsinki: Schildts, 1997.
Gruenberg, Louis. "Vom Jazz und ander Dingen; Ruckblick und Ausblick." *25 Jahre neue Musik, Jahrbuch der 1926 Universal Edition*. Vienna: Universal Edition, 1926.
Guerrini, Guido. *Ferruccio Busoni: La vita, la figura, l'opera*. Firenze: Casa Editrice Monsalvato, 1944.
Hinton, Alistair. *The Sorabji Archive*. http://www.sorabji-archive.co.uk/hinton/hinton_brochure.pdf. Accessed March 19, 2016.

Hoffmann, E.T.A. *Signor Formica* [1820]. Adelaide: University of Adelaide, 2012. http://ebooks.adelaide.edu.au/h/hoffmann/eta/formica/complete.html. Accessed April 14, 2013.

Jarnach, Philipp. *La Musica Contemporanea in Europa: Saggi Critici di G.M. Gatti, Henry Pruniers, Edward J. Dent, Philipp Jarnach, Boris de Schloezer, Guido Pannain*. Milano: Bottega di Poesia, 1925.

———. *Schriften zur Musik*. Edited by Norbert Jers. Beiträge zur Rheinischen Musikgeschichte 153. Berlin: Merseburger, 1994.

———. "Thematische Analyse." *Neue Musikzeitung* 42:20 (July 21, 1921), 317.

Jolivet, André. "La Musique: plaid pour le vif." *La nouvelle Saison* 2/7 (July 1939), 400–406.

———. "Reponse un enquete." *Counterpoints* 1 (1946).

Jolivet, Hilda. *Varèse, Musiciens de Notre Temps*. Paris: Hachette Litterature 1973.

Julius, Ruth. "Edgard Varèse: An Oral History Project. *Current Musicology* (1978), 38–49.

Kraft, William. "Conversation with Bruce Duffie." http://www.bruceduffie.com/wm-kraft.html. Accessed August 12, 2013.

Krenek, Ernst. "Busoni Then and Now." *Modern Music* 19:2 (January-February 1942), 88–91.

Kuczynski, Paul, *Erlebnisse und Gedanken. Dichtungen zu Musikwerken*. Berlin: Concordia Deutsche Verlags-Anstalt, 1898.

Leichtentritt, Hugo. *Ferruccio Busoni*. Leipzig: Breitkopf und Härtel, 1916.

Luening, Otto. "Conversation with Theresa Bowers." Bennington Summer School of the Dance Project. New York: n.p., 1979.

———. "Essay by Otto Luening." In *1952, Electronic Tape Music: The First Compositions*, by Otto Luening and Vladimir Ussachevsky. New York: Highgate Press, 1977.

———. Interview with Charles Amirkhanian. Other Minds Audio Archive. http://archive.org/details/AM_1981_03_31. Accessed August 9, 2013.

———. *The Odyssey of an American Composer: The Autobiography of Otto Luening*. New York: Charles Scribner's Sons, 1980.

———. "Some Random Remarks about Electronic Music." *Journal of Music Theory* 8:1 (Spring 1964), 93–94.

———. Sonata for Piano in Memoriam Ferruccio Busoni (program notes). http://www.newworldrecords.org/uploads/fileXuPcA.pdf. Accessed August 10, 2013.

———. Suite for Flute solo no. 3 (liner notes). In *Flute Possibilities*. Harvey Sollberger, Flute. Composers Recordings CRI 400 (1979).

———. "Varèse and the Schola Cantorum, Busoni and New York." *Contemporary Music Review* 23:1 (March 2004), 13–16.

———, and Bruce Duffie. *Composer Otto Luening: A Conversation with Bruce Duffie*. http://www.kcstudio.com/luening3.html. Accessed August 6, 2013.

———, and Tim Page. *From the Archives: American Mavericks: Otto Luening Plugs America into Electronic Music (Otto Luening Speaks with Host Tim Page on Meet the Composer from 1985)*. http://www.wqxr.org/#!/programs/from-archives-mavericks/2012/mar/30/. Accessed August 6, 2013.

———, and Vladimir Ussachevsky. *1952 Electronic Tape Music: The First Compositions.* New York: Highgate Press, 1977.

Manzoni, Giacomo. *Il suono organizzato: scritti sulla musica.* Milan: Ricordi, 1985.

Motte-Haber, Helga de la, and Klaus Angermann, eds. *Edgard Varèse: Dokumente zu Leben und Werk.* Frankfurt am Main: Peter Lang, 1990.

Partch, Harry. *Genesis of a Music.* 2nd ed. New York: Da Capo Press, 1974.

Paul, Adolf. *Profiler: minnen av stora personligheter.* N.p.: Fahlcrantz & Co., 1937.

Perl, Max. Antiquariat, *Bibliothek Ferruccio Busoni: Werke der Weltliteratur in schönen Gesamtausgaben und Erstdrucken; Illustrierte Bücher aller Jahrhunderte,* Auction 96. March 30–31, 1925. Berlin: Max Perl, 1925.

Petri, Egon. "How Ferruccio Busoni Taught: An Interview with the Distinguished Dutch Pianist." Interview by Friede F. Rothe. *Etude* 58 (October 1940), 637–710.

Pfitzner, Hans. *Gesammelte Schriften,* vol. 1. Augsburg: B. Filser G.M.B.H., 1929.

Rae, Caroline. "Jolivet on Jolivet: An Interview with the Composer's Daughter." *Musical Times* (Spring 2006), 5–22.

Riemann, Hugo. *Hugo Riemann's Musik-Lexicon.* 9th ed. Edited by Alfred Einstein. Berlin: Max Hesses Verlag, 1919.

Schoen, Ernst. "Die Rundfunkkompsitionen für Baden-Baden." *Melos Jahrbuch für zeitgenössische Musik* 8 (1929), 313–315.

———. "Musikalische Unterhaltung durch Rundfunk." *Anbruch* 11:3 (1929), 128–129.

Schoenberg, Arnold. *Berliner Tagebuch.* N.p.: Propyläen Verlag, n.d.

———. *Entwurf einer neuen Aesthetik der Tonkunst* by Ferruccio Busoni (annotated version) (1916). Frankfurt: Insel, 1974.

———. *The Musical Idea and the Logic, Technique and Art of Its Presentation.* Translated and edited by Patricia Carpenter and Severine Neff. New York: Columbia University Press, 1995.

———. *Style and Idea: Selected Writings of Arnold Schoenberg.* Edited by Leonard Stein. Translated by Leo Black. New York: St. Martin's, 1975.

———. *Theory of Harmony.* 3rd ed. Translated by Roy E. Carter. 1922. Berkeley: University of California Press, 1983.

Schuller, Gunther. "Conversation with Varèse." *Perspectives of New Music* 3:2 (1965), 32–37.

Selden-Goth, Gisella. *Ferruccio Busoni: Der Versuch eines Porträts* (1922). Firenze: Leo S. Olschki, 1964.

Sibelius, Aino, and Jean Sibelius. *Sydämen aamu: Aino Järnefeltin ja Jean Sibeliuksen kihlausajan kirjeitä.* Edited by Suvisirkku Talas. Suomalaisen Kirjallisuuden Seuran toimituksia, no. 821. Helsinki: Suomalaisen Kirjallisuuden Seura, 2001.

———. *Syysilta: Aino ja Jean Sibeliuksen kirjeenvaihtoa, 1905–1931.* Edited by Suvisirkku Talas. Suomalaisen Kirjallisuuden Seuran toimituksia, no. 1133. Helsinki: Suomalaisen Kirjallisuuden Seura, 2007.

———. *Tulen synty: Aino ja Jean Sibeliuksen kirjeenvaihtoa 1892–1904.* Edited by Suvisirkku Talas. Suomalaisen Kirjallisuuden Seuran toimituksia, no. 910. Helsinki: Suomalaisen Kirjallisuuden Seura, 2003.

Sibelius, Jean. *Dagbok: 1909–1944.* Edited by |FCO|HyperlinkFabian Dahlström-Skrifter utgivna av Svenska litteratursällskapet i Finland, no. 681. Helsingfors: Svenska litteratursällskapet i Finland, 2005.

———, and Axel Carpelan. *Högtärade Maestro!, högtärade Herr Baron!: Korrespondensen mellan Axel Carpelan och Jean Sibelius 1900–1919*. Edited by Fabian Dahlström. Skrifter utgivna av Svenska litteratursällskapet i Finland, no. 737. Helsingfors: Svenska litteratursällskapet i Finland. Stockholm: Atlantis, 2010.

———, and Rosa Newmarch. *The Correspondence of Jean Sibelius and Rosa Newmarch*. Edited by Phillip Ross Bullock. Rochester: Boydell Press, 2011.

Spencer, Jon Michael, ed. *The William Grant Still Reader: Essays on American Music*, vol. 6, no. 2. Durham, NC: Duke University Press, 1992.

Steuermann, Eduard. *The Not Quite Innocent Bystander*. Edited by Clara Steuermann, David Portner, and Gunther Schuller. Translated by Richard Cantwell and Charles Messner. Lincoln: University of Nebraska Press, 1989.

Thomson, Virgil. "'Greatest Music Teacher' at 75." *Music Educator's Journal* 49:1 (September-October 1962), 42–44.

Varèse, Edgard. *Écrits*. Edited by Louise Hirbour and Christiane Leaud-Lacroix. Paris: C. Bourgois, 1983.

———. *Il Suono organizzato: scritti sulla musica*. Milano: Ricordi, 1985.

———. "Performer's Choices—A Symposium." *Listen* (June 1946), 3.

———, and Andrè Jolivet. *Correspondence: 1931–1965*. Edited by Christine Jolivet-Erlih. Geneva: Contrechamps, 2002.

———, and Chou Wen-Chung. "The Liberation of Sound." *Perspectives of New Music* 5:1 (Autumn/Winter 1966), 11–12.

Varèse, Louise. *Varèse: A Looking-Glass Diary, vol. 1: 1883–1928*. New York: W. W. Norton and Co., 1972.

Varga, Balint. *Conversations with Xenakis*. London: Faber and Faber, 1996.

Vogel, Wladimir. *Schriften und Aufzeichnungen über Musik: "Innerhalb—Ausserhalb."* Edited by Walter Labhart. Zurich: Atlantis, 1977.

Wen-Chung, Chou. *"And the Fallen Petals."* http://www.chouwenchung.org. Accessed October 31, 2013.

———. "Independent Is the Key Word." *World New Music Magazine* 4 (1994), 35.

———. "Varèse: Who Is He?" *Grand Street: Crossing the Line*, no. 63 (Winter 1998), 106.

Wuorinen, Charles. "Bamboula Squared." http://www.charleswuorinen.com/audio.php. Accessed December 5, 2013.

———. "The Outlook for Young Composers." *Perspectives of New Music* 1:2 (Spring/Summer 1963), 55–56.

Zimmermann, Bernd Alois. *"Du und Ich und Ich und die Welt": Dokumente aus den Jahren 1940 bis 1950*. Archive zu Musik des 20. Jahrhunderts, Band 4. Berlin: Stiftung Archiv der Akademie der Künste, 1998.

SECONDARY SOURCES

Adamo, Mark. *John Corigliano: A Monograph*. Todmorden, Lancs: Arc Music, 2000.

Antonini, Andrea. "Busoni and Varèse." http://www.rodoni.ch/busoni/telharmonium.html. Accessed October 8, 2012.

Appleton, Jon H., and Ronald C. Perera. *The Development and Practice of Electronic Music*. Englewood Cliffs, NJ: Prentice-Hall, 1975.

Association des amis d'André Jolivet. *André Jolivet: Guide des Oeuvres*. Paris: Association des amis d'es Andre Jolivet, 2006.
Beaumont, Antony. *Busoni the Composer*. Bloomington: Indiana University Press, 1985.
———. "Busoni's 'Doctor Faust': A Reconstruction and Its Problems." *Musical Times* 127:1718 (April 1986), 196–199.
———. "Sibelius and Busoni." *Proceedings from the First International Jean Sibelius Conference*. Helsinki: Sibelius Academy, 1995.
Beeson, Jack. "Otto Luening," *Bulletin of the American Composers Alliance* 3:3 (1954), 4.
Berliner Actionair, ed. *Ein Nachschlagebuch für Banquiers und Capitalisten: 1885–1886*. Berlin: Ernst Siegfried Mittler und Sohn, 1885.
Berlioz, Hector. *Grand traité d'instrumentation et d'orchestration modernes*. Paris: Schonenberger, c. 1844.
Beyer, Anders, and Jean Christiensen, eds. *Voice of Music: Conversations with Composers of Our Time*. Burlington, VT: Ashgate, 2000.
Boatwright, Howard. "Paul Hindemith as Teacher." *Musical Quarterly* 50:3 (July 1964).
Borio, Gianmario, Mauro Casadei, and Turroni Monti, eds. *Ferruccio Busoni e la sua scuola*. Nuovi percorsi musicali 3. Lucca: Una cosa rara, 1999.
Brent-Smith, A. "Ferruccio Busoni." *Musical Times* 1 (February 1934), 113–116.
Burbank, Richard D. *Charles Wuorinen: A Bio-Bibliography*. Bio-bibliographies in Music, no. 49. Westport, CT: Greenwood Press, 1994.
Burk, John N. "A Composer of the Future." *Harvard Musical Review* 3:6 (March 1915).
Burkholder, J. Peter, Donald J. Grout, and Claude V. Palisca. *A History of Western Music*. 8th ed. New York: W. W. Norton and Co., 2010.
Burnham, Scott G. *Musical Form in the Age of Beethoven: Selected Writings on the Theory and Method*. Cambridge: Cambridge University Press, 1997.
Campbell, Don G. *Master Teacher: Nadia Boulanger*. Washington, DC: Pastoral Press, 1984.
Cantfield, Susan. "Review of *The Witch of Brocken*." *Music Supervisor's Journal* 18:5 (May 1932), 79.
Chang, Peter M. *Chou Wen-Chung: The Life and Work of a Contemporary Chinese-Born American Composer*. Composers of North America, no. 25. Lanham, MD: Scarecrow Press, 2006.
Chisholm, Alastair. *Bernard van Dieren: An Introduction*. London: Thames Publishing, 1984.
Clark, Edward. *The Forest's Mighty God*. N.p.: British Sibelius Society, 1997.
Clarkson, Austin. "Varèses *Déserts*, Wolpes Symphony und Busonischer Modernismus." Translated by Caroline Kliemt and Thomas Phelps. *Stefan Wolpe II* 152/153 (2011), 136–157.
———. "Wolpe, Varèse, and the Busoni Effect." *Contemporary Music Review* 27:2/3 (April/June 2008), 361–381.
Collins, Nick, and Julio d'Escriván, eds. *The Cambridge Companion to Electronic Music*. Cambridge: Cambridge University Press, 2007.
Conrad, Brigid F. "The Sources of Jolivet's Musical Language and His Relationship with Varèse." PhD diss., City University of New York, 1994.

Couling, Della. *Ferruccio Busoni: A Musical Ishmael*. Lanham, MD: Scarecrow Press, 2005.

Crispin, Judith Michelle. *The Esoteric Musical Tradition of Ferruccio Busoni and Its Reinvigoration in the Music of Larry Sitsky: The Operas Doktor Faust and the Golem*. Preface by Larry Sitsky. Lewiston, ME: Edwin Mellen Press, 2007.

Dahlhaus, Carl. *Die Musik des 19. Jahrhunderts: Mit 75 Notenbeispielen, 91 Abbildungen und 2 Farbtafeln*. Akademische Verlagsgesellschaft Athenaion. Wiesbaden: Laaber Verlag, 1980.

———, ed. *Festschrift für eine Verleger Ludwig Strecker zum 90. Geburtstag*. Mainz: B. Schott's Sohne, 1973.

Dahlström, Fabian. *Jean Sibelius: Thematisch-bibliographisches Verzeichnis seiner Werke*. Wiesbaden: Breitkopf und Härtel, 2003.

Davis, Richard Beattie. "Belyayev, Mitrofan Petrovich." *Grove Music Online*. Oxford Music Online. Oxford University Press. http://www.oxfordmusiconline.com/subscriber/article/grove/music/02622. Accessed January 7, 2013.

De Jong, Diederik. "Madetoja: Comedy Overture, Symphony 3. Okon Fuoko Suite and Ostrobothnians Suite." *American Record Guide* (January/February 1993), 114.

Dieren, Bernard van. *Down among the Dead Men and Other Essays*. London: Oxford University Press, 1935.

Dufallo, Richard. *Trackings: Composers Speak with Richard Dufallo*. New York: Oxford University Press, 1989.

Dümling, Albrecht. "What Is Internal Exile in Music?" http://orelfoundation.org/index.php/journal/journalArticle/what_is_internal_exile_in_music/#fn19. Accessed February 14, 2014.

Ekman, Karl. *Jean Sibelius: His Life and Personality*. Translated by Edward Birse. London: A. A. Knopf, 1938.

Epstein, Joseph. *Masters: Portraits of Great Teachers*. New York: Basic Books, 1981.

Erickson, Robert. *Sound Structure in Music*. Berkeley: University of California Press, 1975.

Ewen, David. *American Composers Today*. New York: H. W. Wilson, 1949.

Feliciano, Francisco F. *Four Asian Contemporary Composers: The Influence of Tradition in Their Works*. Quezon City: New Day Publishers, 1983.

Fleet, Paul. *Ferruccio Busoni: A Phenomenological Approach to His Music and Aesthetics*. Cologne: Lambert Academic Publishing, 2009.

Fontaine, Susanne. *Busonis "Doktor Faust" und die Ästhetik des Wunderbaren*. Kassel: Bärenreiter, 1998.

Freeman, Robin. Review of "The Music of Louis Gruenberg." *Tempo* 180 (March 1992), 61.

———. "Three 'Years', and Louis Gruenberg." *Tempo* 180 (March 1992), 58–60.

Frisch, Walter. "Music and Jugendstil." *Critical Inquiry* 17:1 (Autumn 1990), 138–161.

Fux, Johann Joseph. *Gradus ad Parnassum: sive Manuductio ad compositionem musicæ regularem, methodo novâ ac certâ, nondum antè tam exacto ordine in lucem edita*. Vienna: Joannis Petri van Ghelen, 1725.

Gauss, Rebecca B. "O'Neill, Gruenberg and *The Emperor Jones*." *Eugene O'Neill Review* 18:1/2 (Spring/Fall 1994), 38–44.

Glahn, Denise von. *The Sounds of Place: Music and the American Cultural Landscape.* Boston: Northeastern University Press, 2003.
Goss, Glenda Dawn. *Jean Sibelius and Olin Downes: Music, Friendship, Criticism.* Boston: Northeastern University Press, 1995.
———. *Sibelius: A Composer's Life and the Awakening of Finland.* Chicago: University of Chicago Press, 2009.
———. "Sibelius Letters in the Helsinki University Library." *Fontes artis Musicae* 52:3 (July-September 2005), 145–156.
Gray, Cecil. *Sibelius.* London: Oxford University Press, 1931.
Griffiths, Paul. *Peter Maxwell Davies.* London: Robson House, 1982.
Grimes, Ev. "Interview: Education." In *Writings on Glass: Essays, Interviews, Criticism.* Edited by Richard Kostelanetz and Robert Flemming. New York: Schirmer Books, 1997.
Grimley, Daniel, ed. *The Cambridge Companion to Sibelius.* Cambridge: Cambridge University Press, 2004.
———. *Jean Sibelius and His World.* Princeton, NJ: Princeton University Press, 2011.
Grosch, Nils. "Das 'Volksliederbuch für die Jugend' Volkslied und Moderne in der Weimarer Republik." *Lied und populäre Kultur/Song and Popular Culture* 48 (2003), 207–239.
Gut, Serge. *Le Groupe Jeune France.* Paris: Honore Champion, 1977.
Hartsock, Ralph. *Otto Luening: A Bio-Bibliography.* Bio-Bibliographies in Music, no. 35. Edited by Donald L. Hixon. New York: Greenwood Press, 1991.
Häusler, Josef. *Spiegel der Neuen Musik: Donaueschingen.* Stuttgart: J. B. Metzler, 1996.
Heinonen, Eero. "Introduction." Translated by Jaakko Mäntyjärvi. In Sibelius, *Florestan.* N.p.: Warner/Chappell Music, 2001.
Helm, Everett. "Current Chronicle." *Musical Quarterly* 36:4 (October 1950), 602.
Hentschel, Frank. "Ferruccio Busonis *Doktor Faust:* Eine 'Oper, die keine Oper' ist." *Archiv für Musikwissenschaft* 62:4 (2005), 303–326.
Hepokoski, James. *Sibelius: Symphony no. 5.* Cambridge Music Handbooks. Edited by Julian Rushton. Cambridge: Cambridge University Press, 1993.
Herbst-Köln, Kurt. "Philipp Jarnach." *Die Music* 23 (1930–1931), 86–92.
Hewett, Ivan, et al. *Iannis Xenakis: Composer, Architect, Visionary.* N.p.: Fleet Center at RISD, n.d.
Hinton, Stephen. *Weill's Musical Theater: Stages of Reform.* Berkeley: University of California Press, 2012.
Holländer, Hans. *Musik und Jugendstil.* Zurich: Atlantis-Verlag, 1975.
Holmes, Thom. *Electronic and Experimental Music: Technology, Music, and Culture.* 3rd ed. New York: Routledge, 2008.
Hong, Barbara. "The Friends of Lesko, the Dog: Sibelius, Busoni, Armas, and Eero Järnefelt." In *Sibelius in the Old and New World: Aspects of His Music, Its Interpretation, and Reception.* Edited by Timothy L. Jackson, Veijo Murtomäki, and Timo Virtanen. Interdisziplinäre Studien zur Musik, edited by Tomi Mäkelä and Tobias R. Klein, vol. 6. Frankfurt am Main: Peter Lang, 2010.
Howell, Tim. *Progressive Techniques in the Symphonies and Tone Poems.* New York: Garland, 1989.

Hugill, Andrew. "The Origins of Electronic Music." In *The Cambridge Companion to Electronic Music*, edited by Nick Collins and Julio d'Escriván. Cambridge: Cambridge University Press, 2007.

Ikonen, Lauri. *Säveltaiteellis-Kirjallinen Julkaisu: 1925, Omistettu Suomen Säveltaiteen Suurelle Mestarille, Professori Jean Sibeliukselle Hänen 60-vuotispäiväkseen*. Helsinki: Suomen musiikkilehti, 1925.

Jackson, Timothy L., Veijo Murtomäki, and Timo Virtanen, eds. *Sibelius in the Old and New World: Aspects of His Music, Its Interpretation, and Reception*. Interdisziplinäre Studien zur Musik, edited by Tomi Mäkelä and Tobias R. Klein, vol. 6. Frankfurt am Main: Peter Lang, 2010.

"Jean Sibelius." http://www.sibelius.fi/english/omin_sanoin/index.htm. Accessed December 29, 2012.

Jelmoli, Hans. *Ferruccio Busonis Zürcherjahre*. Zürich: Art Institut Drell Füssli, 1929.

Johnson, Harold E. *Jean Sibelius*. New York: Faber and Faber, 1959.

Karvonen, Arvi. *Sibelius-Akatemia 75 vuotta: Helsingin Musiikkiopisto 1882–1924, Helsingin Konservatorio 1924–1939. Sibelius-Akatemia*. Helsinki: Kustannusakeyhtiö Otava, 1957.

Kayas, Lucie. *Andrè Jolivet*. N.p.: Fayard, 2005.

Keislar, Douglas. "History and Principles of Microtonal Keyboard Design." Stanford University, Center for Computer Research in Music and Acoustics (April 1988), 4. https://ccrma.stanford.edu/STANM/stanms/stanm45/stanm45.pdf. Accessed April 23, 2014.

Keller, Johanna. "Trying to Put a Proper End to 'Doktor Faust.'" *New York Times*, January 7, 2001, 40.

Kelly, Barbara L., ed. *French Music, Culture, and National Identity 1870–1939*. Eastman Studies in Music, edited by Ralph P. Locke. Rochester: University of Rochester Press, 2008.

Kendall, Alan. *The Tender Tyrant: Nadia Boulanger, A Life Devoted to Music*. London: Macdonald and Jane's, 1976.

Kliemann, Helga. *Die Novembergruppe*. Berlin: Gebr. Mann Verlag, 1969.

Knyt, Erinn. "Ferruccio Busoni and the Absolute in Music: Form, Nature and Idee." *Journal of the Royal Musical Association* 137:1 (May 2012), 35–69.

———. "Ferruccio Busoni and the New England Conservatory: Piano Pedagogue in the Making." *American Music* 31:3 (Fall 2013), 277–313.

———. "Ferruccio Busoni and the Ontology of the Musical Work: Permutations and Possibilities." PhD diss., Stanford University, 2010.

———. "'How I Compose': Ferruccio Busoni's Views about Invention, Quotation, and the Compositional Process." *Journal of Musicology* 27:2 (Spring 2010).

Konold, Wulf. *Bernd Alois Zimmermann: Der Komponist und sein Werk*. Köln: Dumont, 1986.

———, ed. *Bernd Alois Zimmermann: Dokumente und Interpretationen*. Köln: Wien- and Verlag, n.d.

Krämer, Ulrich. *Alban Berg als Schüler Arnold Schönbergs: Quellenstudien und Analysen zum Frühwerk*. Alban Berg Studien, vol. 4. Edited by Rudolf Stephan. Vienna: Universal Edition, 1996.

Krellmann, Hanspeter. *Studien zu den Bearbeitungen Ferruccio Busonis*. Regensburg: Gustav Bosse Verlag, 1966.

Kunz, Andreas. *Civil Servants and the Politics of Inflation in Germany, 1914–1924*. New York: De Gruyter, 1986.

Kyr, Robert. *Between the Mind and the Ear: Finding the Perfect Balance*. Boston: League-ISCM, 1990.

Lagus, Hugo. "Några Musikminnen." *Finsk Tidskrift* 118 (1935), 39–48.

Lai, Eric C. *The Music of Chou Wen-Chung*. Burlington VT: Ashgate, 2009.

Lappalainen, Seija, and Erkki Salmenhaara. *Leevi Madetojan Teokset*. Helsinki: Suomen Säveltäjät, 1987.

Laquai, Clara. *Kultur und Gesellschaft Seit der Jugendzeit: Musiker-Memoiren von Reinhold und Clara Laquai*. Zurich: Kreisverlag, 1979.

Ledoux, Charles. *From the Philosophical to the Practical: An Imaginary Proposition Concerning the Music of Tristan Murail*. Translated by Joshua Fineberg. *Contemporary Music Review* 19:3 (2000), 41–65.

Legge, Walter. "Conversations with Sibelius." *Musical Times* 76:1105 (March 1935), 218–220.

Lelong, Guy, and Gérard Grisey. *Écrits, ou, L'invention de la musique spectrale edition*. N.p.: Repercussions, 2008.

Lembke, Hans H. *Die Schwarzen Schafe bei den Gradenwitz und Kuczynski: Zwei Berliner Familien im 19. Und 20. Jahrhundert*. Berlin: Verlagsgruppe Dr. Wolfgang Weist, 2008.

Levas, Santeri. *Sibelius: A Personal Portrait*. Translated by Percy M. Young. Lewisburg, PA: Bucknell University Press, 1973.

Levitz, Tamara. "Ferruccio Busoni and Hhis European Circle in Berlin in the Early Weimar Republic." *Revista de Musicología* 16:6 (1993), 3705–3721.

———. "Jarnach, Philipp." *Grove Music Online. Oxford Music Online*. Oxford University Press. http://www.oxfordmusiconline.com/subscriber/article/grove/music/14193. Accessed January 15, 2014.

———. "'Junge Klassizität': Zwischen Fortschritt und Reaktion: Ferruccio Busoni, Philipp Jarnach und die Deutsche Weill-Rezeption." In *Kurt Weill-Studien*, edited by Nils Grosch, Joachim Lucchesi, and Jürgen Schebera. Kurt-Weill Gesellschaft, vol. 1, 9–37. Dessau: M & P, 1996.

———. "Teaching New Classicality: Busoni's Master Class in Composition, 1921–24." PhD diss., University of Rochester, 1993.

———. *Teaching New Classicality: Ferruccio Busoni's Master Class in Composition*. European University Studies, Series 36. Vol. 152. Berlin: Peter Lang, 1996.

Liebert, Tobias, et al. "Ernst Schoen: Biographische Skizze und Nachlass." *Studienkreis Rundfunk und Geschichte Mitteilungen* 2/3 (April-July 1994).

Lobe, J. C. *Lehrbuch der musikalischen Komposition*, 4 vols. Leipzig: Breitkopf und Härtel, 1858–1867.

Lopatnikoff, Nikolai. "Independents in Central Europe." *Modern Music* 8:4 (May-June 1931).

Lott, R. Allen. "'New Music for New Ears': The International Composers' Guild." *Journal of the American Musicological Society* 36:2 (Summer 1983), 266–286.

Louis, Rudolf, and Ludwig Thuille. *Harmonielehre*. 7th ed. Stuttgart: Carl Gruninger, 1920.
Macdonald, Malcolm. *Ronald Stevenson: A Musical Biography*. Edinburgh: National Library of Scotland, 1989.
———. *Varèse: Astronomer in Sound*. London: Kahn and Averill, 2003.
Macpherson, Elizabeth. *The Bennington School of the Dance: A History in Writings and Interviews*. Jefferson, NC: McFarland, 2013.
Mäkelä, Tomi. *Jean Sibelius*. Translated by Steven Lindberg. Woodbridge: Boydell Press, 2007.
———, ed. *Topics, Texts, Tensions: Essays in Music Theory*. Magdeburg: Otto-von Guericke Universität, 1999.
Marx, Adolf Bernhard. *Die Lehre von der musikalischen Komposition, praktisch-theoretisch, zum Selbstunterricht, oder als Leitfaden bei Privatunterweisung und öffentlichen Vorträgen*. Leipzig: Breitkopf und Härtel, 1837.
Matthews, Joseph. "Busoni's Contributions to Piano Pedagogy." PhD diss., Indiana University, 1977.
Matthews, Paul, ed. *Orchestration: An Anthology of Writings*. New York: Routledge, 2006.
Matthis, Olivia. "Edgard Varèse and the Visual Arts." PhD diss., Stanford University, 1992.
McCredie, Andrew, ed. *Art Nouveau and Jugendstil and the Music of the Early 20th Century*. Miscellanea Musicologica. Adelaide Studies in Musicology. Vol. 13. Adelaide: University of Adelaide, 1984.
———, and Marion Rothärmel. "Bernd Alois Zimmermann." *Grove Music Online. Oxford Music Online*. Oxford University Press. http://www.oxfordmusiconline.com/subscriber/article/grove/music/30977. Accessed December 16, 2013.
McCutchan, Ann. *The Muse That Sings: Composers Speak about the Creative Process*. New York: Oxford University Press, 1999.
McGregor, Richard, ed. *Perspectives on Peter Maxwell Davies*. Burlington, VT: Ashgate, 2000.
Messing, Scott. *Neoclassicism in Music: From the Genesis of the Concept through the Schoenberg/Stravinsky Polemic*. Rochester: University of Rochester Press, 1998.
Meyer, Felix, and Heidy Zimmermann, eds. *Edgard Varèse: Composer, Sound Sculptor, Visionary*. Woodbridge: Boydell Press, 2006.
Meyer, Hans. "Eine stilkritische Untersuchung der Werke Ferruccio Busonis aus den Jahren 1880–1890." PhD diss., Universität Graz, 1962.
Morgan, Paula. "Egon F. Kenton." *Grove Music Online. Oxford Music Online*. Oxford University Press. http://www.oxfordmusiconline.com.silk.library.umass.edu/subscriber/article/grove/music/14897?q=egon+kenton&search=quick&pos=1&_start=1#firsthit. Accessed October 24, 2012.
Morgan, Robert P. "'A New Musical Reality': Futurism, Modernism, and 'The Art of Noises.'" *Modernism/Modernity* 1:3 (1994).
———. "Notes on Varèse's Rhythm." In *The New Worlds of Edgard Varèse: A Symposium with Papers by Elliott Carter, Chou Wen-Chung Robert P. Morgan*, edited by Sherman van Solkema. ISAM Monographs, no. 11. Albany: State University of New York Press, 1979.

Moricz, Klára. *Funeral Games in Honor of Arthur Vincent Lourié*. New York: Oxford University Press, 2014.

Murchison, Gayle. "'Dean of Afro-American Composers' or 'Harlem Renaissance Man': The New Negro and the Musical Poetics of William Grant Still." *Arkansas Historical Quarterly* 53:1 (Spring 1994).

———, and Catherine Parsons Smith. "Still, William Grant." *Grove Music Online. Oxford Music Online.* Oxford University Press. http://www.oxfordmusiconline.com/subscriber/article/grove/music/26776. Accessed November 5, 2013.

Neff, Severine. "Otto Luening (1900–) and the Theories of Bernhard Ziehn (1845–1912)." *Current Musicology* 39 (1985), 21–41.

Niggli, Arnold. *Arnold Jensen: 1843–1927*. Berlin: Harmonie, 1900.

Nisbett, Robert Franklin. "Louis Gruenberg: His Life and Work." PhD diss., Ohio State University, 1979.

———. "Louis Gruenberg's American Idiom." *American Music* 3:1 (Spring 1985), 25–41.

———. "Pare Lorentz, Louis Gruenberg, and *The Fight for Life*: The Making of a Film Score." *Musical Quarterly* 79:2 (Summer 1995), 231–255.

Noble, David. "Louis Gruenberg." In *The Music of Louis Gruenberg*. Gunther Schuller, conductor. Newton, MA: GM Recordings, n.d. GM2015CD.

Oja, Carol J. *Making Music Modern: New York in the 1920s*. New York: Oxford University Press, 2000.

———. "'New Music' and the 'New Negro': The Background of William Grant Still's *Afro-American Symphony*." *Black Music Research Journal* 12:2 (Fall 1992), 145–169.

Orledge, Robert. *Debussy and the Theater*. Cambridge: Cambridge University Press, 1982.

Orr, Robin. "A Note on Nadia Boulanger." *Musical Times* 120:1642 (December 1979), 999.

Otto Luening Centennial. N.p.: Otto Luening Trust, 2000.

Ouellette, Fernand. *Edgard Varèse*. Translated by Derek Coltman. New York: Orion Press, 1966.

Palmer, Andrew. *Encounters with British Composers*. Rochester: Boydell Press, 2015.

Patterson, Nick. "The Archives of the Columbia-Princeton Music Center." *Notes* (March 2011), 483–502.

"Peter Maxwell Davies Introduces and Conducts Sibelius: Symphony no. 6." Vredenburg, Utrecht, November 10, 1996. https://www.youtube.com/watch?v=X3LL_zFAoBM. Accessed November 2, 2015.

Petrak, Albert M. "Ferruccio Busoni: His Life and Times." http://www.rprf.org/PDF/Busoni_Bio.pdf. Accessed April 9, 2013.

Petrobelli, Pierluigi. "Dallapiccola e Busoni." *Lettere e prospettive: Atti del Convegno Internazionale di studi (Empoli-Firenze 16–19 febbraio 1995)*, 25–34. Milan: Ricordi, 1997.

Polignac, Armande de. "Musique." *La Rénovation Esthétique: Revue de l'Art le Meilleur* 9 (January 1906), 165.

Pollack, Howard. *Marc Blitzstein: His Life, His Work, His World*. New York: Oxford University Press, 2012.

Potter, Caroline. *Nadia and Lili Boulanger*. Abingdon: Ashgate, 2008.

Ray, Lee. "On Developing the Electronic Tracks for Bamboula Squared." http://www.charleswuorinen.com/Writings/Lee_Ray/Lee_Ray.pdf. Accessed November 15, 2013.

Renihan, Colleen. "'History as It Should Have Been': Haunts of the Historical Sublime in John Corigliano's and William Hoffman's *The Ghosts of Versailles*." *Twentieth-Century Music* 10:2 (September 2013), 249–272.

Rickards, Guy. *Jean Sibelius*. London: Phaidon Press, 1997.

Riethmüller, Albrecht, ed. *Busoni in Berlin: Facetten eines kosmopolitischen Komponisten*. Stuttgart: F. Steiner, 2004.

———. *Ferruccio Busonis Poetik*. Mainz: Schott, 1988.

Roberge, Marc-André. "Busoni in the United States." *American Music* 13:3 (Autumn 1995), 295–332.

———. *Ferruccio Busoni: A Bio-bibliography*. Bio-bibliographies in Music, no. 34. New York: Greenwood Press, 1991.

———. "Ferruccio Busoni, His Chicago Friends, and Frederick Stock's Transcription for Large Orchestra and Organ of the *Fantasia contrappuntistica*." *Musical Quarterly* 80:2 (Summer 1996), 302–331.

Rodoni, Laureto. "Die Gerade Linie ist Unterbrochen: L'esilio di Busoni a Zurigo (1915–1920)." In *La Svizzera: Terra d'Asilo*. Atti-Kongressbericht-Ascona, 1998. Bern: P. Lang, 2000.

Rubin, Emanuel. "Jeannette Meyers Thurber and the National Conservatory of Music." *American Music* 8:3 (Autumn 1990), 294–325.

Sablich, S., and R. Dalmonte, eds. *Il Flusso del Tempo: Scritti su Ferruccio Busoni*, Quaderni di Musica, 11. Milan: Edizioni Unicopli, 1986.

Salmenhaara, Erkki. *Leevi Madetoja*. Helsinki: Kustannusosakeyhtio Tammi, 1987.

Sariola, Petri. "Doktor Faustus of the Keyboard and the Discreet Charm of Stella Polaris." *Finnish Music Quarterly* 1 (1999), 46–51.

Sechter, Simon. *Die Grundsätze der musikalischen Komposition*. Leipzig: Breitkopf und Härtel, 1853–1854.

Sitsky, Larry. *Busoni and the Piano: The Works, the Writings and the Recordings*. 2nd ed. Distinguished Reprints, no. 3. Hillsdale, NY: Pendragon Press, 2009.

———. *Music of the Twentieth-Century Avant-Garde: A Biocritical Sourcebook*. Westport, CT: Greenwood Press, 2012.

Smith, Catherine Parsons. *William Grant Still: A Study in Contradictions*. Berkeley: University of California Press, 2000.

———. "William Grant Still, Darker America, and Symphony no. 2." http://americansymphony.org/darker-america-1924-africa-1930symphony-no-2-1937/. Accessed November 1, 2013.

Solkema, Sherman van, ed. *The New Worlds of Edgard Varèse: A Symposium with Papers by Elliott Carter, Chou Wen-Chung, Robert P. Morgan*. ISAM Monographs, no. 11. Albany: State University of New York Press, 1979.

Southern, Eileen. "America's Black Composers of Classical Music." *Music Educators Journal* 62 (November 1975), 46–59.

Spycket, Jerome. *Nadia Boulanger*. Translated by M. M. Shriver. Stuyvesant, NY: Pendragon Press, 1991.

Steiner, George. *Lessons of the Masters*. Cambridge, MA: Harvard University Press, 2003.

Stempel, Larry. "Not Even Varèse Can Be an Orphan." *Musical Quarterly* 60:1 (January 1974), 46–60.

Stenzl, Jürg. "Busonis Sohn: Zur Genese von Varèse's Musikaesthetik." In *Edgard Varèse: Die Befreiung des Klangs: Symposium Edgard Varèse*, edited by Helga de la Motte-Haber. Hamburg: Hofheim, 1992.

Still, Judith Anne, Michael J. Dabrishus, and Carolyn L. Quinn. *William Grant Still: A Bio-Bibliography*. Bio-bibliographies in Music, no. 61. Westport, CT: Greenwood Press, 1996.

Stuckenschmidt, H. H. *Ferruccio Busoni: "Chronicle of a European* [1967]." Translated by Sandra Morris. New York: St. Martin's, 1970.

Sundberg, Gunnar. "Der Begriff Klassizität in den Symphonien von Jean Sibelius." PhD diss., Universität Vienna, 1987.

Szendy, Peter, and Risto Nieminen. *Magnus Lindberg*. Translated by Nick le Quesne. Helsinki: n.p., 1996.

Tawaststjerna, Erik. *Sibelius*. Translated by Robert Layton. 3 vols. Berkeley: University of California Press, 1976.

———. "The Two Leskovites." *Finnish Musical Quarterly* 3 (1986), 2–9.

Törne, Bengt de. *Sibelius: A Close Up*. Boston: Houghton Mifflin, 1938.

Upper, Nancy. *Ballet Dancers in Transition*. Jefferson, NC: McFarland, 2004.

Walton, Chris, ed. *Adolf Brunner: Erinnerungen eines Schweizers Komponisten aus der Schule Philipp Jarnachs und Franz Schrekers*. Zurich: Hug and Co., 1997.

Wegelius, Martin. *Konstnärsbrev*. Helsingfors: Senare Delan, 1919.

Weidenaar, Reynold. *Magic Music from the Telharmonium*. London: Scarecrow Press, 1995.

Weindel, Martina, ed. "Busonis 'Berlin Orchesterabende': Eine Nachlese Unveröffentlichter Briefe von Schönberg, Mahler, Bartók und Sibelius." *Schweizer Jahrbuch für Musikwissenschaft* 23 (2003), 323–324.

———. *Ferruccio Busonis Ästhetik in seinen Briefen und Schriften*. Edited by Richard Schaal. Wilhelmshaven: Heinrichsofen-Bücher, 1996.

Weiss, Stefan. "Die Gründung der hamburger Musikhochschule und ihr erster Direktor Phiipp Jarnach." In *Kunsträume Studium Innenansichten*, edited by Hanns-Werner Heister and Wolfgang Hochstein, 158–169. Hamburg: Bockel Verlag, 2000.

———. *Die Musik Philipp Jarnachs*. Cologne: Christoph Dohr, 1996.

Wen-Chung, Chou. "Varèse: Who Is He?" *Crossing the Line* (Winter 1998), 106.

Winfield, George A. "Ferruccio Busoni's Compositional Art: A Study of Selected Works for Piano Solo Composed Between 1907 and 1923." PhD diss., Indiana University, 1982.

Wis, Roberto. "Ferruccio Busoni and Finland." *Acta Musicologica* 49:2 (July-December 1977), 250–279.

Wissmann, Friederike. *Faust im Musiktheater des zwanzigsten Jahrhunderts*. Berlin: Mensch und Buch Verlag, 2003.

Zimmermann, Walter, ed. *Morton Feldman Essays*. Koln: Beginner Press, 1985.

INDEX

Note: Page numbers in *italics* indicate musical examples.

Abendroth, Hermann, 272n69
Abraham, Max, 66
Adamo, Mark, 306–307
Adler, Guido, 134n107
A. Durand & Fils, 262
Akademie die Künste (Berlin), 2, 29, 31
Allgemeiner Deutschen Musikverein, 259
Amar, Licco, 262
Amar Quartet, 262
American Composers Alliance, 222, 231n98
American Dance Festival, 230n78
American Music Guild, 171, 186n111, 186n113
Anderson, Julian, 63, 77, 314
Andreae, Volkmar, 190
Ansermet, Ernest, 98
Antonini, Andrea, 92
Arel, Bülent, 303
Artaud, Antonin, 332n87

Babbitt, Milton, 189, 218, 281, 303, 304
Bach, Johann Sebastian: Aria mit 30 Veränderungen ("Goldberg Variations"), BWV 988, 11–12, 192; Boulanger's pedagogical use of works by, 32; Busoni's pedagogical use of works by, 11–13; Chaconne from the Violin Sonata in D Minor, BWV 1004, 11–12, 141; Concerto in D Minor, BWV 1052, 56; contrapuntal exceptions, 12; Fantasy and Fugue in D Minor, BWV 905, 255; Fugue no. 2 in C Minor, BWV 871, 13, *15*; *Die Kunst der Fuge*, BWV 1080, 26; Lobe's pedagogical use of works by, 34; Passacaglia in C Minor for Organ, BWV 582, 11–12; Prelude and Fugue no. 2 in C Minor, BWV 871, 12; Prelude no. 1 in C Minor, BWV 870, 12–13; Prelude no. 3 in C-Sharp Major, BWV 872, 13, *14, 16*; Prelude no. 5 in D Minor, BWV 874, 13; Toccata and Fugue in D Minor, BWV 565, 82n30; transcriptions of, 13, 56, 82n30, 141–42, 170, 178n15; *Das Wohltemperierte Klavier*, book I, BWV 846–869, 12, 141; *Das Wohltemperierte Klavier*, book II, BWV 870–893, 12–13
Bachmann String Quartet, 121
Baeiloff publishing firm, 66–67
Baker, Ray Stannard, 104
Baker, Theodore, 99
Balmer, Luc, 2, 263, 315
Bancock, Granville, 76
Bancquart, Alain, 78
Barbirolli, John, 314

359

Bartel, Suzanne, 302, 333n98
Bartók, Béla: 14 Bagatelles, op. 6, 139; Busoni's mentorship and promotion of, 3; Busoni's programming of, 68, 119; as pianist, 139
Baudrier, Yves, 332n82
Bauer, Jürg, 260
Bauer, Marion, 186n111; Sonata for Violin and Piano, op. 14, 301; *Turbulence*, op. 17, 301
Bauhaus, 42n62
Beaumont, Antony, 8n3, 46, 67, 87n116, 271n62
Becker, Albert, 45, 49, 77
Beer-Walbrunn, Anton, 190
Beethoven, Ludwig van, 34; orchestration techniques, 201; Piano Concerto no. 5, "Emperor," 22; Piano Sonata in B-flat Major, op. 106, 49; string quartets, 248; Symphony no. 3, op. 55 ("Eroica"), 71
Behm, Eduard: *Im Frühling*, 120
Beklemishev, Gregor, 129n23
Beliaev, Mitrofan, 67, 85n82
Bellini, Vincenzo, 18
Benjamin, George, 78
Bennington College, 220–21, 222
Berg, Alban, 31, 33, 259
Berkeley, Lennox, 32, 43n76
Berkowitz, Sol, 302
Berlin master classes, 2–3, 10n9, 28, 42n62, 278
Berlioz, Hector, 22; as model for orchestration, 34; orchestration techniques, 201; *Roméo et Juliette*, 248; *Les Troyens*, 248
Bernardoni, Virgilio, 236
Bertoglio, Chiara, 46
Bertrand, René, 106
Beyer, Fred, 303
Bing, Suzanne, 92, 128n16, 129n26
Bizet, Georges, 248
Blanchet, Émile R., 141, 164
Bleuse, Marc, 299, 332n82
Blitzstein, Marc, 31, 43n74
Blum, Robert, 2, 275n115

Boccioni, Umberto, 21
Bodansky, Artur, 153, 182n66
Bodky, Erwin, 2
Borio, Gianmario, 9n3, 278, 324nn7–8
Bösendorfer, Ludwig von, 140, 178n17
Bossi, Marco Enrico, 328n45
Boulanger, Nadia: institutional affiliations, 42n64; pedagogical method, 2, 29–31, 32, 223; personal friendships with students, 33; promotion of students, 33; structural vision important to, 33–34; on Varèse, 95–96
Boulez, Pierre, 90, 281, 317
Bowers, Theresa, 213
Brant, Henry, 281
Braunfels, Walter, 232
Breitkopf und Härtel publishing firm, 67, 69, 170, 262–63
Britten, Benjamin: *Paul Bunyan*, 229n67
Brown, Earle, 288, 292
Brunner, Adolf, 275nn113–14
B. Schott's Son, 263
Buber, Martin: *Chinesische Geister- und Liebesgeschichten*, 239
Buffett, Gabrielle, 281
Buhler, Carlos, 225
Burg, Jacques, 143
Burkhardt, Heinrich, 263
Burston, Winifred, 319
Busoni, Benvenuto (son), 126–27, 128n15
Busoni, Ferdinando (father), 10n8
Busoni, Ferruccio, 73, 139–40, 262; appreciation of, 1–2; attitude toward commodification of music, 29, 95, 129n30, 143, 322–23; avant-garde and experimental composers influenced by, 317–19; Berlin contemporary orchestral music concerts, 28, 34, 68–70, 118–19; books owned by, 39n23; as conductor, 69–70; contrapuntal technique, 12–13, 61–62; in Helsinki, 46–49, 51–53, 76; Alistair Hinton influenced by, 315–16; home concerts of new works, 28, 118; interest in architecture, 27, 42n54, 109, 144, 287; libretto for Gruenberg's

INDEX 361

Götterbraut, 152, 153–54, 239; Lourié and, 288–89; *Maximen und Aphorismen*, 320; multiple versions of works, 108; musical training of, 10n8; notation viewed by, 107–108; orchestration treatise project, 17, 44n85, 59, 60, 83n59, 270n47; as pianist, 1, 48–49, 50, 52–53, 76, 82n41, 94, 120, 139, 192–93; polystylistic composers influenced by, 314–17; primary documents on, 6; reception of works, 76–78; spectral composers influenced by, 312–13; Stevenson influenced by, 316–17; textural composers influenced by, 313–14; United States disliked by, 142, 193; unpredictability of, 29; women viewed by, 39n28; Ziehn's influence on, 205–207

Busoni, Ferruccio, aesthetic vision, 19, 21–27, 229n60; absolute music viewed by, 47, 108–109, 238; "absolute orchestration" concept, 17, 58–59, 107; on adaptability of music, 238; dislike of systematization, 28–29; electronic instruments in, 23, 104, 106, 203, 204–205, 212, 305; *Entwurf einer neuen Ästhetik der Tonkunst*, 3, 23–24, 57, 62, 64, 66, 93, 99–100, *101–103*, 104, 106, 125, 144, 204, 303; *The Essence of Music*, 237, 243, 278, 317; evolution of thought, 3, 278–79; formal organization, 3, 12, 26–27, 57–58, 62–63, 99–100, 108–109, 131n69, 144, 162–63, 202–203, 242, 286–88, 327n39; future of music predictions, 21, 37, 98–99, 117, 141, 172, 174; Gruenberg influenced by, 143–64, 172, 177; Jarnach influenced by, 233, 237–38, 266, 268n18; Luening influenced by, 189, 190, 199, 201–205, 222–23, 225–26, 277; melodic integration theory, 113–14; Mozart's operas admired by, 17, 61, 207; Mozart's orchestration admired by, 61, 201, 245, 247; new instruments, 3, 24–25, 104, 107, 124, 204–205, 212, 281, 324–25n9; new scales and tonal expansion, 3, 23, 24–25, 100, 106–107, 131n63, 145, 285; non-musical influences, 19, 21; opera aesthetics, 155, 156, 183n72, 190, 207–208, 239; opera subjects preferred by, 19, 150; opera viewed as highest art form, 27; orchestral pedal concept, 59, 157–58; originality viewed by, 25–26, 33, 77; rhythmic simultaneity, 110; Sibelius influenced by, 57, 59, 61–63, 66, 321; stylistic pluralism, 24, 62, 125, 150, 156, 190, 203–204, 219, 237–38, 253–55, 282, 284–85, 306, 317; syncretism, 21; textural ideas, 201; "Ur-Musik" theory, 23–24; Varèse influenced by, 91–92, 98–106, 124–27, 222, 321; Young Classicality, 3, 19, 25, 62–63, 125–26, 144, 236, 237–38, 253, 266, 278, 310–11, 319

Busoni, Ferruccio, as pedagogue, 277–88; aesthetic vision, 19, 21–27, 35–36, 57–59, 96, 98–99, 278–88, 320; as authority figure, 36–37, 42n62; avoidance of political or economic topics, 39n22; avoidance of routine, 28–29, 203, 238–39, 322; Bach's works used by, 11–13, 26; Berlin master class, 2–3, 10n9, 28, 42n62, 278; as composition competition judge, 164–65; contrapuntal technique emphasized, 12–13, 196, 198, 202, 264, 278; critique of students, 36; dialogue approach, 21–22, 37; edition of Bach's *Wohltemperiertes Klavier*, book II, 12–13; evolution preferred to revolution, 33; expectations of students, 201–202; impact, 277–78; institutional affiliations, 2, 70, 94, 178n9; Italian opera composers' works used by, 18; literary and artistic discussions, 22–23, 203, 239, 303; mentorship of nonstudents, 3; methods compared with Boulanger, 29–31; methods compared with Schoenberg, 29–30; Mozart's use of form admired by, 62; Mozart's works used by, 11, 13, 16–17, 245, 247; organic connectedness, 12, 27; performance as instruction, 27–28, 47; personal friendships with students, 33, 72, 74,

76–77, 110, 121, 124, 171–72, 261–64, 265–66, 276n121, 276n123, 322–23; piano master classes in Vienna, 9n5, 138–42, 139, 178n9; promotion of students, 33, 49, 51, 66–72, 98, 116–19, 121, 124, 164–66, 168–70, 220–23, 251, 262–64, 274–75n107; *Schwarzer Kaffee* hours of, 2, 9n4; score critique by, 18–19, 20, 26, 55–56, 95–97, 240; sonority and orchestration, 13, 16–17, 58–59, 61, 126, 226, 244–45, 247–48, 270n47, 279–82, 306; structural vision important to, 33; students of students, 4, 288–312; teaching method, 4–5, 11–18, 286–88; transcription's importance to, 13, 41n47; unconventional approach of, 4–5, 34, 96, 320–23; under-appreciation of, 1–2. *See also specific students*

Busoni, Ferruccio, compositions of: *All'Italia! in modo napolitano*, 178n15; *An die Jugend*, BV 254, 141, 263; *Arlecchino*, BV 270, 145, 150, 192, 201, 248, 264, 315; Bach transcriptions, 13, 56, 82n30, 141–42, 170, 178n15; *Berceuse élégiaque*, BV 252, 56, 61, 64, 82n40, 110, 111, 126, 132n75, 159, 207, 219; *Die Brautwahl*, BV 258, 150, 248; Concerto for Piano, Orchestra, and Male Chorus, BV 247, 56, 120, 145, 201; *Concertstück*, BV 236, 51, 82n30; Divertimento for Flute and Orchestra, BV 285, 271n59; *Doktor Faust*, BV 303, 126, 135n116, 145, 150, 156, 201, 213, 225, 239, 248, 249, 255, 271n59, 271n62, 309, 315, 318–19, 319; *Fantasia contrappuntistica*, BV 256, 26, 41n48, 56, 64, 66, 108, 109, 144, 179n29, 206; *Fantasia contrappuntistica* two-piano version, BV 256b, 145; *Fantasia nach Bach*, BV 253, 113, 113–14; *Geharnischte Suite*, BV 242, 72, 74, 75; *Idomeneo* suite, 70–71; *Indianische Fantasie*, BV 264, 87n116; *Indianisches Tagebuch*, 315; Jarnach's completion or orchestration of, 249; *Kleine Ballet-Szene*, BV 235/2, 148; *Lied des Brander*, BV 299, 249, 250; *Lied des Unmuts*, BV 281a, 271n59; *Meine Seele bangt und hofft zu dir*, BV 249, 64; *Nachdichtungen*, 255, 315–16; *Nocturne symphonique*, BV 262, 64, 159; orchestral edition of Busoni's *Lied des Brander*, 249, 250; orchestrations by, 146; Piano Concerto, op. 39, 315, 316, 319, 323; piano sonatinas, 64; Sonatina 1910, BV 257, 249; Sonatina no. 3, "Ad usum infantis," BV 268, 248; Sonatina no. 4 ("In diem nativitatis Christi"), BV 274, 271n59; Sonatina no. 5, *Sonatina in Brevis "In Signo Joannis Sebastiani Magni,"* BV 280, 255; Sonatina no. 6 ("Super Carmen"), BV 284, 255, 271n59; *Sonatina seconda*, BV 259, 3, 126, 142, 145, 213, 315, 319; *Toccata: Preludio-Fantasia-Ciaccona*, BV 287, 142, 145; *Turandot*, BV 273, 150, 152, 192, 219, 248–49, 260, 264, 309; *Turandots Frauengemach (Intermezzo)*, 178n15; *Vierte Ballet-szene*, BV 238, 148–49, *149*; Violin Concerto in D Major, BV 243, 56, 249; Violin Sonata in E Minor, BV 244, 145, 201; *Das Wandbild* collaboration with Jarnach, 239–40; *Zigeunerlied*, op. 55, no. 2, 262

Busoni, Gerda, 275n115
Busoni, Rafaello (son), 126–27, 128n15, 225
Butting, Max, 232

Café Society Band, 174
Cage, John, 304, 329n54; Varèse's influence on, 318–19
Cahill, Thaddeus, 25, 40n41, 104, 130n51, 205, 212
Carlos, Walter, 302
Carpenter, John Alden, 186n108
Carter, Elliott, 32, 304, 316
Caruso, Enrico, 170
Casella, Alfredo, 121, 134n107; *O toi suprême*, 120
Caspar, Walther, 262
Cervantes, Miguel de: *Don Quixote*, 22, 74
Chadwick, George W., 186n108

INDEX   363

Chevillard, Camille, 128n11
Chopin, Fryderyk: Ballade no. 4, op. 52, 316; ballades, 193
Chou Wen-Chung, 223, 280, 288, 293, 329n54, 330nn58–59; *All in the Spring Wind*, 293, 294–95; *And the Fallen Petals*, 293
Clarkson, Austin, 5, 92, 288, 324n7
Closson, Louis, *140*, 140–41, 169
Columbia Broadcasting System, 187n122
Columbia-Princeton Electronic Music Center, 189, 217, 218, 303, 304
Columbia University (New York), 214–15, 261
Cominos, Joan Gruenberg, 166, 178n7, 301
Copland, Aaron, 33, 231n98
Copley, Alfred Lewin, 329n54
Corigliano, John, 4, 190, 223, 225, 302, 306–9, 335n118, 335n123; *The Ghost of Versailles*, 307–308, *309*; *Kaleidoscope*, 306, *307*; stylistic pluralism, 306–309
Corner, Philip, 302
Cortot, Claude, 97, 128nn16–17, 129nn26–27
Cottlow, Augusta, 95
Cowell, Henry, 331n75
Crispin, Judith, 24, 319, 324n1; *Leonardo: The Italian Faust*, 338n158
Csillag, Hermann, 53
Curtis, Natalie, 87n116, 326n18

Dada movement, 281
Dahlhaus, Carl, 77
Dallapiccola, Luigi, 126, 135n116
Damrosch, Walter, 143, 179n34, 186n107, 186n108
Daniel-Lesur, Jean-Yves, 332n82
David, Constantin, 121
Davidovsky, Mario, 190, 218, 223, 288, 303
Davies, Peter Maxwell, 78, 314–15; Sinfonia for Chamber Orchestra, 314; Symphony no. 1, 314, 315; Symphony no. 5, 315
Debussy, Claude, 68, 124, 129n28; advocacy for Varèse, 128n11; Jarnach influenced by, 233, 237; *Pelléas et Mélisande*, 90, 128n8; Three Nocturnes, L. 91, 57; Varèse and, 91, 92
de Jong, Paul, 194
de la Motte-Haber, Helga, 92, 130n37
Delius, Frederick, 71, 76
Dent, Edward, 127, 129n24, 171
de Törne, Bengt, 289
Dieren, Bernard van, 121, 134n107; as Busoni's student, 3, 18–19, 21–22, 25, 28; *Carnavalesque*, 19
Dieudonné, Mademoiselle, 30, 42n64
d'Indy, Vincent, 68, 119, 328n45; *Symphonie sur un chant montagnard*, op. 25, 120
Dlugoszewski, Lucia, 288, 329n54
Dodge, Charles, 303
Donaueschingen Festival, 232, 251, 253, 263, 266–67n2
Donizetti, Gaetano, 18
Downes, Olin, 210–12
Drogoz, Philippe, 332n82
Druckman, Jacob, 303
Duffie, Bruce, 190, 203–204, 210, 223–24
Dufort, Hughes, 78
Dusapin, Pascal, 78
Dynamophone, 106

Eisler, Hanns, 232
Ekman, Karl, 46, 79n5, 81n27
El-Dabh, Halim, 303
Elgar, Edward, 68; "Enigma" Variations, 316
Erdmann, Eduard, 121, 134n107
Erickson, Raymond, 230n92

Feigin, Joel, 31, 302, 333n106, 334n107; *Mysteries of Eleusis*, 304
Feldman, Morton, 78, 288, 317–18, 329n54, 339n168
Ferneyhough, Brian, 338n145
Finnissy, Michael: Busoni's influence on, 315; *History of Photography*, 315; *Verdi Transcriptions*, 315
Fleet, Paul, 8n3, 25, 110

Flesch, Carl, 165
Frank, Maurits, 262
Freeman, Robin, 187n114
Friedman, Ignaz, *140*, 141
Fried, Oskar, 56, 70
Fuchs, Robert, 45, 51, 81n29, 84n68, 328n45
Furtwängler, Wilhelm, 251
Furuhjelm, Erik, 329n51
Futurism, 21, 105, 287, 288
Fux, Johann Joseph, 31, 34; *Gradus ad Parnassum*, 43n71

Galston, Gottfried, 174, 238
Ganz, Rudolph, 186n108, 300
Geiser, Walther, 2, 18, 38n15
Glass, Philip, 30
Glazunov, Alexander, 67
Godesberger Musiktagen (Cologne), 260
Goethe, Johann Wolfgang von, 19, 39n23; *Faust*, 22
Goldmark, Karl, 45, 51, 77, 81–82n29, 84n68
Goldmark, Rubin, 186n107
Goldstein, Malcolm, 302
Goode, Daniel, 302
Goossens, Eugene: Violin Sonata no. 1, 121
Goss, Glenda Dawn, 72, 80n8
Graf, Herbert, 272n73
Grainger, Percy: Busoni's mentorship and promotion of, 3, 325–26n18; experimentation of, 281
Gray, Cecil, 46, 79n1
Grisey, Gérard, 78, 312, 313, 337n143, 338n145
Gruenberg, Abraham, 178n7
Gruenberg, Louis, *139–40*; American characteristics in music, 156–57, 172; background and education, 137–38; Berlin composition concert, 1912, 165–66; on Busoni's admiration for Sibelius, 76; Busoni's aesthetic influences, 127, 143–64, 172, 177; Busoni's mentorship and promotion of, 164–66, 168–70; as Busoni's student, 3–4, 19, 136–37, 138–43, 171, 179n34; at Chicago Musical College, 300–301; composers' organizations founded by, 171; composition prizes won, 186n108; familiarity with Busoni's compositions, 145–46; formal innovations, 162–63; formal models inspired by architecture, 144–45, 287; friendship with Busoni, 171–72, 261–64, 322–23; future of music envisioned by, 174–75, 176–77; new scales and tonal expansion, 145, 285; in New York, 170–71; orchestral pedal concept, 157–58; orchestration ideals, 157–58, 279; personal copy of Busoni's *Entwurf*, 40n33, 144; as pianist, 121, 140–42, 168–70; Sibelius and, 71, 164; students of, 300–301; stylistic pluralism, 156–57, 284–85; use of electronic mediums, 4, 281–82
Gruenberg, Louis, compositions of: *The Creation*, op. 23, 136, 171; *The Daniel Jazz*, op. 21, 136, 171, 187n114, 284; *The Emperor Jones*, op. 36, 157, 186n108, 285; *The Fight for Life* documentary score, 172–74, 187n120, 285; film music, 172–75, 173, 282; *Die Götterbraut*, op. 2, 153–56, 239; *The Great Liar*, 152; *Green Mansions*, op. 39, 175–76, 187n122, 282, 283; *The Hill of Dreams*, op. 10, 136, 143, 159, *160–62*, 161–64, 279, 287; *Impressionen–Dreizehn Klavierstücke*, op. 4, 165; Intermezzo, op. 13, no. 1, 146–47, *147*; *Jack and the Beanstalk*, 186n108; *Jazzberries*, op. 25, 284, 301; libretto sources, 151–52; operas and stageworks, 150–57, 172; Piano Concerto, 171, 322–23; piano sonata, 19, *20*; *Piccadillymädel*, 143; *Polychromatics*, op. 16, 170; *Polychrome*, 120; popular music of, 143; radio music, 172, 175–76, 282; *Scène de Ballet*, *148*, 148–49; *Sechs Lieder*, op. 5, 165–66; *Signor Formica*, 152–53, *154*; string quintet, 186n108; Suite for Violin and Piano, op. 3, 165, 166, *167*, 170, 184n94; symphonic works by, 157–64,

158, 172; Violin Concerto, 136; *The Witch of Brocken*, op. 1, 182n65; works for stage, 151; works written while studying with Busoni, 146–55, 150
Guerrini, Guido, 3, 5, 10n11, 18, 23, 26, 36, 38n16, 316

Hába, Alois, 2, 121, 134n107
Handy, W. C., 297
Hanson, Howard, 330n62
Harmati, Sandor, 171, 186n111
harmony of the spheres, 24
Haubiel, Charles, 186n111
Havemann, Gustav, 232, 273n83
Haydn, Franz Joseph, 34
Heifetz, Jascha, 136
Heininen, Paavo, 337–38n145
Heinsheimer, Hans, 306, 335n119
Helm, Everett, 260
Helmholtz, Herman von: *Sensations of Tone*, 213, 312
Helsinki Music Institute, 2, 46–49, 80n10, 81n13, 178n9, 327–28n44
Henselt, Adolf von, 142
Hepokoski, James, 63, 286
Hersant, Philippe, 299, 332n82
Herzogenberg, Heinrich, Freiherr von, 51
Hesse, Hermann, 232
Hindemith, Paul, 121, 134n107, 223, 259, 260–61, 262, 264
Hinton, Alistair, 315–16; *Sieben Charakterstücke*, 316
Hinton, Stephen, 9n3
Hirsch, Hans, 2
Hochschule für Musik (Basel), 9n5
Hoffmann, E. T. A., 19, 53, 152–53
Hoffmannsthal, Hugo von, 114, 129n27; *Oedipus und die Sphinx*, 96–97
Hollaender, Gustav, 164, 183n87
Holm, Hanya: *Trend*, 214, 220–21, 230n78
Holstein, Jean-Paul, 332n82
Honegger, Arthur: *Three Fragments*, 120
Hong, Barbara, 46
Horenstein, Jascha, 232
Hudson, W. H., 175–76

Hugill, Andrew, 288
Hug music publishers, 263

International Composers' Guild, 119–21, 170
International Gesellschaft für neue Musik, 259
International Society for Contemporary Music, 171, 179n29, 227n20
Internationale Componisten-Gilde, 116–17, 119, 120–21, 121, 122–23, 124, 126, 259
Ives, Charles, 282, 284

Jacobi, Frederick, 171, 186n111
Jadassohn, Salomon, 228n37
Jarnach, Philipp, 134n107, 262; Busoni connection sources, 236; as Busoni's assistant, 264; Busoni's *Doktor Faust* completed by, 249, 271n62; Busoni's mentorship and promotion of, 251, 262–64, 268n18, 274–75n107, 276n121, 276n123; as Busoni's student, 3–4, 24, 38n13, 233, 236–49; collaboration on Busoni's orchestration treatise project, 17, 83n59, 270n47; contrapuntal technique, 233, 242–44, 264; electronic music viewed by, 261, 325n13; essay "Mechanische Musik," 261; formal experimentation, 4, 242–44, 286; German Nazi government and, 253, 259–61, 272n69, 272n71; increasing experimentalism of, 251–53, 265–66; as Internationale Componisten-Gilde member, 121, 124; lecture "Electronic Music in the USA," 226; Luening and, 190, 191–92, 193–94, 199, 220, 225, 226, 259, 261, 309, 325n13; Mozart's influence on, 255–57, 259; new music promotion of, 259–60; *Novembergruppe* and, 232, 251, 253; orchestration techniques, 244–45, 247–48, 270n47, 279, 310–11; post-war activities, 260; reception of, 232, 251; Sibelius and, 71; students of, 259–60, 264–65, 309–12; stylistic plu-

ralism, 4, 233, 237–38, 242–44, 253–57, 261, 284, 310; tonal expansion, 285; Young Classicality and, 237–38, 253–54, 259, 266, 310–11; in Zurich, 232, 236–37, 263–74, 267n15; as Zurich Stadttheater Kapellmeister, 263–64

Jarnach, Philipp, compositions of: *Ballata für Orchester*, 244–45, 275n108; *Clown Songs*, op. 24, 251; *Concertino nach Giovanni Platti in E moll*, op. 31, 254–55; *Drei Klavierstücke*, op. 17, 251; early, 267n15; Flute Sonata, 225; Konzertstück für Orgel (*Romanzero III*), op. 21, 251, 252, 252–53; *Morgenklangspiel (Romanzero II)*, op. 19, 251; *Musik mit Mozart*, 255–57, 258, 259; post-war, 273n92; *Prolog zu einem Ritterspiele*, 242; *Sinfonia Brevis*, op. 14, 240, 242, 247, 263, 266, 279; Sonatina for Piano (*Romanzero I*), op. 18, 251–52; Sonatine for Flute and Piano, op. 12, 234, 235; String Quartet, op. 16, 240; String Quartet, op. 22, 275n108; String Quintet, op. 10, 232, 242–44, 244–45, 253, 261, 263, 274–75n107, 286; *Vier Orchesterlieder*, op. 15a, 253; Violin Sonata, op. 9, 233–34, 234; *Das Wandbild* collaboration with Busoni, 239–40, 241, 276n123; *Winterbilder*, op. 15, 275n108

Järnefelt, Armas, 47, 74, 81n13, 329n51
Järnefelt, Eero, 47, 74, 76, 81n13
Jelmoli, Hans, 236
Joachim-Loch, Heinz, 2
Jolivet, André, 293, 298–300, 329n54, 332nn79–82; Boulez and, 317; *Concerto pour Ondes Martenot et orchestra*, 299–300; sonority and textural focuses, 298–300; works with ondes martenot, 299
Jonson, Ben, 152
Jugendstil movement, 21, 287

Kaim, Franz, 166, 168
Kalischer, Fritz, 121
Kander, John, 190, 223

Kenton, Egon, 118, 133nn95–96
Kessler, Harry Graf, 232
Klein, Lidus, 275n108
Kneisel, Frank, 186n108
Koch, Friedrich, 137–38
Konold, Wulf, 310, 311
Korte, Karl, 302
Koussevitzky, Serge, 33, 186n108
Kraft, William, 223–24, 302
Kramer, A. Walter, 186n111
Krenek, Ernst, 2, 121, 134n107, 266
Kuczynski, Pawel, 116, 126
Kurth, Ernst: *Grundlagen des linearen Kontrapunkts*, 264
Kuula, Toivo, 289, 328n45; Piano Trio, op. 7, 292

Laderman, Ezra, 223
Lanier, Harriet, 170, 185–86n107
Laquai, Reinhold, 3, 263
Lavignac, Albert, 267n14
League of Composers, 171, 186n112
Le Corbusier, 281
Leichtentritt, Hugo, 42n54, 198, 247
Leipp, Émile, 337n143
Lejet, Edith, 332n82
Levalle, Pierre Yves, 332n82
Levitz, Tamara, 2, 9n3, 36–37, 83n59, 236, 251, 268n18, 278, 324n8
Lewinger, Max, 70
Liceo musicale (Bologna), 2, 70
Lichtenstein, Alfred, 272n73
Ligeti, György, 337n143
Lindberg, Magnus, 78, 312–13, 337n145, 338n148; *Kinetics*, 313
Liszt, Franz: *Faust Symphony*, S. 108, 56–57; *Mephisto Waltz*, 170; orchestration techniques, 248; Piano Sonata in B Minor, S. 178, 140, 141; *Totentanz*, S. 126, 22, 264
Lobe, Johann Christian: *Lehrbuch der musikalischen Komposition*, 34–35, 80n10
Longfellow, Henry Wadsworth, 208, 210
Louis, Rudolf, 35

Lourié, Arthur, 121, 134n107, 288
Luening, Otto, 92, 127; approach toward opera, 190, 207–12; belief in well-rounded education, 303; Busoni's aesthetic influences, 189, 190, 199, 201–205, 222–23, 226; Busoni's mentorship and promotion of, 220–23, 225–26; as Busoni's student, 3–4, 277, 286; collaboration with Ussachevsky on *King Lear* score, 308; contrapuntal technique, 196, 198, 202; as flautist, 190, 191, 193, 214, 215, 216; Jarnach and, 190, 191–92, 193–94, 199, 220, 225, 226, 259, 261, 309, 325n13; new scales and tonal expansion, 285; notational difficulties, 193–94; *The Odyssey of an American Composer*, 190; orchestration techniques, 303–304; promotion of American opera, 229n67; rhythmic and metric fluidity, 198; serialism viewed by, 302; sonority and textural focuses, 213, 215–18, 226, 302, 306, 308–309; students of, 190, 223–25, 302–309; stylistic pluralism, 190, 203–204, 208, 210, 219, 302, 306; teachers of, 190; teaching methods, 223–25, 231nn102–103; treatment of counterpoint, 190; Varèse and, 220–23, 326n19; Ziehn's influence on, 205–7; in Zurich, 190–205

Luening, Otto, compositions of: acoustic compositions, 189, 226, 279; *Alleluia*, W. 130, 222; Aria for Cello and Piano, W. 124, 226; arrangement of "Poor Wayfaring Stranger," 222; as Busoni's student, 192–99; *Chorale Fantasy for Organ*, W. 43, 217, 284; early songs, 192; electronic compositions, 4, 189–90, 203, 204–205, 212–18, 226, 261, 279, 281, 302, 303, 304, 308; *Evangeline*, W. 85, 207–208, 209, 210–12, *211*, 222; *Fantasy in Space*, W. 148, 214, 215, 216, 226n1, 279; *Fugue and Chorale Fantasy with Electronic Doubles for Organ and Tape*, W. 224, 217–18, 284; *Fugue for Organ*, W. 221, 217, 284; *Invention in Twelve Tones*, w. 149, 215, 216–17; *Low Speed*, W. 150, 214, 215, 279; Lyric Suite for Flute and Strings, W. 171, 220; *Requiescat*, W. 25, 190–91, *191*; *Rhapsodic Variations for Tape Recorder and Orchestra*, W. 159, 216, 226n1, 281; Sextet, W. 32, 192, 193–94, 198; Sonata for Piano in Memoriam Ferruccio Busoni, W. 162, 206, 207, 218–20, 221, 230n92, 326n19; String Quartet no. 1, W. 38, 192, 193, 194, 196, *196–97*, 198, 199, *200*; Suites for Flute Solo, 220; Symphonic Fantasia no. 1, W. 56, 206–207; *Synthesis for Orchestra and Electronic Sound*, 218; Trio for Violin, Cello, and Piano, W. 42, 213; Violin Sonata no. 1, W. 26, 192, 193, 194, *195*, 198–99; Violin Sonata no. 2, W. 46, 206

Macdonald, Malcolm, 90, 92
Macmillan, Ann, 329n54
Madetoja, Leevi, 289–90, 328n45, 329n48, 329n51; Symphonic Suite, op. 4, 290; Symphony no. 3, op. 55, 290, 291, 292
Magnard, Albéric: Troisième Symphonie, 120
Mahabharata epic, 154, 182n68
Mahler, Gustav, 61, 68, 82n40; *Das Lied von der Erde*, 32; Symphony no. 6, 32
Mäkelä, Tomi, 46, 79n5
Maler, Wilhelm, 275n113
Malipiero, Gian Francesco: Ariette, 120
Mamlok, Ursula, 288
Margulies, Adele, 137, 178n7
Martenot, Maurice, 106
Marx, Adolf Bernhard, 31, 34; *Die Lehre von der musikalischen Komposition*, 43n72, 80n10
master-apprentice guild model of learning, 42n62
Matthews, Joseph, 9n3
Matthis, Olivia, 92
Mauzey, Peter, 214, 215
Mayer-Rémy, Wilhelm, 10n8
McClure's Magazine, 104
McDowell, John Herbert, 302

McGregor, Richard, 314
McPhee, Colin, 329n54
Melos Konzerten für Neue Musik, 259
Meltzer, Charles Henry, 155
Mendelssohn, Felix, 61
Mengelberg, Willem Joseph, 133n97
Menotti, Gian Carlo: *The Medium*, 229n67
Messiaen, Olivier, 317, 332n82, 337n143
Meyerbeer, Giacomo, 22
microtonal scales and music, 25, 40n40, 104, 106–107, 285, 288–89
Middelschulte, Wilhelm, 206
Miller, Dayton: *The Science of Musical Sound*, 213
Mitropoulos, Dimitri, 2, 10n15
Molière: *School for Wives*, 207
Monteverdi, Claudio, 71
Morris, Harold, 186n111
Moscow Conservatory, 2, 178n9
Mozart, Wolfgang Amadeus: approach toward spacing and voice leading, 16–17; Boulanger's pedagogical use of works by, 32; Busoni's pedagogical use of works by, 11, 13, 16–17; Divertimento in D Major, K. 334, 255; *Don Giovanni*, 17, 61; dramatic principles, 17–18; formal organization, 62; Lobe's pedagogical use of works by, 34; *Le Nozze di Figaro*, 17, 150, 245; orchestration techniques, 61, 62–63, 64, 201, 245, 247; Piano Concerto in A Major, K. 488, 256; Piano Trio in E Major, K. 542, 256, 257; Piano Trio in G Major, K. 496, 246, 247; Requiem, K. 626, 238; String Quintet, K. 593, 256; *Die Zauberflöte*, 17, 61, 150, 207, 245
Mugmon, Matthew, 30
Murail, Tristan, 78, 312, 313, 337n143
Murchison, Gayle, 297
Museum of Modern Art (New York), 214–15
Mysakowsky, Nikolai, 124

Nazism: Jarnach and, 253, 259–61, 272n69, 272n71; Sibelius and, 77

Neff, Severine, 132n70, 190, 206, 213, 229n56, 304, 333–34n107
Neisser, Ferdinand, 69
Nelson, Georgina, 129n23
neoclassicism, 30, 62, 125–26
Neue Gesellschaft für Musik, 260
Neue Sachlichkeit, 238
New England Conservatory of Music, 2, 178n9
New Symphony Orchestra, 119
Nicódé, Jean Louis, 68, 85n88
Nietzsche, Friedrich, 19, 39n23
Nikisch, Arthur, 266n2
Nisbett, Robert Franklin, 137, 138, 148, 173–74, 178n7
Nono, Luigi, 317
Nørgård, Per, 78, 88n125
Nováček, Rudolf, 56, 66, 68; as conductor, 119, 120; Sinfonietta in D Minor, op. 48, 120
Novembergruppe, 232, 251, 253

Oboussier, Robert, 275n113
Oehlenschläger, Adam Gottlob, 99
Oja, Carol, 296
Ojanperä, Abraham, 53, 82n33
ondes martenot, 106, 131n68, 299–300
O'Neill, Eugene, 157
Oppens, Ursula, 230n92
Otava publishing firm, 66
Ouellette, Fernand, 90, 117

Page, Tim, 190, 212
Pan American Association of Composers, 119
Pan (magazine), 21
Partch, Harry, 107, 288
Paul, Adolf, 47, 56, 71, 74, 81n13
Penderecki, Krzysztof, 313
Perrin, C. H., 185n97
Peters edition, 66
Peterson, William, 185n97
Petri, Egon, 5, 11, 47, 56, 98, 131n63, 140, 165, 276n123, 319, 324n1
Petyrek, Felix, 121, 134n107, 232

INDEX

Petzold, Rudolf, 260
Pfitzner, Hans, 71, 266n2; Scherzo for Orchestra, 120
Phillips, O'Neill, 168, 184n96
Picabia, Francis, 281
Piccardi, Carlo, 9n3
Pizzetti, Ildebrando: *I Pastori*; *La Madre al figlio lontano*, 120
Plato, 21
Platti, Giovanni Benedetto, 254, 272n73
Polah, Andre, 121
postmodernism, 77
Poulet, Gaston, 332n79
Praeger and Meier concert agency, 183n86
Press, Vera Maurina, 129n23
Puccini, Giacomo: *Madama Butterfly*, 21–22

Rautavaara, Einojuhani, 337–38n145
Ravel, Maurice, 124, 129n26, 237; Piano Trio in A Minor, 316
Reger, Max, 260
Renihan, Colleen, 308
Renner, Willy, 164
Rénovation esthétique, La, 90
Reynolds, Roger, 292
Riethmüller, Albrecht, 9n3
Rimsky-Korsakov, Nikolai, 49
Risler, Edouard, 267n14
Risset, Jean-Claude, 332n82
Roberge, Marc-André, 9n3
Rodoni, Laureto, 236
Rosenfeld, Paul, 297
Rowe, Theresa, 185n97
Rubinstein, Anton: Theme and 12 Variations in G Major, op. 88, 142
Runeberg, Johan Ludvig, 66
Russolo, Luigi, 21

Saal, Max, 169
Salzedo, Carlos, 121
Salzman, Eric, 106, 288, 318–19, 329n54
Samaroff, Olga, 186n108
Sariola, Petri, 46
Satie, Erik, 128n8

Schaeffer, Pierre, 281
Scharwenka, Philipp, 164
Scherchen, Hermann, 259
Schlesinger music publishers, 263, 274–75n107
Schnabel, Arthur, 133n97
Schnebel, Dieter, 317
Schoenberg, Arnold, 25, 124, 259, 266, 285; as authority figure, 36; Berlin composition concert, 1912, 168–70; Busoni's mentorship and promotion of, 3; compositional texture, 61; *Fünf Orchesterstücke*, op. 16, 288; Gruenberg and, 168–70, 185n100; *Harmonielehre*, 31–32, 35; Jarnach's correspondence with, 253; *Kammersymphonie* no. 1 in E Major, op. 9, 57; *Klangfarbenmelodie*, 287–88; pedagogical method, 1–2, 29–30, 31–33, 35, 324n7; personal copy of Busoni's *Entwurf*, 40n33; personal friendships with students, 33; *Pierrot Lunaire*, 118, 133n96, 170; structural vision important to, 33; stylistic pluralism, 282; transcriptions viewed by, 41n47; Varèse influenced by, 91; Wind Quintet, op. 26, 32
Schoen, Ernst, 116–17, 121
Schopenhauer, Arthur, 19
Schreker, Franz, 134n107
Schubert, Franz: Lieder of, 238
Schuller, Gunther, 97, 98
Schumann, Robert: "Belshazzar" Ballad, op. 57, 53; *Carnaval*, op. 9, 82n35, 140; *Kreisleriana*, op. 16, 52, 53; Piano Quintet in E-Flat Major, op. 44, 52; Sonata in D Minor for Violin and Piano, op. 121, 52–53; *Symphonic Etudes*, op. 13, 52, 301
Schwartz, Elliott, 302
Schwarzwald, Eugenie, 31, 43n71
Scriabin, Alexander, 128n8
Sechter, Simon, 31, 34; *Die richtige Folge der Grundharmonien*, 43n71
Selden-Goth, Gisella, 3, 17, 164
Serato, Arrigo, 133n97

Sessions, Roger, 231n98, 302, 333n104
Shakespeare, William, 152
Shapey, Ralph, 288
Shifrin, Seymour, 223
Sibelius, Jean, 73; aesthetic ideals, 62–63; Berlin visit, 1894, 55–56; Busoni's influence on, 51–66, 321; Busoni's mentorship and promotion of, 66–72; as Busoni's student, 3–4, 45–49; composition career beginnings, 45–46, 80n10; as conductor, 119, 120; Davies influenced by, 314–15; early teachers, 45, 46, 77, 81–82n29, 84n68; expansion of musical contacts, 71–72; formal innovations, 52, 53–55, 57–58, 62–63, 66, 286, 314–15; friendship with Busoni, 72, 74, 76–77; influence on later composers, 77–78; Liszt viewed by, 56–57; Lobe's composition treatise studied by, 34–35; Mozart's orchestration admired by, 61; orchestral pedal concept, 59; orchestration of, 64, 289–90, 292; performance weaknesses, 48; post-Helsinki contacts with Busoni, 55–57; publishers for, 66–67; reception of works, 76–78; rejection of Nazi solicitations, 77; sonority and textural focuses, 4, 58–59, 61, 64, 66, 77–78, 279–80; spectral composers influenced by, 77–78, 312–13; students of, 289–92, 327–28nn44–45; style of, 45, 284; symphonies conducted by Busoni, 71; tonal language, 64, 66, 314–15; Wagner viewed by, 56
Sibelius, Jean, compositions of: *En Saga*, op. 9, 68–69, 85nn89–90, 120; *Finlandia*, op. 26, 68, 69; *Florestan* Suite, 51, 53–55, 54–55; *Illale*, op. 17, no. 6, 63; *King Christian II*, op. 27, 67; *Lemminkäisestä*, 68; Overture in E Major, 51, 82nn29–30; Piano Quintet in G Minor, 51; *Pohjola's Daughter*, op. 49, 70, 85n89, 87n116; *Serenad* for voice and piano, 66; String Quartet in A Minor, 48; String Quartet in D Minor, op. 56 ("voces intimae"), 70; Suite in A Major for String Trio, 47–48; *Swan of Tuonela*, 72; Symphony no. 2, 48, 69–70, 85n89, 120; Symphony no. 4, 63, 64, 65, 66, 67, 70; Symphony no. 5, 61, 63–64, 70, 76–77, 78, 286, 314; Symphony no. 6, 314, 315; Symphony no. 7, 315; *The Tempest*, op. 109, 314; *Tulen Synty*, op. 32, 56; *Valse triste*, op. 44, no. 1, 69; Violin Concerto in D Minor, op. 47, 69, 70
Signale für die musikalische Welt, 164–65
Silverman, Faye-Ellen, 302
Singer, Otto: Piano Concerto in A Major, op. 8, 120
Sirota, Leo, 129n23, *140*, 140–41
Sitsky, Larry, 8n3, 324n1, 338n158; Busoni's influence on, 319; completion of Busoni's *Doktor Faustus*, 319; *Sonatina Seconda in Extremis*, 319
Skalkottas, Nikos, 275n113, 309
Smith, Catherine Parsons, 297, 331n74
Society of Friends of Music, 185–86n107
Sollberger, Harvey, 302
Southern, Eileen, 330n60
spectral music, 77–78, 312–13
Springer, Hermann, 121, 134n107
Stančić, Svetislav, 2
Steffens, Walter, 309–10
Stempel, Larry, 90, 91
Stenzl, Jürg, 92, 105
Steuermann, Eduard, 10n15, 118, 169
Stevenson, Ronald, 316–17; *Fantasy on Doktor Faust*, 316; *Motus Perpetuus Temporibus Fatalibus*, 316–17; Piano Concerto no. 2, 317
Still, William Grant, 4, 293, 296–98, 329n54, 330nn60–62; *Afro-American Symphony*, 296–97; *Darker America*, 296, 298, 331n74; essay "The Art of Musical Creation," 296; form, style, and sonority in works of, 296–98; *From the Land of Dreams*, 297, 330n62, 331n71
Stock, Frederick, 18, 186n108, 206
Stockhausen, Karlheinz, 313, 337n143
Stoessel, Albert, 171, 186n111, 301
Stokowski, Leopold, 186n108, 214–15

Strauss, Richard, 61, 114, 124, 128n8, 266n2; *Elektra*, 91; Jarnach influenced by, 233; orchestra series, 68, 69, 119; *Der Rosenkavalier*, 91; Varèse influenced by, 91
Stravinsky, Igor, 232; neoclassical style, 62; *Pulcinella*, 254–55; stylistic pluralism, 282; Varèse influenced by, 91
Stuckenschmidt, Hans Heinz, 18, 37, 137, 232
Sullivan, Joe, 174
surrealism, 332n87
Szigeti, Josef, 56

Tagliapietra, Gino, 3
Taira, Yoshihisa, 332n82
Tamba, Akira, 332n82
Tawaststjerna, Erik, 46, 57, 59, 71–72, 79n5, 81n12, 81n27
Taylor, Deems, 186n111
telharmonium, 25, 40n41, 104, 130n51, 205
Tenney, James, 288, 329n54
theremin, 106, 176, 282, 319
Theremin, Léon, 105–106, 280
Thomson, Virgil, 30, 231n98; *The Mother of Us All*, 229n67
Thuille, Ludwig, 35, 133n93
Tiessen, Heinz, 121, 124, 134n107, 232, 259
Titian, Fred, 217
Törne, Bengt von, 59
Torpadie, Greta, 121
Toscanini, Arturo, 72, 182n66, 186n107
Turczyński, Józef, *140*, 140–41

Universal Editions, 187n114
Ussachevsky, Vladimir, 189, 214, 218, 226n1, 303, 304, 308; *Sonic Contours*, 215
Ussher, Bruno David, 176

van de Velde, Henry, 232
Varèse, Edgard: absolute music preferred by, 108–109; aesthetic ideas, 90, 104–14, 124–27; annotated copy of Busoni's *Entwurf*, 40n33, 93, 99–100, *101–103*, 104; artistic credo, 89–90; in Berlin, 92–99, 114, 116–19, 128n17; Berlin social network expansion, 117–18; Busoni connection sources, 92–93; Busoni's aesthetic influences, 98–106, 124–27, 222; Busoni's influence on, 89, 91–92, 321; as Busoni's student, 3–4, 93–98, 114, 116, 124–25; composers influencing, 91, 124, 128n8; composers' organizations founded by, 116–17, 119–21, 122–23, 124, 170, 231n98, 259; contact with Busoni's sons, 126–27; early works destroyed by, 96–97; first marriage, 92, 93, 95; formal innovations, 78, 108–109, 131n69, 132n71, 287; friendship with Busoni, 121, 124; Gruenberg and, 168, 170; instrumentation diversity, 105–106, 284; interest in past music, 222; lack of writings by, 104–105; Luening and, 220–23, 326n19; melodic integration theory, 113; microtonal scales used by, 106–107; multiple versions of works, 108; new scales and tonal expansion, 285, 292–93; notation viewed by, 107–108; "Organized Sound for the Sound Film," 318; pedagogical method, 35; rhythmic layering, 104, 109–10, 113; Sibelius and, 71–72; siren used by, 105, 124; slow pace of composing, 95–96; sonority and textural focuses, 78, 114, 279–80, 284, 292–93, 317–19; spectral composers influenced by, 312–13; students and followers of, 116–17, 288, 292–300, 317–18, 327n43, 329n54, 329n57; style change, 90–91; use of electronic instruments, 4, 105–106, 203, 280
Varèse, Edgard, compositions of: *Amériques*, 90, 91, 107, 108, 124, 285, 332n79; *Arcana*, 91, 312; *Astronome*, 318–19; *Bourgogne*, 97–98; *Les Cycles du Nord*, 93–94, 96–97, 129n18; *Density*, 21.5, 132n70; *Déserts*, 106, 216, 280–81, 313, 334n112; *Ecuatorial*, 106, 131n68, 280, 284; "Un grand sommeil noir," 90; *Hyperprism*, 109, 124, 287; *Intégrales*, 109, 287; *Ionisation*, 97, 110, 112, 113, 124, 220–21, 317, 331n75; *Nocturnal*, 90, 107;

Octandre, 109, 114, *115*, 221, 287; *Ödipus*, 93–94, 96–97, 129n18; *Offrandes*, 121, 124; *Poème électronique*, 281, 317
Varèse, Louise, 90, 91, 92, 93, 121, 126
Vecsey, Franz von, 70
Verdi, Giuseppe, 18; *Falstaff*, 21–22, 207
Verlaine, Paul, 90
Vianna da Motta, José, 139
Vienna Conservatory: Busoni's piano master classes, 9n5, 94, 138–43, *139–40*, 178n9; Busoni's studies, 10n8
Violette, Andrew, 302–303, 304, 323, 333n105
Vogel, Wladimir, 2, 232, 275n115

Wagner, Richard: leitmotif use disliked by Busoni, 28; orchestration techniques, 201, 248; *Parsifal*, 29, 42n61; Sibelius's disillusionment with, 56; *Tristan und Isolde*, prelude, 22
Wassermann, Jakob, 232
Webern, Anton, 31, 169, 185n100
Wegelius, Martin, 45, 46–47, 49, 56, 68, 77, 81n13, 81n14, 84n68
Weill, Kurt, 2, 266; as Busoni's student, 4, 10n9; *Die Dreigroschenoper*, 275n115; *Fantasia, Passacaglia, und Hymnus*, op. 6, 275n115; Jarnach and, 259, 264, 309; *Mahagonny-Songspiel*, 275n115; *Novembergruppe* and, 232
Weimar era in Germany, 121, 124, 232–33, 238, 251–53, 265–66
Weindel, Martina, 8n3, 24
Weiss, Stefan, 236, 242, 243, 253, 254–55, 263, 266, 267n3, 272n71
Weisshorn, Hermann, 165
Weissmann, Adolf, 198
Welles, Orson, 308
Whiteman, Paul, 297
Whithorne, Emerson: *Three Greek Impressions for String Quartet*, 120

Widor, Charles-Marie, 96
Wilde, Oscar, 190–91
Winfield, George A., 84n77
Winternitz-Dorda, Martha, 169
Wis, Roberto, 9n3, 46
Wolffheim, Werner, 121, 134n107
Wolf, Hugo, 68
Wolpe, Stefan, 2, 92, 232, 288, 317, 329n54
Wood, Henry, 72
Wuorinen, Charles, 4, 223, 288, 302, 303, 304–306, 329n54, 334nn108–109; *Arabia Felix*, 305; *Bamboula Squared*, 305; *Consort from Instruments and Voices*, 304; electro-acoustic compositions, 304–305, 334n109, 334–35nn115–16; *New York Notes*, 305; *Orchestral and Electronic Exchanges*, 304; *Time's Encomium*, 304–305

Xenakis, Iannis, 313–14, 337n143; *Metastasis*, 313–14; *Pithoprakta*, 314

Young Classicality, 3, 19, 25, 62–63, 125–26, 144, 236, 237–38, 253–54, 266, 278, 310–11, 319
Ysaÿe, Eugène, 119; *Poème élègiaque*, op. 12, 120; *Rêve d'enfant*, op. 14, 120

Zadora, Michael, 98, 276n123
Ziehn, Bernhard, theories of, 18, 132n70, 190, 205–207, 219, 229n56, 316
Zierfuss, Ferdinand, 262
Zimmerman, Hans, 193
Zimmermann, Bernd Alois, 4, 260, 309, 310–11; *Die Soldaten*, 312, 336n133; stylistic pluralism, 311–12, 336n133; temporal philosophy, 311–12; Trio for Violin, Viola, and Cello, 311; Young Classicality and, 310–11
Zweig, Stefan, 1

ERINN E. KNYT is Assistant Professor of Music History at the University of Massachusetts Amherst. Knyt specializes in nineteenth- and twentieth-century music, aesthetics, and performance studies and has written extensively about Ferruccio Busoni. She has published articles in the Journal of the Royal Musical Association, the Journal of Musicological Research, American Music, the Journal of Musicology, the Journal of Music History Pedagogy, and Twentieth-Century Music.

www.ingramcontent.com/pod-product-compliance
Lightning Source LLC
Chambersburg PA
CBHW052010290426
44112CB00014B/2190